WAKE-UP CALLS

Wake-Up Calls

Classic Cases in Business Ethics

Second Edition

LISA H. NEWTON, PH.D.
Department of Philosophy
Fairfield University

DAVID P. SCHMIDT, PH.D.
The Charles F. Dolan School of Business
Fairfield University

THOMSON
TM
SOUTH-WESTERN

Australia · Canada · Mexico · Singapore · Spain · United Kingdom · United States

Wake-Up Calls: Classic Cases in Business Ethics, 2e
Lisa H. Newton and David P. Schmidt

VP/Editorial Director:
Jack W. Calhoun

VP/Editor-in-Chief:
Michael P. Roche

Executive Editor:
John Szilagyi

Developmental Editor:
Molly Flynn

Marketing Manager:
Rob Bloom

Production Editor:
Starratt E. Alexander

**Manufacturing
Coordinator:**
Rhonda Utley

**Media Developmental
Editor:**
Kristen Meere

Media Production Editor:
Karen L. Schaffer

Production House:
Argosy Publishing

Design Project Manager:
Rik Moore

Cover Designer:
Rik Moore

Cover Images:
© Digital Vision

Printer:
Webcom Ltd.
Toronto, Ontario
Canada

To the Spice (of life):
Victor J. Newton
and
Norma Schmidt

Contents

PREFACE   **XV**

INTRODUCTION   **XVII**

Scope of This Work   xvii

Introductory Note: The Tocsin   xviii

The Discipline of Ethics: An Introduction   xix

     The Vocabulary of Ethics   xix

     The Moral Commitments of Ethics   xx

     Subjective Relativism as a Challenge to Ethics   xxi

     Ethical Principles and Human Nature   xxiii

     The Basic Imperatives   xxvii

     *A Complementary Approach: The Forms of
     Moral Reasoning*   xxix

     Levels of Reasoning: A Case to Consider   xxxii

     The Need for Clarity   xxxiv

Capitalism and the Business System   xxxv

The Historical Moment   xxxviii

     Reference Points   xxxix

In Brief: Through the Chapters   xl

Questions to Keep in Mind   xli

Readings   xlii

Endnotes   xlii

1   **IS IT RIGHT TO CHANGE NATURE FOR A PROFIT? THE CASE OF GENETICALLY MODIFIED AGRICULTURE**   **1**

     Questions to Keep in Mind   1

Unlimited Possibilities   2

Genetically Modified Crops: The Controversy over the "Frankenfoods"   3

     The Special Problems that Attend the New Biotechnology Industry   4

     A Success Story Suddenly Goes Sour: A Brief History   5

     Accounting for the Reaction   8

     The Terminators and the Lordly Monarchs   10

Fighting a Netwar: The Legacy of Mad Cows   13

     NGOs and PR   15

     The Wall Street Waffle   20

The Precautionary Principle vs. the Risk Benefit Ratio: Why Public Relations Is Not the Only Problem   23

Where We Go from Here   24

Questions for Reflection   26

Endnotes   26

2 WHO WILL PROTECT THE BABIES? THE LONG ORDEAL OF NESTLÉ'S INFANT FORMULA **31**

    Questions to Keep in Mind   31

The Skeleton of the Case: A Chronology of the Nestlé Boycott   32

    Development, Use, and Production of Infant Formula (1867–1998)   32

    Emergence of a Public Health Controversy: A Collegial Inquiry (1966–1973)   32

    Crunch Time: The Debate Goes Public (1973–2002)   35

    Back to the International Context: WHO Code Development (1979–1981)   37

    End of an Era: The Resolution of the Boycott (1980–1984)   39

    Peace Is Illusion: The Conflict Renewed (1985–12002)   40

The Blood and Guts of the Case: What Really Happened, and Why   46

    Facts: Was the Jelliffe Scenario a Mistake?   46

    More Facts: Where Did the Jelliffe Scenario Come From?   51

What Did the Activists of the NGOs Really Want?   55

What Was Nestlé Doing Wrong?   62

Questions for Reflection   67

Endnotes   67

3 MUST WE MAINTAIN A FRIENDLY WORKPLACE? SEXUAL HARASSMENT ON THE JOB **71**

    Questions to Keep in Mind   71

A Costly Complaint   74

Charges and Defenses   75

Sexual Harassment: The Legislative History   77

Quid Pro Quo and Hostile Work Environment   79

Differences in Perception   82

The Jury Decides   83

Questions for Reflection   84

Suggestions for Further Reading   84

Endnotes   84

**4   WHOSE JOB IS IT TO PROTECT
CONSUMER HEALTH? TOBACCO'S
LAST STAND   87**
　　　Questions to Keep in Mind   87

The Tocsin Sounds: Luther Terry's Report   88
　　　The Road to the Report   88
　　　The Tobacco Industry's Response: Back to Bed 91

Tobacco and Health   93
　　　Mortality and Morbidity: A Medical Overview 93
　　　The Scientific Controversy on Smoking and Health 95

The Uses of the Law   96
　　　On Liberty   96
　　　On Lawsuits   98
　　　On Harm to Others   101
　　　On Street Drugs and Addiction   102
　　　Whistleblowers   103

Conclusion   105
　　　The Economic Issues   105
　　　The End   107

Questions for Reflection   107

Suggestions for Further Reading   108

Endnotes   108

5   HOW SHALL WE KNOW IF OUR
     PRODUCTS ARE SAFE? DIVERSE
     PERSPECTIVES ON TIRES
     AND AUTOMOBILES   111

        Questions to Keep in Mind   111

     Three Deaths in Indiana   114

     A Historical Perspective: The Controversial
        Achievement of the Pinto   116

     An Engineering Perspective: Business
        Pressures on Design and Production   118

     An Economic Perspective: Weighing
        the Costs and Benefits   120

     A Political Perspective: Who Sets the Consumer
        Safety Standards?   123

     The Outcome of the Trial   125

     Questions for Reflection   126

     Suggestions for Further Reading   126

     Endnotes   126

6   WHO SHOULD CLEAN UP THE MESS?
     LOVE CANAL AND CORPORATE
     RESPONSIBILITY FOR OLD POLLUTION 129

        Questions to Keep in Mind   129

     Love Canal, the Event: A Chronology   130

     Introduction   132

     A Brave History, a Shattering Revelation   133
        Background   133
        The Event   134
        Trouble Materializes   136
        The Chemicals, the Illnesses, the Tests   137
        Legislation   139
        Liability   140
        Resettlement   142

Concluding Reflection   143

Questions for Reflection   145

Suggestions for Further Reading   146

Endnotes   147

7   HOW SHALL WE DEAL WITH
    UNLIMITED GREED? THE INSIDER
    TRADING SCANDALS   149

    Questions to Keep in Mind   149

    An Arrest on Wall Street   152

    Background on Wall Street   153

    Wigton's Friend: Marty Siegel   156

    Why Insider Trading Is Wrong: The Law   158

    Using Regulations to Achieve Ethical Markets   161

    Is Insider Trading Unethical?   164

    What Happened to Wiggy   166

    Questions for Reflection   168

    Suggestions for Further Reading   168

    Endnotes   168

8   WHICH HAT MUST THE ENGINEER
    WEAR? THE CHALLENGER CASE   171

    Questions to Keep in Mind   171

    Why Did Columbia Fail?   172

    The Tragic Explosion of Space Shuttle Challenger   173

    Something Was Not Right   175

    Growing Concern about O-Rings   177

    The Teleconference between Morton Thiokol
        and NASA   179

Organizational Features of NASA and Morton Thiokol   181

The Problem of Whistleblowing   184

Perspective, Risk, and Responsibility   186

Questions for Reflection   189

Suggestions for Further Reading   189

Endnotes   189

9   **WHAT RESPONSIBILITIES DO WE HAVE FOR FOREIGN MANAGEMENT? UNION CARBIDE AND THE DISASTER AT BHOPAL**   **191**

Questions to Keep in Mind   191

The Story of a Disaster   192

Union Carbide in India: Chemistry for Disaster   192

The Factory in a Foreign Land   194

What Went Wrong?   194

The Victims, Workers, and Squatters   196

The Immediate Reaction: The Corporation's Response   197

Response and Frustration: Dealing with India   198

The Investigation, Within and Without   200

Accident or Sabotage?   201

Sorting Out the Demands for Compensation   203

The Entrance of the Lawyers   204

The Incident Continues   205

Some Provisional Conclusions   206

The Chemicals Industry's Reaction: Responsible Care   206

The History of the CMA   206

Bhopal Imperatives   207

Responsible Care   208

CAER: The First Step   208

The Canadian Modifications   210

The Adoption of Responsible Care   210

Preliminary Reflections   211

Questions for Reflection   212

Suggestions for Further Reading   212

Endnotes   213

10   WHO WILL WATCH THE WATCHERS? THE SAVINGS AND LOAN DISASTER   217

Questions to Keep in Mind   217

A $400 Million Settlement   220

The Savings and Loan Industry   221

The Audit of Lincoln Savings   223

Background on Ernst & Young   225

Standards in the Accounting Industry   227

A Changing Culture   229

Consequences for Ernst & Young   230

Questions for Reflection   232

Suggestions for Further Reading   232

Endnotes   232

EPILOGUE   235

Preface

The first edition of this book grew from the authors' conviction that ethics is not just about abstract principles; it is also about stories or narratives that help display the practical dimension of ethical principles. We were also guided by our perception that ethics education benefits from the ready availability of classic cases that have set the terms of contemporary discussions of business ethics. We needed a book of rich, vivid case studies that we could use in our classrooms. For these reasons, we authored the first edition of *Wake-Up Calls*.

No one doubts there still is a need for engaging, thoughtful depictions of business issues that are accessible to students of ethics. Even more, we believe that the current business situation has only heightened the need for ethics education and for thoughtful engagement of business issues. As of this writing, it has been one year since Enron filed for bankruptcy. Since then, our society has watched aghast as one company after another self-destructed from ethical and legal misconduct. We have moved quickly from talk about cleaning up isolated bad apples to suspicions that the ethical crisis in business today may be pervasive, even systemic in nature. The need for ethical analysis of business has never been more urgent.

For this reason, we have updated and revised *Wake-Up Calls* to make it more relevant to educators and students who wish to understand better the leading issues now driving business. Many of the classic cases are still here, for the lessons they impart are timeless. However, these classic cases have been linked to current, breaking issues, helping the instructor and student to apply the lessons of the past to today's problems. Some new cases have been introduced as well, to broaden the usefulness and applicability of this text. Taken as a whole, these readings sound a wake-up call to which we must ever be alert.

We would like to thank all those who have helped us bring this volume together: our colleagues in the field of business ethics, the editors from Thomson Learning, and above all our families, without whose patient support the completion of this project would not have been possible.

Introduction

SCOPE OF THIS WORK

In this text are cases about important business issues that will introduce you to the ethical dimensions of business conduct and policy. The focus is comprehensive. We describe industry problems and societal dilemmas, as well as actions of individual companies and managers. We have tried to offer a general introduction to essential issues in the challenging world of business.

Our basic goal is to stimulate your curiosity about ethics in business, to make you more alert to ethics issues you might encounter at work, and to deepen your general understanding of what is at stake in these issues. We also provide a basic ethics vocabulary that may help you analyze and discuss the cases with some measure of sophistication and clarity. Though it is not a management text in how to make particular business decisions, this book may enhance your capacity for sound business *judgment*, which will guide your future decisions and actions.

The issues described in this book are too important to be left to the experts alone. For that reason, these cases are presented in terms that any competent layperson can understand. In plain English, we have told the *stories* that make these issues come alive. We have been selective in telling these stories. We have avoided the extensive quantitative and technical exposition that is more appropriate to an MBA-level text. These tales delve into the financials of the companies discussed only when that information contributes to the overall flow of the narrative and understanding of the issues. Any unavoidable technical terms are always explained. At the end of each case there are references to guide the inquiring reader who seeks a deeper understanding of certain aspects of the case.

INTRODUCTORY NOTE: THE TOCSIN

The tocsin was the main bell for a European village from early medieval into early modern times. It was rung whenever danger—invasion, wolves, fire, or storm—confronted the town. The ringing of the bell warns of an impending crisis and is a call to pay attention to something new and alarming, and to be prepared to do something about it. We all know what an alarm clock sounds like; it is never a welcome sound but it gets our attention and we must respond to it. (If we ignore it, turning over and going back to sleep, we face later consequences.) The cases in this book are significant because each is a tocsin ring—a "wake-up call" to the business community as well as to the general public. We can choose to try to ignore the alarm, but we will pay dearly, one way or another, if we do.

The "wake-up calls" in this book were selected because each is a classic in business ethics. Significance for business practice, not time alone, makes a classic; the stories told here are milestones in business experience, even if the news is still breaking. You might be able to think of other cases that you consider classic. That is as it should be. Expanding this book to include them all would result in an immensely bigger book. We tried to make sure the cases we included were truly significant and representative of the broad terrain of business practice.

There are many reasons to teach business ethics from case histories rather than from a didactic text. There is, first, the traditional business school rationale— "because wisdom can't be told" and only by observing management at work can the student learn decisionmaking.[1] But there is more to the matter than teaching future managers. A story is inherently richer than an argument, and every time it is told, new facets of the human actions and deliberations come to light. These stories are all particularly rich, therefore worth continuing to talk about. Their terms and ideas have become part of the essential vocabulary for knowledgeable and effective managers today. You are being initiated into a serious and society-wide conversation that has been going on for some time on these cases; the material of this book should enable you to hold up your part of the conversation intelligently and compassionately.

Readers of this book can use these cases to chart their own standards for ethical business conduct and to interpret new situations that they will face long after the book has been put down.

THE DISCIPLINE OF ETHICS: AN INTRODUCTION

1. The Vocabulary of Ethics

Of all matters in ethics, the meanings of the terms have caused the most acrimony and dispute. Since the earliest of the Socratic dialogues, we have argued about the meaning of key terms like *morals, ethics, virtue, piety, justice,* and others. Given the very limited purposes in this introduction, we will simply stipulate at this point how we intend to use the key terms of ethics, observing only that our usage is reasonably widely accepted and as far as possible, theory-free. More than that no philosopher will claim. In what follows you may expect the following words to be used in general in these ways:

- Morals or Morality: The **rules** that govern our **behavior as persons to persons**. Also, **duties**. Examples:
  - Don't hurt people.
  - Don't tell lies.
  - Don't take more than your fair share.

  A note on morals: all you really need to know you probably learned in kindergarten. The rules are easy to know and remember—but very hard to follow consistently.
- Values: **States of affairs** that are **desired by and for people** and that we want to increase; **ends, goals**. Examples:
  - Health (vs. sickness)
  - Wealth (vs. poverty)
  - Happiness in general
  - Freedom, justice, respect for human rights
- Virtues: **Conditions of people** that are desirable both for the people themselves (as part of a fully human life) and for the good functioning of the society. Examples:
  - Wisdom (vs. ignorance or irrationality)
  - Courage (vs. weakness or unreliability)
  - Self-control (vs. greed or violence)
  - Justice (vs. egoism, favoritism, or dishonesty)
- Ethics: Properly speaking, **the study of morals, values, and virtues** to discover:
  - Their theoretical links and relationships
  - How they work (or don't work) together in practice

Other understandings of the term **ethics**:

More generally, the whole field of morals, values, and virtues—**the whole study of our attempts to order human conduct toward the right and the good**.

More specifically, a **professional ethic** is a **particular code of rules** and understandings worked out by the members of a profession to govern their own practice.

- Ethical Principles: Very general **concepts that sum up a range of morals, values, and virtues** from which moral imperatives can be derived. In ordinary conversation we make no distinction between the notions of "morality" and "ethics," "moral obligations" and "ethical duties," "moral codes" and "codes of ethics." But in philosophy, as above, we may distinguish "morals" from "ethics," according to the level of analysis intended. "Morality" governs conduct, tells us to "obey the rules," the rules that attach to our social roles or arise from our traditional communities or govern civil relationships generally. Morality calls our attention to the fundamental commitments with which we order our lives. Morality tells us not to steal: One tempted to steal is morally bound not to steal, and one who habitually succumbs to that temptation is an immoral person. "Ethics," on the other hand, is primarily an academic discipline; it has to do with forms of reasoning rather than conduct; it reflects on, compares, and analyzes rules, and it traces the logical connections between fundamental principles and the moral commitments that guide us. Ethics derives the principle of respect for the property of others from which we further derive the rule that we should not take the property of others without authorization. Ethics describes the conditions under which the principle fails to apply or can be overridden. We can live moral lives without knowing ethics, but we cannot discuss the morality of our lives, defend it, put it into historical context, without the intellectual tools to do so. Ethics provides those tools.

2. The Moral Commitments of Ethics

Morality is a precondition for ethics, in two ways. First, morality, as a shorthand way of referring to all our transactions with each other, is the subject matter of ethics, just as our transactions with the physical world form the subject matter of science. Second, ethics is an activity, and any activity requires certain moral commitments of those who take part in it. We cannot do anything well without moral commitments to excellence, or anything for any length of time without the moral virtue of perseverence. The practice of ethics also has moral commitments appropriate to it. These commitments, to **reason** and to **impartiality**, can rightly be demanded of any person who would take ethics seriously.

In any troubling case, we have first an obligation to think about it, to examine all the options available to us. We must not simply act on prejudice, or impulsively, just because we have the power to do so. We call this obligation the commitment to **reason**. The commitment to **reason** entails a willingness to critically scrutinize one's own moral judgments, and to submit them for public scrutiny by others; further, to change those judgments and modify the commitments that led to them if they turn out (upon reflection) to be not the best available. This commitment rules out several approaches to moral decision-making, including several versions of "intuitionism" (a refusal to engage in reasoning about moral judgment at all, on grounds that apprehension of moral truth is a simple perception, not open to critical analysis), and all varieties of "dogmatism" (an insistence that all moral disagreements are resolved by some preferred set of rules or doctrines; that inside that set there is nothing that can be questioned, and that outside that set there is nothing of any moral worth).

Second, we have an obligation of **impartiality**, a duty to examine the options from an objective standpoint, a standpoint that everyone could adopt, without bias. We want to take everyone who has a stake in the outcome ("stakeholders," we will call them) into account. Since this consideration for other persons is the foundation of morality, we sometimes call this perspective the **moral point of view**. The commitment to impartiality entails a willingness to give equal consideration to the rights, interests, and choices of all parties to the situation in question. This commitment to impartial judgment has one essential role in the study of ethics: Once we have decided that all persons are to count equally in the calculations and that each is to count as one and as no more than one, we have the unit we need to evaluate the expected benefit and harm to come from the choices before us, to weigh the burdens placed and the rights honored. We also know that if anyone's wants, needs, votes, or choices are to be taken seriously and weighed in the final balance, then everyone's wants and needs of that type must be weighed equally. That is, if anyone is accorded respect and moral consideration, then all must be. We can derive most of the moral imperatives that we use from this single commitment.

By way of example, the familiar Golden Rule, that we ought to treat others as we would have them treat us, is a fine preliminary statement of those commitments. With regard to anything we plan to do that will affect others, we ought not just to go ahead without reflection. We ought to ask, how would we like it if someone did this to us? That consideration is perfectly adequate as a satisfaction of the moral commitments that precede ethics. In general it may be said, that *if we will not agree to submit our decisions to reason, and to attempt to see the situation from the point of view of all who are caught up in it, ethics is impossible.*

3. Subjective Relativism as a Challenge to Ethics

One obstacle to doing ethics of any kind, business or otherwise, in the contemporary Western community, is the prevalence of a superficial ethical orientation known as "subjective relativism." Subjective relativism violates the commitments to reason and impartiality, and has the effect (usually intended) of making ethics impossible. To make the commitments clearer, it may be worthwhile examining the errors of subjective relativism.

Relativism denotes any approach to ethics which holds that there are no absolute or unchanging moral principles, that the rules governing each situation are to be determined by their *relation* to something else—the customs or culture of the country, for instance, or the desires of the participants. Subjectivism insists that the sole source of knowledge or authority is in the perception of the individual. "Subjective relativism," then, as a philosophical position, declares that each person is his own authority on the moral life and the source and measure of his own moral principles. On this reasoning, each person has the right to decide on all matters of right and wrong. According to subjective relativism, what's right for you may *not* be right for me; no one has any right to impose morality on anyone else. So there is really no point, the doctrine continues, in arguing about decisions on matters of morals or learning about justifying moral judgments according to reason, because there is no need to justify them in any way at all. And that is why, subjective relativism concludes, there is no need to study ethics.

Note that the position is both anti-reason (there is no need, or way, to subject moral judgment to reasonable criticism) and dogmatic (on the areas of morality that affect me, my opinions constitute an absolute and final authority, not to be questioned by others). We will get nowhere with ethics as long as this view is taken seriously. But it *is* taken seriously, in that world that lies outside our classrooms and committees, and it is instructive to see why.

The common public justification of subjective relativism (setting aside the philosophers' more elaborate analysis) seems to follow this line of reasoning: First, we live under a constitutional government, protected by a firm Bill of Rights. "Freedom of speech" is the name of one of our fundamental beliefs. Freedom of speech entails freedom of conscience: Each person has the right, indeed the obligation, to think out ethical and political issues and to come to reasoned conclusions on ethical and political matters. (True enough.) Further, each person has the right (within certain obvious limits) to express that opinion without anyone else having the right to object to, or anyway interfere with, such speech. (Also true.) Further, we live in a pluralistic democracy. We are a collection of very different cultures, but we agree on two basic principles: first, the innate dignity of each individual and second, the right of each cultural community to maintain its identity, including its characteristic beliefs and teachings (as long as these are within the law). That means that we have a duty to treat all citizens with respect. We also have the duty to promote tolerance, or acceptance, of all our citizens, for what they are and for the culture from which they come. (So far, so good.)

Meanwhile, we consider it very bad manners to go around telling people that we think they are wrong, especially *morally* wrong. But if we have many different cultures, we are bound to have disagreements, including serious disagreements, about matters of morality.

All these points add up to a national culture of "respectful disagreement": In America, it is one of our proudest boasts that **citizens can very seriously disagree with each other on matters of policy and moral right, and yet each will treat the other with respect and no instrument or agent**

of the state will attempt to suppress either of them. (Nothing wrong so far; as a matter of fact, that statement is a good start for any American ethic.)

But it is psychologically a very short step, and a very wrong step, from respectful disagreement to "indifferentism" or subjective relativism. We make a very large mistake when we confuse a constitutionally guaranteed "right" with the moral category of "rightness." There is no *logical* connection between *what you have a right to do*, and *the right thing to do*; but there is a *psychological* temptation to move from one to the other. Let's say that again: In logic, there is no connection between *"You have the right to think what you like,"* and *"Anything you like to think is right."* You have the right, after all, to contradict yourself; you have all the right in the world to think "2 + 2 = 5." That doesn't make it correct. But psychologically, once you have told me that no one has the *right* to correct me when I claim certain sorts of opinions, you certainly *seem* to have told me that any such opinions *are right*, or at least as right as opinions can be. That is the error we must avoid.

In mathematics, of course, at least at the levels most of us learned in school, there is one right answer. In ethics there may not be, since ethical concepts are logically independent (more on that presently), and the question of what weight to assign to them must often be decided on the configurations of a particular case. That is why there can be honest, and possibly irreconcilable, disagreement on matters of ethics. But there are always better and worse answers, answers more or less in conformity with our accepted values, real moral values. *Several of these real values, by the way, are evident in the argument in defense of subjective relativism, given above*: the integrity of the human conscience, the sanctity of individual rights, the autonomy and dignity of the human person, the appreciation of cultural variety, and general good manners.

Subjective relativism is not self-contradictory as a position. It makes perfectly good sense to posit the individual as a moral authority in his own case in all instances. But the thesis is self-annihilating: It is impossible to defend it without ceasing to be a relativist (since a defender must argue from a basis of absolute values like democracy and freedom), and it is impossible to maintain a consistently subjective relativist position without admitting the legitimacy of the attempts to impose moral beliefs that the proponents of subjective relativism aim particularly to oppose.

4. Ethical Principles and Human Nature

Since ethics is about human beings, we should be able to discover its ruling concepts in the lives of human beings and derive them from fundamental aspects of human nature. The human being, and human nature, are endlessly complex, of course, yet the human being is universally recognizable to others of the species and it seems that humans everywhere, if they have to, can work together. So, avoiding the complexities of the outer limits of human potentiality, it should be possible to learn about the fundamentals of human morality just from the easily discoverable truths about the human being. In the course of the discussion, we will make some initial attempts to foreshadow the major ethical orientations that philosophers have, through our history, adopted as re-flective of these most basic moral principles.

What are human beings about? Given the normative premise, that moral principles must be appropriate to human life if they are to govern human life, three basic, simple, readily observable facts about human beings determine the structure of our moral obligations.

A. People Are Embodied

People are animals. They have bodies. They are matter. They exist in time and space and are subject to physical laws. These bodies are organic processes, re-quiring regular sustenance internally, and suffering all manner of slings and ar-rows of violent change externally. They experience pain, deprivation, and danger. They are prone to periodic failure unpredictably and to ultimate fail-ure inevitably; they are mortal.

People have needs that must be satisfied if they are to survive. They need at least food, water, and protection from the elements and natural enemies. That means that they must control the physical environment to make from it the means to those ends. Failure to do so will lead quickly to pain and suffering.

The first and immediate implication for ethics is that, if we have any reason to care about human beings, then the relief of that suffering and the satisfaction of those needs should be our first concern. In philosophical terms, human need and vulnerability to harm give rise to duties of *compassion* (for suffering), *non-maleficence* (avoiding harm), and more generally, *beneficence* (working to satisfy human need, maximize human happiness, optimize human interests in all re-spects). In general, the moral reasoning that takes help and harm to human be-ings as the primary determinant of the rightness of action is called "utilitarianism," following John Stuart Mill's description of that reasoning.[2]

B. People Are Social

Social animals regularly live in large groups of their own kind (i.e., in groups containing several to many active adult males). Individuals raised apart from such groups exhibit behavior that is abnormal for the species. Whatever prob-lems, therefore, that people have with their physical environment, they will have to solve in groups. They will soon discover that this necessity produces a new set of problems. They must cope with a social environment as well as the physical one. That social environment produces two further needs: for a social structure to coordinate social efforts and for a means of communication ade-quate to the complex task of such coordination. The need for communication is fulfilled by the evolution of language.

The implication for ethics is that, given that there are so many of us, we must take account of each other in all our actions. We come saddled by nature with obligations, to the group in general and to other members of the group in particular, that we cannot escape or evade. Normal people (not psychopaths) seem to know this without being told. By nature, human beings try to do good and avoid evil, in advance of knowing just what counts as good or evil. The at-tempt to do good, to others as to oneself, involves the adoption of "the moral point of view," or a stance of impartiality with regard to the distribution of benefits and burdens. *Fairness*, or *justice*, demands that we subject our actions to rule, and that the rule be the same for all who are similarly situated. What will make an act "right," ultimately, is not just that it serves individual happiness but that it serves the whole community; people are equal and society must deal with them equally unless good reason is given for differential treatment. As John Rawls points out, the duty of justice may require us to favor just those persons who would not succeed in getting their claims recognized if personal power, or even majority benefit, were to determine the distribution.[3]

C. People Are Rational

Normal adult human beings are able to consider abstract concepts, use language, and think in terms of categories, classes, and rules. *Rationality*, of course, in our ordinary discourse, means a good deal more than the basic ability to think in terms of abstract categories. Ordinarily we use the word to distinguish calm and dispassionate decision-making from "emotional" or disorganized decision-making; we use it to distinguish people capable of making good decisions from people who are not. But for our purposes, we need go no further with the word. The creature that is rational will think, on occasion, in *general* terms about classes and laws extending over time, space, and possibility, while the creature that is not rational will think, if at all, only about *particular* (individual) objects or events.

Since people are rational, they can make *rational choices*. When people think about action they think in terms of classes of acts as well as individual acts. For instance, if my neighbor has a particularly attractive knife, and I desire to take it from him and am currently making plans to do so, I shall make my plans based on what I already know about all cases of people taking things from other people. And I can contemplate not only those past acts of taking and the present plan to take that knife, but all cases that will ever be of taking, especially of knives—future acts as well as past and present acts. But in that case I am thinking of action not yet taken, of action therefore undetermined, for which real alternatives exist. Since people can conceive of alternatives, they can choose among them—having thought over the circumstances and deliberated on the outcomes, they can decide what to do. Put another way: I do not *have* to take that knife, if I have not yet done it. People are *free*, as we say, or *autonomous moral agents*. But then people can also realize that they could have done differently—I did not have to take the knife, and given my neighbor's understandable grief and anger at its loss, maybe I *should* not have. That is, I can feel guilt and remorse and assume *responsibility* for having chosen as I did.

As far as we know, we are alone among the animals in possession of this ability. And since people can conceive of classes of acts for which alternatives exist, they can make *laws* to govern acts in the future, specifying that the citizens (or whoever may be bound by the law) *ought* to act one way rather than another: For instance that no one ought to take things that do not belong to them, and that such takings, henceforth to be called "theft," shall be collectively punished. General obligations can be formulated and articulated for a whole society. Collectively (acting in their groups), people make collective choices, especially choices of rules, rather than relying on instinct, and they are then collectively responsible for those choices and individually responsible for abiding by them.

Rationality's implication for ethics is that, since freedom of choice is the characteristic that sets humans apart from the other animals, if we have any duty to respect human beings at all, it is this *choice* that we must respect. Persons are categorically different from the things of the physical world. As Immanuel Kant put it, people have *dignity*, *inherent worth*, rather than mere price or dollar value; they are bearers of *rights* and subjects of *duties* rather than mere means to our ends or obstacles to our purposes.[4] Our duty of *respect for persons* or respect for persons as autonomous beings requires that we allow others to be free, to make their own choices and live their own lives. We are required not to do anything to them, even for their own benefit, without their consent.

In summary: By *C*, above, humans have minds or, as the philosophers say, a rational nature and by *A*, above, humans have an apparently limitless capacity for physical and psychological suffering. Rationality and suffering are not found together anywhere else; possibly angels have the first and surely all beasts possess the second, but only human beings appear to be able to reflect upon their own suffering and contemplate the suffering of others of their kind, and that sets them apart from all creation. By virtue of rationality, human possess *dignity* and command respect. Ultimately, that respect entails the willingness to let other people make their own choices, develop their own moral nature, and live their lives in freedom. By virtue of that abysmal capacity for suffering, the human condition cries out for compassion and compels attention to human *well-being* and the relief of pain. And by *B*, above, this condition is shared. We are enjoined not only to serve human need and respect human rights, but to establish *justice* by constructing a political and legal structure that will distribute fairly the burdens and benefits of life on this earth in the society of humans. These most general concepts: *human welfare*, *human justice*, and *human dignity*—are the source and criteria for evaluation of every moral system authored by human beings.

The same concepts are the source of every moral dilemma. Attention to human welfare requires us to use the maximization of human happiness (for the greatest number of individuals) as our criterion of right action; attention to the needs of groups and of social living requires us to set fairness for all above benefit for some, yet duty can require that we set aside both the feelings of the groups and the happiness of the individual in the name of respect for human dignity. To protect the welfare of many it is often necessary to limit the liberty of the individual (the liberty to operate dangerous or noisy vehicles without a license, for instance). On the small scale as well as the large, to respect the liberty of persons is not always to further their best interests, when they choose against those interests (for instance, by taking addictive drugs or by spending themselves into debt). To maintain a rough equality among persons, it is often necessary to put unequal demands on the interests of some of them (by progressive taxation, for example). To preserve the community, it is sometimes necessary to sacrifice the interests of the few—but that course seems to discount the worth of the few, and so to violate justice.

5. The Basic Imperatives

Such conflict is fundamental to ethics and is the major reason ethics is famous as the discipline that has no clear answers. The human being is a complex creature, and when we extract human values from that complexity, we find them logically independent at the least—that is, there is no logical priority among the values, and no way to derive them from each other—and often in opposition. There are, by tradition, two ways to formulate the opposition (see "Vocabulary of Ethics" in this Introduction):

1. As a conflict of *values*: A value is a desired state, which we try, in our dealings, to advance or enhance or promote. The concepts so far discussed can be treated as values that are difficult to pursue simultaneously—the happiest society, the fairest or most equal society, the freest society or the lifestyle incorporating the most freedom. Our most fundamental political commitments turn on opposed views of this priority: Traditionally, the political left chooses justice as its priority, the political right chooses liberty, and both claim to maximize happiness.

2. As a conflict of *imperatives*: An imperative prescribes a duty to do or to forbear. It is occasionally more useful to see ethical conflict as a conflict of injunctions or prescriptions telling us what to do in any given situation. We are *told*—by the law, by our religion, by our parents, by our employers, by the civil law—that we must respect the rights of others, be fair to everyone, and serve each other's needs. Sometimes it is not possible to do everything at once.

For every clear value, there is another value, which sometimes conflicts. For every clear imperative, there is a contrary imperative, equally clear, which sometimes applies. Ethics is the discipline that derives these values and imperatives, works out the consequences of our efforts to protect them, and musters what light it can to show us the possible reconciliations and the necessary compromises that attend their application in practice.

The three concepts elucidated above—human welfare, human justice, and human dignity—correspond to three imperatives for human conduct.

1. *Do no harm, and where possible do good*: Because we must live, and because we can suffer, we must value life and happiness: safety, protection from harm, absence of pain, hunger, or suffering of any kind; enjoyment, pleasure. That is, we have an obligation to help and protect each other, to relieve suffering, to choose each action, or rule of action, according to the amount of pain it will relieve or happiness it will provide. This general duty we may call *beneficence*, or *concern for welfare*.

This imperative is often broken down into logically related but different prescriptions:

a. Do no harm (the duty of *non-maleficence*). In the pattern of duties to do good and to avoid harm, this duty is the negative, individual, and immediate part. (For instance, no matter how much fun it would be, do not blow up the bridge.)

b. Prevent harm wherever possible. This duty generalizes the one before, enjoining us to attempt to keep agencies besides ourselves from doing harm. (If the bridge is near collapse, act to shore it up and keep people off it until it is fixed.)

c. Remedy harm wherever possible. This duty is the proactive equivalent of the two before, enjoining *compassion* for suffering and positive efforts to relieve it. (If the bridge has collapsed, pull the people out of the water.)

d. Do good, provide benefit, wherever possible. (Build better bridges.)

In this pattern of duties, the duty of non-maleficence takes moral priority (i.e., if you can provide benefit to many people, only at the cost of doing harm to a few, there is a presumption *against* doing whatever would result in the benefit and harm). The second two follow from the same presumption and the last comes into play only when the others are taken care of. That presumption can, of course, be overridden, as when the state takes my property to build a road, but only on proper authority, with at least an attempt to provide compensation, and presentation of compelling reasons.

2. *Observe the requirements of justice.* Because we must live together, we must adhere to rules of equal treatment, justice, fairness, equality before the law trust and trustworthiness, and honesty in word and deed. Then we have an obligation to acknowledge our membership in, and dependence on, the human community and the community in which we live—to contribute to its life; to obey its laws, customs, and policies; to be honest in all our dealings with our fellows; and above all to hold ourselves accountable to them for our actions, especially as they affect others. This duty we may call the duty of *justice*.

3. *Respect persons (as autonomous beings).* Because we aspire to the full potential of humanity, we must value freedom. We take liberty, autonomy, and rationality to be ideals and value them in others as much as we prize our own. The human enterprise is an endless quest to become better, wiser, more loving people, and we must cultivate people and institutions that will protect that quest. We have an obligation to respect the choices of others, to allow them the space to live their lives, to the end, the way they see fit. For ourselves, we have the obligation to realize our own potential, not only to discern for ourselves the moral course of action and to take responsibility for the moral choices we make, but also to extend our knowledge and the scope of our reason to become as fully as possible autonomous persons. This duty we may call the duty of *respect for persons*.

Clearly none of these imperatives is optional. We cannot choose to not have bodies. We cannot choose to not need each other. Although we may sometimes wish we could, we cannot choose to not choose, to not be free. And these imperatives are logically independent one from another. They can conflict.

6. A Complementary Approach: The Forms of Moral Reasoning

Ethical debate ordinarily employs two contrasting forms of moral reasoning, or reasoning to conclusions on the problems under discussion. The first we may call *consequentialist* (or utilitarian or teleological) reasoning, in which ends are identified as good and means are selected that will lead to those ends; the second is generally called *nonconsequentialist* (or deontological) reasoning, in which rules are accepted as good and acts are judged according to their conformity to those rules. A third form of reasoning, complementary to the first two but not yet included in the decision processes, is called *virtue-based* (or ontological) reasoning, in which the type of person one is, and the type of moral community one belongs to, determines the obligations to act. In consequentialism, the rightness of an act is linked with the goodness of the state of affairs that it brings about; in non-consequentialism, rightness is linked with the act's derivability from a rule; in virtue-based reasoning, it is linked with the character of the agent.

A. Reasoning from Rule: Deontological Reasoning

We suggested above that moral principles usually take the form of an imperative, setting a duty sufficient in itself to justify action. An imperative serves as the major premise for a line of *deontological*, or *nonconsequentialist*, reasoning. Deontological reasoning states a duty, observes that the present instance, real or hypothetical, falls under that duty, and proceeds to derive the obligation to carry out that duty in this instance. For example, presented with a particularly nice necklace left unguarded on a jewelry counter at the department store, I might be very tempted to snatch it and run. But my duty not to do that is very clear:

(major premise)	Thou shalt not steal.
(minor premise)	Taking this necklace would be stealing.
(conclusion)	Thou (in this case, I) may not take the necklace.

If I take it anyway, and am confronted at the door by the store owner asking if I paid for that necklace, and want very much to say "Yes sir, I certainly did pay for the necklace, but I seem to have dropped the receipt," again my duty is clear:

(major premise)	Lying is wrong.
(minor premise)	To say I paid for it would be lying.
(conclusion)	I may not say that I paid for it.

Connoisseurs of logical form will note a certain falling short of the strict subject-predicate form demanded by Aristotelean logic, but the point should be clear enough. In deontological reasoning (literally, reasoning from duty), we assume that we are obligated to do what is *right*, that *moral laws* correctly demarcate what is right and what is wrong, and that we can deduce the moral status of a contemplated action by finding what moral laws apply to it. (By those laws, an act may have one of three moral statuses: It may be *prescribed* (obligatory), *proscribed* (forbidden), or *permitted* (neither prescribed nor proscribed).

There are problems with this approach, as you may have noted. What, for instance, is the *grounding* of the major premises? Deontological reasoning starts with the assertion of duties, but those duties must be justified externally. In this case, we can go back to our basic principles and derive the prohibitions of stealing and lying without too much difficulty. Occasionally, however, in order to justify a premise, we are forced to fall back on consequentialist reasoning— the reason why we mustn't trade shares of stock on the basis of inside information cannot be traced directly from the original principles, but involves understanding of the stock market and, ultimately, the assertion that (a very small minority of economists dissenting) insider trading is harmful to the market and thus to the free enterprise system. (Insider trading is usually represented as a violation of "justice." But of course it would not be "unjust" to deal as an insider if the rules permitted it. It would just be conducive to bad consequences, or so the general belief goes.)

B. Reasoning from Consequences: Teleological Reasoning

Note, however, that we could often just as easily couch the same moral argument in goal-oriented or *consequentialist* terms. In such an argument we treat the principles as values rather than as imperatives, and as *ends* to be achieved in society rather than laws governing action directly. Moral argument then becomes an exercise in evaluating the *means* to the end of the best possible society. The *good*, as opposed to the *right* of right action, becomes the benchmark of moral prescription. Good is generally understood as the greatest happiness of the greatest number of persons in the society in the long run. Action is right insofar as it brings about *good* results. The most familiar form of consequentialist reasoning is the "cost-benefit" analysis familiar from the business world: To find the right thing to do, you add up the benefits of each option, divide the benefits of each course of action by its costs, and select the option with the highest ratio of benefits to costs.

Can we deduce the same conclusions as above using consequentialist reasoning? Yes, somewhat more elaborately:

(major premise)	If everyone took objects from stores without paying for them, the economy would collapse; therefore the practice of taking objects without paying for them is contrary to the greatest good of the society.
(minor premise)	Taking this necklace without paying for it would therefore be contrary to the greatest good of the society.
(conclusion)	This act is not right and I should not do it.

We don't have to go through this procedure every time we find a necklace lying around within reach, of course. The experience of the whole human race is that respect for property, however property may be defined in different cultures, is essential for the stability of society, and therefore, on those grounds, such taking of property without payment is appropriately forbidden everywhere (as is lying on matters of commercial interest). Once the act is prohibited, the reasoning proceeds exactly as it did in the nonconsequentialist framework. Most of us find *rule utilitarianism* (consequentialism that establishes rules and then reasons from them) easier to work with on a day-to-day basis than *act utilitarianism* (consequentialism that evaluates every individual act on the basis of its consequences). But any consequentialist will insist on the point that *every legitimate major premise* for moral reasoning *is based on consequentialist reasoning*; we need no divine commands, unverifiable intuitions, or arbitrary pronouncements to give us the principles from which we derive the moral status of the act in question.

C. Reasoning from Virtue: Aretological or Ontological Reasoning

A third form of reasoning is customarily couched in the terms of *virtue* or character. In such argument we appeal to the principles as *character traits* rather than as goals or as rules, as virtues inherent in the moral agent rather than as characteristics of the act. Every time we act we simultaneously define ourselves (as the type of person who acts that way) and change ourselves (toward that type of person), whether for better or for worse. Our objective in moral action, by this reasoning, is not only to adhere to rules (a minimal prescription) and achieve good ends, but also to become a good person, especially the kind of person who performs right actions by habit and by desire. We go beyond cost/benefit and rule adherence to aim at *ideals* of conduct and personhood.

Virtue ethics does not define, initially, just what virtues are worth pursuing most and by whom. In this lack of specificity, virtue ethics is no worse than utilitarianism, which wavers among definitions of happiness (welfare objectively determined? felt pleasure? preference as expressed in the market?), or deontology, which is indifferent among several sources of rules (natural law? human law? the form of moral reasoning itself?). By tradition, humans should seek to become temperate, courageous, wise (prudent), and just; additionally, in our religious traditions, they should try to acquire faith, hope, and charity—not to mention kindness, patience, equanimity, magnanimity, modesty, and a sense of humor. For moral action, it is essential to acquire just those virtues that will make immoral conduct impossible; for professional ethical conduct, it is essential to acquire the virtues appropriate to the profession. These virtues should differ depending on the function of the profession in the community. Presumably, the physician will seek to acquire compassion (professional benef-icence) before justice, the judge will seek justice first. The businessman will value prudence (professional wisdom) most highly, the military officer will cultivate courage. The Greeks always linked virtue to function—you are the right person for what you do when you have the character traits that permit you to do it well—and that link continues to make sense.

Can we put the same examples in virtue ethics? Yes, even more easily:

(major premise)	I aspire to be an honest person, I hate the idea of being a thief.
(minor premise)	Taking this necklace without paying for it makes me a thief.
(conclusion)	Therefore I may not take this necklace.

Whatever its theoretical merits, it is worth observing that virtue ethics is as practically effective as we are likely to get. It is close to its subject and highly motivational; most of us in fact abstain from crime because we hold ideals (im-ages) for ourselves that are incompatible with petty crime, not to mention its punishments.

7. Levels of Reasoning: A Case to Consider

It is very rare that a person trying to puzzle through a personal moral dilemma will begin by considering the relative merits of ontological or teleological rea-soning or will appeal directly to beneficence, justice, or respect for persons as a basis for a decision. It is almost as rare for a practicing professional to make such an appeal. We "do ethics" at several levels. For the sake of convenience, we may summarize them here as three, distinguished by the levels of reflection required to apply them:

A.   The level of unreflective taught, or consensus, morality
B.   The level of intermediate rules and principles
C.   The level of first principles and fair procedure

To make these levels clear, an example may be helpful. Easy, or first level, cases might include the following:

You are the production manager of a pharmaceutical company under a lot of competitive pressure. Your boss suggests that you could double produc-tivity if you filled half the penicillin ampules with saline solution instead of penicillin. To be sure, the patients wouldn't get the penicillin prescribed, but most penicillin prescriptions are unnecessary anyway, so probably it wouldn't do anyone any harm.

Harder, or second level, cases along the same line might include:

In the same situation as above, your boss suggests only that you speed up the penicillin production process from culture to filling the ampules, raising a 2 percent probability that the drug dispensed will not be up to the company's standard strength (although still as good as some other products on the market). The quality control manager has just retired, and the company is "searching" for another, so you have a probable three-week window during which you can get the infinitesimally-below-standard drug on the market.

And the cases get still harder, into the third level:

As above, but the company will have to close the plant, cutting 10,000 jobs, unless productivity takes a marked turn for the better in the next quarter.

In practice, the first case would probably not go beyond level A, the level of commonly accepted "taught" morality—the morality of absolute rules. One does not deliberately adulterate product runs or market trash under a product's label. If one is asked for reasons, the simple A-level reasons will suffice: basically, "That simply is not acceptable"; personally, "I couldn't look at myself in the mirror if I did anything like that"; spiritually, "My religion forbids me even to consider anything like that"; or ominously, "I don't look good in orange jumpsuits and neither do you." Note that the conclusion reached is very much in accord with accepted rules and principles and with the ultimate principles that ground them (in this case, non-maleficence, "do no harm").

Principles and reasoning based entirely on consensus morality are not always sound. Recall the Third Reich and the fact that in Germany in Adolf Hitler's time, it was accepted practice, in accord with the religious intuitions of the leaders of the country, and definitely in accordance with law, to kill Jews wherever you found them. That is why we have to know ethics; to know when the principles and reasoning that we ordinarily use need to be reexamined, criticized, and maybe changed.

By the time we get to level B, the need for higher-level reasoning is evident. The harm caused by the acceleration of the manufacturing process is not at all certain—even if penicillin was never prescribed unless it was needed, the mix of batches would ensure that no patient actually got perceptibly less than the proper dose. Here an appeal to a middle-level principle is necessary. The manager must ask himself not, what are the consequences of this action but what would happen if everyone did this? What would be the general consequences of a rule that permitted or required this action? The Golden Rule, "do unto others as you would have them do unto you," is a similar principle.

At level C we have fundamental principles definitely in conflict. Product quality considerations appear in a different light when the fate of the enterprise is at stake. The solution is not immediately clear, and intermediate principles do not really solve the problem (try applying the Golden Rule to this level of the case, letting first the workers and then the customers fill the role of "others"). Here the balance must be struck between the obligation to continue the business enterprise for the sake of shareholders, workers, the local community, and others, and obligations to customers, reputation, society at large, and others with a stake in the integrity of the procedures. The principles of concern for the welfare of those affected by a decision—primarily the employees, in this case—and of justice in following the rules applicable to all no matter what the consequences are logically independent, and there is no safe formula for deciding which shall take priority in a given case. This is the type of case where the articulation of a just or fair *process* for decision is extremely important.

In general, in making moral judgments, we operate by rules of thumb. Depending on the activity in question, we first apply intermediate-level rules derived from the duty of beneficence (what will do the patient the most good? what will maximize profit? what will best serve the client's interests?) or from the duty of respect for persons (what does the client want to do? what career choice does the student feel is best? what do the voters in my district prefer?), then modify those conclusions with each other and with considerations of justice (should states that had no part in generating the savings and loan crisis be taxed to clean up its results? could the money we are allocating to organ transplants be better spent on primary and prenatal care in poorer neighborhoods?). When first principles do enter the discussion, it is often to show how middle-level questions can be answered by supplements from elsewhere in the principle. The rule allowing the student to choose his own courses, for instance, can operate to satisfy the further demand that the student take courses that will benefit him in his future career, by the provision of thorough counseling for the student. The perceived injustice of assessing nonoffending states for the misdoings of the operators of the defunct thrift institutions can be ameliorated, and justice and the interests of the country served besides, by particularly vigorous prosecutorial efforts to bring the criminals among those operators to justice and use their gains to supplement the funds available for paying off the creditors.

8. The Need for Clarity

No one form of reasoning is inherently superior to the other. We may use them all and usually, in the course of a discussion involving ethics, we do. But *it is important to note the differences among them,* for if we do not, we condemn ourselves to talk past each other and frustrate our dialogue. For example, at a dinner party some years ago, we came across a heated debate on the problem of providing special work-training programs for African American employees. One side of the debate, primarily businessmen, maintained that African Americans in that region were no more disadvantaged than the Canadian immigrant majority, and that it was *unjust* to expend resources on one group alone. The other side, made up primarily of schoolteachers, argued that education and training provided the only *decent prospects for the future* for a group concededly underrepresented in the workforce, and indeed, provision of such programs was the only way to achieve real diversity in the workforce and a leg up for the next generation.

Were these two groups really arguing against each other? No. Each could easily have conceded the other's point (and sometimes did) while maintaining its own. Rather, they were arguing *past* each other, one arguing consequentially (toward the future, bleak or somewhat brighter, depending on the means, especially educational means, adopted now), and the other deontologically (from justice). Both, by the way, were making excellent points. You might want to warm up your minds at this point by joining that debate, in imagination, trying to see where virtue ethics might come into the debate, and trying to find a reconciliation.

CAPITALISM AND THE BUSINESS SYSTEM

Capitalism as we know it is usually traced to the work of Adam Smith (1723–1790), a Scottish philosopher and economist, and a small number of his European contemporaries. The fundamental "capitalist act" is the **voluntary exchange**: Two adults, of sound mind and clear purposes, meet in the marketplace, to which each repairs in order to satisfy some felt need. They discover that each has that which will satisfy the other's need—the housewife needs flour, the miller needs cash—and they exchange, at a price such that the exchange furthers the interest of each. The *marginal utility* to the participant in the free market of the thing acquired must exceed that of the thing traded, or else why would he make the deal? So each party to the voluntary exchange walks away from it richer.

Adding to the value of the exchange is the **competition** of dealers and buyers; because there are many purveyors of each good, the customer is not forced to pay exorbitant prices for things needed (it is a sad fact of economics that, to the starving man, the marginal value of a loaf of bread is very large, and a single merchant could become unjustly rich). Conversely, competition among customers (typified by an auction) ensures that the available goods end in the hands of those to whom they are worth the most. So at the end of the market day, everyone goes home not only richer (in real terms) than when he came—the voluntary nature of the exchange ensures that—but also as rich as he could possibly be, since he had available all possible options of goods or services to buy and all possible purchasers of his goods or services for sale.

Sellers and buyers win the competition through **efficiency**, through producing the best quality goods at the lowest possible price, or through allotting their scarce resources toward the most valuable of the choices presented to them. It is to the advantage of all participants in the market, then, to strive for efficiency—to keep the cost of goods for sale as low as possible while keeping the quality as high as possible. Adam Smith's most memorable accomplishment was to recognize that the general effect of all this self-interested scrambling would be to make the most possible goods of the best possible quality available at the least possible price. Meanwhile, sellers and buyers alike must keep an eye on the market as a whole, adjusting production and purchasing to take advantage of fluctuations in **supply and demand**. Short supply will make goods more valuable, raising the price and bringing more suppliers into the market, whose competition will lower the price, to just above the cost of manufacture for the most efficient producers. Increased demand for any reason will have the same effect. Should supply exceed demand, the price will fall to a point where the goods will be bought. Putting this all together, Smith realized that in a system of free enterprise, you have demonstrably the best possible chance of finding for sale what you want, in good quantity and quality, at a reasonable price. Forget benevolent monarchs ordering things for our good, he suggested; in this system we are led as by an **"invisible hand"** to serve the common good even as we think we are being most selfish.

Adam Smith's theory of economic enterprise and the "wealth of nations" emerged in the Natural Law tradition of the eighteenth century. As was the fashion for that period, Smith presented his conclusions as a series of iron laws: the law of supply and demand, which links supply, demand, and price; the law that links efficiency with success; and the laws that link the absolute freedom of the market with the absolute growth of the wealth of the free market country.

To these laws were added others, specifying the conditions under which business enterprise would be conducted in capitalist countries. The laws of **population** of Thomas Malthus concluded that the supply of human beings would always reach the limits of its food supply, ensuring that the bulk of humanity would always live at the subsistence level. Since Smith had already proved that employers will purchase labor at the lowest possible price, it was a one-step derivation for David Ricardo to conclude that workers' **wages** would never exceed the subsistence level, no matter how prosperous industrial enterprise should become. From these capitalist theorists alone proceeded the nineteenth-century assumption that society would inevitably divide into two classes, a tiny minority of fabulous wealth and a vast majority of subsistence level workers.

That condition hardly satisfies our intuitions about justice. As a young nineteenth-century philosopher, Karl Marx, pointed out, the situation could only, by the same laws, get worse. It was in the nature of capital-intensive industry to concentrate capital within itself: Its greater efficiency would, as Adam Smith had proved, drive all smaller labor-intensive industry out of business, and its enormous income would be put to work as more capital, expanding the domain of the factory and the machine indefinitely (at the expense of the cottage and the human being). Thus would the wealth of society concentrate in fewer and fewer hands, as the owners of the factories expanded their enterprises without limit into mighty industrial empires, dominated by machines and by the greed of their owners.

Meanwhile, Marx went on to argue, all this wealth was being produced by a new class of workers, the unskilled factory workers. Taken from the ranks of the obsolete peasantry, artisans, and craftsmen, this new working class, the "proletariat," expanded in numbers with the gigantic mills, whose "hands" they were. Work on the assembly line demanded no education or skills, so the workers could never make themselves valuable enough to command a living wage on the open market. They survived as a vast underclass, interchangeable with the unemployed workers (recently displaced by more machines) who gathered around the factory gates looking for jobs, *their* jobs. As Ricardo had demonstrated, they could never bargain for any wage above the subsistence level. In Marx's scenario, as capitalism and its factories expanded, the entire population, excepting only the wealthy capitalist families, sank into this hopeless pauperized class.

So Marx took from Ricardo the vision of the ultimate division of Western society under capitalism into a tiny group of fabulously wealthy capitalists and a huge mass of paupers, mostly factory workers. The minority would keep the majority in strict control by its hired thugs (the state—the army and the police), control rendered easier by thought control (the schools and the churches). The purpose of the "ideology" taught by the schools and the churches—the value structure of Capitalism—was to show both classes that the capitalists had a right to their wealth (through the shams of liberty, free enterprise, and the utilitarian benefits of the free market) and a perfect right to govern everyone else (through the shams of democracy and equal justice). Thus the capitalists could enjoy their wealth in good conscience and the poor would understand their moral obligation to accept the oppression of the ruling class with good cheer.

Marx foresaw, and in his writings attempted to help bring about, the disillusionment of the workers: He predicted a point when the workers will suddenly ask, *why* should we accept oppression all our lives? Marx believed the search for answers to this question would show them the history of their situation, expose the falsehood of the ideology and the false consciousness of those who believe it, show them their own strength, and lead them directly to the solution that would usher in the new age of socialism—the revolutionary overthrow of the capitalist regime. Why, after all, should they not undertake such a revolution? People are restrained from violence against oppression only by the prospect of losing something valuable, and the industrialized workers of the world had nothing to lose but their chains.[5]

As feudalism had been swept away, then, by the "iron broom" of the French Revolution, so capitalism would be swept away by the revolt of the masses, the irresistible uprising of the vast majority of the people against the tiny minority of industrial overlords and their terrified minions—the armed forces, the state, and the church. After the first rebellions, Marx foresaw no lengthy problem of divided loyalties in the industrialized countries of the world. Once the scales had fallen from their eyes, the working class hirelings of army and police would quickly turn their guns on their masters, and join their natural allies in the proletariat in the task of creating the new world.

After the revolution, Marx predicted, there would be a temporary "dictatorship of the proletariat," during which the last vestiges of capitalism would be eradicated and the authority to run the industrial establishment returned to the workers of each industry. Once the economy had been decentralized, and each factory turned into an industrial commune run by its own workers and each landed estate into an agricultural commune run by its farmers, the state as such would simply wither away. Some central authority would certainly continue to exist, to coordinate and facilitate the exchange of goods within the country (one imagines a giant computer, taking note of where goods are demanded, where goods are available, and where the railroad cars are, to take the goods from one place to the other). But with no ruling class to serve, no oppression to carry out, there will be no need of state to rule *people*; what is left will be confined to the administration of *things*.

Even as he wrote, just in time for the European revolutions of 1848, Marx expected the end of capitalism as a system. Not that capitalism was evil in itself; Marx did not presume to make moral judgments on history. Indeed, he believed capitalism was necessary as an economic system to concentrate the wealth of the country into the industries of the modern age. So capitalism had a respectable past, and would still be necessary in the developing countries, to launch their industries. But that task completed, Marx asserted, capitalism had no further role in history, and the longer it stayed around, the more the workers would suffer and the more violent the revolution would be when it came. The sooner the revolution, the better; the future belonged to communism.

As the collapse of the Communist governments in Eastern Europe demonstrates, if demonstration were needed, the course of history has not proceeded quite as Marx predicted in 1848. In fairness, it might be pointed out that no other prophet of the time had any more luck with prognostication; the twentieth century took all of us by surprise. But there is much in Marx's analysis that is rock-solid, possibly for reasons, especially ethical reasons, that he himself would have rejected. He pioneered the moral critique of capitalism, and made it possible for us to subject business enterprise, in whole or in part, to moral scrutiny. That reflection brings us to the present time.

THE HISTORICAL MOMENT

The recent past—from the middle of the 1960s to the first years of the third millennium—has shown as much ferment about business and its proper place in our society as did Karl Marx's time. It is not an accident that all the alarm bells seemed to go off at once. The time of the cases in this volume—generally, the last three decades of the twentieth century—has been a time of political and ethical as well as economic ferment. Alive with the idealism of the "soaring sixties," the victories of the civil rights movement, and the first stirrings of the environmentalist movement, **the inheritors of the mantle of liberalism had been promised something that was not true: that concerted and reasonable moral effort could change the world permanently for the better**. As the 1970s began, the nation saw also the defusing of the worst terrors of the Cold War, which had paralyzed the fifties. In the intoxication of this heady new tonic, this new vigor, the engagement in Vietnam came to seem intolerable, and the peace movement was born. When the scandals of bribery and corruption that accompanied Richard Nixon's election in 1972, terminating with Watergate, came to light, the protests swept him out of office. Incriminated in that scandal were all the professions (especially the legal profession), all American business (especially those that had profited from the war effort and contributed, illegally, to Nixon's campaigns), and the entire structure of trust and authority that had cemented society during the rapid industrialization and technologization of the United States during the greater part of the twentieth century. There was a new revolution of rising moral expectations for American business. To meet the challenges, we would need a whole new way of doing business.

Reference Points

It is very hard to summarize the triumph and torment of a generation. Let us focus on a few of the threads that made up the weave of that fabric.

Picket lines and confrontation were adopted as tools for change. A picket line is a military practice. When an army pitches camp for the night or for a period before battle, it rallies a detachment of soldiers (or "pickets"). They march to posts in a circle around the camp, to watch for enemies and to make sure none cross the line. The point of a picket line is that none shall cross. So when the labor movement instituted the practice of a labor strike, they adopted the picket line: Union workers would be posted in a circle to ensure that none should pass into the workplace and that all work would be halted. Once the picket line was established, workers could not enter the worksite and all others who sympathized with the union would also refuse to cross that line. The "rallies" before the picket line were also absorbed into the labor movement, to encourage workers who had every reason to fear that a strike would be dangerous for their livelihood and lives. Leaving military practice behind, the workers also carried signs identifying themselves, the union, and their cause, to inform and to alert the public to their cause. The public aspect of the picket line was picked up by the demonstrators in the civil rights movement, who carried signs around places that refused to serve African Americans or that otherwise countenanced racist policies; the same signs were hoisted in the rallies that accompanied the march and the picketing. The peace movement, which extended from the civil rights movement, used the same signs, organizing them in rallies and parades for public effect, only rarely actually picketing a military establishment, corporate headquarters, or plant. By the time the cases that interest us were current, the picket line, the protest demonstration, and the seizure of buildings were well established in the repertory of all activists.

The circle of community widened and environmentalism became a force on the political scene during these decades. The movement had been around since John Muir, of course, and had its early adherents, but they were confined to organic gardeners and birdwatchers, and lacked any political influence. Laughed at in the 1940s, ignored in the 1950s, the writings of Aldo Leopold, Rachel Carson, and to some extent the Ehrlichs (*The Population Bomb*) began to be taken seriously in the 1960s.[6] By 1970, at the first Earth Day, environmental claims would have a hearing in any forum in the land, and by 1980 all businesses knew they had to take them seriously.

So as a people, as a national community, we were well prepared for the possibility that corporate America might turn out to be an alliance of wrongdoers that would have to be actively opposed, by public condemnation and by public demonstration, in order for morality to survive. This new tone, known for obvious reasons as "Post-Watergate Morality," has pervaded the interactions of business and public since the mid-1970s. We are still learning how to deal with it.

IN BRIEF: THROUGH THE CHAPTERS

It is tempting to divide the cases into classics—the Pinto case, the *Challenger* decision, all the others we've always known—and contemporaries, like sexual harassment. We have resisted the temptation in this edition. All these cases are classics. They deal with the stuff of human nature—greed, bullying, weakness of will, shame, social pressure, complacency—as it shows up on the business scene.

So we begin the book with the newest case, but the oldest human story. Suppose we decide to tamper with the basic stuff of nature, the fundamental instructions of Creation, DNA: Can we, should we, make a profit from modified crops? Is such tampering progress or unendurable *hubris*—defiance of the gods, dangerously wrong?

When forces rally to protect the old way, the natural way, are they always right? The problems that Nestlé S.A. had with the NGOs is now the stuff of legend.

Sexual harassment has to fight for headlines, if only because it is such an old story, and in a world where some nations subject women to death by stoning for "adultery" (often rape), it can hardly seem unusual. But can men harass men? The story keeps taking bizarre turns.

The story of tobacco is a standard in the business ethics curriculum, as a very successful industry that fought to stay alive when its product was found to be inevitably harmful to human health.

The classic Pinto case, modified through the Bronco and the Explorer, is different—there is no earthly reason why your family car should be hazardous to your health, but sometimes it is. Whose fault is that?

With Love Canal, we come upon one of the phenomena that drive businessmen nuts. Whatever Hooker Chemical did in the 1940s, it was completely legal; the company was very careful to specify that no buildings could be put on the site of the dump; the provisions were forgotten, the buildings were built, and the company was held responsible. Some days it doesn't pay to get out of bed.

Where the insider trading scandals are concerned, we have the other side of the business coin: What the players did was illegal, and they knew it, but they calculated that in a relaxed regulatory climate, they could get away with it. The parallels with breaking cases in 2002 will be striking.

The case of the space shuttle *Challenger*, and the decision process that preceded its disastrous launch, has been scheduled to remain unchanged from the first edition. It stands, forever, as an example of the kind of pressures that can drive business in ways that it will later regret, and we had hoped there would never be a need for another chapter in the story. The tragic loss of the Space Shuttle *Columbia* changed the schedule; overtones of the same problems echo through this new disaster.

Union Carbide takes us abroad. How shall we decide what is adequate governance for a foreign partner—especially when the chemicals are dangerous and lives could be at stake?

The savings and loan debacle and the questions raised about the accounting industry in its wake, return us to today's headlines. The accountants have served us well for most of the twentieth century. Is their day over? Will we have to find other watchers?

These cases are all classics in that the central problem for each is bound to recur in some form in many others. Each is one of a kind yet exemplary of its own field and of the difficulties facing corporate executives in the contemporary world. Enjoy the book, learn from the cases, and get out there and do better.

QUESTIONS TO KEEP IN MIND

1. What is the purpose of business? Are human beings a means of production, or is production a means of being human? What about business practice follows from your answer to this question?

2. Why is return on investment (ROI) so often taken to be the core value and test of a business ethic? Are there circumstances in which ROI should be ignored?

3. Where do the appropriate responsibilities of business begin and leave off? After the return on shareholder investment, what may a company strive for? Diversity in the workforce? Mutual help and job satisfaction in the employees? Community service?

READINGS

The following works are major works in ethics and excellent sources for your continued exploration. Most are available in several editions and all can be found at your local library.

Thomas Aquinas, *Summa Theologica,*
   IA–IIAE, QQ 55–67; 90–96

Aristotle, *The Nicomachean Ethics.* Aristotle,
   The Politics

Bernard Gert, *Morality: A New Justification
   of the Moral Rules*

Stanley Hauerwas, *A Community of
   Character*

Thomas Hobbes, *Leviathan*

Immanuel Kant, *Groundwork of the
   Metaphysics of Morals*

John Locke, *Second Treatise: Of Civil
   Government*

Alasdair MacIntyre, *After Virtue*

John Stuart Mill, *Utilitarianism*

John Stuart Mill, *On Liberty*

John Rawls, *A Theory of Justice*

W. D. Ross, *The Right and the Good*

ENDNOTES

1. Charles I. Gragg, "Because Wisdom Can't Be Told," *Harvard Alumni Bulletin* (October 19, 1940).

2. John Stuart Mill, *Utilitarianism,* Mary Warnock, ed. (Cleveland, OH: World Publishing Co. 1962). Many editions are available.

3. John Rawls, *A Theory of Justice* (Cambridge, MA: Harvard University Press, 1971).

4. Immanuel Kant, *Foundations of the Metaphysics of Morals,* Lewis White Beck, tr., Robert Paul Wolff, ed. (Indianapolis, IN: Bobbs-Merrill, 1969). Many editions are available.

5. Karl Marx and Frederick Engels, *The Communist Manifesto,* authorized translation (New York: International Publishers, 1948 [1975]). Many editions are available.

6. Rachel Carson, *Silent Spring* (Boston: Houghton Mifflin, 1962); Aldo Leopold, *A Sand County Almanac* (New York: Oxford Press, 1946); Paul and Anne Ehrlich, *The Population Bomb* (New York: Ballantine Press, 1968).

See also, following on the pioneers, Barry Commoner, *The Closing Circle* (New York: Knopf, 1971).

1

※

Is It Right to Change Nature for a Profit?

The Case of Genetically Modified Agriculture[1]

Questions to Keep in Mind

1. What is genetic modification? How do you create a genetically modified organism (GMO)? When did we start developing them?

2. How did Monsanto get into the business of making GMOs? What economic factors recommended the move to GMOs? Have these factors changed?

3. What is Greenpeace? How and why did Greenpeace get involved in the controversy over GMOs?

4. Where does the controversy over GMOs stand today? What ought Monsanto and other suppliers in this field to do next?

I. UNLIMITED POSSIBILITIES

The use of genetically modified agricultural products (known as GMOs) is increasing in the Canadian farmlands, according to an article in the *Guelph Mercury*. Mary Lou Garr, a spokesman for a consortium of Ontario farmers (AGCare, or Agricultural Groups Concerned About Resources and the Environment), thinks that the current upswing of GMO use comes from their obvious benefits—you can use less pesticide (if the crop has a pesticide engineered into it), you can use less herbicide (if the crop has herbicide tolerance engineered into it so you can get rid of weeds in one spraying), and you use less time—all big savings. Peter Pauls, a professor of plant agriculture at the University of Guelph, agrees. "If we look at how farmers survive," he says, "it's not through price increases for their commodities. They really haven't increased over the years. They've been able to survive by becoming more efficient, more productive."[2] There is no question that GMOs help efficiency by cutting the costs to the farmer to produce the same amount of crops, or more, on the same land. Agriculture has been around for 10,000 years, and breakthroughs in productivity are harder to come by; this one is significant.

But GMOs aren't good only for making money for the farmers. They can save lives and make a serious dent in the hunger and poverty of the developing world, according to Florence Wambugu, daughter of a subsistence farmer in Kenya. Wambugu used her education to discover ways to alleviate the desperate poverty in which she was raised and which still assails sub-Saharan Africa. She describes, with more hope and enthusiasm than we are accustomed to seeing from that part of the world, the work of the Kenyan Agricultural Research Institute (KARI) in helping farmers develop new varieties of bananas, sugar and pyrethrum (a natural insecticide exported by Kenya) and fight maize streak virus (MSV) in the central highlands. Sweet potatoes, a major source of nourishment, also stand to profit from protection against viruses.[3]

What is genetic modification? It is one of a series of techniques for inserting genetic material into the genome of any organism for the purpose of changing the traits of that organism. There are plants, for example, that naturally (without human intervention) have a gene that sickens the insects or caterpillars that would eat them. Finding that gene, agricultural scientists carve it out and insert it in the seeds of another plant that regularly is eaten by those bugs. (It doesn't go quite like that, but that's the general idea.) When those seeds sprout, the resulting plant is resistant to the insects; farmers won't have to spray it with pesticide and won't have to share the crop with the insect life. Similarly, scientists may find a way to make a valuable crop resistant to an herbicide, so the herbicide doesn't hurt it. Now farmers can spray the field with the herbicide; weeds will die but the plant won't, and that saves enormous amounts of work. What could be wrong with that? But the use of GMOs in agriculture has turned out to be very controversial. This is (part of) the story of Monsanto, the company that first attempted to sell GMOs to the farmers of the world.

II. GENETICALLY MODIFIED CROPS:
THE CONTROVERSY OVER
THE "FRANKENFOODS"

The industry, or industries, dependent on biotechnology bear an unwanted distinction. They have been the targets of moral attack since well before they came into being. Only slavery, in the history of free market capitalism, aroused a more intense conviction that the entire motive of an industry is morally flawed. From the first, we have had doubts about the manipulation of the basic materials of life itself for the purpose of making a profit. Part of the doubts seem to be based on quasi-theological grounds, calling attention to the sacred nature of life itself (human, animal, or plant) and expressing serious (if nameless) fears about tinkering with it. In a revealing article in The New York Times international section in July of 1998, Michael Specter quotes a traditional farmer in Germany, denouncing the United States. attempts to "change the basic rules of life" by the production of GMOs. Such changes were not for him, he insisted. "Here we are going to live like God intended."[4] Why should God dislike GMOs so much more in Europe than in the United States? It's a good question, but not one we can take on in this chapter, which deals with the ethics of for-profit operations of the corporations and individuals of the free-market economy. We must, however, take seriously the effects of public perception on market behavior, and the complex shaping of public perceptions by market-related communications.

More doubts come from the environmental perspective. These objections focus not on the consequences of the problematic technology for human rights and interests (the ordinary focus of business ethics)—at least not in the foreseeable future. They focus instead on the values that Aldo Leopold associated with the ethic of the land itself.[5] These values include biodiversity (the preservation of all existing natural species in the environment), the integrity of the ecosystem (freedom from invasion by human activity or exotic species), and resilience (the ability of the ecosystem, or the biosphere, to recover from natural shocks). Such objections, for instance, are raised against many GMOs, including genetically engineered salmon, which gain weight much faster than wild salmon and are therefore more profitable to raise and sell. If they get loose from their pens, however, they might mate with the wild salmon. As the engineered salmon are bigger, they would have an evolutionary advantage (female salmon prefer larger males), and might eventually replace the wild salmon. From the human point of view, so much the better. From the point of view of biodiversity and the integrity of the ecosystem, so much the worse, for a natural species will have been forever altered by human meddling.[6]

We will consider objections that seem to take into account species other than human only when they raise symbolic or other issues that directly affect public welfare or perceptions. For instance, one apparently environmental objection is raised with respect to crops engineered to carry new traits, whose pollen, flying freely among the wild plants, may carry the new traits to plants in the wild. A cardinal example of such an objection was the claim that when pollen from corn engineered to contain insecticide hostile to certain kinds of insect larvae blows upon the milkweed the larvae of monarch butterflies feed on, the monarch larvae might be sickened or killed.[7] To the extent that we are talking only about butterflies and milkweed, the objections might seem to be solely environmental (and not well taken at that: The results of the single study that claimed such damages are disputed, and even if the results are valid, the pollen transfer threatens neither milkweed nor monarchs). But the monarch butterfly is more than an insect. Like the bald eagle, it is a powerful symbol of the beauty of the wild environment, and is closely linked with our perception, often felt more than articulated, that that beautiful environment is fragile and threatened. For this reason, any perceived threat to the monarch arouses reactions that go well beyond the self-interested calculations of the relative advantages and disadvantages of engineered corn, and for this reason we will have to take it seriously as impacting the market.

1. The Special Problems that Attend the New Biotechnology Industry

Why, with all the possibilities open before us, does this industry seem to have so many problems? First, the "products" of biotechnology are difficult to define, let alone evaluate for safety and effectiveness. Genetically modified corn is not like the Pinto car, one of a huge and known species, whose variations can be investigated against a background of known characteristics and government standards. The magnitude of the distance between an established line of automobiles and a new one is usually calculable (and usually small). The distance between regular corn and a GMO just is not calculable: It is either infinitesimal (amounting to no more than a normal variation that might occur in nature) or immense (amounting to the distance between Nature and the untested assumptions of ignorant humans). If the former is true, there is no need to distinguish the new from the old, and the GMO is hardly a "product" at all. If the latter is correct, what kind of testing would ever be reassuring? Unfortunately, the decision to regard the GMO as one or the other is, at present, in the hands of the media and the political process. How should a company that markets such products ensure their safety for the ultimate consumer, meet the objections of competitors and nongovernmental organizations (NGOs) in their proposed markets, and define the directions and limits of future products of this sort? These questions are not separable from other, larger questions, involving world trade in agricultural goods and the World Trade Organization (WTO) that regulates it, the economic situation of the small farmer, and the future of agriculture in every country in the world.

Second, the free market system depends upon the protection of the institution of private property; we cannot buy or sell unless we own, unquestionably, what we sell prior to the sale and will safely own what we buy after it. Intellectual property is like any other property: If an idea or process is my idea, my discovery, my product, I can take out a patent on it. I have a free and exclusive right to the use and licensing of that process or discovery during the life of that patent, and any party who would use it must pay me for a license. Does that include the genes discovered during the process of sorting out the human genome? How about the proteins that the genes turn out to be responsible for synthesizing? Above all, does that include drugs and other modes of therapy developed from all this new knowledge? Does it matter that much of the information assembled by the private parties taking out the patent was actually uncovered by a taxpayer-financed project? Who ultimately has the "right" to all of this new information? The question of the legitimacy of patenting genetic discoveries cannot be separated from larger political and economic questions about the pharmaceutical industry in general. Are its profits too high? Does the burden of drug costs lie unfairly on the backs of senior citizens, who consume a disproportionate share of pharmaceuticals in the United States? (Should such costs be borne by the taxpayer?) What are the obligations of pharmaceutical companies (as opposed to toy companies, for example) to subsidize the purchase of their products for the poor in this country and across the world? In any survey of the moral implications of new uses of genetic knowledge in pharmaceuticals, there is very little solid moral ground in the pharmaceuticals industry on which to plant the surveyor's transit.

Novel and troubling as they may be in and of themselves, the dilemmas of biotechnology are also inseparable from the most intractable and polarizing political and economic disputes of this nation and the world at this time. We *do not know* what to do about the overwhelming march of world free trade and the plight of the small farmer (or any small producer) worldwide. Nor do we know what to do about world hunger. We have no formula for the just and responsible provision of health care in this country, including regulation of the industries that profit from it. These larger contexts and these difficult times must be kept in mind in consideration of the industry-specific problems that follow.

The first problem concerns the warrant of merchantability of genetically modified foods: What responsibilities do Monsanto and its competitors have for assuring their safety? The second concerns the place in the private property system for knowledge of the genome: Should Incyte and its competitors be allowed to patent genes, proteins, and other basic elements of life? We will not get certain answers at this time, but at least we may ask the questions.

2. A Success Story Suddenly Goes Sour: A Brief History

The problem and the possibilities that led to the genetic engineering of market crops are not new. For more than fifteen years we have known that crops could be engineered by the techniques of recombinant DNA to have characteristics that would be desirable—even that it was possible to take a beneficial gene (that repels insects, for instance) out of one species and put it into another, which thereafter, with all its progeny, would have that trait. That crops could be engineered to resist weed killers—saving farmers, in the case of genetically engineered tomatoes, potentially $30 per acre each season by reducing the need for hand or mechanical tilling—was announced in March 1986, in a two-page article in *Science* authored by Marjorie Sun. At that time, the Department of Agriculture was expected to announce very soon its approval of the first outdoor tests of the engineered plants. The article discussed the potential of such a development, especially the business opportunities that awaited the chemical companies that engineered seeds resistant to their own herbicides. There was some discussion of the risk of vertical monopolies as chemical companies acquired seed companies to create the fit they were looking for; there was some talk of the possible environmental problems if farmers became less careful with herbicides; there was a concern over regulation by the EPA. None of the concerns seemed to be serious.[8] As for the concern that people might not want to eat foods known to be genetically modified—that did not come up. No one suspected that at the time.

The need for improvement in the world's agriculture was well known. Up to 40 percent of the world's crops are destroyed as they grow or before they leave the field. Right now it takes one hectare, two and a half acres of land, to feed four people, according to Maria Zimmerman, who is in charge of agricultural research for the sustainable development department of the United Nations Food and Agricultural Organization. A projected increase in demand, stemming from a higher population living at a higher standard of living, means that hectare of land will have to support six people in about twenty years. Working harder will not get the job done; technology has to help. We have the technology. "Scientists can now tell with precision which of 50,000 genes in a plant governs a particular trait. If it is beneficial, they can take that gene out of one species—something that wards off a common insect, for instance—copy it and stick it into another organism, to protect it. That organism, and its offspring, will then have a genetic structure that lets them resist such pests."[9]

By the end of 1986, MIT's prestigious *Technology Review* had reported the development of new and safer herbicides, especially Monsanto Co.'s glyphosate and contributions from Du Pont and Cyanamid. But these are broad-spectrum herbicides, lethal to all plants, which had spurred research to engineer crop plants that will not suffer from the herbicide. The article notes a huge potential payoff should such plants be developed.[10] A year and a half later, Jane Brody reported new developments in hormone production: Designer livestock, created by altering hormones produced by genetic engineering, can create cows with more beef and less fat.[11] The most impressive advance to date was announced a year after that—plants that contained their own insecticide. Understandable enthusiasm greeted the plants with *Bacillus thuringiensis* (Bt), a natural insect killer, engineered into them. There were muted worries that there might be health and safety problems, both for humans and the environment, if more exotic forms of molecule were to be used and got loose; the concern that bugs might become immune to Bt surfaced even then.[12] Environmentalists fought the use of bioengineered Bt, in part on behalf of organic farmers, who would use nothing else and were worried about acquired resistance. When it came to cotton, however, even environmentalists had to concede that biotech is better than the alternative. *Forbes*, a business booster, treated the cotton issue as a success story. In a 1990 article (entitled, of course, "The Lesser of Two Weevils"), *Forbes* reported that cotton farmers in the United States had put 100 million pounds of agricultural chemicals, most of it insecticide, on their crops each year for the past several years. Monsanto's cotton, with Bt engineered into it, resists bugs without all the spraying, saving the environment. The article noted signs that cotton pests were beginning to show resistance to the sprayed insecticides; this fate may well await Bt.[13] But for the time being, agribusiness, in the form of Monsanto, the cotton farmers, and the environment, profited from the new developments.

Before entering controversial ground, it should be noted that the progress of GMOs continued from that point and was widely accepted. "A decade ago," Michael Specter reported in April 2000, "no transgenic crops were commercially available anywhere on earth; in 1995, four million acres had been planted; by 1999, that number had grown to a hundred million. In the United States, half of the enormous soybean crop and more than a third of the corn are the products of biotechnology."[14] And the trend continues.

Tomatoes may have led the way to the present impasse. In 1993, John Seabrook, writing in *The New Yorker*, introduced the Flavr Savr, a tomato with a longer shelf life, developed by Calgene. Almost everyone was enthusiastic about the long-lived tomato, especially Wall Street. Jeremy Rifkin, president of the Foundation on Economic Trends and an anti-technology activist of long standing, well known in technological circles for unflagging opposition to biological research and change, was not. He was already organizing a boycott against the Flavr Savr. Seabrook further wrote that the Mycogen Corporation was even then developing a corn with Bt in it, and that such a corn would be helpful in cutting the use of pesticides (which amounted to 25 million pounds of chemicals per year on corn alone in the United States). That development also was opposed by Jeremy Rifkin and by Environmental Defense (formerly The Environmental Defense Fund), both citing the possibility of cultivating insect resistance to Bt.

Rhone-Poulenc, meanwhile, wanted to make money selling its bromoxynil herbicide, so it was helping Calgene develop a bromoxynil-resistant cotton plant. That meant, in the activists' understanding, more herbicide use. (The growers disagreed, pointing out that if they didn't have to worry about the crop dying from the herbicide, they could use the herbicide once, thoroughly, and have done with it. The activists, most notably Rebecca Goldburg of Environmental Defense, pointed out that when the local weeds acquired the herbicide resistance, you'd have to use all kinds of *other* herbicides to get rid of *them*.)[15] Meanwhile, the Flavr Savr tomato contains an antibiotic to cut down on bacterial attack. Just as regular exposure to an insecticide will lead to insecticide-resistant insects, regular exposure to an antibiotic will lead to resistance among the microbes, a very costly development in terms of human health. Jeremy Rifkin saw the whole genetic modification development as a move to help the drug and chemical manufacturers cash in on the food business. "What we're seeing here is the conversion of DNA into a commodity, and it is in some ways the ideal corporate commodity—it's small, it's ownable, it's easily transportable, and it lasts forever. . . .Genetic engineering is the final enclosure movement. It is the culmination of the enclosure of the village commons that began five hundred years ago. As we have developed as a society and we have moved from an agricultural to a pyrochemical to a biotechnical culture, we have seen that whoever controls the land or the fossil fuels or, now, the DNA, controls society."[16]

By the middle of 1998, the battle was joined. Michael Specter wrote an extensive and thoughtful article, quoted above, on the European rejection of "genetically modified organisms" in the summer of that year. Why is Europe so conservative about its food, he wondered, and came up with three independent answers. First, because Europe has many small farmers, who are threatened by the new agribusiness crops; these farmers are too small to buy into the revolution, and will be driven out of business if it is successful. Second, because Europe, and notably Germany, has a strong environmental movement, the "Green Party" of most European nations. This movement is committed to preservating natural species, and therefore opposing the introduction of new ones, especially species that, spreading through the wild, might threaten natural species; since the movement was born of opposing chemical pollution, it is reflexively antibusiness. The third and most telling reason is "recent history": "The shadow of the Holocaust is dense and incredibly powerful still," said Arthur Caplan, the American ethicist now at the University of Pennsylvania. "It leaves Europe terrified about the abuse of genetics. To them the potential to abuse genetics is no theory. It is a historical fact."[17]

3. Accounting for the Reaction

The Holocaust? How big a deal is it really, Specter asked, to genetically engineer a tomato, corn, or potato plant? Joseph Zak, under contract to the American Soybean Association to calm Europeans, minimized the change, putting it in the line of all advances in agriculture, for instance "when we moved to breeding to make a better product." But another observer said that Europeans see genetic engineering as "tampering with their food," and the perception of manipulation "drives people crazy."[18]

In the fall of 1998, *The Ecologist* devoted an entire issue to the controversy. Entitled *The Monsanto Files: Can We Survive Genetic Engineering?* and featuring on its cover the skeleton of a horse half buried in the endless sand of a lifeless desert, it was a scathing attack on business in general and Monsanto in particular. "This is the company that brought us Agent Orange, PCBs and Bovine Growth Hormone; the same company that produces Roundup, the world's biggest selling herbicide, and the highly questionable 'Terminator Technology.' . . . Can we allow corporations like Monsanto to gamble with the very future of life on Earth?" The issue continues with allegations of threats to health from every GMO on the market, hormone-produced milk, the herbicide Roundup, and all the dioxins and PCBs that Monsanto has sown into the environment from its varied operations. There are several direct attacks on Robert Shapiro, then the CEO of Monsanto.[19]

Why this reaction? Is "the very future of life on Earth" really at stake? It is significant that high on the list of relevant objections to bioengineering is "Mad Cow Disease," referring to an episode of bovine spongiform encephalopathy (BSE) in the U.K. some years ago. (The latest European outbreaks of the disease were not foreseen when *The Ecologist* went to press.) But BSE is a simple transmissible disease, not a product of genetic engineering (or genetic at all). What does BSE have to do with it? The associations with GMOs are interesting:

1. Profit-oriented innovations had led farmers to include the offal of slaughtered animals in feed for their herds of beef cattle; cows are normally herbivores, so we have a violation of nature. That violation is how (we think) the cows became infected in the first place.

2. Even when infected cattle staggered and fell before the television cameras of three continents, scientists plausibly argued (backed up by government health officials) that such disease could not possibly affect humans, so British beef was quite safe.

3. After all the scientists promised it wouldn't happen, some people who ate that beef became very sick, and some died.

These associations prove that reassuring scientists and government officials are not always right, and may not always be honest. BSE has no other role in this controversy, but its supporting role is very strong: The BSE controversy served to undermine the authority of regulatory authority and scientific pronouncements, and that undermining turns out to be very important in the conduct of the GMO debate.[20] We'll see those cows again.

"We have eaten the apple and now we will have to live with the knowledge it gives us," said Gian Reto Plattner, a professor of physics at the University of Basel. "If you look at this as a question of risks it's pretty clear that these crops are safe," he went on. "Explosions and fire are far more dangerous, and we use them every day. But nobody is looking at the use of genetics that way. This is a religious discussion we are having. Many people feel nature is immutable. This work tells them they are wrong, and then they are being told to forget about their basic beliefs. It's really asking a lot."[21]

Of course the objections were answered. No less a personage than former U.S. President Jimmy Carter argued the safety and acceptability of genetically modified organisms, "everything from seeds to livestock." Protesting the regulations proposed for adoption by signatories to the Biodiversity Treaty forged at the 1992 Earth Summit at Rio de Janeiro, Carter argued that the requirement that recipient nations approve, item by item, the importation of any GMOs, would leave food and vaccines rotting on docks all over the world. A farmer himself, Carter points out that "for hundreds of years virtually all food has been improved genetically by plant breeders," by the simple techniques of selective breeding. There is no evidence of any harm from any genetically engineered products, some evidence of much benefit, and if the technology is halted at this point, the real losers will be the developing nations and the poor of the world.[22] But where science and regulators had not been totally effective, Jimmy Carter's influence added little; the controversy continued. In October 1998, Michael Pollan wrote an extensive account of a potato (New Leaf Superior) from development to planting in his own garden; the controversy that enveloped his account, including a gripping description of his own uneasiness with this unregulated, unexplained organism, foreshadows all later problems with this technology.[23]

4. The Terminators and the Lordly Monarchs

In the middle of 1999, the volume of the war increased noticeably. Popular literature was beginning to notice the controversy, and the consumer movement checked in on the side of the environmental activists.[24] Meanwhile a new controversy erupted. Monsanto had engineered a new kind of gene, instantly dubbed the "terminator gene," one that would make sure that its bioengineered plants had no progeny. Why do this? An unsigned editorial in *The Economist* explained: "Terminator is a set of genes that act as a series of molecular switches. These switches are set off by a chemical signal sprayed on genetically tinkered seed. Although the plant springing forth from that seed is healthy and can go about its business of producing grain, say, quite normally, the grain that it produced will not grow if planted, because the activated terminator gene has killed off the seed's reproductive bits. This means that farmers who want to grow a plant with the same genetically engineered traits next season have to go back to the company for more seeds."[25] A new uproar greeted the news. First, how mean of Monsanto to deprive poor farmers of the developing world the possibility of saving their seeds! More ominously, would these genes spread, by pollen, to the fields of neighboring farms? If they did, would they inject themselves into the seeds of traditional crops, making it impossible for farmers planting them to save their seeds from year to year? How would these farmers know that their seeds were contaminated until a new crop simply failed to germinate, and their family starved? What new death spores was science (for profit) loosing on the world?[26]

The publicity was immense. Still in development, and long in advance of being used anywhere, terminator genes were already being blamed for crop failures all over the world. The Rockefeller Foundation, which sponsors agricultural projects across the world, strongly objected to their use. Monsanto CEO Robert Shapiro, by now used to progress blowing up in his face, formally promised not to commercialize the genetic engineering of seed sterility. "Given its parlous public image, Monsanto must be hoping that its move will buy it a little goodwill. The terminator technology has raised such interest in the industry, and caused such an outcry in society, because it is a neat and potentially powerful way for biotechnology firms such as Monsanto to protect the intellectual property locked in genetically modified seeds. . . ."[27] As Laura Tangley indicated in "Seed Savers Get a Break": "More than 1.4 billion people, most of them in poor, developing countries, rely on farm-saved seed as their primary seed source and are unable to afford repeated annual expenditures for new seeds." As a result, terminator seeds could be a real "threat to world food security," according to Hope Shand of the Rural Advancement Foundation International, a farmer's advocacy organization. Monsanto, Tangley pointed out, is not the only company working on them. "The battle highlights the difficulty of protecting intellectual property when the products are sophisticated genetic technologies. Monsanto and other firms have said the terminator is a legitimate way to recoup the billions of dollars they have poured into developing bioengineered crops with traits such as insect resistance."[28]

That's a good point. How *do* we protect real intellectual property?[29] The controversy also underscores the difference between developed world and undeveloped world patterns of agriculture. Yearly buying of new seeds is the way farmers do business in the United States now. The hybrid seeds that farmers use to produce the wonder crops to which we have become accustomed do not breed true—do not produce the uniform crop we expect—so we have to buy new each year. But in poorer countries, they often recycle whatever seeds they have, hybrid or not. They have no choice.

In high-technology agriculture, in developed countries, terminator genes could have their uses. In experimental fields, where we are trying to introduce new hybrids, the use of a terminator could save the time and effort of "tasseling," removing the male pollen before the plant can self-fertilize. If we can get the formula specific enough, we can shut down genes (like the engineered gene to produce the pesticide Bt) when we don't need it, turn it on when we do. The uses are tantalizing. But in the present world uproar, they are not open for discussion.[30]

The controversy rapidly grew. It did not stay in Europe: Brazil suddenly, in the middle of 1999, discovered reasons to dawdle over the approvals needed for growers to plant genetically modified ("Roundup Ready") soybeans and to build a Roundup herbicide factory. Why? European resistance was cited; that sort of fear is highly contagious, and Brazil wanted to make sure that their farmers could sell their crops. Monsanto, which had just invested $550 million in Brazil, was less than happy; why not let growers make the decision, they asked?[31] In an article tellingly entitled "Tampering with the Natural Order," Mark Nichols told the story of a farmer who grows canola (rape) on his farm near Bruno, Saskatchewan, who never, to the best of his knowledge, bought seed from Monsanto, but now finds Roundup Ready (herbicide resistant) canola on his farm, and Monsanto suing him for the royalties. How did it get there? How much control over farmer's crops should Monsanto have? At this time there is little controversy in Canada or the United States about genetically modified foods, but will Canada follow the example of the U.K.? Nichols also suggested that the approval process for these crops is probably compromised, since Canada has poured $300 million into biotech research and development.[32]

What's the farmer to do? An editorial in *Farmers Guardian* April 1999 groused that "in the middle of claims and counter-claims, speeches, demonstrations, and a High Court decision that environmental protestors could not be banned from interfering in GM crops, farmers were 'piggies-in-the-middle' in all of this," unable to plant competitive crops or rely on the government to protect their income if they didn't. This is essentially a public relations battle, the *Farmers Guardian* commented, and if it were a soccer match, "the score so far is about 7-0 to the environmentalists and we haven't even got through the first quarter."[33]

In May of 1999, the soccer match turned even more decisively against Monsanto, as engineered corn was discovered (so it was claimed) to be dangerous to Monarch butterflies.[34] Suddenly, wrote John Carey, covering science from Washington for *Business Week*, "foes of bioengineering in the food supply have their own potent symbol: the beloved monarch butterfly. In mid-May, Cornell University researchers reported that pollen from corn altered to slay corn-borer pests can land on neighboring milkweed plants, where it can kill monarch butterfly caterpillars. The finding has biotech foes exulting. 'The monarch butterfly experiment is the smoking gun that will be the beginning of the unraveling of the industry,' says Jeremy Rifkin. . . . The findings cast genetically altered food plants in a new light. They may benefit farmers and consumers, but now opponents have evidence that there could be worrisome ecological effects on other species." Both Greenpeace and the Union of Concerned Scientists are now asking the EPA to pull the seeds off the market.[35]

Monsanto and Novartis, Carey wrote, are worried that this sort of problem could cause the European fear of gene-altered food to cross the Atlantic. Right now the European Commission will not approve pest-resistant corn, or other GM products. "The industry is in big trouble," according to agriculture consultant Charles Benbrook. "It misplayed its hand by overstating its command of the science and its knowledge of the consequences." If biotech companies had considered unintended side effects years ago, they would not, he argued, be on the defensive now. Carey wrote: "The industry 'asked for trouble, and they got it,' says monarch expert Lincoln Brower of Sweet Briar College."[36] The judgment seems harsh; who could have suspected damage to monarchs? Who knew how to refute the charge that monarchs were being damaged? But that is just the point, of course.

"If the current British furore over genetically modified foods were a crop not a crisis," chortled *The Economist* in June of 1999, "you can bet Monsanto or its competitors would have patented it. It has many of the traits that genetic engineers prize: it is incredibly fertile, thrives in inhospitable conditions, has tremendous consumer appeal, and is easy to cross with other interests to create a hardy new hybrid. Moreover, it seems to resist anything that might kill it, from scientific evidence to official reassurance. Now it seems to be spreading to other parts of Europe, Australia and even America. There, regulators will face the same questions that confront the British government: how should the public be reassured, and how can the benefits of GM foods be reaped without harm, either to human beings or to the environment?"[37] At least, U.K.-based

The Economist consoled us, the U.S. doesn't have to deal with the Prince of Wales, who had taken a very public position against GMOs. The editorial went on to point out that this unforeseen consumer backlash "threatens to undermine both this new technology and the credibility of the agencies that regulate it." That, recall, was the major effect of the fallout from Mad Cow disease (those cows again). By repeated infections of scandal, and general suspicion (fanned by NGOs) that government is in league with the biotech industry, food fears seem to have developed a resistance to official reassurance, much as insect species develop resistance to pesticides.

Through the summer and fall of 1999, the media continued its barrage, following the continuing battles in Europe,[38] tracking the damage to U.S. farmers from the boycott,[39] studying the potential for GMOs to spread to the wild,[40] questioning the ability of bioengineered crops to feed the world as claimed,[41] chronicling the new kinds of "crops" being brought on to the GM line (including leaner pigs and extra-meaty hogs, "Enviropig," a porker with replicated mouse genes that produces manure with less phosphorus),[42] and most ominously, tracking the growing trend in the United States to demand proof that GM food is really safe.[43] By October, Monsanto found itself answering charges that its central weed killer, Roundup (glyphosate), caused cancer. Apparently a "confidential" European Commission report had concluded that glyphosate had "harmful effects" on mites and arthropods that consume harmful insects. Humans exposed to glyphosate, according to a 1999 *Farmers Guardian* report, are three times as likely to get non-Hodgkin's lymphoma. The report was a blow to Monsanto: General acceptance of Roundup is essential if Roundup Ready crops are to be marketed. Monsanto spokesmen dismissed the scientific basis of the studies, pointing out that the studies were conducted in 1995, were badly designed then, and had never been taken seriously.[44]

III. FIGHTING A NETWAR:
THE LEGACY OF MAD COWS

Monsanto was doing something wrong, and nothing in the management manuals could explain just what. It seemed to have science on its side, government regulatory agencies had been supportive, and Monsanto management thought they could really improve the nutritional status of the world (while making money for their shareholders). Where did all this hostility come from? The major factor, as anyone could see by the fall of 1999, was that in none of their calculations had they anticipated the reaction to GMOs from the large privately funded nongovernmental organizations (NGOs) like Greenpeace and Environmental Defense. After all, to whom is a business—a for-profit publicly held corporation—accountable? Two accounts dominate the literature.[45] One holds that the corporation is accountable only to its owners, the shareholders. This view is generally propounded by the Wall Street–oriented business commentary and upheld by a significant stream of our legal tradition. The other, associated with the liberal reform movement that infused the corporate world in the 1970s and into the 1980s, holds that good management must weigh the claims of all the "stakeholders," all who will be affected by the decisions of the corporation.[46] Both views are logically consistent, and both are widely espoused. The latter is generally accorded, among business ethics academicians, some moral superiority to the former. But neither one includes, in theory or in practice, the NGOs as parties who will demand an accounting, and so the NGOs, from case to case, continue to take corporations completely by surprise. Monsanto, Novartis, and the other players in the biotech farming industry were no exception. Eventually the companies—especially Monsanto, the main target—realized that they had to talk to the NGOs directly.

Barry Came, of *Maclean's*, documented the historic conversation between Robert Shapiro, CEO of Monsanto, and Peter Melchett, executive director of Greenpeace U.K., by transatlantic satellite. Melchett, in his glory, accused Shapiro of every form of insensitivity and monopolistic practice, and finally of "bullying" Europe, to force GM foods on them. Shapiro answered dourly that if he was a bully, he sure wasn't very successful at it. This was, according to Came, the "first high-profile acknowledgement that the world's biotech industry, based largely in the United States, is losing the global battle to convince the public of the benefits of genetic engineering." All their efforts had antagonized more than persuaded Europeans. Shapiro identified his own sin: He forgot to listen. It was his fault, and the result was the public rejection of GM products. Canada, Came noted, may be next on the list to boycott GMOs. Already items were being taken off the shelves for suspected GM content. Shapiro had already been forced to agree not to market the Terminator seeds. Investors were unhappy and the boycott was spreading. "Increasingly, genetically 'improved' crops are trading at deep discounts, while European processors have been willing to pay premiums of as much as $1.50 a bushel for non-GM crops. In September, the huge U.S. grain processing corporation, Archer-Daniels-Midland, advised American grain farmers to begin segregating GM and non-GM crops. At the same time, the two main U.S. baby food manufacturers, Gerber Products Co. and H. J. Heinz Co., declared they would no longer use genetically modified corn or soybeans in any of their products."[47] Echoing a theme that underlies the entire conflict, Came wrote:

> The problem is as much about public perceptions as it is about science. In Europe, the anti-GM battle has been waged against the backdrop of a series of European food scares that began with BSE, of 'mad cow' disease, in Britain, and has escalated with scandals over carcinogenic dioxins in Belgian poultry and dairy products and the use in France and elsewhere of sewage slurry in animal feeds. The aggressive stance of U.S. based agribusiness giants has not helped. The U.S. government, responding to pressure from the powerful agribusiness lobby in Washington, has taken the Europeans to court at the World Trade Organization, winning successive decisions against Europe's restrictions on Caribbean bananas and growth

hormone additives in beef. The Americans have threatened similar challenges to European resistance to the free import of genetically engineered grains. . . . The combined effect has been to shatter Europeans' confidence in what they are eating and drinking as well as fostering deep resentment about the unrestrained power of U.S. multinational corporations. 'There has been an unprecedented, permanent and irreversible shift in the political landscape,' Greenpeace's Lord Melchett told Shapiro last week. 'People are increasingly aware and mistrustful of the combination of big science and big business.' . . .

Where will this go next? Newly elected president of the European Commission, Italy's Romano Prodi singled out food safety as the top priority of his infant administration. He proposed a pan-European food agency to deal with issues such as those involving British beef, Belgian chickens, and U.S. genetically modified products. "We have to provide answers," he said, "to those who are wondering if official information can be trusted these days, or is it all being manipulated for economic and political purposes?"[48]

1. NGOs and PR

What do you do with a public relations disaster? Came pointed out that the problem was one of public perception, so Monsanto hired a "perception management," (public relations) firm to take care of the problem. Burson-Marsteller has been retained to pitch genetically modified foods as safe for people and nature. It is, indeed, a novel attempt to reach out to the critics. Shapiro recently "admitted that Monsanto's former hard-ball tactics with critics has backfired against the company, which has been called 'Monsatan' and 'Mutanto' by its biotech opponents. He now wants to establish a dialog. . . ."[49] In the name of dialogue, Shapiro has agreed to meet (privately) with Jeremy Rifkin at the Greenpeace London office. Ralph Nader will arrange the meeting. Meanwhile, no one at B-M will talk to reporters. B-M's job is to counter hysteria; now B-M is getting some hysterical picketing of its own, accused of "deception management," and aiding and abetting polluters.[50] There is a pattern here. All attempts to solve the problem, initiated by the target of the problem, are liable to instant condemnation by the targeters as part of the problem. We will see it again.

Rick Mullin, writing in *Chemical Week* in the last month of 1999, drew one clear lesson from the fracas: ". . . successful corporations will begin taking consumers and the public as seriously as they take Wall Street and shareholders. It shows that while U.S. consumers understand that the role of business is to make profits and create jobs, they also believe the most important goal for companies will be to help build a better society."[51]

"Any lawyer will tell you," Mullin went on, "and any scientist will dispute—that perception is reality. In this case, the lawyers are right. If a majority of the U.K.'s population feels genetically modified seeds pose a threat as severe as eventual global famine, that concern had best be reckoned with. There are good examples of how to handle this, and how not to. While Monsanto fell on its sword by dismissing concerns as typical public ignorance of scientific fact, DuPont chairman and CEO Chad Holliday publicly avowed his company's need to respect public opinion. Addressing the Chief Executives' Club of Boston in September, Holliday said, 'We have to listen to the people who are raising alarms. We don't have all the answers, and to pretend we do, or to brush off concerns as unfounded, is to be arrogant and reckless.'" It took a little longer, but Monsanto eventually came to the same insight. "David Morley, senior v.p./plant sciences at Monsanto, admitted in a speech to the Commercial Development and Marketing Association that, 'Greenpeace effectively made [genetic modification] a consumer issue. We made it a science and regulatory issue. We were behind the curve.' . . . Against a widely perceived threat, Monsanto's calculated efforts to gain trust based on its mastery of science failed. In essence, Monsanto repeated the fatal public relations error made by the nuclear energy industry in the 1970s."[52]

Mullin is not alone in drawing that analogy. Paul Magnusson and co-authors had made the same comparison to the nuclear industry in *BusinessWeek* in October 1999. They went on to point out that the huge PR war is not without consequences. To avoid the EC boycott, Archer-Daniels-Midland (ADM), the United States largest dealer in agricultural products, had demanded that all its suppliers segregate GM grain from "natural" grain. Consider the dilemma of farmer Dave Boettger: He has 280 acres, half in GM crops. ADM will pay eight cents a bushel more for the natural product. But if testing reveals even a tiny amount of altered genes in the higher priced shipment, he has to pay ADM to dump the whole load. Pollen blows over all his fields; he can make no guarantees that none of the GM pollen blew into a natural field. Now, how does he sell his crop? [53]

GM crops were sold to the farmers, after all, as an "agricultural revolution: The new corn, soybeans, potatoes, oilseeds, and cotton promised to fight pests, boost yields, and cut chemical use. . . . Now they find that the fierce backlash in Europe . . . is cutting off billions of dollars in export sales." Even as the battle goes on, with everyone swearing the GM foods are safe, all food processors are going back to buying conventional foods.[54] This retreat from the new crops hurts farmers and incidentally undermines the battle against protectionism in world trade. The United States could, after all, retaliate for this irrational prejudice against our crops more than it has. It could demand "safety guarantees" for French wine and cheese, after all. What about the French practice of "using animal blood to draw solids from its red wines"? "Allowing public sensitivities to decide these highly technical issues is a very dangerous slope," said Clinton administration chief agricultural negotiator Peter L. Scher. The demand for "labeling," as far as Scher was concerned, was a non-starter. It's like placing a skull-and-crossbones on each package and invites exclusion.[55]

The stakes are high. Overseas shipments of U.S. crops came to $46 billion in 1998, giving us a $5 billion trade surplus in farm products. Half of U.S. soybeans and one third of U.S. corn are genetically modified. About 60 percent of processed food and virtually all candy, syrup, salad dressing, and chocolate, have GM material in them. Monsanto had hoped to reap $881 million by 2003 in licensing fees for its high-tech seeds. It appears that it will fall far short of that target.[56]

The controversy is not just a matter of anti-U.S. sentiment, although that helps. Activists go after European companies too, like Switzerland's Novartis. The companies, scientists, and governments agree that GM food is safe. The FDA has ruled that no special labels on GM food are needed since the new strains are not different from hybrids developed by cross-breeding. The World Health Organization (WHO) also has approved GM food. "But science is no match for public opinion in Europe, where debacles such as Britain's mad cow disease [there go those cows again] and other food-contamination problems have eroded confidence in government regulators. Now, the bio-food phobia is catching on in Japan. Brewers have sworn off GM corn, and the government is mandating labeling for 28 different products containing GM food. Japanese tofu makers, responding to public sentiment, are switching to non-GM soybeans, jeopardizing some 500,000 tons of imports, most of them from the U.S." U.S. companies, by now, approve of Romano Prodi's suggestion for an EU equivalent of the FDA, on grounds that it might restore government credibility.[57]

As the battle continued through winter and spring, a measured defense of biotechnology was heard. John Carey and others presented a solid examination of the whole topic ("Are Bio-Foods Safe?") in *Business Week* toward the end of 1999;[58] Margaret Kriz did the same in "Global Food Fights" in *The National Journal*.[59] Both pieces pointed out that genetically engineered foods had indeed been tested, certainly much more than conventional foods were ever tested, and that time and again, the proof of the pudding had been in the safe eating. Paul Krugman, a columnist for *The New York Times*, poured contempt on the whole biotech protest, pointing out that GM foods have indeed been tested, and have been shown to be safe and really useful, while the "dietary supplement" industry, which retails without prescription all kinds of megavitamins and the like, is entirely unregulated, unwatched, and potentially really dangerous.[60] But the trend was still strongly the other way. Carey Goldberg reported a huge protest march in Boston that raised serious questions about the level of information available to activists. The protest was timed to coincide with Bio2000, a meeting of biotechnology scientists and business promoters (7,000 participants were expected in Boston for five days.) The businessmen and scientists did their best to contain the uproar: "In a pre-emptive salvo against the protesters, about 2,000 scientists from around the world, including two Nobel laureates, signed a 'Declaration in Support of Agricultural Biotechnology,' said AgBioWorld.com, an advocacy group that released the declaration on Thursday. It quoted the declaration's organizer, Dr. C.S. Prakash of Tuskegee University, as saying that 'biotech crops allow farmers to grow more food on less land with less synthetic pesticides and herbicides.'"[61]

But Prakash was outnumbered. " . . . Protesters argued today that the agricultural biotechnology industry, fueled by greed, was placing human health—possibly the health of the biosphere—at risk. 'These are the people who gave us thalidomide babies,' Sarah Seeds, a protester who also trains others to protest nonviolently, said of the participants in the Bio2000 convention. 'Now they want to give us genetically modified food.'"[62] Thalidomide?

If 2,000 scientists are ineffective, can a "perception management" firm do any better? The spring of 2000 blossomed with truly lovely full-page full-color ads in the newspapers ("Biotechnology gives her a better way to protect her crop—and her grandchildren's planet"), and a wonderful, brightly colored and well-written brochure, "Good Ideas Are Growing" sponsored by the industry association, the Council for Biotechnology Information. Will this campaign work? Ross S. Irvine, in a special article in *O'Dwyer's* PR Services Report, thinks the whole campaign is ridiculous. "The Council for Biotechnology Information is spending more than $50 million for an advertising campaign to convince consumers that biotech food is safe to eat and not a threat to the environment," in an effort, probably useless, to keep Frankenfood fear out of the U.S. There is nothing wrong with biotechnology, he points out; it holds out great hope for the world. But this isn't the way to defend it:

> They are basically throwing the money away because feel-good image ads just don't make it in the era of the Internet. Corporate PR people need to engage in a 'netwar' to succeed in today's fast-paced communications arena. It's hard to believe that the corporate PR people who are supposed to be laying the foundation for public and regulatory acceptance of biotechnology stubbornly rely on communication strategies and tactics that were effective 20 years ago. Corporate PR pros who want to update their PR effectiveness should look at the strategies and tactics used by activist groups. The challenge is to adapt those strategies for the corporate world. . . . reliance on traditional communications tools such as brochures, toll-free phone lines, and advertising is out-of-date in cyberspace. It's worth noting that anti-biotech activists and other non-governmental organizations have gained the upper hand in the biotech debate without the use of paid advertising. They have mastered the power of the Internet to make their argument and forge alliances.[63]
>
> "Information is power" is the lesson learned by non-governmental organizations during the past 15 years. They learned that if they provided their supporters with information, those supporters felt knowledgeable and empowered. With that sense of empowerment, supporters were comfortable taking a public stand on issues. The NGOs also learned that as supporters were given more information, they became increasingly autonomous and took the initiative to undertake their own PR campaigns. Through the use of the Internet—and its ability to distribute vast amounts of information quickly and inexpensively—local grassroots groups have enormous resources at their disposal. In any community, a small group of activists with an Internet connection could become an informed, effective, and powerful champion of a cause. . .[64]

For example, there's the NGO that Monsanto should have known well, The Pesticide Action Network of North America (PANNA). Its mission is to replace pesticides with environmentally friendly, less dangerous, means of pest control. By now it links "local and international consumer, labor, health, environment and agriculture groups into an international citizens' action network [that] challenges the global proliferation of pesticides, defends basic rights to health and environmental quality, and works to insure the transition to a just and viable society." (This from the PANNA Web site http://www.panna.org) All organizations in that coalition can reinforce each other with regard to pesticides or their home cause, and with the level of communication they have, they can easily take on any new related cause, constructing links to the home interests of all their affiliates. Biotechnology does admirably as such a new cause.

As far as activism is concerned, the move to the net is a paradigm shift, which has already attracted the attention of the American military:

> In the early and mid-1990s, RAND, the American military think tank, started looking at the Internet and its impact on modern conflicts, including those involving social activists and NGOs. Biotech opponents are a recent example of the type of social activists RAND discusses. RAND notes:'The information revolution is leading to the rise of network forms of organization, whereby small, previously isolated groups can communicate, link up, and conduct coordinated joint actions as never before. This, in turn, is leading to a new mode of conflict—netwar—in which the protagonists depend on using network forms of organization, doctrine, strategy, and technology. Many actors across the spectrum of conflict from terrorists, guerillas, and criminals—who pose security threats—to social activists—who do not—are developing netwar designs and capabilities.' From the concept of netwar, RAND coined the word 'netwarrior' which can be either an individual or an NGO. At the heart of a netwar is the dense, free and broad distribution of information to a variety of activists who have an interest in an issue. . . .[65]

The corporation's traditional functional hierarchy, it turns out, is its worst enemy. "RAND has this to say about netwars, which are now an established and recognized form of social conflict: 'The information revolution favors and strengthens networks, while it erodes hierarchies. Hierarchies have a difficult time fighting networks. It takes networks to fight networks. Whoever masters the network form first will gain major advantages.' The messages to the controllers of the biotech industry's campaign are clear," Irvine concludes. "Enter the 21st century. Learn from past and ongoing netwars in which you have been defeated in the battle for public understanding and acceptance. Give up your hierarchical, command-and-control approach to communications. Adapt to the realities of the Internet. Master the network form of organization. Become netwarriors!"[66]

The Council for Biotechnology Information now has a Web site, http://www.whybiotech.com, in addition to its full-page ads and booklets. Maybe it will do the industry some good. But it will be catch-up all the way.

2. The Wall Street Waffle

Investors look at matters from a narrow, but very well focused, perspective. Is this company, this industry, a good investment? If I add these shares to my port-folio, will they make money for me? The answer to this question, where ge-netically engineered agricultural products are concerned, has been one largely of ambivalence. It is not possible to pick a time before which all accounts were bullish on biotech stocks, after which they were bearish. Rather, enthusiasm and disenchantment seem to coexist in the same financial universe, with the latter holding a distinct edge.

The bulls make a convincing case, for instance, through Tim Stevens in "Sowing Seeds of Success." Stevens is enthusiastic about the emergence of the "industry of life science . . . a convergence of chemistry, pharmaceuticals, biotechnology, agrobusiness, and nutrition." Its value, he said, comes from syn-ergy among those enterprises, all of which are working with DNA, recombi-nant processes, the very stuff of life itself. Of course the industry will have "growth spurts and growing pains . . . divestitures and myriad acquisitions. . ." and the like, but with a strong technology base, this very diverse enterprise presents an "enormous" opportunity for value creation (here Stevens cites Gary Pfeiffer, CFO of Du Pont, Wilmington, DE).[67] This sentiment is echoed in a substantial account of the industry by Ray A. Goldberg, in "Transforming Life, Transforming Business: The Life-Science Revolution." While generally enthusiastic about the new "life-science industries," Goldberg emphasized the transition problems that the industry would have to confront. Essentially, a life-science company merges a pharmaceutical enterprise (drugs) with an agricul-tural enterprise (seeds). Both will be using recombinant DNA technology, so the combination makes sense. But drug companies moving into agriculture must remember that they are moving from a very high profit industry with no cycles to a cyclical industry with a much lower return. The corporate cultures of the industries are very different. Monsanto and Novartis are cited in the ar-ticle as examples of life-science companies that ran into financial difficulties that they had not foreseen. For some reason there are problems gaining the foreseen efficiencies in marketing and distribution. Goldberg acknowledged that the major problem seems to be overcoming resistance to the product.[68]

While the bulls are formal and tentative, the bears are scathing. Wall Street has little patience with corporations that cannot manage their public relations problems. As early as April 1999, Amy Barrett was warning investors not to "sow their seeds too soon" in the emerging life-science industry. Monsanto was praised as a good investment individually, only because of its new drug, Celebrex, selling in the infinitely rich market of remedies for arthritis. But as for the rest of the industry, ". . . life-sciences business has limitless potential. But for those looking for an opportunity to invest, the key word is 'potential'—the big payoff from biotech agriculture will likely be years in coming."[69]

By the end of the summer of 1999, Deutsche Bank was advising investors to get out of the industry: ". . . The public's rejection of genetically modified foods in Europe may lead to a share price collapse for genetically modified

seeds firms," such as Pioneer Hi-Bred and Monsanto. "Today, the term genetically modified organism has become a liability," said Timothy S. Ramey, analyst
at Deutsche Bank (New York). "We predict that genetically modified crops,
once perceived as the driver of the bull-case for this sector, will now be perceived as the pariah."[70] At that point, Monsanto's Shapiro apparently gave up,
not for the first or last time, and started looking for a good buyer to sell the
company to.[71]

After listening to both sides, *The Economist* joined the bears. "The world's
leading 'life-sciences' firms, among them Novartis, AstraZeneca and Monsanto,
which have put together agricultural products and drugs, are wondering if
they got their cross right. Much-vaunted exchanges of technologies and joint
development have yet to materialize. Compared with agriculture, making
drugs is so profitable that many life-sciences firms find agrochemical divisions
a drag on their share prices." Along with Monsanto, many life-science companies were planning to sell off their agricultural division. The life-science combination, *The Economist* observed, should have worked because both need
recombinant DNA information and processes. But basic research is only one-
fifth of the development cost; the rest is field trials and marketing, and at that
point the two industries are very different. "As Tray Thomas, head of Context
Consulting, points out, consumers will pay the earth for a new medication,
but farmers balk at a new, expensive chemical. Agriculture is inherently less
profitable than pharmaceuticals, with profit margins of around 10%, about a
third of what drugs earn. Few pesticides fetch more than a billion dollars; and
indeed the worldwide market in chemical pesticides and seeds is $35 billion,
roughly a tenth of global drug sales." The present slump in commodity prices
due to years of good harvests hurts more; the consumer backlash against GM
foods makes matters worse. The American market may be next for consumer
backlash. And there may be crossover boycotts: Some German doctors have
threatened to boycott Novartis' drugs because of its GM crops. Under those
circumstances, it is wise for drug companies to divest themselves of their agricultural divisions. Matters are not helped by a financial backlash, as investment
analysts urge once-enthusiastic investors to head for the door.[72]

By December 1999, GMO enthusiasm was under full attack. "If you're
making up your New Year's tally of what's in and what's out, add the once-
trendy term 'life-sciences company' to the latter list," wrote Amy Barrett in
BusinessWeek. Novartis and Monsanto were once stars in any portfolio of businesses. "These days, however," Barrett wrote, "many of those same companies
are scrambling to cast off the life-sciences moniker. They're all shedding their
agricultural divisions to concentrate on their pharmaceutical divisions. Monsanto is obviously trying to do the same.

> Why the sudden reversal? For one thing, the consumer backlash against
> genetically engineered foods continues to grow in Europe, and it shows signs
> of gaining traction in the U.S. That makes the business of marketing geneti-
> cally engineered seeds a tricky one. At the same time, the U.S. farm economy
> remains in the dumps, hurting sales of traditional herbicides and pesticides.
> The vaunted "synergy," Barrett concluded, never really materialized.[73]

A Christmas article in *The Economist* chronicled Robert Shapiro's fall from grace with scornful wonder. "How could a master of marketing and an exponent of business ethics get things so spectacularly wrong?" By that time, Monsanto had merged with Pharmacia & Upjohn, and *The Economist* confidently expected that soon the agribusiness would be history, as would Shapiro. To his defenders, *The Economist* opined, Shapiro was a visionary trying to save the world's environment and feed the world's people. To his detractors, he was blind. "He failed to understand the nature or the magnitude of the mess that Monsanto is in, or the way to extricate it, until it was too late."[74] There was some bad luck, the article conceded. After all, he wasn't responsible for mad cow disease (there they are again). But he failed as a businessman. He moved too fast buying up seed companies "to have a lock on the science from laboratory to farm." As a result, he paid too much, he got the company in much too much debt, and simultaneously attracted the attention of farmers, activists, and the Justice Department for monopolistic tendencies. When Shapiro withdrew Monsanto's offer for the last seed company, Monsanto was $6 billion in debt, which would have been all right if the biotech industry had taken off as it was supposed to do, which it did not. Investors deserted him all the more quickly.

Shapiro's major mistake, according to *The Economist*, was to attempt to carry on business as usual when the NGO attacks began. He and his managers

> were convinced that those whose ignorance led them to reject biotechnology would eventually be swayed by Monsanto's assurances of safety and its research, which is highly praised in both industry and academia. Company officials have doggedly defended the firm's genetically tinkered seeds and high-tech agrochemicals by trotting out studies on increased crop yields and falling pesticide outlays. *Yet the public wants to talk about social values, not soyabean statistics.* Mr. Shapiro now acknowledges that he was naïve, especially when it came to fighting the criticism of pressure groups and the press by scientific arguments alone. What Mr. Shapiro seemed to forget was that scientific certainty often sounds like corporate arrogance.[75]

The message is significant. Business ethicists and concerned citizens alike have tried everything to get the owners and managers of very large corporations to listen to messages of consumer need, morality, caution, attention to the environment. We have tried persuasion, and persuasion usually lands on deaf ears. We have tried regulation, and watched corporate campaign contributions distract legislators from taking regulation seriously. We tried in desperation tying ourselves to trees. Now, finally, here is a successful effort. It is no shining model: The activists know much less about the science than we could have wished, their targets are not always well chosen, and this whole debate has *nothing at all to do with Mad Cow disease.* Meanwhile, activists may have poisoned the atmosphere so that later developments that might bring real good, especially to the poor of the world, will not be brought to market. But they have, finally, succeeded in convincing the business press and at least one industry that environmental concerns must be taken seriously or the consequences may be disastrous for the market, the corporation, and the investor.

The conclusion, as far as the business world is concerned at this point, was articulated in June 2000, again in *BusinessWeek*. Shapiro had failed at Monsanto. The company had changed focus from limitless visions to cutting costs. All revenue was threatened by "global backlash against genetically engineered foods." The $30 billion deal that had merged Monsanto with Pharmacia & Upjohn in March had spun off Monsanto as the agribusiness section. Should investors consider putting their money into that agribusiness spinoff from the new company? "Our overall view is to stay away," advised a portfolio manager at Dresdner RCM Global Investors. Especially since the backlash seems to be spreading to Brazil, Monsanto must prove that it can deliver solid earnings growth now before investors will be interested in it again.[76]

IV. THE PRECAUTIONARY PRINCIPLE VS. THE RISK BENEFIT RATIO: WHY PUBLIC RELATIONS IS NOT THE ONLY PROBLEM

Is there more here than meets the eye? Europeans are not normally less rational than Americans; there is no *a priori* reason why Europeans should be terrified of food that we have been eating for years without apparent harm. Three other factors in the profoundly hostile European reaction are worth mentioning before we pass to the future.

First, there is the possibility that Europeans have a preference for what is known as the "precautionary principle," the conservative principle according to which no new thing is to be accepted until it has been proved beyond a reasonable doubt to be safe and better than the present products. Americans, on the other hand, more trusting of novelty, may be inclined to go with a risk-benefit calculation, placing the new idea (product, whatever) on a par with the old and comparing them for safety and advantage. So Americans may accept an unknown innovation while Europeans greet it with skepticism.

Second, even if Europeans had in this case used a risk-benefit calculation, weighing whatever risks there might be with the benefits of genetically altered food, no one ever suggested to them that there were any consumer benefits. Monsanto did not think any risks were associated with the foods. But were there any benefits? All the benefits mentioned were for the growers, who could cut dramatically their costs for chemicals and labor, and so make a bigger profit. Presumably some of the profit would be passed on to consumers, but the corn that benefited went mostly to hog and cattle feed (i.e., to other producers, not to consumers), and the rape plants were all ground up for canola oil that went into processed food, not to supermarket shelves. At no point did the consumer get in on the cost savings, and no one ever suggested that these GM foods were healthier, safer, or better tasting.[77]

Third, there is the question of the small farmer. Europe has many of them, and they are a powerful political force. GM crops, with the high expense for seed and the economies to be realized in savings on tillage, are not for the small farmer. Their profit is in volume. GM crops, like all large-scale agribusiness, do best in depopulated areas like the Great Plains in the United States, where small towns turn to ghost towns as the Atlantic and Pacific coasts gain population. In the United States, the small farmer is not a political force; the "farm vote" is cast by the enormous automated farms that have inherited the heartland. Is this move to agribusiness, away from the small farmer, a good idea? The question has force in the United States—where sentiment at least remembers the family farm—and political weight in Europe, but is of terrible portent in the developing world. Across India, the Philippines, and other nations of Africa, Asia, and South America, the search for market access has given priority to huge plantings of single crops for export only. Ironically, these large farms, owned by multinational corporations, often share the region with the farmers they displaced, now without enough food to feed their children.[78] Ultimately, the issue whether it is better for the consumer and for the farm family to carry on agriculture through small local farms providing local markets with a variety of crops or through huge monocultures supplying global markets through worldwide transportation networks is larger than we can consider here. But it's worth thinking about.[79]

V. WHERE WE GO FROM HERE

What future can we expect for genetically modified food? Both sides of the dispute are in motion. A cover story in *Time* on the new "golden rice," genetically modified to contain beta-carotene (vitamin A) proclaimed, "This rice could save a million kids a year," and proceeded to present a convincing argument for the assertion, based on the extent and consequences of malnutrition in the developing nations. The article rehearsed the by now familiar arguments against uncritical acceptance of genetic modifications, and does a nice job of capturing the European suspicions of multinational companies bearing gifts of new products.[80] But its focus on Ingo Potrykus, professor of plant science at the Swiss Federal Institute of Technology, who worked for years to develop the rice, put a human face on the development of transgenic organisms for the first time. Potrykus really does want to save the world, or at least to feed a significant portion of its children with a more nutritious diet. Before the world writes off GMOs as an idea whose time will not come, someone has to explain why it is not necessary to save children from blindness and depressed immune systems.[81]

Meanwhile, all the controversy has finally stirred the regulatory agencies into action; we may expect more attention to the testing and marketing of

GMOs in the U.S.[82] Until recently, the controversy faced off European GMO opponents against U.S. GMO supporters; now reports of "eco-terrorism" on Long Island suggest that the battle may be crossing the pond more quickly than we thought.[83]

The industry continues to develop new technologies, possibly in hopes of finding one that will not arouse the ire of the activists and U.S. and Canadian farmers are still planting genetically modified crops on their farms.[84] By now, cotton and corn protected by Bt are widely grown, Canola and Roundup Ready soybeans are still popular, and in many circles, new transgenic crops are defended. When a ringspot virus attack on Hawaiian papayas in 1994 almost destroyed the orchards, with no chemical or "natural" remedy available, only the introduction of transgenic papaya saved the crop. Hawaiian papaya growers are now very enthusiastic supporters of GMOs. Similar viruses afflict many crops in Africa, according to Kenyan plant scientist Florence Wambugu, cited at the beginning of this chapter. She hopes that the introduction of a transgenic sweet potato that is resistant to the feathery mottle virus will help Africa double its sweet potato harvest. There seems to be no other option. Bananas may be next. In Africa, nearly half the fruit and vegetable harvest is lost because it rots on the way to market; bananas that ripened more slowly could yield 40 percent more bananas. Herbicide-resistant plants would improve education: "We could liberate so many people if our crops were resistant to herbicides that we could then spray on the surrounding weeds. Weeding enslaves Africans; it keeps children from school."[85] Wambugu's opinion of the European flap on "Frankenfood"? "Ludicrous."[86]

And for all our doubts, our policies on buying, using, even thinking about, GMOs, are substantially inconsistent. There is still no fully satisfactory explanation for the fact that GMOs have been a non-issue in the U.S. and anathema in Europe. And why is it such a problem in Japan, even trace amounts previously unsuspected?[87] There is no separating worries about food safety and worries about public relations. Genetically modified crops are now widely grown (52 percent of soybeans are modified), even as the conflicts multiply. Novartis, a Swiss pharmaceutical giant, makes and sells genetically modified corn and soybean seeds, while Gerber Products, one of its subsidiaries, has virtuously banned all genetically modified ingredients from its baby-food formulas. Heinz has banned GMOs from its baby foods but not its other products. McDonald's will not accept genetically modified potatoes for its fries, but it cooks them in vegetable oil made from modified corn and soybeans. Pepsi Cola uses corn syrup made from genetically modified corn, but Pepsico's Frito-Lay division won't use that corn in its chips.[88] Right now confusion reigns. The experiment seems destined to continue; we may hope that some combination of common sense from science, government, and the market will eventually sort out the real cautions from the hype.

QUESTIONS FOR REFLECTION

1. Is there something wrong in creating economic value out of "natural" life materials? Compare:

   The breeding of cocker spaniels
   for desirable traits

   Selecting tall, dark-haired men for
   movie stardom

   Coaxing bell peppers to grow in
   many colors for the market

   Cosmetic surgery

2. Did Monsanto have any *obligation*
   to Greenpeace? Why or why not?
   If it did, what kind of obligation
   was it?

3. If Monsanto's conflict with
   Greenpeace was just a management problem, how should it have
   been handled? If the conflict was
   more than a management problem, what was it really about?
   Discuss the role of the NGO in
   contemporary business management.

4. If the flap over GMOs was just a
   PR problem, how should it have
   been handled? What would you
   have done? If it was more than
   that, what was it?

ENDNOTES

1. An earlier version of this chapter, em-
phasizing the environmental rather than
the business aspects of the dilemma, is
found in Newton and Dillingham, *Watersheds*, Belmont, CA: Wadsworth Publishing Co., 2001.

2. *Guelph Mercury,* July 24, 2002.
http://www.guelphmercury.com/news/
news_0207189561.html

3. Information taken from Florence
Wambugu's Web site, http://www.
modifyingafrica.net. Incidentally, the
contact information on that site seems to
be incorrect (as of July 2002), and the
book *Modifying Africa* does not appear in
Books in Print.

4. Michael Specter, "Europe, Bucking
Trend in U.S., Blocks Genetically Altered
Food, *The New York Times* (July 20,
1998): p. A1, A8.

5. Aldo Leopold, "The Land Ethic," in *A
Sand County Almanac* (New York: Oxford
University Press, 1949): pp. 201ff. See
especially p. 224: "A thing is right when it
tends to preserve the integrity, stability,
and beauty of the biotic community. It is
wrong when it tends otherwise."

6. Carol Kaesuk Yoon, "Altered Salmon
Leading Way to Dinner Plates, but Rules
Lag," *The New York Times* (May 1, 2000):
pp. A1, A20. The fears were aired in a
National Public Radio broadcast on May
12, 2000, featuring Becky Goldburg of
Environmental Defense.

7. Carol Kaesuk Yoon, "Altered Corn
May Imperil Butterfly, Researchers Say,"
The New York Times (May 20, 1999): pp.
A1, A25. See also the next day's editorial,
"A Warning from the Butterflies," May
21, 1999. See also John Carey, (Carey
Covers Science from Washington), "Im-
periled Monarchs Alter the Biotech Land-
scape," *BusinessWeek* (June 7, 1999):
pp. 36.

8. Marjorie Sun, "Engineering Crops to
Resist Weed Killers," *Science* 231 (21
March 1986) pp. 1360-1361.

9. Michael Specter, "Europe, Bucking
Trend in U.S., Blocks Genetically Altered
Food," *The New York Times* (July 20,
1998): pp A1, A8.

10. Charles M. Benbrook and Phyllis B.
Moses, "Engineering Crops to Resist

Herbicides," *Technology Review* (November/December 1986): pp. 55 ff.

11. Jane E. Brody, "Quest for Lean Meat Prompts New Approach," *The New York Times* (April 12, 1988): pp. C1, C4.

12. Amal Kumar Naj, "Can Biotechnology Control Farm Pests? Specialty Plants May Cut Need For Chemicals," *The Wall Street Journal* (May 11, 1989): p. B1.

13. Gary Slutsker, "The Lesser of Two Weevils," *Forbes* (October 15, 1990): pp. 202–203.

14. Michael Specter, "The Pharmageddon Riddle," *The New Yorker* (April 10, 2000): p. 58–71.

15. Rebecca Goldburg, "Biotechnology's Bitter Harvest: Herbicide-Tolerant Crops and the Threat to Sustainable Agriculture," Biotechnology Working Group of the Environmental Defense Fund, 1990.

16. John Seabrook, "Tremors in the Hothouse: The Battle Lines Are Being Drawn for the Soul of the American Consumer as Agribusiness Launches the First Genetically Altered Supermarket Tomato," *The New Yorker,* Brave New World Department (July 19, 1993): pp. 32–41 (quote at 38–39).

17. Michael Specter, "Europe, Bucking Trend in U.S., Blocks Genetically Altered Food," *The New York Times* (July 20, 1998): p. A1, A8.

18. Specter, loc. cit.

19. *The Ecologist: Rethinking Basic Assumptions* 28(5) (September–October 1998).

20. The "Mad Cows" have raised a floating panic about such mysterious brain disease. Consider U.S. government plans to destroy nearly 400 sheep because there is a chance that they *may* have been exposed to Belgian sheep that *may* be infected with some variant of BSE (as opposed to scrapie, a disease of the same family which often shows up in sheep and is not transmissible to humans). Carey Goldberg, "U.S. Planning to Destroy Sheep at Risk of an Infection," *The New York Times* (July 18, 2000): p. A12. Consider also "mad squirrel disease," the flap over which is chronicled by Burkhard Bilger in "Letter from Kentucky: Squirrel and Man," *The New Yorker* (July 17, 2000): pp. 59–67.

21. Specter, op. cit.

22. Jimmy Carter, "Who's Afraid of Genetic Engineering?" *The New York Times* Op-Ed (August 26, 1998).

23. Michael Pollan, "Playing God in the Garden," *The New York Times Magazine* (October 25, 1998): pp. 46 ff.; see his new treatment in *The Botany of Desire: A Plant's-Eye View of the World,* (New York: Random House, 2001).

24. Ralph Nader wrote the Foreword to Genetically Engineered Foods: Changing the Nature of Nature (What You Need to Know to Protect Yourself, Your Family, and Our Planet) by Martin Teitel and Kimberly Wilson (Rochester, VT: Inner Traditions International, Ltd., 1999).

25. "Fertility Rights," *The Economist* (October 9, 1999).

26. Barnaby J. Feder, "Plant Sterility Research Inflames Debate on Biotechnology's Role in Farming," *The New York Times* (April 19, 1999): p. 18.

27. "Fertility Rights," *The Economist* (October 9, 1999).

28. *U.S. News and World Report* (October 18, 1999): p. 83.

29. See the Darden School (U. of Virginia) case study, "Monsanto and Intellectual Property," and subsequent discussion in *Teaching Ethics* 2(1) (Fall 2001): 91–117.

30. "Fertility Rights," *The Economist* (October 9, 1999). "Terminator Terminated," *Farm Industry News* (November 1999).

31. Kara Sissell, "European Consumers Stunt Brazilian Crops," *Chemical Week* (April 21, 1999): p. 48.

32. Mark Nichols, "Tampering with the Natural Order: Genetically Altered Foods Are Filling North American Shelves with Startling Speed—and Scant Publicity," *Maclean's* (May 17, 1999): p. 59.

33. "Red Faces over Genes in Greens," *Farmers Guardian* (April 23, 1999): p. 10.

34. Yoon, "Altered Corn." "A Warning From the Butterflies," *The New York Times* (May 21, 1999).

35. John Carey, "Imperiled Monarchs Alter the Biotech Landscape," *Business-Week* (June 7, 1999): p. 36.

36. Ibid.

37. "Who's Afraid?" *The Economist* (June 19, 1999).

38. Diane Johnson, "France's Fickle Appetite," *The New York Times* Op Ed (August 2, 1999). Warren Hoge, "Britons Skirmish Over Genetically Modified Crops," *The New York Times* (August 23, 1999): A15.

39. Melody Petersen, "New Trade Threat for U.S. Farmers," *The New York Times* (August 29, 1999): pp. 1, 28.

40. Charles C. Mann, "Biotech Goes Wild," *Technology Review* (July–August 1999): pp. 36ff. Solid coverage of the whole issue, beginning with the concerns that engineered crops might spontaneously breed with wild relatives, creating super-weeds. See also Carol Kaesuk Yoon, "Squash With Altered Genes Raises Fears of 'Superweeds,'" *The New York Times* (November 3, 1999): pp. A1, A18. See also Letters to the Editor, *The New York Times* (November 8, 1999).

41. Peter Rosset, "Why Genetically Altered Food Won't Conquer Hunger," *The New York Times* Op Ed (September 1, 1999).

42. "Seeds of Change: In the U.S. and Elsewhere, the Food Supply Is Being Genetically Altered. Here's Why You Should Care," *Consumer Reports* (September 1999): p. 41.

43. Marian Burros, "U.S. Plans Long-Term Studies on Safety of Genetically Altered Foods," *The New York Times* (July 14, 1999): p. A 18. Jeffrey Kluger, "Food Fight," *Time* (September 13, 1999): pp. 42–44.

44. "Monsanto Denies Cancer Threat from Weedkiller," *Farmers Guardian* (October 15, 1999): p. 7.

45. For purposes of this essay, the accounts will be referred to by name only. A rich literature awaits those who would enter the discussion.

46. The term stakeholder was coined and the theory developed by R. Edward Freeman, primarily in *Strategic Management: A Stakeholder Approach* (Boston, MA: Pitman, 1984).

47. Barry Came, "The Food Fight," *Maclean's* (October 18, 1999) p. 44.

48. Ibid.

49. Ibid.

50. Kevin McCauley, "B-M Engineers Biotech PR Drive by Monsanto," *O'Dwyer's* PR Services Report, (December 1999): p. 1.

51. Rick Mullin, "Mob Rule," *Chemical Week* (December 8, 1999): p. 5.

52. Ibid.

53. Paul Magnusson, Ann Therese Palmer, and Kerry Capell, "Furor Over 'Frankenfood,'" *BusinessWeek* (October 18, 1999): p. 50.

54. Ibid.

55. Ibid.

56. Ibid.

57. Ibid.

58. John Carey, Ellen Licking, and Amy Barrett, "Are Bio-Foods Safe?" *BusinessWeek* (December 20, 1999): p. 70.

59. Margaret Kriz, "Global Food Fights," *The National Journal* 32(10) (March 4, 2000): 688.

60. Paul Krugman, "Natural Born Killers," *The New York Times* Op Ed (March 22, 2000).

61. Carey Goldberg, "1,500 March in Boston To Protest Biotech Food," *The New York Times* (March 27, 2000): p. A14.

62. Ibid.

63. Ross S. Irvine, ePublic Relations Ltd., (http://www.epublicrelations.org),"'Netwarriors' Fight Way to Top in Corporate PR," *O'Dwyer's* PR Services Report (May 2000): p. 1. Copyright © 2000 by J.R. O'Dwyer, Inc. Used with permission.

64. Ibid.

65. Ibid.

66. Ibid.

67. Tim Stevens, "Sowing Seeds of Success," *Industry Week* (September 6, 1999): p. 68.

68. Ray A. Goldberg, "Transforming Life, Transforming Business: The Life-Science Revolution," *Harvard Business Review* (March/April 2000): 94.

69. Amy Barrett, "Investors, Don't Sow Your Seeds Too Soon," *BusinessWeek* (April 12, 1999): p. 74.

70. Alex Scott, "Deutsche Bank Advises Investors to Sell Crop Companies' Shares," *Chemical Week* (August 25, 1999/September 1, 1999): p. 32.

71. Robert Westervelt, "Monsanto Back on the Block," *Chemical Week* (August 25, 1999/September 1, 1999): p. 9.

72. "Hybrid Rigour," *The Economist* Editorial (September 11, 1999).

73. Amy Barrett, "Gene Is a Four-Letter Word on Wall Street," *BusinessWeek* (December 20, 1999): p. 76. See also "The De-merging of Life Sciences," *Farm Industry News* Editorial (January 2000).

74. "Grim Reaper," *The Economist* Editorial (December 25, 1999).

75. Ibid. Emphasis added.

76. Amy Barrett, "Rocky Ground for Monsanto?" *BusinessWeek* (June 12, 2000): p. 72.

77. Goldberg, "Transforming Life."

78. Vandana Shiva, "Small Scale Farming: A Global Perspective (South)" *The Ecologist* 30(4): (June 2000) 37.

79. A fair amount of such thinking is found in "Facing the Farm Crisis," *The Ecologist* 30(4) (June 2000): pp. 28 ff.

80. "Trojan Horse" is what that golden grain is usually called. See Andrew Pollack, "A Food Fight for High Stakes," *The New York Times* Week in Review (February 4, 2001): p. 6.

81. J. Madeleine Nash, "Grains of Hope: Genetically Engineered Crops Could Revolutionize Farming. Protesters Fear They Could Also Destroy the Ecosystem. You Decide," *Time* (July 31, 2000): pp. 38–46.

82. Melody Petersen, "U.S. to Keep a Closer Watch on Genetically Altered Crops," *The New York Times* (May 4, 2000): p. A23.

83. Michael Cooper, "Wave of 'Eco-Terrorism' Appears to Hit Experimental Cornfield," *The New York Times* (July 21, 2000): pp. B1, B8.

84. "New Gene-Altering Strategy Tested on Corn," *Science News* 157 (May 6, 2000): p. 294-295; David Barboza, "U.S. Farmers Still Planting Biotech Crops: Only a Slight Dip in Use of Gene-Altered Seeds," *The New York Times* (July 1, 2000): p. C1.

85. Nash, "Grains of Hope," p. 46.

86. Wambugu, *loc. cit.*

87. Stephanie Strom, "Altered U.S. Corn Found in Samples Sent to Japan," *The New York Times* (January 18, 2001): W1.

88. For a company to maintain even a limited ban successfully, it must have extraordinary knowledge of its sources. Most companies buy products on the open market, and most food suppliers have no idea whether or not there are GMOs in the mix. A labeling regimen would be very hard to carry out even if everyone thought it was a good idea.

2

Who Will Protect
the Babies?

The Long Ordeal of Nestlé's
Infant Formula

Questions to Keep in Mind

1. What *facts* are relevant to the infant formula controversy? What facts were alleged by Nestlé's critics? What facts were found by the anthropologists? What facts are relevant to the health of the babies of developing nations?

2. What is a nongovernmental organization (NGO), of the sort that we find in INFACT and IBFAN? How is an NGO defined? What are the internal principles of its operations? What are the imperatives that drive it (as "profit" drives a business)?

3. What global factors and forces did Nestlé encounter that led to the conflict? Was there anything Nestlé could have done to avoid these factors, or mitigate their impact?

4. What mistakes did Nestlé make that companies in similar situations should avoid?

I. THE SKELETON OF THE CASE:
A CHRONOLOGY OF THE NESTLÉ BOYCOTT

1. Development, Use, and Production
of Infant Formula (1867–2002)

As it is with all mammals, human mothers have always suckled their infants; as with all mammals, sometimes the milk fails or is insufficient. What shall we feed the infant when that happens? Historically, mothers who could not breast-feed have tried primarily milk from other animals, but also almost any substance associated with food that the infant could fit in its mouth and keep down. In 1867 Henri Nestlé developed the first commercial infant food (a milk and cereal pap). In 1869, he said why:

> During the first months, the mother's milk will always be the most natural nutriment, and every mother able to do so should herself suckle her children ... [but] there will never be enough woman's milk to nourish all the children that are born. We must then seek some suitable substitute. ... I have endeavored to make a food suitable for infants, and fulfilling all the conditions sought for by physicians.[1]

From the 1860s to the early 1960s, sweetened condensed milk was the most used commercial breast-milk substitute in developing countries. From the 1950s to the 1970s, sweetened condensed milk was gradually replaced as a breast-milk substitute, first by full cream and half cream (low fat) powdered milk, then by modern infant formula from the United States, Europe, and Japan. Beginning in the 1970s and to the present, pediatricians and public health agencies have advised against the use of unmodified milks for infant feeding; infant formula has grown steadily in popularity. Since the 1960s, the developed world has generally enjoyed a choice between breast-feeding and a range of good formulas for feeding newborn babies. Proportions vary by region, but about half of all new mothers in the developed world choose formula. In that choice, the developed world is being joined by the urbanized and prosperous areas of the developing world, especially in places like Hong Kong, Singapore, Taiwan, and Malaysia.

Infant formula is increasingly made in the developing world. Nestlé began local dairy product manufacture in developing countries in 1921, with production in Brazil. By 1998 more than 100 Nestlé factories in over 40 developing countries were manufacturing dairy products (including infant foods) using local milk; other companies, international and local, are also involved in this enterprise.

2. Emergence of a Public Health Controversy:
A Collegial Inquiry 1966–1973

In 1966 Dr. Derrick B. Jelliffe, an expert in child nutrition and Director of the Caribbean Food and Nutrition Institute, published under the auspices of the

World Health Organization (WHO) a pamphlet, *Child Nutrition in Developing Countries*, calling attention to the dangers of bottle-feeding in "traditional and semi-sophisticated populations." In 1969 the United Nations Protein Advisory Group (PAG) (working group on child nutrition) met in Bogotá, Colombia; Jelliffe's testimony, by then a serious condemnation of infant formula companies, took center stage. Jelliffe hypothesized a train of events that made the formula industry responsible for infant mortality, based on the following scenario, hereinafter the Jelliffe scenario (note: this is our summary, based on many accounts):

> We know that infant mortality is rapidly increasing in the developing world. We also know that breast-feeding is decreasing throughout the developing world, while sales of infant formula are increasing by leaps and bounds. There is alarming evidence that the sales of infant formula are leading directly to the infant deaths, and that the formula industry's promotional practices are primarily to blame. Consider how it happens: A poor mother with a new baby is gently urged by "mothercraft" or "milk" nurses at the hospital in which the baby was born, not to breast-feed her infant. Instead, she is told, she should adopt the modern, scientific infant feeding practice of bottle-feeding formula, the same kind of formula advertised on the radio and on billboards and flyers, with pictures of fat happy babies sitting beside cans of powdered formula—just the way all the better educated mothers did these days. Unaware that the "nurse" was being paid a commission to sell the formula, the mother takes her "expert advice," allows her breast milk to dry up and takes the baby home with free bottles and nipples and several cans of formula generously provided by the hospital. Alas, she is illiterate and cannot read the instructions that tell her to sterilize the bottles, the nipples, and the water that she mixes with the formula. Even if she could read, how is she to carry out the sterilization procedures on her three-stone stove (fireplace)? But the water supply is contaminated, and soon the baby develops diarrhea. That lowers his ability to absorb nutrients from the formula. Then, of course, the formula given by the hospital rapidly runs out, and she finds that it is very expensive to buy. So she does not buy enough, and extends it with too much water—contaminated water. Now the infant has malnutrition added to his intestinal illness, and between them, he dies of malnutrition and dehydration. In order to make a profit on this hitherto untapped market, the infant formula industry, especially Nestlé S.A., has adopted deceptive hard-sell promotional practices (including undermining the mother's confidence in her ability to produce enough milk for her baby) that deliberately disrupt the new mother's breast-feeding in order to sell their product. That disruption was the cause of that child's death—death by "commerciogenic malnutrition."

Jelliffe followed up in 1972 with "Commerciogenic Malnutrition? Time for a Dialogue," in *Food Technology*,[2] reinforcing his scenario.

The PAG's working group issued its Statement No. 23, "Promotion of Special Foods (Infant Formula and Processed Protein Foods) for Vulnerable Groups," on July 18, 1972, with a revised edition issued on November 28, 1973. According to this statement (hereinafter PAG 23)

Governments were called to

Encourage industrial investment for the development of highly nutritious foods

Reduce fiscal burdens on processed infant formulae and weaning foods

Consider subsidy programs (including free distribution) to provide nutritious infant formulas and weaning foods to the poorest groups;

Stimulate the use of mass media channels for both education and responsible product promotion.

Pediatricians and other physicians, for their part, were urged to

Keep informed of developments in infant and child feeding, including the promotion of breast-feeding but also the use of processed foods and home-prepared weaning foods;

Meet with representatives of the food industry to discuss progress in child nutrition, with particular emphasis on the needs of low-income populations.

Industry was asked to

Ensure that breast-feeding be stressed in its own employee training programs and that sales and promotional methods discouraging appropriate breast-feeding be avoided;

Avoid direct promotion to new mothers, recognizing that the hospital nursery was not appropriate for any promotion of infant foods directed at other than professional personnel;

Develop "unambiguous" standard directions for the preparation of commercial formulas, taking into account the needs of illiterate persons;

Use product labels and literature as a means of encouraging better hygiene practices in infant food preparation.[3]

Throughout this period, Dr. Jelliffe was really the only voice for significant restraint of the infant formula companies, and even he was calling for "dialogue." PAG 23 was, as we can see, a moderate document, asking everyone to work together for the health of the infants and specifically recommending the use of infant formula as appropriate. Until 1973, virtually every participant in the debate was a pediatrician, an industry expert, or a member of an international commission charged with studying the subject, and on the whole, they worked together as colleagues.

3. Crunch Time: The Debate Goes Public (1973–1978)

In **August 1973** *The New Internationalist* published "The Baby Food Tragedy," an interview with two leading child nutritionists, Dr. Ralph G. Hendrickse of the Tropical Child Health Department at Liverpool University and Dr. David Morley, an expert on Third World nutrition. The article begins with a disclaimer insisting that there are many instances in which formula can "supply a vital need"—famine, disaster, sick infants, or other situations where the mother cannot breast-feed—and that the editors were interested only in those cases where bottle-feeding was inappropriate. The pediatricians interviewed added similar disclaimers, and volunteered on occasion that they noticed promotional practices had changed for the better since the controversy had begun in 1970. But the burden of the interview, and the message of the editorial that preceded it, was a condemnation of the infant formula industry on account of the disruption of breast-feeding caused by the infant formula promotions—in short, the Jelliffe scenario. Nestlé was given a chance to reply to the article and, in the course of the reply, invited the authors or anyone else to come to Nestlé headquarters in Vevey, Switzerland, to learn about Nestlé's approach to infant formula sales in the developing world. In **December 1973** Mike Muller, from the British organization War on Want, took Nestlé up on the invitation and spent several days in Vevey researching infant formula. Then he returned to London and wrote *The Baby Killer*, published in **March 1974**—essentially a restatement of all the charges in "The Baby Food Tragedy" with fewer of the qualifications. The pamphlet got a very wide circulation, and was soon picked up by the Arbeitsgruppe Dritte Welt (ADW) ("Third World Working Group"), a tiny left-wing student organization, which published an altered "translation" of the pamphlet (leaving out *all* the qualifications) as *Nestlé Totet Babys* ("*Nestlé Kills Babies*") in **June 1974**.

In **June 1974** Nestlé sued the ADW for libel on several counts, which eventually narrowed to the issue of the title alone. The trial, which took place in Berne, Switzerland, was a classic mismatch: The ADW turned out to consist of seventeen unknown activists who thoroughly enjoyed skewering the giant Nestlé in public for the two years of the trial. In **July 1976** Nestlé won its case—but at a terrible public relations cost. The trial positioned Dr. Jelliffe, who testified for the ADW, as the world's favorite authority on infant nutrition; it gave worldwide currency to his scenario of the poor third world mother duped (by Nestlé, for its own profit) into using formula rather than breast-feeding; and it made *The Baby Killer*, in which that scenario played a central role, known in the United States.

The battle was crossing the Atlantic. In **September 1974** the Consumers' Union published an editorial critical of the infant formula industry.[4] In the course of **1975** the Interfaith Center on Corporate Responsibility (**ICCR**), led by Timothy Smith and based on Riverside Drive in New York City, encouraged Leah Margulies, a young activist committed to the cause of justice for the third world, to make the infant formula cause her own.[5]

Public education continued: An emotion-engaging and very influential film, *Bottle Babies*, came out in 1975 and was widely used for grass-roots organizing—spreading the word. Finally in **1975** (after about a year of discussions following the publication of PAG 23) the infant formula industry realized that it would be well advised to adopt a modicum of organization to prepare responses to these attacks, and eight companies, including Nestlé, joined to put together the International Council of Infant Food Industries (**ICIFI**). Meanwhile members of the ICCR bought stock in Ross/Abbott to force that company to negotiate under threat of a shareholder resolution to be submitted at the annual meeting in 1976. Eventually Ross/Abbott did get the ICCR the information it wanted and agreed to policy changes for its overseas marketing; claiming its policy was stricter than that of ICIFI, it declined to join ICIFI. In 1975 the ICCR also demanded that Bristol-Myers furnish information on its sales and promotional practices.[6] In reply, Bristol-Myers published a 19-page report (August 7, 1975). The report did not satisfy anyone, especially the Sisters of the Precious Blood, also shareholders in Bristol-Myers, so they brought up another shareholder resolution in 1976, and eventually sued the company on September 27, **1976**, for filing a false proxy statement. U.S. District Court Judge Pollack threw out the case in May **1977**; the Sisters appealed. Faced with such persistent critics, U.S. companies decided to negotiate with the Infant Formula Action Coalition (INFACT) and the Sisters. By mid **1978**, Borden had agreed to scale back powdered milk promotion, Ross/Abbott scaled back its use of milk nurses, and Bristol-Myers ordered all its employees to cut off all contact with new mothers (in addition to giving the Sisters opportunity to to present their case in the company's quarterly report and directly to the Board of Directors). Nestlé, the giant, had no shareholder meetings in the U.S.; something else would have to be done with Nestlé.

On **July 4, 1977, INFACT**, brand-new on the scene, and led by Douglas A. Johnson of the Newman Center in Minneapolis, Minnesota, started a boycott against Nestlé, urging consumers not to buy any of Nestlé's U.S. products (which did not include infant formula). The demonstration leafleted churches, erected a huge puppet baby bottle in front of Nestlé USA's offices, and used coffins and banners, all announcing the boycott and the goals of the drive—to stop public formula promotion, mass media advertising of formula, distribution of free samples, "milk nurses," and promotions to medical professionals. Beyond that, they demanded that Nestlé "prevent artificial formula foods from getting into the hands of people who do not have the means or facilities to use them safely."[7] As soon as the boycott was established, INFACT and its allies started a campaign for U.S. Senate hearings, working to persuade Senator Edward Kennedy to hold public hearings on the infant formula issue before the Subcommittee on Health and Scientific Research of the Committee on Human Resources of the U.S. Senate, which he chaired. "Before long, more than 50 letters a day were pouring into Senator Kennedy's office."[8] Moved by genuine concern for the babies of the third world, and briefed extensively by the activists, Kennedy scheduled Hearings on the subject for May 1978.

On **May 23, 1978**, the hearings began. A parade of critics of industry, primarily from the ICCR, presented the case against Nestlé alleging that Nestlé's promotional practices were disrupting breast-feeding and killing babies in the third world. In his opening remarks, Kennedy set the tone of the hearings by asking,

> Can a product which requires clean water, good sanitation, adequate family income, and a literate parent to follow printed instructions be properly and safely used in areas where water is contaminated, sewage runs in the streets, poverty is severe, and illiteracy is high?[9]

The opening witness for industry, Dr. Oswald Ballarin, chairman of Nestlé-Brazil, criticized the boycott's charges as "misleading and inaccurate," and accused its leadership of "an indirect attack on the free world's economic system," and of having "the stated purpose of undermining the free enterprise system." Kennedy attacked Ballarin vociferously, everyone else followed suit, and Nestlé had to swallow another public relations disaster born of its efforts, as it saw the matter, to defend itself against unjustified attack. Prakash Sethi reports that

> it soon became apparent to everyone—even those who were not in on the writing of the script—that Nestlé was on the road to creating another major strategic blunder and public relations fiasco in the United States, a blunder of greater magnitude that the one that befell the company not too long ago at the Berne trial and the ensuing adverse publicity against Nestlé in Europe.[10]

Of possibly greater public effect than the "blunder" was the testimony of Dr. Jelliffe. In the testimony that he had submitted in advance to Kennedy, he had repeated his scenario of infant death-by-formula and offered as a "guesstimate"—his word—that a return to breast-feeding worldwide would prevent 10 million cases of marasmus (malnutrition) and diarrhea. When Kennedy questioned him on this point, it came out, "you believe that there would be a saving of 10 million infant lives a year with the return of breastfeeding . . . ," to which Jelliffe answered "Yes." Jelliffe went on to explain, qualify, and retract, but that Yes created the next activist publications—"10 million babies dead each year . . . because of industry's marketing and promotional practices."[11]

May 1978 also saw the issue of Bill Moyers' influential documentary, "Into the Mouths of Babes," highly critical of the industry and Nestlé in particular; in **November 1978** the National Council of Churches endorsed the boycott. The controversy by now was anything but collegial, and it was not going well for Nestlé.

4. Back to the International Context: WHO Code Development (1979–1981)

But at least the conflict was changing scene, always a relief. In **July 1978**, Kennedy met with representatives of AHP, Ross/Abbott, Bristol-Myers, and

Nestlé to determine what to do next. At the request of ICIFI President Ian Barter of Cow & Gate (a U.K. milk producer), to which Nestlé added a supporting letter delivered by Jacques Paternot, a Nestlé executive,[12] Kennedy asked the director general of the World Health Organization (**WHO**) to sponsor an international conference to discuss the issue and come up, if possible, with an international recommendation for marketing infant formula in the third world. Thereafter the action lay with WHO and the other agencies of the United Nations. By the time WHO and UNICEF held the Meeting on Infant and Young Child Feeding in **October 1979**, Nestlé had already developed internal guidelines, limiting advertising and sales promotions, curbing free samples and supplies, spelling out the content of informational materials and ending all financial incentives for health professionals to sell formula. The conference developed a (somewhat strained) "consensus" on the subject of formula promotions, urging limitation of many types of promotions and calling upon WHO to develop a full code for the governance of the marketing practices of the infant formula industry. Immediately after the "consensus" was announced, ICIFI announced that an industry-generated voluntary code would be drafted as a working model, and proceeded to put one in place, working with the governments of Malaysia and Singapore to link with their national codes. The activists of INFACT and the ICCR, banding together as the International Baby Foods Action Network (**IBFAN**) announced that the consensus did not go far enough, and that it was time to internationalize the U.S. Nestlé boycott through the new International Nestlé Boycott Committee (**INBC**). World organizations have to move more slowly: WHO can do nothing without the express approval of its governing body, the World Health Assembly (**WHA**), and had to wait until its May 1980 meeting for the specific instruction (to its Director General) to draft an international code. The drafting began immediately, and proceeded through 1980. In **January 1981** the WHO executive board approved a draft of its new International Code of Marketing of Breast-milk Substitutes; it was adopted by the WHA on **May 21, 1981**. A portion of that code appears here.

> In pursuit of its aim (Article 1), the International Code sets out detailed provisions with regard to:
>
> products within its scope (Article 2), in keeping with definitions formulated for the purposes of the Code (Article 3);
>
> the appropriate dissemination of information and education on infant feeding (Article 4);
>
> the marketing of breast-milk substitutes and related products to the general public and mothers (Article 5);
>
> measures to be taken in health care systems, and with regard to health workers and employees of manufacturers and distributors (Articles 6, 7, and 8);
>
> the labeling and quality of breast-milk substitutes and related products (Article 9 and 10);
>
> the Code's implementation and monitoring (Article 11).[13]

The United States delegation voted against adopting the Code, on several procedural grounds and on one substantive ground: The Code did not address any specific issues of infant health, nor—absent any proof that there was any connection between infant formula promotions and infant health, a connection that the U.S. delegation doubted existed—did it address any issues at all having to do with WHO's mandate. In general, "WHO had no business telling private business how to sell its products," nor was "WHO an international Federal Trade Commission."[14] Meanwhile, the industry had cast about for some more direct defense. Throughout **1980** Nestlé-U.S. continued to attempt to defend itself and the West's economic system in the manner of the 1950s, strategizing for better media exposure and accusing the National Council of Churches, through distribution of an anti-NCC article from *Fortune*, of being anti-business.[15] As far as public relations was concerned, much of the activity backfired; there was no sympathy for "painting them Red," here or abroad.[16] But Nestlé ran into a piece of good fortune when the United Methodists, asked to endorse the boycott at their **1980** general meeting, decided to defer the decision and appoint a task force to find out what was going on. The Methodist Task Force instructed Dr. Paul Minus to write a background paper, which he completed (114 pages) in September 1980;[17] the Task Force set about its inquiries immediately. Meanwhile Nestlé, under new leaders (Helmut Maucher and Carl Angst), not burdened by the less-than-fully-successful strategies of the past, decided on a genuinely new strategy of communication: In **January 1981** it hired Rafael Pagan to head up a new entity in Washington, DC, the Nestlé Coordination Center for Nutrition (**NCCN**), to serve as an information source concerning key issues in nutrition which are of interest to professional and lay publics alike; coordinate Nestlé's grants to universities and organizations in the U.S. and developing nations for research in nutrition and the training of nutrition specialists;[18] act as a receiver and organizer of information to aid Nestlé in instituting real organizational change to meet new and unforeseen conditions; engender greater credibility for the company's actions on the part of its critics and other constituencies;[19] in general, to be the face and voice of Nestlé during a very troubled time. NCCN resolved to avoid all confrontation and confrontational rhetoric, to seek out dialogue with all responsible parties, and as a first step to establishing that credibility, to disseminate the information that Nestlé would accept the new WHO code as its own.

5. End of an Era:
The Resolution of the Boycott (1980–1984)

In **February 1982** in Dayton, Ohio, Nestlé presented the Methodist Task Force with a set of detailed instructions for its employees in the developing world to ensure compliance with the WHO code. NCCN pursued a strategy of dialogue with the hundreds of organizations that had endorsed the boycott.

Communications emphasized that the changes in market strategy in Nestlé were genuine, not just window-dressing. In **May 1982** NCCN engendered an independent monitoring agency, the Nestlé Infant Formula Audit Commission (**NIFAC**), chaired by former Secretary of State Senator Edmund Muskie and "charged with the responsibility for ensuring compliance by the company's field offices with code provisions and the company's own instructions."[20] By **October 1982** consultations with NIFAC led to a thorough revision of the company's instructions; in that month, the Methodists decided against joining the boycott. That changed the political scene: The *Washington Post* withdrew its editorial support for the boycott; in **January 1983** the American Federation of Teachers withdrew its support for the boycott. Despite increasingly frantic attacks from the core boycott organizations (also in January 1983, IBFAN issued a report accusing infant formula manufacturers of "14,985,160" violations of the WHO code, including more than 4 million by Nestlé[21]), support waned quickly in the course of **1983**.[22] With the partial resolution of the few remaining issues, and Nestlé's firm commitment to strong national codes to regulate the marketing of infant formula, all parties gathered to celebrate the official suspension of the boycott in **January 1984**, finalized on **October 4, 1984**. Douglas Johnson himself, coordinator of INFACT from its beginning, praised Nestlé as "a model for the whole industry, a model which creates a new standard for corporate behavior."[23] Not everyone was happy. Leah Margulies, the ICCR's Program Coordinator for the infant formula issue, was not there. Some activists grumbled about not being sufficiently consulted. And there was one real issue that awaited WHO definition: "infants who have to be fed on breast-milk substitutes," for whom free supplies were permitted by the code. But the momentum of peace was not to be stopped. It was over— except, of course, for making sure that Nestlé and the others adhered to the code. So after October, the INBC reconstituted itself as the "International Negotiators for Babyfood Code Compliance," and silently settled in for the long haul.

6. Peace Is Illusion: The Conflict Renewed (1985–2002)

The next portion of the case lacks the drama of the first, if only because it has no beginning, middle, or end: It just drags on—for a purpose, as we shall see. The opening stages of the next act look like the end of the first: NCCN was disbanded a little more than a year after the boycott ended. Rafael Pagan founded his own consulting firm, Pagan International, with Nestlé as a client. ICIFI was disbanded and a new organization, the Infant Formula Manufacturers (**IFM**), more inclusive than ICIFI, was created after about a year to represent the industry. After that, the anticipated dialogue—or bickering— continued, for *years*. WHO held consultations and published guidelines on "infants who have to be fed breast-milk substitutes" in **1986**. WHA resolution 39.28 enunciated a policy on "free and low priced supplies" (free or inexpensive cases of formula sent to hospitals) in the same year. Activists called on Nestlé to withdraw all "supplies" unilaterally; Nestlé declined, on the grounds that competitors still sent them, and the IFM tried to institute direct dialogue with the ministers of health of the developing world, without much luck. In **September 1988** two new activist organizations, Action for Corporate Accountability (**ACA**) in the United States and Baby Milk Action (**BMA**) in the U.K., relaunched the Nestlé boycott. Immediately Nestlé UK formed an issues management team and launched a communications strategy like NCCN, to communicate with BMA. In the U.S., NIFAC (the Muskie commission) denounced the Boycott renewal as unjustified, and instituted a dialogue with the major UN agencies and Nestlé. By **April 1989** Nestlé had published a plan of action to resolve the outstanding issues, and agreed to withdraw free supplies from the Ivory Coast and Thailand as a pilot. An IFM proposal to talk out remaining problems with the activist NGOs was rejected in **August 1989**. By the next year the U.S. boycott had disappeared, while the U.K. one, with the backing of Church of England (**CE**) leaders, continued.[24]

With the U.S. boycott now history, the IFM appointed an ombudsman to handle all further complaints of non-compliance in **January 1991**; six months later, NIFAC decided its work was done and disbanded. Nestlé continued to study and modify its policies to conform more closely to the code, in continuing dialogue with WHO and UNICEF. The dialogue was initially very successful; eventually, as we shall see, agreement proved elusive.

The stickiest issue was, and remains, "free supplies," cases of formula provided to hospitals without charge (as opposed to "free samples," which go directly to the mother). WHO defines "supplies" as "quantities of a product provided for use over an extended period, free or at a low price, for social purposes, including those provided to families in need." Companies compete to become the favored provider of "supplies," because if a child is to be formula fed, almost invariably the mother will continue the child on the brand he's been fed in the hospital. So no company can afford unilaterally to stop the free supplies—the others will quickly fill the gap and the one stopping the supplies will lose the market.

Hospitals love free supplies; without them, they'd have to pay (or make the mother pay) for the formula fed to the bottle-feeders. Breast-fed babies, of course, are not to be fed formula. They are to be taken to their mothers for breast-feeding when they are hungry. That's where the problem develops. It's much easier for the nurses to bottle-feed the babies, even the ones that are supposed to be breast-fed, when they get hungry, than it is to get them up, change them, and take them to their mothers, especially when they were just brought back twenty minutes ago. So that's what they do. No matter what choice the mother has made, where the nurses are lazy, or ill-instructed, or under-staffed, the infants will be fed formula in the nursery if it's available. With free supplies, it's available. As the activists well know, if those free supplies were just not there, the nurses would have to take the babies to their mothers, and breast-feeding would be marginally more successful. That's why the activists want the formula out of there, and the competitive free market system is why the companies won't take it out, unless some enforceable law is passed that puts the same burden on the competition. No one knows how such a law would read, because somehow we have to allow for the infants—4 percent to 5 percent at the least, up to 50 percent in urbanized areas—that by necessity or the mother's choice are to be bottle-fed. "Negotiations" on the subject are necessarily obscure. For starters, the fault in this (all too real) scenario lies with the health care facilities—not the companies, the mothers, or anyone else—and neither activists nor companies can change the practices of third world health facilities. At the end of the day the law as it stands prevails: Only the governments of the developing nations (not the industry and not the activists of the NGOs) can make binding law for their people, and the companies have no legal right to "sacrifice" profits that by right belong to the shareholders. No wonder the issue is intractable.

Nevertheless, Nestlé had committed in 1989 "to end all supplies of infant formula in developing countries except for the limited number of infants who need it," and the conflict over the interpretation of the commitment continued. On **August 1, 1990**, several infant nutrition organizations, including La Leche League, joined together in Florence to issue the "Innocenti Declaration," stating that "all infants should be fed exclusively on breast-milk from birth to 4-6 months of age." The United Nations (WHO and UNICEF) continued to work toward the goal of universal breast-feeding (so far as possible), launching the Baby Friendly Hospital Initiative (**BFHI**) in 1991–1992.[25]

Interim agreements on distribution of free supplies had been reached in Mexico in **1991**, extended to twelve lead countries by mid-**1992**. A meeting between IFM and WHO/UNICEF in **November 1992** seemed to be successful, but a follow-up memo from UNICEF to IFM complaining of "failure to honor agreements" was embarrassingly leaked to U.K. church leaders (**October 1993**), damaging the mood of cooperation—not for the first or last time. For instance, in July 1993 UNICEF issued a directive entitled "An End to the Ambiguities," expanding on the 1981 Code without consultation either with WHO or with anyone from the industry. In the view of the infant formula industry, the directive contradicted the Code. Incidentally, that's where Leah Margulies turned up again: Employed by UNICEF as the person to consult (as the legal advisor to the BFHI) if you had any questions about the Code. Such communication as continued was punctuated by harsh memos and canceled meetings, accusations (*Breaking the Rules 1994*, a volume of allegations of code violations put together by IBFAN) and denials, in an increasing atmosphere of distrust. Despite this, the Church of England decided to suspend its support of the U.K. boycott in **July 1994**, rousing protests from UNICEF that Nestlé had misled the Church, and detailing allegations of misdoings from October 1993. By the beginning of **1995** UNICEF expressed interest in restarting the meetings with IFM, but in March of that year UNICEF blocked IFM participation in the preparations for the 4th World Conference on Women, on the grounds that business interest nongovernmental organizations (BINGOs), such as the IFM, should not participate in meetings with public interest NGOs (PINGOs). Ambivalence and confusion reigned in **May 1995** when Carol Bellamy took office as UNICEF Executive Director.

Dialogue swiftly deteriorated even further, as an agenda of separation and exclusion took form. Bellamy's initial replies to Nestlé's invitation to talk were hostile, and in **December 1995** UNICEF issued Programme Instructions recommending development of a policy on UNICEF association with the infant food industry:

> the focus should be on minimizing any association with companies that would compromise UNICEF's unambiguous support of breastfeeding and child well-being.

Through 1996 IFM and UNICEF jousted over Bellamy's proposal for a meeting in which all the members of IFM would sit around a table and talk about all their marketing and sales practices, including country-by-country data. Lawyers blanched. The meeting would result, in their view, in jail sentences for most of the IFM executives on conviction for violations of the anti-trust laws. No alternative type of meeting was acceptable to Bellamy. In **April 1996** the Zimbabwe Ministry of Health declined Nestlé support for an international conference on the elimination of Iodine Deficiency Disease in Africa, in accord with Bellamy's Programme Instructions. Meanwhile, a new ad hoc activist coalition had been forming—the Interagency Group on Breastfeeding Monitoring (**IGBM**), claiming independence from all factions (but with overlapping memberships with other activist groups, and not particularly willing to meet with IFM). In **January 1997** IBFAN issued a massive "Code Handbook," including a "Model Law" that it thought countries should adopt. Its foreword is informative:

> . . .The ultimate aim of *The Code Handbook* is to give the right to breastfeed back to the mother. The multiple advantages of breastfeeding known today dwarf what was known in 1981 when the Code was adopted by the World Health Assembly. Yet even now, 16 years later, too few governments have enacted legislation in order to protect breastfeeding from commercial competition by manufacturers of breastmilk substitutes, feeding bottles and teats.
>
> Breastfeeding is not like a tap which can be turned on and off. Mothers need to have confidence in their capacity to provide milk. Breastmilk allows babies to thrive without any other food or drink until the child is about six months old. As with most things, the start is the most sensitive. The mother's hormones are already active before birth, triggering the various production mechanisms. The delivery of the milk, however, depends on the "let-down reflex" and that is very susceptible to psychological and emotional stress.
>
> A mother's confidence is easily upset by subtle messages. Companies understood this a long time before objective researchers established the link. For instance, suggestions about "not enough milk" will cause the mother anxiety and will most likely result in her not having enough, leaving the baby hungry and crying, the mother upset and uncertain. The doubts and pressures invariably lead to artificial feeding, a vicious circle, cleverly fostered by company booklets, advertisements and even product labels. . . .[26]

With an opener like that, the contents may be imagined. This document concluded that, adopting the position of La Leche League as expressed in the Innocenti Declaration, any food that could be fed to a child up to age *two* was to be designated a "breast-milk substitute." IGBM published a set of allegations in the same month ("Cracking the Code"), most of which the IFM contested, but which Carol Bellamy praised and congratulated. In **July 1997**, by way of contrast, the International Pediatric Association adopted a relatively friendly policy for industry relations; six months later UNICEF wrote the editor of *International Child Health* criticizing the policy as directly contrary to UNICEF policy. In **October 1997** Bellamy finally met with Nestlé executives (not in the presence of other companies), for a long presentation on Nestlé's practices in marketing its products, down to the labels used. After the meeting, Nestlé CEO Peter Brabeck wrote a letter thanking her for her time and offering continued help and dialogue in the future; Bellamy replied that having had

> an opportunity to reflect on the situation and discuss the issues more fully
> . . . we have come to the considered conclusion that there do not appear
> to be opportunities for cooperation that would be of mutual benefit to
> our respective organizations at this time. The outstanding and significant
> differences in our views on the content and application of the International code represent a barrier to any such cooperation. . . . It continues to
> be clear that the divergent views are simply not reconcilable in specific
> and critical areas. Therefore, much as we appreciate the opportunity to
> have had the meeting, it does not seem to us to be useful to maintain such
> contact in the future.[27]

There it stood, and basically stands, with UNICEF. Meanwhile in **January 1998** Dr. Tomris Turmen, Executive Director of the WHO unit on family and reproductive health, proposed a process "for identifying, examining and overcoming the main obstacles to implementation by all countries of the International Code" and in July 1998 Dr. Gro Harlem Brundtland took office as Director General of WHO. The process continues.

Meanwhile, demons undreamt of by Jelliffe stalk the developing world and change the entire understanding of the infant formula issue. In **April 1998** the United Nations Task Force on the Acquired Immune Deficiency Syndrome (UNAIDS) met in Geneva to plan a conference aimed at developing directives to protect people in developing nations from the spread of the Human Immunodeficiency Virus (HIV). Some WHO and UNICEF officials tried, unsuccessfully, to keep infant formula industry representatives out of the discussions, even though they would be centrally involved in any effort to feed the babies of HIV-positive mothers. The conference took place in **June 1998** and did indeed conclude that a change in policy was needed. The account of the change, appearing on the front page of *The New York Times* on **July 26, 1998**, is worth quoting at length, as much for its summary of conflicts past as for its account of the change:

AIDS Brings a Shift on Breast-Feeding:

U.N. Discouraging Practice for Women Infected With H.I.V.

GENEVA, July 25. Countering decades of promoting "breast is best" for infant nutrition, the United Nations is issuing recommendations intended to discourage women infected with the AIDS virus from breast-feeding. The much-debated step aims at preventing transmission of H.I.V., the AIDS virus, from mothers to babies in what United Nations officials say is "a runaway epidemic" in many developing countries.

United Nations officials said they were reluctant to issue a blanket warning because the decision should be left to each mother and because no simple message could encompass the diversity of environments where women live. Women may become stigmatized for not breast-feeding in some cultures, and in some places alternatives like formula can be unaffordable or unsafe, but the United Nations wants that to change.

In its directive, the United Nations said it was deeply concerned that advising infected mothers not to breast-feed might lead many mothers who are not infected to stop breast-feeding. To reduce that possibility, it is advising governments to consider bulk purchases of formula and other milk substitutes and to dispense them mainly through prescriptions.

The compelling reason for the action is the soaring H.I.V. infection rates in much of the world, said Dr. Tomris Turmen, a United Nations official. As many as 70 percent of women at a prenatal clinic in one city in Zimbabwe and 30 percent of women in major urban areas in six African countries were found to be infected in recent surveys.

In desperately trying to deal with a crucial aspect of mother-to-child transmission of H.I.V., the United Nations is up against a fundamental, even ideological, pediatric practice. It also risks stirring memories from decades past, when international corporations promoted formula, and babies died after it was mixed under unsanitary conditions.

"Those who have seen babies die needlessly because they were fed with formula made from dirty water are worried that it might happen again," said Dr. Susan E. Holck, an expert on breast-feeding at the World Health Organization. But she added in an interview, "Others say it is unethical to deliberately, consciously breast-feed an infant milk that you know has H.I.V. in it."[28]

All the conflicts rise to the surface in this substantial article. Dr. Peter Piot, executive director of UNAIDS, recognized the "double message" the UN was sending, but said that "we urgently need to find solutions" to the AIDS epidemic. On the other hand, Dr. Felicity Savage of WHO "expressed extreme caution about the new guidelines, citing the risk of contamination of breast milk alternatives in areas that lack clean water and loss of nutrients if a woman mixes water and formula inaccurately."[29] Shall the old fight continue with the new specters looming over us? What about the NGOs? As noted above, in **July**

1998 Gro Harlem Brundtland took office as Director-General of WHO, promising sweeping changes. Will these include an attempt to resolve these long-standing issues? And what, if anything, should Nestlé do at this juncture?

There are enough omens in the material above to cause concern for the next millennium. Let us take note of two of them before attempting analysis of the case. First, the anti-industry move has gone from insisting on dialogue to refusing it. Some international agencies have at this time an agenda of self-isolation that is truly alarming. Second, there has been "de-learning" on the subject of infant feeding. The original interview in *The New Internationalist* began with a disclaimer, acknowledging that some babies really needed formula, and that some mothers honestly chose it for their own interests. By the 1997 *Code Handbook* that recognition is lost. According to the *Handbook*'s philosophy, all mothers are to be nailed to the same Procrustean bed; breast-feed or stand condemned. Ideology has triumphed over health, mother's and child's alike.

It is time to back off and see the case whole, to try to get a better purchase on what has really been happening.

II. THE BLOOD AND GUTS OF THE CASE: WHAT REALLY HAPPENED, AND WHY

1. Facts: Was the Jelliffe Scenario a Mistake?

First we need to get a grip on the facts, particularly the facts of the Jelliffe scenario, which plays a central role in the controversy from 1966 to July 1998. At the height of the boycott, Dr. Benjamin Spock, noted authority on child care and boycott advocate, would put it this way (in publicity distributed by INFACT):

> Nestlé, the largest food processor in the world, is actively encouraging mothers in the developing countries in Africa, Asia, and South America to give up breast feeding and turn to powdered milk formula instead. But in such countries water is contaminated, sterilization procedures are unknown, illiteracy makes proper preparation impossible, and poor people try to stretch the powdered milk supply by over-diluting their baby's formula. The tragic results are widespread malnutrition and severe infant diarrhea that often end in death.

But Spock's statement was largely false. While it cannot be said that *no* illiterate woman ever foolishly opted for formula she could not afford, and proceeded to misuse it until her child predictably died—in a world full of poverty, illiteracy, and pollution, how could anyone say that?—important and uncontradicted evidence runs straight to the contrary. For soon after the Jelliffe scenario was presented to the public in the early 1970s, the U.S. Agency for International Development (USAID) commissioned the Human Lactation

Center (HLC) of Connecticut, a research institute dedicated to breast-feeding, to find out if it was so. Dana Raphael, director of the HLC, described the origins of the study, the only one at the time commissioned to address the question directly:

> At the time [the summer of 1976, when the study was commissioned] researchers and health officials worldwide had suddenly become concerned because breastfeeding seemed to be declining in the developing countries and infant mortality to be on the increase. They put the two together—no breastfeeding leads to infant death. Many, including myself, were convinced that breastfeeding was being undermined by bottle feeding with commercial formula and that when mothers fed their babies this way they lost their breastmilk. Now the equation ran: Modern feeding methods, loss of breastmilk, dying babies.[30]

In short, it is the Jelliffe scenario. Raphael continued:

> ...We had expected to confirm certain assumptions: Breastfeeding was declining; as a result, more babies were dying; and the multinational companies' aggressive marketing of their products in the developing countries was responsible.[31]

The study was carried out in a series of third world locations—India, the Philippines, Sardinia, Jamaica—by experienced anthropologists already in the developing world, piggybacking Raphael's breast-feeding study on their own work. And the results?

> Yet, in the cultures we studied, much to our surprise, a decline was not a major part of the problem. In some, breastfeeding was still universal. . . . Furthermore, the very poor seldom used processed milk to bottle-feed their babies. The simple reason: they couldn't afford it. . . . Most important, we learned that mixed feeding was common. Babies were breastfed but they were given other foods as well from a very early age. . . .
>
> Was it possible that the particular cultures we had studied systematically were atypical, that elsewhere in the world breastfeeding was threatened in the way we had anticipated? Not so. A WHO/UNICEF two-year Collaborative Study on Breast-feeding (1979) a survey of 22,857 women in nine countries, revealed these same patterns . . . the clinical data from the nine-country survey [showed] that one-third of the lactating mothers used supplemental food on a regular basis by the end of three months.[32]

One of the more encouraging findings of Raphael's study was that, as far as the anthropologists and their informants could tell, infant mortality was not only not increasing in the developing world, it was significantly decreasing. Infants continued to get sick, largely from malnutrition, bad water, and simple environmental contamination. But increasingly, mothers were able to take sick babies to clinics for rehydration, vitamins, and antibiotics, and these simple remedies were saving children who otherwise would have died.

Contrary to popular beliefs, the figures revealed a decline in infant and maternal mortality in the last two decades. . . . The folk wisdom so often reported in our field data supported the demographic trend on child survival. Again and again, older women sang the virtues of the good old days, but, when pressed further, sadly admitted that far more of their children died than their daughters' children.[33]

In the less rural areas, not all women decided to breast-feed. What influences the decision to breast-feed or not, to stop breast-feeding earlier or later? The factors recited by the women being interviewed by Raphael's team of anthropologists could be duplicated in all but the wealthiest neighborhoods of the first world: Can I afford formula? (Usually not.) Do I have to go right back to work in order to support my family? (Often yes.) What are my long-range plans, aspirations, and the immediate demands that flow from these? (Variable, but dependent upon the proximity of the city and its jobs and education.) Can I get someone reliable and affordable to watch the children if I go to work? (The most difficult question to answer.) In certain conditions of third world poverty, a mother's decision to breast-feed exclusively could doom both her baby and herself to death by starvation, since no workplaces would accept babies and no source of income except work could be found. In very few cases did the women interviewed in the study feel that they had a real choice in the matter. In the rural areas, with no outside work and no access to formula, the women had to breast-feed; in the more urban areas, where work was an imperative, the women could not, or could not exclusively.

What did the promotion of infant formula have to do with the choices made by the women? As far as the study was able to determine, nothing whatsoever. The interviewers were under specific instructions to ask their informants about such promotions, and they did; the most common answer given was that since they couldn't afford formula anyway, and didn't need it, they took no notice of such promotions. They were not totally unaware of the product. Reporting from Melwal, in India, Raji Misra noted that:

> No infant formula was available in the village; few families had the money to buy it. The women knew about processed milk because they had sisters in Mysore who used it, but when Raji asked them to recall any brand names, they couldn't.[34]

If brand recall is that poor, advertising is nowhere near as effective as the controversy presupposes.

So in this study, commissioned specifically to discover whether Jelliffe's scenario was on the mark, most of the scenario was disconfirmed: Where the study was carried out, infant mortality was *decreasing*, not increasing. Breast-feeding was not decreasing at all in the illiterate rural areas. It was decreasing in the urban areas, in nations that prohibited advertising as well as nations where advertising was permitted, so that women could pursue goals incompatible with breast-feeding. Infant formula promotions had nothing to do with it.

The study bears out the observations of the WHO publication, "Women and Breast-feeding":

> For large numbers of women, time and work are critical to their decisions about breast-feeding—especially about the length of time they breast-feed. In both developed and developing countries, women are increasingly part of the labour force, whether in the formal or informal sectors. This usually involves work away from the home so that women are separated from their infants.[35]

The essay goes on to observe that the money earned outside the home is necessary for the family's living; that few workplaces have crèches or other places for women to breast-feed at work; that they have not the job security or employment opportunities to simply take time off; that the shaky infrastructure, especially with regard to mass transit, makes work arrangements even more time-consuming for the women; and that many of them, bound especially by traditional divisions between men's work and women's work, are required to double their employment time at home in housework unaided by technical marvels like dishwashers—often without clean running water.

> These pressures on women's time and energy are growing at the very same time that family patterns are changing rapidly. In many developed and developing countries, family norms and household patterns are changing to match new economic and social realities. An important change has been migration: the flight to the cities from rural areas by both women and men, as well as large scale international migration in search of jobs. Urbanization brings with it many changes in life-style that have detrimental effects on breast-feeding.[36]

To get back to basics: How many mothers simply cannot breast-feed? The *Code Handbook*, as we saw, insists that all mothers can provide adequate milk for their babies until six months, and that any who would hold otherwise are trying to undermine the woman's confidence so she will have to buy formula. The devastating effects of such belief can be found even in the first world: A front-page report in *The Wall Street Journal* entitled "Dying for Milk" recounted a series of cases of infant malnutrition, even death by starvation and dehydration, because wealthy and well-educated women, unable to produce enough breast milk to feed their babies, refused, on ideological grounds, to turn to formula.[37] The best estimate comes from the American Academy of Pediatrics, which suggests that 4 percent of mothers will not be able to breast-feed—but in the context: "given adequate instruction, emotional support, and favorable circumstances, 96 percent of new mothers can breastfeed successfully."[38] In short, if the woman does not have to go to work, and has friends and family to support her, the chances are 96 percent. There's more to success, in other words, than just putting your mind to it and staying clear of formula ads.

The simplistic conclusions on infant death and bottle-feeding do not survive a look at the quality of the evidence. Again citing the American Academy of Pediatrics,

> if a breast-fed infant is not doing well, the infant is likely to be switched to partial or complete bottle-feeding. This factor is of great importance in assessing the superiority of breast-feeding over bottle-feeding in such matters as infectious morbidity because it has the effects of keeping the breast-fed group healthy and adding "non-healthy" infants to the bottle-fed group. Even if the infants lost from breast-feeding were not added to the bottle-fed group, the selective removal of non-thriving infants from the breast-fed group would tend to maintain the selectivity for healthy infants.[39]

In short, the investigators cited by the industry critics, who have confidently associated bottle-feeding with infant sickness, have made the error of those who attempted to determine if aspirin caused headaches: Noting that people who did not take aspirin generally did not have headaches, and that those who did take aspirin very often did have headaches, they concluded that aspirin indeed is responsible for headaches. The infant formula issue is more complex than the aspirin case, but the error is the same.

The Code Handbook insists not only that all mothers can breast-feed, but also that all babies will thrive on breast-milk alone "for about six months" and prohibits the introduction of "complementary foods" until after that time. With this estimate the American Academy of Pediatrics Committee on Nutrition agrees, as do other authorities, with qualifications.[40] The rest of the world disagrees. In most societies, as it turns out, "it is quite usual and normal to supplement the supply of breast milk quite early in lactation, sometimes in the first month, and certainly in the first 2-3 months."[41]

Raphael's study, too, suggests that breast-feeding women do not breast-feed exclusively after the first few weeks or months, in the third world any more than in the first. And this is a good thing, because the quantity of breast milk available for the child levels off at about three months, going into a slow decline thereafter.[42] As the child grows, breast milk must be supplemented by something or the child won't get enough to eat. In addition, then, the question of when a child should be weaned from the breast to other foods is misguided. There is, Raphael suggests, no age of "weaning." Weaning is very gradual, over a long period of time, in every culture, in normal circumstances. There is no minimum age for it, she suggests, and no international agency should try to set one.

A confounding factor in the estimation of optimal length of breast-feeding, with or without supplements, is of course the nutritional status of the mother. While the attack on industry made no allowances for failure of lactation (or of sufficient milk) on account of malnutrition—even citing sunny predictions of "95% success"[43] for all mothers, no matter what their state of health—the clear fact is that the calories available to the baby are taken from the body of the mother, and that she cannot supply what she does not have.

Even the Jelliffes[44] agreed on this one, based on their own extensive work in the third world: By the age of three months, the baby of a malnourished mother will not be getting enough food, and the diet must be supplemented with other foods if the baby is to thrive.[45]

2. More Facts:
Where Did the Jelliffe Scenario Come From?

Let's summarize that last section. First, professional women in the cities of the developing world seem to appreciate the choice provided by the availability of infant formula. If their pediatricians disagree, they may comfort themselves that pediatricians in the developed world suffer from the same frustrations. Second, the illiterate women with the three-stone stoves, objects of so much suburban pity, seem to be universally breast-feeding, even as they always did, with some important exceptions. First, if they run out of milk, from malnutrition or illness, and have to turn to breast-milk substitutes (as they would always have had to), formula provides a costly but nutritious substitute. If they can get formula, their babies have a good chance of surviving, which they would not have otherwise. Second, if their babies develop infant diarrhea for some reason (eventually, every baby has to drink the local water, even if breast-feeding), the diarrhea is no longer a death sentence; the child can be taken to a clinic for oral rehydration and antibiotics and, again, will likely live. (Recall that most of the sick babies were over one year of age, when the mother would surely have had to supplement breast-feeding with local fare.) Third, the babies most at risk were those born to mothers who had left the three-stone countryside for the slums around the cities, and who had to work outside the home immediately after giving birth. What the grandmothers fed the babies is not known—probably rice water, as much formula as they could afford, goat's milk, and "bush tea," a mixture of herbs boiled in water. Water in these slums is more corrupt than in any countryside, infants are sicker, and clinics are nearer. Thereon hangs the rest of the tale.

Jelliffe himself had felt the need of some empirical backup for his scenario, soon after he had advanced it. He was in contact with many clinics and pediatricians in developing nations, since before becoming convinced that infant formula was harmful, he had himself trained Nestlé's "milk nurses" at his Caribbean Food and Nutrition Institute in Jamaica. In 1972 he wrote many of the clinics, asking them to fill in a "survey" generally inquiring into the prevalence of breast-feeding and bottle-feeding in their areas. The letter's wording is instructive (remember, this is several years after the first publication of his scenario):

> In many parts of the world, malnutrition is on the increase. Among the factors implicated, the decline in breast feeding appears to play a major role.
>
> The present Questionnaires, A1 and A2, have been designed by the undersigned in order to gain up-to-date data regarding the prevalence and trends in breast feeding in different parts of the world.

In Questionnaire A1, we would be most grateful if you could record your personal experience in the field of infant nutrition in your country with specific emphasis on breast feeding trends and blocks to this method of feeding, as you see them.

Questionnaire A2 has been designed to record the impressions and/or data which colleagues from other parts of the country would be willing to provide in order to give more of a complete picture of the actual breast feeding situation in the country.

We are hoping to analyze the data by April 15, and would be most grateful if you could return the completed questionnaires by March 1. We are aware that work pressure is great and that you have many commitments, but we can assure you that your valuable contribution would be of great benefit to all of us who, like yourself, are attempting to stem the increasing rates of child mortality in this world.

With many thanks, we remain, Sincerely yours,

And three signatures follow: Derrick B. Jelliffe, M. D. and E. F. P. Jelliffe, SRN, MPH, both of the School of Public Health of UCLA, and D. Raphael, Ph.D., Human Lactation Center, 666 Sturges Highway, Fairfield, CT.[46] The surveys asked for all manner of demographic data, extensive medical data on delivery and breast-feeding—length of time, ease or difficulty—and for very detailed information on the type and price of formula available in the area. Note that the factual assertion, that infant mortality is increasing—the assertion that Raphael's 1977 study proved to be flatly false—is included in two different places in the covering letter. The "survey" was clearly designed to prove one thing and one thing only, and that was the Jelliffe scenario.

Not many physicians responded to the survey, but they supplied enough anecdotes of dying babies brought in by desperate mothers, still feebly sucking on filthy bottles, to encourage Jelliffe to continue—to Berne, to Washington to speak to the Kennedy Committee, and the rest is history.

How can honest people get it so wrong? (Most people who knew the Jelliffes are sure they were honest, and Dana Raphael was the one who finally disproved the scenario.) There are two answers, one from epistemology and one from sociology. In epistemology, specifically in philosophy of science, we distinguish carefully between "anecdotes," stories that illustrate a point, and "observations," data gathered in response to a set of hypotheses and detailed methods. In this first "survey," the investigators asked for anecdotes. Raphael's anthropologists took the hypotheses of the Jelliffe scenario and made observations.

What distinguishes an anecdote from an observation? An anecdote is a story told by someone about his own experience in the past, which seems to him to be particularly important to the discussion now occurring. It may not have struck him as important at the time it happened, but now that someone else has raised a question that seems relevant, he is reminded of it, and contributes it to the discussion. An observation, on the other hand, is made in order to answer a previously formed question, conceived to contribute to a particular discussion, framed in the terms of that discussion. Put another way, The anecdote *precedes* the question it is supposed to answer, and the observation *follows* the question. Why does science trust observations and not anecdotes? There are many reasons, some having to do with the accuracy of documentation. With the question right there, observers will document all relevant aspects of the observed phenomenon, positive or negative, while documentation may be scanty for the anecdotes. But most of the reasons have to do with the selectivity of memory. Human memory is a very unreliable and overly cooperative instrument, cheerfully bending to any new agenda, gladly releasing memory-images that correspond to the currently preferred scenario, and conveniently losing those that do not. When the controversy began—with the first publication of the Jelliffe scenario in 1971—many frustrated pediatricians working in third world countries leaped on the activist-advocacy wagon. The scenario fit all their predilections: It explained the malnutrition, diarrhea, and death with which they coped on a daily basis, and it focused their anger at the filthy bottles and other paraphernalia brought in with the sick babies, all without forcing them to blame the poverty-stricken and helpless mothers with whom they dealt. Amid all the tiny communities of poverty and the callous and remote governments, it gave them someone large and rich to blame—the great corporations that dominated the infant formula market. The anecdotes followed immediately, and sets of them formed the message of the first publications: *The New Internationalist* and the film *Bottle Babies*. But no number of anecdotes can add up to an observation. Unless there is a question asked beforehand—unless we are observing, therefore, whether in fact

1. an infant formula promotion influenced any decisions the mother made
2. the baby was started on formula or switched to it when he became too sick and weak to nurse
3. formula or some other substitute was in the filthy bottle
4. the formula was beyond the means of the woman who selected it, causing insufficient use and consequent malnutrition
5. the mother on account of illiteracy could not understand, because of poverty, could not implement, or as a result of human frailty (laziness) simply ignored instructions to sterilize the water to mix the formula (three distinct scenarios)

—we really do not have the kind of information we need to draw any conclusions about the role of formula whatsoever.

The second reason Jelliffe and others persisted in believing his scenario is sociological. For this we must put ourselves in a pediatrician's office, perhaps one of the pediatricians who responded to Jelliffe's survey. He (usually) runs a clinic; poor women with sick babies line up outside in the morning. If the babies are sick enough, he can put them in the hospital; some of those babies have been there many times. The infants are very young, and he is very frustrated. He knows the babies would be better off if they were breast-fed, yet the women keep insisting on bottle-feeding! Why do they do that? Unwilling to share information about the relatives at home putting pressure on them to get back to work, the women timidly avoid answering. But let him suggest that they thought bottle-feeding was better for the baby because of all the pretty advertisements, and they quickly agree; more data for the survey.

One of the problems of the Jelliffe scenario is that it presumes that women (1) are not very bright, and (2) never talk to each other. Both presumptions are patently false, as Raphael's study proves. The real women in her study, as opposed to the suppositious women of the activists, have wide access to networks of practical knowledge on caring for their babies, and they are geniuses at keeping their infants alive under very difficult circumstances. Jelliffe may have forgotten that new mothers tend to look and sound not very bright when talking to their doctors, especially important male doctors in their offices; Raphael's field anthropologists, all women, talking to them in their homes, saw them in quite a different light. That brings us to one of the central problems in the infant formula controversy—from the perspective of ethics, *the* central problem. Where is the voice of the mother in the Jelliffe scenario? The mother's voice is not heard in this controversy, except in Raphael's work, which was not easily accessible until 1985. What Raphael learned in her study was that women grow and live in communities of women, and that childbirth and infant feeding are among the most discussed subjects. In that context, it would be absurd to suppose that woman after woman would traipse innocently into hospitals to be misled by "milk nurses" into a course of action detrimental to her child.

So Jelliffe's pediatricians are not to be blamed for drawing the wrong conclusions from their clinic experience; it was not scientific, it was wrongheaded, but there was no reason why they would know that. But there is one anomaly totally unexplained. In 1976, when USAID commissioned the study that disproved the scenario, it chose one of the signatories of the survey cover letter, Dana Raphael, the first woman ever to write a doctoral dissertation on breast-feeding and the founder and Director of the Human Lactation Institute. She did a truly scientific study that answered the question: Is the Jelliffe scenario true? As noted above, her study demonstrated it was not. Yet a survey of business ethics literature even today, twenty-six years later, will yield an almost universal agreement that it *was* true. Indeed, *is* true. Why?

The long answer appears in Part III of this chapter, a study of the work and agenda of NGOs in general and INFACT in particular. The short answer is that Raphael's study and the knowledge it provided were buried. Raphael herself was loath to publish, in 1977; for her, after all, the results were negative, contrary to everything she had hoped to find. USAID required publication, so she brought out the results as inconveniently as possible in the smallest conceivable type in her *Lactation Review.* She saw the results as damaging to third world mothers. Only in 1984, when Flora Davis started helping her edit the results, did she begin to see them as a powerful affirmation of the ingenuity, intelligence, and resourcefulness of the mothers of poverty. And by that time, Dana Raphael's part in the infant formula controversy was history. The formula companies had all seized on her results to defend themselves before the Kennedy Committee. Raphael was called a traitor, one who had turned against the women of the developing nations by saying that the formula companies were not to blame for their children's illness. The NGOs insisted immediately that Raphael had been paid by the formula companies to reach the results she had—and immediately she found herself excluded from the discussions as they continued. The accusation that she sold out to the formula companies, especially Nestlé, for money pursues her to this day, firmly believed by her former allies in the effort to help the nutrition of the babies of the developing nations.

There has to be more to the story than meets the scientific eye. Given that the Jelliffe scenario had a certain amount of surface plausibility (and arose innocently enough), given that pediatricians in the developing world may be excused for misinterpreting what they saw in their practices, and given that Raphael did not publicize the results as widely as she might have, still a great deal of human effort went in to suppressing the evidence that disproved Jelliffe. Why? To answer that question, we are going to have to step back and look a bit more at the position of the NGO on the current world scene.

III. WHAT DID THE ACTIVISTS OF THE NGOS REALLY WANT?

In the course of the Kennedy hearings Oswald Ballarin suggested that the NGOs, especially the churches allied against Nestlé through the ICCR, harbored an "anti-business" agenda beneath their apparent concern for little babies, and was laughed out of the Senate. It might be worth observing that there was a fair amount of evidence, from the perspective of those who wrote the statement, that Ballarin was right on the money. First, the statements emerging from the camps of the enthusiastic proponents of the Nestlé boycott certainly sounded left-wing. Mark Ritchie, on his way to becoming national INFACT coordinator, summed it up later in a Clergy and Laity Concerned (CALC) meeting in August 1978:

> It's not just babies, it's not just multinational corporations, it's class conflict and class struggle. . . .I think ultimately what we're trying to do is take an issue-specific focus campaign and move it in conjunction with other issue-specific campaigns into a larger, very wide, very class-conscious campaign and reassert our power in this country, our power in this world.[47]

Other activists, church related and otherwise, had not been shy about suggesting left-wing opinions and, by implication, affiliations; "revolution" was part of every speech, and strong anti-capitalist sentiments part of the daily bread fed to the followers. In retrospect, more than twenty years later, we can see the "class consciousness," "class struggle" rhetoric of the activists as imitative, amateurish, and not really serious. But they can hardly object to being taken at their word.

Another set of questions is raised by the activists' choice of strategies. The chronology reveals a sharp break in NGO activity, so startling a break that it requires an explanation. In retrospect, it seems that from 1974 to 1984 the activists are convinced that the Jelliffe scenario is largely true. They are convinced that corporations are heartlessly profiting from irresponsible marketing activities, and they are trying to get those companies to modify those activities for the sake of the infants of the third world—in short, exactly what they said they were doing. They were not dewy-eyed idealists. They were top flight organizers with strong organizational histories in the civil rights movement, the anti-war movement, and the anti-nuclear demonstrations; they had picked up tactics from the Black Power movement, ideology from La Leche's breast-feeding campaign, a dislike of large corporations, and a preference for confrontational politics from all of the above. (It has been suggested that one reason that the infant formula controversy blew up in 1974 was that the war in Vietnam came to an end, releasing battalions of experienced activists for new causes.)[48]

During this period, astute organizers used their resources to maximum effectiveness to achieve their ends. With the combination of the boycott and the Kennedy hearings, they scored their finest victory before Nestlé and the other manufacturers had really got organized. With the WHO Code in 1981 they achieved the major part of their objectives. They would have preferred to have IBFAN (for instance) officially appointed monitor of Code compliance, but they were above all realistic in estimating what they could and could not achieve. As soon as the wind started to blow the other way (with the United Methodist decision not to join the boycott), the activists began to look for closure; after the defections of 1983 they moved very quickly to get the boycott to a successful end. Both managements, Nestlé's and INFACT's, effectively isolated their extremist wings to make peace in 1984. It is a story with a beginning, middle, and end. The activists emerged triumphant and the company emerged wiser (if sadder).

But then why, after 1984, did the controversy re-emerge? After a few years of quarrels over definitions and interpretations of the Code, suddenly new organizations (ACA and BMA) came up with a new boycott. The boycott had no hope of the kind of success enjoyed by the first one, and it was counterproductive in terms of the 1974–1984 objectives, since it was launched against a company that had pledged to join in open discussions of all further objections to its marketing practices, and to cooperate in all projects aimed at improving infant nutrition. Futile and misdirected, the new boycott didn't make sense. The senselessness continues. From 1988 to 1998, UNICEF resisted all association with the IFM, setting impossible conditions for meeting that prevented all meaningful dialogue, indeed prevented any setting in which work might actually be accomplished. The activists, now closely associated with UNICEF, have adopted positions on the medical aspects of infant feeding that can only be characterized as dangerously wrong (as noted previously, if women took seriously their injunctions not to consider formula feeding for six months, *at least* 4 percent of all infants born would be doomed to an entirely unnecessary death by starvation and dehydration). They attempted to influence other organizations to hinder the indisputably good work of the companies and IFM in conducting educational activities and donating money for research and education, and in general they substituted hostile posturing for the dialogue that had characterized earlier dealings. Why?

Clearly a new agenda had emerged. It had little to do with infants or milk, and a great deal to do with power. As Jessica Tuchman Mathews points out, there had been a

> novel redistribution of power among states, markets and civil society. National governments are not simply losing autonomy in a globalizing economy. They are sharing powers—including political, social, and security roles at the core of sovereignty—with businesses, with international organizations, and with a multitude of citizens groups, known as nongovernmental organizations (NGOs). *The steady concentration of power in the hands of states that began in 1648 with the Peace of Westphalia is over, at least for awhile.*[49]

Why the change? Mathews cites several trends: the absence of international war or (especially since 1990) the credible threat of international war; the consequent disentanglement of erstwhile third world nations from binding alliances with developed nations and the consequent disempowerment of the governments that derived their strength—if not their existence—from those alliances; renewed interest in seizing control of the resources of the developing world for the purpose of nonpolitical participation in the global market; and the renewal of racial and ethnic conflicts that had been forgotten in the forty-year face-off between East and West. Armed conflict is now an intrastate affair.

Under these circumstances, new notions of "security" begin to take hold, centering on the conditions of "daily life—food, shelter, employment, health, public safety—rather than flowing downward from a country's foreign relations and military strength." Because of the technological revolution cited above, governments no longer have a "monopoly on the collection and management of large amounts of information."[50] NGOs can have just as much information, and can deploy it in many cases much more quickly and effectively than newly formed national governments, which are often struggling with corruption and incompetence among its office holders. An NGO with a grasp of some central issue of daily life can rapidly assume a leadership role in the troubled developing world. As Mathews wrote:

> NGOs' role and influence have exploded in the last half-decade. Their financial resources and—often more important—their expertise, approximate and sometimes exceed those of smaller governments and of international organizations. "We have less money and fewer resources than Amnesty International, and we are the arm of the U.N. for human rights," noted Ibrahima Fall, head of the U.N. Centre for Human Rights, in 1993. "This is clearly ridiculous."[51]

So often the U.N. agencies become the public faces of the NGOs, adopting their agenda, as we have seen in the infant formula issue. National states are often in the same position:

> NGOs deliver more official development assistance than the entire UN system (excluding the World Bank and the International Monetary Fund). In many countries they are delivering the services—in urban and rural community development, education, and health care—that faltering governments can no longer manage.[52]

"Increasingly, NGOs are able to push around even the largest governments," Mathews pointed out. The day when governments could make their deals quietly and carry them out unopposed is over: Consider the fate of the North American trade deals, which had to be reopened to include labor and environmental considerations.[53] Witness the case of Shell Oil's oil buoy Brent Spar. Just when Shell thought it had covered all the bases and got all the permits from all the legitimate authorities, an enormous "environmentalist" public campaign made it impossible to dump the platform at sea.[54] Mathews suggests that governments, with their hierarchical structure and assumptions, may be the *least* qualified to address new issues that affect the daily life of its citizens. All the other players—corporations, NGOs, even ethnic societies and crime cartels, are way ahead of government in the decentralized, node-centered, multi-interaction world of the Web site, the network, and the chatroom.

We will need a new set of expectations about the locus of power. We have become accustomed to clear differentiations between private and public sector, with the corporation operating for profit in the private sector without spending too much time worrying about the "public good," and the public good administered by the sovereign state, duly elected, its sole and legitimate guardian. Let businesses go tearing off after profits; the state could always pull them up if what they did went counter to public interest. In the United States, for instance, if a corporation was polluting the environment, the state in which the offending plants were located could pass laws against pollution, applying to that corporation and all its competitors, and the pollution would have to stop. If the corporation threatened to move the plant and all its jobs to another, more lenient state, federal environmental law could be introduced to stop companies from playing states against each other. And legally, *only* the state could limit private enterprise. Other organizations trying to tell corporations how to do their business could be ignored, or carted off by the police for interfering in the legal tasks of a private citizen. The state is defined as the entity with a monopoly on the use of force, the right to deprive people of life, liberty, or property. Only the state can arrest you, try you, put you in jail or other captivity, destroy your property, or kill you. Anybody else who tries that is a terrorist.

But the system has broken down. The globe is our community, and what is its legitimate government? When the UN was formed, it was planned as a very weak confederacy, subject to whim of member states. Early attempts to make the UN a real international authority (by the United World Federalists, for example) failed. But often its agencies have real influence, and could command human efforts well beyond power to reward (it had no power to coerce), simply by moral suasion. That is how NGOs worked at their inception, and the method on which they continue to depend.

But the real breakdown of system came with expansion of private enterprise to other nations. If the multinational corporations (MNCs) want to complain about these bothersome internationalized NGOs, they will do well to remember that MNCs were first to extend their reach over, through, and despite the Westphalian national boundaries. Now a global enterprise, with its head in New York (or Houston or London or Geneva) and tentacles in many places, can play nations against each other as they used to play states against each other in the United States, only without a federal government to trump it.

How do we handle this new situation? The first attempt on the part of ethicists who concern themselves with such matters was a call for corporate responsibility across borders, in the absence of any ability to enforce it.[55] In a novel initiative, Clinton's first Secretary of Labor Robert Reich attempted to organize the garment industry into a "No Sweat" campaign against sweatshops abroad; that campaign continues.[56] The agreements or collective undertakings that come from these appeals are very unstable, and with U.S. companies at least, must tread a very fine line between cooperation for moral reasons and violation of the antitrust statutes. Whether they can find and stay on that line, it could be argued that MNCs have neither the expertise nor mandate to enforce international morality. Luther Gerlach adds that even if MNCs fiduciary duties could be modified to include international good works, we might want to think twice before leaving global morality up to the denisons of the boardroom.[57] Meanwhile, the MNCs' partners in the developing world have legitimate interests in profitability, and have shown a certain amount of impatience with American agony over non-economic issues.

But it gets worse. It turns out that moral arrangements for the good of the world are worse than unstable, they're illegal. For a while the American citizenry thought, as noted above, that we could still enforce laws restricting private enterprise for the public interest in our own country, if we were willing to absorb the consequences to the economy, in terms of lost jobs. But it doesn't seem that way now.

> The threat that stands head and shoulders above the others . . . is the legal
> effect of international Free Trade agreements: NAFTA, GATT, and the
> approaching Multilateral Agreement on Investments, MAI. All such agree-
> ments have provision forbidding tariffs *or any other legal devices that have the*
> *effect of tariffs* by stopping or slowing or otherwise hindering the free pas-
> sage of goods among the nations signatory. It is not clear that any laws
> adopted by the U.S. to forbid the importation of goods made in sweat-
> shops (for example) or animal products from endangered species (like
> ivory) could be compatible with such trade agreements. Already the
> "dolphin-safe" restrictions on methods of catching tuna fish have been

ruled discriminatory by a GATT board, which invalidated the Pelly
Amendment to the Fisherman's Protective Act, since they forbid the importation of tuna from Mexico, whose fishers do not adhere to the procedures recommended to spare the endangered spinning dolphin, by
releasing the dolphins from the tuna nets before they are closed.[58]

Nor, it seems, can we ban imports of shrimp that are caught in ways that endanger the sea turtles. All attempts to protect anyone or anything from the rav-
ages of the MNCs are now illegal by the terms of the agreements. The only
sanction, since the WTO cannot use force against a party to the agreement
(the state still has that monopoly), is expulsion from the agreements and with-
drawal of its advantages, but that's an economic cost few nations would want
to pay.

Nations with really powerful charismatic leaders might be able to insist on
their own agenda on the world scene—to stand up against this economic
dictation—for the protection of their citizens and their values. Such insistence
is difficult enough when national leadership is strong. But now, legitimate governments worldwide are saddled with weak leadership, for any and all purposes;[59] for purposes of implementing the WHO Code, the nations that the
Code was meant to protect seem to have little interest in adopting it. So the
situation as it stands is terrible, from any perspective of social responsibility.
The market seems to have it all its own way, and any attempt to limit the pursuit of profit in the name of the public good, even if all the company's shareholders have signed off on it, is forbidden. Now what? Reaction and protest
can take only strictly illegitimate forms, since the legitimate ones are blocked.
Increasingly, the choice is, in Benjamin Barber's inspired terms, between Jihad
and McWorld: Jihad (Arabic for holy war) is irrational nationalism, usually violent in content and religious in origin; McWorld is the homogenized U.S.
version of friendly private enterprise, unopposed in its profit-seeking peddling
of goods and services for private consumption, worldwide.[60]

Must we just let the Market alone, forget social responsibility for the moment, and let free enterprise raise the standard of living of the world as Adam
Smith said it would? It is not clear the free market can do that. The ham-
handed internationalism practiced by Wall Street and the International Monetary Fund does not work very well:[61] witness Russia and large parts of
Southeast Asia.

This is where the NGOs come in. Like the MNCs, they are international,
capable of organizing, capable of raising money across borders. They can es-
pouse any cause they like and organize a constituency around it. They can protect the environment and lobby for international treaties that supersede or
limit trade agreements because they are international. They can perform services that are beyond the means of third world countries, and they can lobby
first world countries, they can mobilize through the Internet citizenry that are
not reachable by any standard organization. Mathews points out that NGOs
can significantly influence the way states treat their citizens, even without the
legitimacy conferred by law.[62] And that, of course, they do not have: The

NGOs are not elected or appointed, do not operate with charters from any legitimate governing body (although they use governments for their purposes—witness the Kennedy hearings), possess no expertise (although they hire experts on occasion), and seem to be above the rules of doing business. They have no mandate from those they claim to represent, and they operate extralegally much of the time. How can this be right? What's the difference between an activist and a terrorist?

Yet in NGOs lie the salvation of the world. In law, in the Westphalian system, they have the status of garden clubs. In practice, only the choice not (for the moment) to use violent means to achieve their ends distinguishes them from terrorist organizations—NGOs par excellence. (This border has been crossed by anti-abortion and animal-rights activists). But NGOs are the hope for the future.

A world that is more adaptable and in which power is more diffused could mean more peace, justice, and capacity to manage the humankind's burgeoning interconnected problems. At a time of accelerating change, NGOs are quicker than governments to respond to new demands and opportunities. Internationally, in both the poorest and richest countries, NGOs, when adequately funded, can outperform government in the delivery of many public services. Their growth, along with that of the other elements of civil society, can strengthen the fabric of the many still-fragile democracies. And they are better than governments at dealing with problems that grow slowly and affect society through their cumulative effect on individuals—the "soft" threats of environmental degradation, denial of human rights, population growth, poverty, and lack of development that may already be causing more deaths in conflict than are traditional acts of aggression.[63]

In short, NGOs are better than governments at dealing with all of the problems that bedevil the mothers of the developing world. Already the international organizations, powerless as they are, are working with NGOs, becoming in some cases extensions of them, borrowing or absorbing their effective methods, superior networks, and expert personnel. When they're good, they're very good, and are the only hope we have. When they're misguided, their very lack of legitimate status makes them, as Nestlé amply discovered, very difficult to deal with.

Now we are in a position to answer the question posed in the title of Part 3: The activists want power. That is why they relaunched the boycott and made their demands more stringent even though neither would help the babies of the third world; it explains the strategy of distancing from dialogue, a strategy that accomplishes nothing for the health of infants but does very well at keeping the organizations in existence and prominent. In organizational terms, the external task agenda of 1974–1984 has been replaced by an internal organizational agenda—to remain a player on the international scene, and to strengthen the position from which the power game is played. The "Breaking the Rules" publications have nothing to do with Code adherence (which is one reason why the details of Code adherence have not been discussed in this section) and everything to do with maintaining the image of the NGO in a position of moral judgment vis-a-vis Nestlé and the other MNCs.

If we now have some idea of how we got to this point—why the players on the international business field act as they do—what ways are open to ensuring the protection of the infants and peace and quiet for legal economic enterprise? We are left at this point with a tripartite agenda:

1. The governments of the nations of the developing world are still the only legal authorities charged with the protection of the health of the mothers and infants of their own lands. They must take a more responsible role in the regulation of their health care facilities and the monitoring of the operations of the MNCs in their jurisdictions.

2. The MNCs somehow must work with the NGOs. The history of the Nestlé case reveals periods when intelligent corporate officers and focused activists worked very well together and accomplished good work for the world. Those success stories should be studied by all parties to find the basis for more of the same. We know that it can be done.

3. Eventually the new trade alliances may be—must be—brought into the conversation. Right now the WTO sees no mission grander than the protection of the total freedom of capitalists to enrich themselves at the expense, if necessary, of every other value in the world. That has got to change.

What basis have the MNCs and the trade alliances to work with the NGOs? Let's retrace our steps and pick up the business perspective.

IV. WHAT WAS NESTLÉ DOING WRONG?

What kind of company was accused of such wrongdoing in the third world? In fulfilling what obligations had Nestlé failed?

Let's begin with some general assumptions about the obligations of a private corporation in a modern nation state. We have outgrown, most of us,[64] the crude nineteenth century view of the corporation that held it to be solely the plaything of the shareholders, beholden to no one else. We now speak, more generally, of the "stakeholders" in the corporation—those whose interests are affected by corporate actions and who therefore have some legitimate say in what goes on. The private corporations are accustomed to dealing with these parties—allies or potential adversaries—and know how to deal with them effectively. These parties may be categorized as follows:

> *The shareholders, the investors—the true owners of the company.* They elect a Board of Directors, to whom all the managers are accountable. They are owed, by all managers, a fiduciary duty of good stewardship of their funds, generally interpreted as the highest feasible rate of return on their investment (ROI) with allowances

for obedience to law, custom, and reinvestment for the future. They are also owed an annual report on that stewardship, and if they don't like what they see, they can attend the annual meeting of the corporation, and either get resolutions accepted that will reform the managers' stewardship practices (remember the Sisters of the Precious Blood) or, if necessary, throw out the whole Board of Directors and elect new ones. It's their company, and they can run it as they like.

The customers. By preferring the company's product and expressing that preference by purchasing it in the open market, customers provide the profits, the ROI, that the shareholders want. They are owed a good product that is safe to use in accordance with its instructions and will do what it claims; they are owed honesty and concern and responsiveness to their complaints. If they are dissatisfied with the company's performance with respect to their needs, they have a much quicker and more effective way of expressing their dissatisfaction than have the shareholders: They can stop buying the product and the company will go out of business. If the product turns out to be unsafe, they can sue for damages under the law of torts, and (at least in the United States) the courts have not been kind to companies accused of marketing an unsafe product. On the other hand, if they are satisfied with the product, their purchases make up the company's income; the company is bound by its fiduciary duty to its shareholders, as above, to keep that income stream as large as may be.

The employees. Employees are owed what their contract says they are owed, and consideration for further pay and benefits at stated intervals. If they don't like what they find at the bargaining table, they can go on strike, and if they do not put the company out of business, at least they significantly cut into its ROI, meaning that the obligation to settle a strike on fair terms can also be derived from the fiduciary obligation to the shareholders. They are also owed a safe workplace. If it is not safe, the company may incur legal trouble and may also be open to civil suit from the injured employee.

The law and the regulators. Regulators are owed compliance with law and regulation. Since there are distinct financial penalties attached to noncompliance, the obligation to obey the law can be derived also from the obligation to the shareholders.

The communities. The area where the company's facilities are located are owed general neighborliness: concerns for all kinds of pollution, not only those regulated by law; occasional donations of services; and above all open communications. These obligations are in part prudential, since good will translates into an easier time before the zoning board and the tax assessors, and in part derived from the general obligation of living in society.

Others. More generally, suppliers and others with whom business relations are maintained, who are owed strict adherence to a contract, honesty, and faithfulness in all dealings. These obligations are enforced only in part by contract law; for the most part, they are enforced by the prospect of a very difficult time doing business (translated into higher costs of doing business) with a reputation for dishonesty and faithlessness.

Each stakeholder group has mechanisms for settling disputes and other problems, either through direct negotiation, through arbitration, or through adjudication. The ultimate arbiter is the state, which grants the charter, runs the courts, and enforces the laws. The first obligation is the fiduciary obligation to the shareholders; most of the rest of the obligations are covered by contract, tort law, and the recognition that honesty is the best policy.

The company in turn has rights, under the same laws that create its obligations. It is a citizen, with civil rights under the law, including the right to sue for damages if its rights are infringed; it is a contractor, with the right to have its agreements honored and protected. It has a general right that business customs and obligations will be adhered to by all parties.

"Can a Corporation Have a Conscience?" asked Kenneth Goodpaster and John Matthews in a groundbreaking 1982 essay.[65] Strictly speaking, on the model just given, the answer is no. The corporation is a mechanism by which people invest their money in order to make more money, by any activities that fall within the law. The only caretaker of the public good is the state, the central government of the country in which the business activity is carried on. "Social Responsibility" may occupy only a very small space in the corporate agenda, and if pressed, the corporate officers should be able to show that all social responsibility activities positively affect ROI (the "bottom line"), if only in the very long run. Note: If state law undertakes to limit the corporation (and all its competitors), then the corporation is limited; it must obey the law. Only let the rules be fair and fairly applied; the corporation will comply. But if "guidelines" from some local garden club, environmental group, NGO, or international organization not only hinder profit-making but violate science and common sense, then the company *may not* follow the guidelines without violating its fiduciary obligations.

A strongly argued defense of a company's right and duty to concentrate on profits and not to be distracted by the "corporate responsibility" agenda of the NGOs was published recently. "Corporate Irresponsibility," authored by Robert Halfon, bears a copyright date of 1998, suggesting that the author had access to the lessons that Nestlé learned in the course of the boycott. Little evidence of such learning appears in his confident advice on strategy and tactics of resistance to the NGOs:

Business needs to form alliances, to establish its own think tanks, pressure groups and college professorships, vigorously to put forward the argument for corporate capitalism and to expose the inaccuracies of its opponents. The background of the individuals behind and the activists who work for these groups should be investigated and, if suspect (i.e., if they have a history of opposition to the operation of the free economy), their motives and real objectives should immediately be laid bare. In doing so, the credibility of the activist group will be undermined.[66]

Nestlé, it seems, had been there and done that, and it didn't really work. But Halfon's major message—that the corporation's present obligations under the law exclude genuine concessions to NGOs (except those that can be justified on traditional grounds)—is absolutely correct.

Then what can be done about the NGOs' demands? For the sake of the image of the product (and for the sake of fending off unpleasant lawsuits, shareholder resolutions, bad press etc.) the company may certainly talk to NGO leaders, examine its own practices, try to grant the NGO's requests. As Nestlé spokesmen pointed out to Mike Muller, cited in *The Baby Killer:* "It is a very bad advertisement for our product if [infant death from bottle feeding] happens with our product."[67] So the whole system is open to be reasoned with, to change practices if the evidence suggests it, and a constructive dialogue can accomplish a good deal. But the dialogue is not easy going, as we saw in Part I. As early as 1978, Luther Gerlach correctly described the dilemma faced by a corporation trying to deal with an NGO:

> Established orders are accustomed to dealing with relatively centralized institutions directed by an identifiable and permanent leadership with whom it usually shares many common understandings and values and with whom it thus can negotiate binding agreements in routine fashion. [NGOs] characteristically have many and often changing leaders and groups and their values and understandings are different from established orders. Agreements with one or more such leaders may be rejected by others as a sell-out. When it suits them, movement groups and leaders can also disclaim responsibility for acts and decisions of other groups and leaders which may seem to have failed. Yet movement groups and participants will also stand together against a common foe and profit from the successes or the martyrdom of others. . . . Dealing with such a force will increasingly frustrate the challenged multinationals. . . .
>
> Protestors . . . will threaten the entire multinational by attacking its proud name and reputation and by building public opinion against it. Eventually, they may threaten its cash flow. A multinational is more vulnerable than a[n NGO] because it does have more visible power and capital which can be disturbed. It has also promised more to the public. It has everything to lose in a conflict with a[n NGO], nothing to gain except survival.[68]

In this light, we can see the problems Nestlé had in dealing with the activists' demands: What right had they to ask any of this? Who elected them? Where did they get the right to tell a private individual how to conduct its lawful business? Where did they get the right to speak for the mothers and the infants of the third world? And how on earth to deal with them when there were no patterns of interaction that were legitimate and effective?

What did Nestlé see itself as doing, on the way to the Kennedy hearings? Correcting misinformation, asserting its rights under the law (Berne), and generously giving its time (especially to Mike Muller) for clearing up misconceptions. But nothing got cleared up, and every constructive move Nestlé made got turned against it. By the time the request came for a representation to testify before Kennedy's Subcommittee on Health and Scientific Research (of the Senate Committee on Human Resources) in the spring of 1978, Nestlé must have been convinced that in the topsy turvy world of the activists, rights counted for nothing, truth counted for nothing, and engaging in constructive international dialogue might be counterproductive—as indeed it turned out to be in Washington. But Nestlé was unwilling to appear to be hiding anything, and it was sure that if its perspective were known it would carry the day, so Nestlé sent its best qualified representatives to Washington to testify before Kennedy, with the results documented in Part I.

Why did Nestlé keep throwing resources—people, money, reputation—against the stone wall of defending its case against the activists? Why did it not do what all the analysts say it should have done, and simply ignore the NGOs until they went away? For the protestors would have done that eventually. A movement needs food. Its natural nourishment is the enraged reactions of the countries or companies attacked. Starving babies is a crime, but starving activist organizations doesn't sound that bad. Why did Nestlé keep responding? Only one answer fits the data: Nestlé didn't want to get rid of this issue; Nestlé wanted to get it right. Such an objective is a stumbling block to the corporate mentality—foolishness to the business school analysts. As an anonymous Nestlé officer, interviewed by Charles McCoy for an earlier retelling of this case, put it

> I believe it is ethical for Nestlé to produce infant formula. But from a business perspective, there are too many problems. It would be better to drop it. That is *my* opinion. But there's no way Nestlé will go against its commitment.[69]

On behalf of the business school analysts, Prakash Sethi found the entire defense effort on Nestlé's part ridiculous: as noted in his comment in Part I of this chapter, Nestlé's tactics amounted to one blunder after another, the major blunder being the attempt to join the debate with such critics at all.[70] Yet Nestlé—suffering no economic damage at all from either boycott, and perfectly positioned to ignore the whole attack—continues to engage anyone who will listen in conversation, to find the consensus on the best nutrition for the infants, to find a really good strategy for the developing world, in short, to get it right. This approach stands in troublesome contrast to the disengagement policy of, for instance, UNICEF. Where do we go from here?

QUESTIONS FOR REFLECTION

1. From a management standpoint, how could Nestlé have handled the situation better? Consider:

   Choice of product lines

   Choice of times, places, manners of reply

   Use of institutes like the NCCN or NIFAC

2. Also from a management standpoint, can you make an argument that Nestlé did everything right?

3. What does the Nestlé case tell us about the place of the MNC in the contemporary world?

4. What is the role of the NGO in the world of "globalized" business?

ENDNOTES

1. Henri Nestlé, *Memorial on the Nutrition of Infants* (Vevey, Switzerland: Loertscher & Son, 1869): pp. 1, 3.

2. Derrick Jelliffe, "Commerciogenic Malnutrition? Time for a Dialogue," *Food Technology* 15 (1971): 55–56.

3. This summary of PAG23 is taken word for word from two sources: Maggie Mc-Comas, "Origins of the Controversy," in *Infant Feeding: Anatomy of a Controversy 1973–1984*, John Dobbing, ed. (London: Springer-Verlag, 1988): pp. 33–34; and S. Prakash Sethi, *Multinational Corporations and the Impact of Public Advocacy on Corporate Strategy: Nestlé and the Infant Formula Controversy* (Boston: Kluwer, 1994): p. 50. Sethi (see note 8, p. 57) took it from Maggie McComas, Geoffrey Fookes, and George Taucher, *The Infant Formula Controversy: Nestlé and the Dilemma of Third World Nutrition* (Nestlé, S.A., Vevey, Switzerland, 1982). The underlined portions are found in McComas but not in Sethi.

4. *Consumer Reports* (September 1974) Editorial based on Robert J. Ledogar, *Hungry for Profits: U.S. Food and Drug Multinationals in Latin America* Chapter 9, "Formula for Malnutrition," (New York: IDOC North America, 1975): pp. 111–126.

5. According to Sethi, op. cit., pp. 62–63.

6. Paul Minus, "A Background Paper on the Infant Formula Controversy: Prepared for the Task Force on Infant Formula," United Methodist (Dayton, Ohio: United Methodist Church September 17, 1980): pp. 14–15.

7. The account is taken from Sethi, op. cit. p. 60, citing "Nestlé and the Infant Food Controversy (A) (Revised)," School of Business Administration, London, Ontario, Canada, 1981.

8. Sethi, op. cit., p. 81.

9. Ibid., p. 82.

10. Ibid., p. 77.

11. Ibid., p. 82.

12. McComas, "Into the Political Arena," in Dobbing, op. cit., p. 76; Sethi, op. cit., p. 91; or perhaps Paternot presented Kennedy with Barter's letter.

13. World Health Organization, Nutrition Unit, "The International Code of Marketing of Breast-Milk Substitutes: A Common Review and Evaluation Framework," (Geneva, Switzerland: WHO). No date of publication is given.

14. William Shaw and Vincent Barry, *Moral Issues in Business*, 7th ed. (Belmont, CA: Wadsworth, 1998): p. 215.

15. For the association of Nestlé USA with Ernest Lefever's Ethics and Public Policy Center, which distributed Herman Nickel's "The Corporation Haters" (originally published in *Fortune* on June 15, 1980) on Nestlé's behalf, and Ernest Saunders' "Nestlégate Memorandum," see

Sethi, op. cit., pp. 102–107, especially note 8, p. 107.

16. Morton Mintz, "Infant-Formula Maker Battles Boycotters by Painting Them Red," *Washington Post* (January 4, 1981): p. A2.

17. Minus, op. cit.

18. Sethi, op cit., p. 222.

19. Ibid., p. 221.

20. Ibid., p. 233.

21. IBFAN, "Breaking the Rules 1982: A Year-End Compilation of Violations of the International Code of Marketing of Breast-Milk Substitutes" (Minneapolis, MN: IBFAN, 1983). Cited in G. Veraldi, in Dobbing, op. cit., p. 131.

22. Disturbed by the tactics of the boycott organizers in this period, the Methodist Task Force included in its report a substantial critique of their actions. See G. Veraldi, "Implementing the WHO Code," in Dobbing, op. cit., pp. 130–132; J. Philip Wogaman, ed. "Fourth Report of the Infant Formula Task Force to the United Methodist General Council on Ministries" (April 28, 1983).

23. Cited in Veraldi, "Resolution of the Conflict," in Dobbing, op. cit., p. 145.

24. For the only U.S. church account of this campaign the authors have found, see Anglican Church News Service "English Bishop Urges Boycott of Infant Formula Companies for Marketing to Third World Countries," *Good News,* Episcopal Diocese of Connecticut (February–March 1997), p. 17. The Nestlé boycott, this article mentions, had been suspended in 1994; it continues: "now Bishop Simon Barrington-Ward of Coventry wants the boycott renewed against several companies, for violation of the International Code of Marketing of Breast-Milk Substitutes. Companies targeted include not only Nestlé, but also Gerber, Milco, Nutricia and Myeth [sic]."

25. "UNICEF, WHO Open Drive to Promote Breast-Feeding," *Boston Globe* (March 10, 1992): p. 15. See Linda Feldmann, "UNICEF and WHO Promote Breast-Feeding Campaign," *Christian Science Monitor* (March 13, 1992): p. 3;

"Breast Milk for the World's Babies,"*The New York Times* Editorial (March 12, 1992): p. A22.

26. Annalies Allain, "Foreword" to Ellen J. Sokol J. D. *The Code Handbook: A Guide to Implementing the International Code of Marketing of Breastmilk Substitutes* (International Code Documentation Centre (ICDC), 1997.

27. Correspondence with Peter Brabeck, November 3, 1997.

28. Lawrence Altman, "AIDS Brings a Shift on Breast-Feeding: U.N. Discouraging Practice for Women Infected with H.I.V.," *The New York Times* (July 26, 1998): p. 1.

29. Ibid., p. 6.

30. Dana Raphael and Flora Davis, *Only Mothers Know: Patterns of Infant Feeding in Traditional Cultures* (Westport, CT: Greenwood, 1985): Preface, p. xiii. Copyright © by Greenwood Press. Reproduced with permission of Greenwood Publishing Group, Inc., Westport, CT.

31. Ibid., p. 23. The results were also published in 1977 as "Mothers in Poverty: Breastfeeding and the Maternal Struggle for Infant Survival" in *The Lactation Review* 2, with an introduction by Dana Raphael.

32. Raphael, op. cit., pp. 23–24.

33. Ibid., p. 138.

34. Ibid., p. 64.

35. "Women and Breast-Feeding," World Health Organization undated.

36. Ibid.

37. Kevin Helliker, "Dying for Milk: Some Mothers, Trying In Vain to Breast-Feed, Starve Their Infants," *The Wall Street Journal* (July 22, 1994): pp. A1, A4. "Ideologenic" starvation continues, on occasion: see Nina Bernstein, "New York Faults Hospital for Denying Checkup to Baby Who Starved," *The New York Times* (October 26, 1998): p. B1.

38. Sethi, op. cit., p. 115.

39. American Academy of Pediatrics, "The Promotion of Breast-Feeding," *Pediatrics* 69 (1982): 654–661.

40. *The Code Handbook*, p. 45; see note 21, p. 52.

41. Dobbing, op. cit, citing B. Lozoff, "Birth and 'Bonding' in Non-Industrial Societies," *Developmental Medicine: Child Neurology* 25 (1983): 595–600.

42. R. G. Whitehead, A. A. Paul, and M. G. M. Rowland, "Lactation in Cambridge and in The Gambia," in *Topics in Paediatrics* 2, Nutrition in Childhood. B. A. Wharton, ed. (Tunbridge Wells: Pitman Medical, 1980): pp. 22–32.

43. "Infant Feeding Today," *Lancet* i (1986): 17–18.

44. Patrice Jelliffe, Darrel's wife, was a nurse and an expert in public health, and collaborated with her husband on much of his research.

45. D. B. Jelliffe and E. F. P. Jelliffe, *Human Milk in the Modern World: Psychosocial, Nutritional and Economic Significance.* (Oxford: Oxford University Press, 1978): pp. 78–80. Cited in Dobbing, op. cit. pp. 21–22.

46. Letter dated 1972 provided by Dana Raphael. As was the custom of the day, Patrice Jelliffe and Dana Raphael signed with initials only, so that they would not be identified (and disregarded) as women.

47. Cited in McComas, "Into the Political Arena," in Dobbing, op. cit., p. 70.

48. See Introduction.

49. Jessica T. Mathews, "Power Shift," *Foreign Affairs* 76(1) (January/February 1997): p. 50. Emphasis added.

50. Ibid., p. 51.

51. Ibid., p. 53.

52. Ibid., p. 53.

53. Ibid., p. 54.

54. R. Grove White, "Brent Spar Rewrote the Rules," *New Statesman* (July 20, 1997).

55. See, for some excellent examples: Thomas Donaldson "Values in Tension: Ethics Away from Home," *Harvard Business Review* (September–October 1996): 48–62; Manuel Velasquez "International Business Ethics," *Business Ethics Quarterly*, 5(4) (October 1995): 865–882; Richard De George, *Competing with Integrity in International Business* (New York: Oxford University Press, 1993); Gerald F. Cavanagh, S.J., *American Business Values with International Perspectives.* 4th ed. (Upper Saddle River, NJ: Prentice Hall, 1998); Joe Skelly, "The Rise of International Ethics: The Caux Round Table Principles for Business Ethics," *Business Ethics* (March–April 1995): supplement, pp. 2–5. (The Caux principles are also appended in Gerald Cavanagh's book.) For an interesting analysis of international business ethics from the point of view adopted in the Caux principles, see Kenneth Goodpaster, "Bridging East and West in Management Ethics: Kyosei and the Moral Point of View," *The Journal of Human Values* (January 1996), adapted from a presentation on kyosei at the United Nations University in Tokyo, Japan, October 20, 1995.

56. See Laura Pincus Hartman, *Perspectives in Business Ethics* (Chicago: Irwin McGraw Hill, 1998): pp. 775–777.

57. Luther P. Gerlach, "The Flea and the Elephant: Infant Formula Controversy," *Society* 17(6) (September/October 1980): 51–57.

58. L. H. Newton, "A Scaffold for Muir," in Patricia Werhane, ed., *Environmental Challenges for Business*, derived from the 1997 Conference on Ethics in Business, Darden School, University of Virginia, Charlottesville, VA. BEQ special issue, pub. Soc. Bus. Ethics, p. 237.

59. Nicholas D. Kristof, "It's a Bad Time for Weak Leadership," *The New York Times: Week in Review* (August 30, 1998): p. WK 1. The article includes a telling caption below pictures of U.S. President William Clinton, Russian Premier Boris N. Yeltsin, German Prime Minister Helmut Kohl, Jiang Zemin of China, and Prime Minister Keizo Obuchi of Japan: "None of these men is Churchill."

60. Benjamin Barber, *Jihad vs. McWorld* (New York: Times Books, 1995).

61. See Joseph Kahn, "The Bear Draws Blood: Clawing at the Markets, Russia's Crisis Reveals the Ugly Side of Globalization," *The New York Times: Money and Business* (August 30, 1998): p. BU 1; Ethan Bronner, "Moscow Dashes American Illusions," *The New York Times: Week in Review*, (August 30, 1998): p. WK 1; and Michael M. Weinstein, "Russia Is

Not Poland, and That's Too Bad," *The New York Times: Week in Review* (August 30, 1998): p. WK 5.

62. Mathews, op. cit., pp. 58–60.

63. Mathews, op. cit., p. 63.

64. But see Milton Friedman, *Capitalism and Freedom* (Chicago, IL: University of Chicago Press, 1962).

65. Kenneth Goodpaster and John Matthews Jr., "Can a Corporation Have a Conscience?" *Harvard Business Review* (January/February 1982) reprint 82104.

66. Robert Halfon, "Corporate Irresponsibility: Is Business Appeasing Anti-Business Activists?" in The Social Affairs Unit (London), *Research Report 26*: p. 7.

67. Mike Muller, *The Baby Killer: A War on Want Investigation into the Promotion and Sale of Powdered Milk in the Third World* (War on Want: 1974): p. 13.

68. Luther Gerlach, "Milk, Movements and Multinationals: Complex Interactions and Social Responsibilities," prepared for presentation at the seminar on Responsibility of Multinational Corporations (June 2, 1978: pp. 19–20.

69. Charles S. McCoy et al., *Nestlé and the Controversy over the Marketing of Breast-Milk Substitutes: How Should a Multinational Corporation Respond to Protests against the Ethics of Its Policies?* (Columbus, OH: Council for Ethics and Economics, 1996).

70. Sethi, op. cit.

3

❂

Must We Maintain a Friendly Workplace?

Sexual Harassment on the Job

Questions to Keep in Mind

1. Concerning the facts of Rena Weeks's court case: Which facts are not disputed and which are? What role does an accurate account play in making an ethical judgment about this case?

2. How costly is sexual harassment for American business?

3. In what sense is this case of sexual harassment a matter of individual responsibility? In what sense is it a matter of corporate responsibility?

4. In Baker & McKenzie's experience in investigating complaints of sexual harassment, what is the primary reason so few complaints result in convictions?

5. What are the chief points pertaining to sexual harassment of Title VII of the Civil Rights Act of 1964 and the 1990 Equal Employment Opportunity Commission (EEOC) definition of harassment?

6. Identify, compare, and contrast the two broad types of sexual harassment, as defined by the EEOC guidelines.

7. What is the "reasonable person standard" and how is it supposed to help deal with differences of perception about harassing behavior? How is a "reasonable woman standard" different?

By any standards, the complaints coming from men working at Long Prairie Packing Company (LPP) were very disturbing. One worker said in court documents that he was attacked by groups of men who pinned him down, sometimes in a bin of raw meat or a trough of blood. They then simulated sex acts on him. He claimed that this mistreatment occurred repeatedly, sometimes daily. He also claimed that a supervisor was involved, and another threatened to terminate his employment when he complained.[1] A federal lawsuit followed, in which LPP employees claimed that their workplace was characterized by a pervasive atmosphere of sexual intimidation. Some men complained that their faces were repeatedly shoved into other men's crotches. Allegedly, steel rods were thrust between men's legs while they were working. In an article about the suit from the January 2000 issue of *Minnesota Monthly*, a former employee commented about the suit, saying, "You don't feel like a person, but more like the meat on the conveyor belts and in the bins."[2]

In August 1999 the U.S. Equal Employment Opportunity Commission (EEOC) settled the first male-on-male sexual harassment class action.[3] It announced that it had reached a voluntary $1.9 million settlement with LLP, which employs about 235 people. This settlement resolved all claims in an EEOC lawsuit filed on behalf of a class of current and former male LPP employees who claimed that they had experienced a pattern of sexual harassment at the company. These men also claimed that when they tried to oppose the same-sex harassment, other men in the company retaliated against them.

The agreement between the EEOC and LLP followed a precedent-setting decision from the U.S. Supreme Court in March 1998, in *Ocale v. Sundowner Offshore Services*. In that case, the Supreme Court held that same-sex harassment is actionable under Title VII of the Civil Rights Act of 1964, which bans sex discrimination in employment. The settlement with LLP was the result of the EEOC's first class action that challenged a pattern of harassment by men against men.

The settlement did not represent any admission of wrongdoing by LPP, nor did it involve any judicial findings of a violation of law. However, the settlement was significant as a clear and tangible step in the evolution of what counts as sexual harassment at work. In the preceding two decades, a number of court decisions had developed and refined what constitutes harassment at work. By the year 2000, it was generally accepted without argument by most workers that sexual harassment does not belong at work. There was also widespread consensus about what constitutes sexual harassment, especially in cases of so-called quid pro quo harassment that involve unwelcome sexual advances, requests for sexual favors, or other verbal or physical conduct of a sexual nature.

But as the 1990s drew to a close, there were clear signs that harassment was not going away. According to the EEOC, it saw during that decade the largest increase in harassment charges in its entire history![4] Thirty-eight percent of these harassment charges were race discrimination. Sex harassment was the next highest form of discrimination—constituting 30 percent of all charges filed in the 1990s. In fact, the charges of sexual harassment in that decade were three times the charges brought forward in the 1980s.

Significantly, as society heightened its awareness of sexual harassment, people became more attuned to other forms of harassment. For example, society also became more sensitive to the problems of religious discrimination at work. Workplace harassment could also take nontraditional forms, thanks to advances in technology. Increasingly, companies have had to deal with harassment via computer and on the Internet.[5]

Trends of harassment may mirror fundamental and lasting changes in society. More than ever, the workforce includes women and people of color. The trend also is toward a more flexible workforce, as evidenced by more part-time, temporary, and contingent employment. Whereas discrimination at work was once conceived in terms of single dimensions (race, gender, age, class—each considered individually), it appears now that discrimination can cross the boundaries of these various dimensions. Thus an adequate understanding of sexual harassment in the workplace must consider how these various factors intersect. Only then can we understand fully how certain groups of persons at work are especially vulnerable.

We no longer can think of harassment as something that happens only to women. From the beginning, the EEOC cautioned that harassment could work both ways: Women could harass men just as men could harass women. (The fact that traditionally men held positions of greater power tended to mean that sexual harassment was primarily something that men did.) But what about men harassing other men? For a long time, this form of harassment just wasn't on the radar screen. However, as the LLP case makes clear, same-sex harassment—something once too taboo or sensitive to talk about openly—now also became a matter that demanded proactive management by business executives.

Harassment at work will most certainly continue to take new forms, demanding ongoing responses from business and government. Legally, the situation continues to be ambiguous. According to a statement from the EEOC, "The complex employment discrimination issues addressed throughout the 35 year history of Commission and court activity have not reduced the number of legal questions still posed by the laws or made the answers easier to find. For each decision or clarification, new and equally perplexing issues have arisen to take its place."[6] Ethically, the situation also continues to be complex. To help us discern what is going on ethically with current trends in workplace sexual harassment, we need to be aware of interpretive principles derived from earlier court decisions.

The wake-up call for this reading comes from a landmark sexual harassment lawsuit brought against the prestigious law firm Baker & McKenzie. It was considered a landmark case because the jury awarded $6.9 million to Rena Weeks, the Baker & McKenzie employee who claimed she had been harassed by a powerful lawyer, Martin Greenstein. After the trial, the judge reduced that award to $3.5 million, an amount that Baker & McKenzie continued to dispute through various appeals. In 1998, however, the California Supreme court upheld the $3.5 million punitive award.[7] That was enough for Baker & McKenzie, which announced it would not seek a review of that decision in the U.S.

Supreme court.[8] Today, we can read the case of Rena Weeks to remind us how harassment principles were developed and to sensitize us to new and emerging forms of harassment that inevitably crop up in the workplace.

I. A COSTLY COMPLAINT

Rena Weeks, a legal secretary, was suing her boss, attorney Martin R. Greenstein, for alleged sexual harassment. She was also suing the law firm where they had worked, Baker & McKenzie, for not responding adequately to her complaints about Greenstein. Only a few summers before, in 1991, the Anita Hill–Clarence Thomas hearings had forced Americans to confront sexual harassment as a burning public issue. The nation was still coming to terms with the trauma of that televised sexual battlefield. And now, in the late summer of 1994, it seemed to be happening all over again.

Rena Weeks's case, which was being heard by Judge John Munter at the San Francisco Superior Court, was covered closely in newspapers across the country. On top of that, cable television's Court TV aired much of the courtroom proceedings to a spellbound national audience. Soon everyone was talking about the "David and Goliath" story of little Rena Weeks standing up to the largest law firm in the world. Businesses everywhere held their breath, waiting for the court decision that could have a wide-ranging impact on *their* accountability for sexual harassment in the workplace.

The sexual harassment stakes for American business are not trivial. Sexual harassment was first recognized as a type of illegal sex discrimination in 1976. Since then, 90 percent of Fortune 500 companies have dealt with sexual harassment complaints. More than a third of them have been sued at least once for sexual harassment; 25 percent have been sued multiple times. According to Bettina Plevan, an attorney who specializes in defending companies against sexual harassment lawsuits, employers spend an average of $200,000 for each harassment complaint that they investigate and find to be valid—regardless of whether the complaint ever gets all the way to court.[9]

The essential facts of the Weeks harassment case are fairly straightforward.[10] Rena Weeks joined Baker & McKenzie as Martin Greenstein's secretary in July 1991. She was transferred a month later. She left Baker & McKenzie in September 1991, less than three months after starting at the firm. The reason given for Weeks's abrupt transfer and departure, and the basis for her lawsuit, was that Greenstein allegedly had sexually harassed her. Weeks claimed that Greenstein had groped her hips and breasts on different occasions when she worked for him at Baker & McKenzie's California offices in Palo Alto. Weeks sued for compensation for unspecified damages due to emotional distress and for punitive damages for the twenty-day period she had worked for Greenstein.

Weeks also claimed that her law firm had done nothing to stop Greenstein from harassing her. Part of her case claimed that there was a broader pattern of sanctioned abuse at Baker & McKenzie. According to Philip Kay (Weeks's lead attorney in the trial), Weeks was not the only one at Baker & McKenzie to complain to the firm about Greenstein. Thus Baker & McKenzie faced a possible multimillion-dollar judgment for allegedly covering up Greenstein's offensive behavior. It is likely that Baker & McKenzie had expected to settle with Weeks out of court, a common way corporations deal with sexual harassment suits. Instead, Weeks pressed her case all the way to trial, which started in late July 1994.

Weeks's case is significant because it involved a prominent lawyer at Baker & McKenzie, the world's biggest law firm with 1,700 lawyers and offices around the world. In 1993 Baker & McKenzie had pulled in $512 million in revenue.[11] It certainly had deep pockets. The case is also significant precisely because it involved a law firm, which many assumed should know better when it comes to dealing with sexual harassment issues. However, in the opinion of many legal experts, law firms as a whole have been slow to establish their own sexual harassment policies, even while they were advising clients about this evolving area of law! Baker & McKenzie *did* have a recently implemented policy on sexual harassment; it was not clear, however, how closely the members of this firm practiced what it preached. Of the Weeks–Baker & McKenzie dispute, one labor lawyer said, "This is a wake-up call about what can happen if you don't have your act together."[12]

In this chapter, we will summarize three important aspects of this sexual harassment case: Weeks's charges, Greenstein's defense, and Baker & McKenzie's defense. To understand the significance of this case as a sexual harassment wake-up call, we will also review the legislative history pertaining to sexual harassment, chiefly Title VII and the Equal Employment Opportunity Guidelines on Sexual Harassment. Important concepts that bear on the Weeks case will be considered—including the notions of "quid pro quo" and "hostile environment." To understand why sexual harassment continues to be such a troubling issue, we will note how the Weeks case and others like it entail differences of perception among people about just what constitutes sexual harassment. Finally, we will underscore that sexual harassment is not really so much about sex as it is about power. With these concepts in mind, we will then be in a position to understand the complex dynamics contributing to the court's judgment against Greenstein and Baker & Mckenzie.

II. CHARGES AND DEFENSES

First we will present in more detail the charges that Rena Weeks brought against Martin Greenstein and Baker & McKenzie. Weeks was forty years old when she was hired by Baker & McKenzie in July 1991 to work for Greenstein. In less than a month she was transferred out of his office. Why?[13]

According to Weeks, the trouble all started when she and Greenstein had attended a departmental lunch at a Sizzler restaurant near their Palo Alto offices. Upon leaving the lunch, Greenstein allegedly grabbed her breast while dropping M&M candies in the front pocket of her blouse. Weeks further testified that Greenstein then proceeded to pin her arms behind her back, thrusting her chest forward, saying "Let's see which one [of your breasts] is bigger." When testifying in court about the M&M incident, a tearful Weeks said, "I didn't believe what happened. I was in shock. This is a guy that is a supervisor in a big department in this firm, and this shouldn't be going on."[14]

Weeks also testified that the M&M incident was not an isolated instance of harassment. She claimed that Greenstein had made her uncomfortable at work, once lunging at her breasts in a hallway.[15]

It was also part of Weeks's charge against Greenstein and the firm that she was not the only woman harassed at work by Greenstein. According to her lawyers, Greenstein had a history of harassing women and his behavior had become more brazen over time. They claimed that he had harassed at least ten women in two Baker & McKenzie offices over six and a half years. For example, according to Weeks's attorney Philip Kay, Greenstein had made sexual passes at Baker & McKenzie attorney Donna Blow back at the firm's Chicago headquarters. Blow had rebuffed Greenstein because she was a lesbian, telling Greenstein, "Marty, if you were a married woman, I might consider it."[16]

Weeks's attorneys argued that Greenstein was able to get away with his harassing behavior only because his firm tolerated it and sometimes covered it up. Even before Weeks had filed her complaint against Greenstein, others had protested his actions. There was a Baker & McKenzie associate who said Greenstein had tickled her feet beneath a library table and there was also a receptionist from a "temp" agency who had refused to go back to work at Baker & McKenzie because Greenstein had invited her to share a hot tub with him.[17]

At the trial, Vicki Gardner (a "temp" hired by Baker & McKenzie in 1989 to work for Greenstein), described other examples of harassment by Greenstein. Gardner testified that Greenstein had told her that he liked her high-collar blouses because they reminded him of his first wife. But, Gardner said, Greenstein went on to add that he liked her low-cut blouses even more. Describing her reaction to this comment, Gardner testified, "I felt stripped and shocked."[18]

At the trial, Greenstein denied these charges of sexual harassment. Forty-nine years old, he had the reputation of being "a swaggering bear of a man with a gift for attracting lucrative clients and a standard of perfection that admitted few mistakes."[19] He admitted that he gave Weeks some M&Ms after the departmental lunch at Sizzlers, but he denied the rest of her version of the story. Testifying about that incident, Greenstein matter-of-factly explained that he had dropped the candies into Weeks's breast pocket at her invitation. He said, "She held out her pocket, and I dropped the M&Ms in it."[20]

Greenstein's attorneys said that Weeks had not written about the alleged M&M incident in her diary. Furthermore, they claimed, Weeks had been "braless" on the day of the departmental lunch.[21] As if that weren't enough, according to Greenstein's attorneys, Weeks had willingly given Greenstein a neck massage at the office, following his alleged lunge for her breasts.

Why would Weeks fabricate a harassment story against Greenstein? In his defense, Greenstein testified that Weeks was doing it to save her job. In his judgment, she was a disgruntled employee who didn't have the basic secretarial skills necessary to perform in a high-pressure job. "I gave her chance after chance to learn," he said. "She was just a slow learner."[22] Also, according to Greenstein, "She had numerous problems. Each time, she explained to me she was new on the job and really wanted the job."[23] Greenstein argued that Weeks was overwhelmed by her new position at Baker & McKenzie, she feared for her job, and so she used her position with him to fabricate a sexual harassment case in order to profit financially.

Baker & McKenzie had a slightly different take on the issue at Weeks's trial. The law firm acknowledged that Greenstein had displayed "clearly unfortunate behavior" with women at work. The firm also maintained that it *had* investigated prior harassment complaints against Greenstein. But in every instance, it claimed, the alleged victims were not willing to come forward publicly with their complaints and so it had not been possible to produce strong evidence against Greenstein.

According to John Bartko, lead counsel for Baker & McKenzie, in his trial brief, "Baker does not deny that Greenstein has had a history of boorish and childish behavior." But Baker & McKenzie's Chicago home office had warned its West Coast representatives to "keep an eye" on Greenstein when he moved to Palo Alto office in 1989. Also, the firm had indeed put a stop to a "foot tickling" consensual relationship Greenstein had with the firm's Chicago office manager.[24]

Under the terms of the firm's sexual harassment policy, Baker & McKenzie transferred Weeks to another department after she made her complaint against Greenstein. They had then investigated her allegations. As a result, they had required Greenstein to seek psychological counseling. And, Baker & McKenzie eventually *did* fire Greenstein in 1993 (although the defense pointed out that this was fully six years after the firm had first received a harassment complaint against Greenstein).

Baker & McKenzie's defense was, therefore, that if Weeks did have a legitimate complaint against Greenstein, she did *not* have a case against the firm, which had done all it should have done to investigate and deal with her harassment complaint.

III. SEXUAL HARASSMENT:
THE LEGISLATIVE HISTORY

Current laws concerning sexual harassment have their basis in Title VII of the Civil Rights Act of 1964. Congress's primary purpose in proposing Title VII was to protect disadvantaged minorities from employment discrimination. Matters of race, religion, color, and national origin were the primary considerations in the debate at that time; gender was included as a protected class only at the last minute, by opponents who sought to use the issue of sex to kill the proposed legislation.[25] The bill passed, despite the opponents' efforts, unexpectedly providing the nation with a law protecting a majority group: women.

While Title VII protected against *discrimination* on the basis of sex, it was not until 1986, when the Supreme Court ruled in *Meritor Savings Bank v. Vinson*, that sexual harassment was clearly established to be a violation of Title VII. Prior to that time, sexual harassment was not a specific violation of federal law. But in this case the Supreme Court ruled that the creation of a "hostile environment" through sexual harassment violates Title VII, even in the absence of economic harm to the employee or a demand for sexual favors in exchange for benefits, such as promotions or raises. Victims of sexual harassment were entitled to compensation including back pay, damages for emotional stress, and attorney's fees.[26]

In 1990 the EEOC defined sexual harassment in the following terms:

> Unwelcome sexual advances, requests for sexual favors, and other verbal or physical conduct of a sexual nature constitute sexual harassment when:
>
> (1) submission to or rejection of this conduct explicitly or implicitly affects an individual's employment,
>
> (2) unreasonably interferes with an individual's work performance, or
>
> (3) creates an intimidating, hostile, or offensive work environment.

Moreover, the EEOC cited the following as circumstances that could constitute sexual harassment:

- The victim as well as the harasser may be a woman or a man. The victim does not have to be of the opposite sex.
- The harasser can be the victim's supervisor, an agent of the employer, a supervisor in another area, a coworker, or a non-employee.
- The victim does not have to be the person harassed but could be anyone affected by the offensive conduct.
- Unlawful sexual harassment may occur without economic injury to or discharge of the victim.
- The harasser's conduct must be unwelcome.

While the EEOC's guidelines went a long way to clarify what behaviors in principle count as sexual harassment, they by no means ended debate about actual harassment in the workplace. Confusion abounds over what is "safe" conduct among men and women at work. As one commentator put it, "It will be a sad day, if it ever comes, when people [at work] are too nervous to ask a pal out for a drink."[27]

To clarify the applicability of the EEOC guidelines on sexual harassment for the Rena Weeks case, it is important to explain two key concepts upon which the guidelines rest: quid pro quo and hostile environment.

IV. QUID PRO QUO AND
HOSTILE WORK ENVIRONMENT

The EEOC guidelines on sexual harassment presuppose two broad types of sexual harassment: "quid pro quo" harassment and "hostile work environment" harassment. First we will consider what constitutes quid pro quo harassment and whether it applies to Rena Weeks's complaint. Then we will consider what is meant by "hostile work environment" and whether this type of harassment applies to Rena Weeks.

In a quid pro quo situation, something is given or received in exchange for something else. For example, a boss might communicate to a subordinate (explicitly or implicitly) that a promotion or raise will be forthcoming in exchange for sexual favors. According to business law professor Terry Morehead Dworkin, quid pro quo harassment must meet the following conditions:[28]

1. Harassment must be committed by a supervisor or other employee who has *power* or control over a job benefit.

2. The supervisor or other employee must expressly or implicitly threaten to exercise his *power* to deny the benefit if the desired behavior does not ensue.

3. Because the employer has *empowered* the supervisor with the control of the job benefit, traditional agency theory holds the employer strictly liable when the power is abused.

4. In addition, because an abuse of *power* in this context is seen as especially egregious, the behavior need occur only once to hold the employer liable.

According to Dworkin:

> The touchstone of proving a sexual harassment case is that the request from the supervisor was unwelcome. Acceding to the request, however, does not show that it was welcome. Because the employee lacks realistic *power* to refuse the request because of a fear of losing the job, a promotion, a raise, and so forth, additional evidence of the request's being unwelcome must be presented. Proving that the advance is unwelcome when "yes" is not enough can be quite difficult.
>
> The right to sue in spite of saying "yes" has caused much confusion and consternation from those who do not understand the theoretical basis of sexual harassment. Anita Hill may not have quit her job, but it did not mean that Thomas's alleged behavior was welcome.[29]

Dworkin also claims that, in quid pro quo harassment, the threat or denial of a job benefit need not be direct or explicit. She suggests that a supervisor's suggestion to a female subordinate that they go out to dinner to discuss her upcoming promotion could be seen as quid pro quo sexual harassment.

If we apply these considerations to Rena Weeks's case, we may discern some aspects of her situation that fall under quid pro quo. For example,

Greenstein and Weeks both agree that he dropped M&Ms into the breast pocket of her blouse. Greenstein claimed that she let him do this, without protest. But Weeks testified that she was made extremely uncomfortable by his actions. From her perspective, the behavior was unwelcome.

But was Greenstein's behavior part of an overture on his part to obtain sexual favors from Weeks, in exchange for some kind of benefit? This feature of quid pro quo does not seem to apply as neatly to Weeks; there was no indication in the trial that Greenstein was threatening Weeks, or offering her some kind of benefit, in order to obtain some kind of sexual response. A classic quid pro quo situation would have had Greenstein saying something like, "If you want to keep your job here, then you are going to have to do the following things." In any event, the reported interaction between Greenstein and Weeks does not emphasize the feature of his trying to strike some sort of bargain with her.

Next to consider is the "hostile work environment" type of sexual harassment. Unlike a quid pro quo situation, here there is no specific exchange between two people. Rather, an employee perceives that his or her work environment is threatening or hostile overall, due to uninvited sexually oriented materials or behaviors in the workplace. An example might be sexually suggestive photographs on view in a person's office, or the widespread telling of sexual jokes at work.

Justice Sandra Day O'Connor's November 1993 opinion in *Harris v. Forklift Systems* reaffirmed what constitutes a sexually hostile workplace environment. The details of that case were straightforward: Teresa Harris, a manager with a Tennessee truck leasing company, alleged that the company president, Charles Hardy, used vulgar language in her presence, that he proposed to discuss her salary at a local motel, and that he suggested in front of others that she had sex with a customer in order to bring in more business. Harris quit and sued her company, but lower courts found Hardy's behavior merely offensive but not sufficiently injurious. By the time the case reached the Supreme Court, the facts were no longer in dispute; the only question concerned their legal significance. What would be the standard of the Supreme Court for determining whether Hardy's behavior constituted sexual harassment?

The relevant case was the 1986 *Meritor Savings Bank v. Vinson*, which affirmed the EEOC guidelines that established unwelcome conduct of a sexual nature as an illegal barrier to equal employment opportunity. Reaffirming the definition of sexual harassment set out in that case, Justice O'Connor articulated a two-fold test to determine if a sexually hostile environment exists at work. First, would a reasonable person find the conduct severe enough to create an environment that is objectively hostile or abusive? Second, does the victim perceive the environment to be hostile or abusive?[30] This two-fold test goes against an earlier standard requiring plaintiffs to show that they suffered *severe psychological injury* as a result of an overly hostile work environment. Instead, the Supreme Court now holds that other factors must be considered, such as whether the defendant's behavior could be considered threatening or humiliating or if it unreasonably interfered with the employee's work.[31] The significance of this opinion is that it will make it easier for a plaintiff to win a sexual harassment claim based on "hostile work environment."

Even though the Supreme Court was unanimous in its judgment on *Harris v. Forklift System*, it has triggered widely different responses from the public. Consider the following excerpts from two leading public opinion pages, the first from *The New York Times*:

> A victim of sexual harassment need not suffer a nervous breakdown to sue an employer for discrimination. A worker has suffered enough, the Supreme Court asserts, if the employer has so polluted the workplace with sexual improprieties that a reasonable person would find it hostile and abusive, a disagreeable, unpromising place to work.
>
> Seems elementary, doesn't it? Yet since 1986, when the high court held that sexual harassment on the job amounted to job discrimination, several Federal courts have contrived to make it more complicated. Justice Sandra Day O'Connor's plain-spoken opinion for a unanimous Court brings a refreshing end to the legalese and resistance to change the lower courts have indulged in.[32]

Contrast that appraisal with the following, taken from *The Wall Street Journal*:

> Barely touched [by *Harris v. Forklift Systems*] were important and troubling questions now being grappled with in the lower courts and in the regulatory arena, questions that arise as notions of political correctness invade the workplace as they have the academy. The court left to another day a number of important questions: If speech harasses and that harassment is in the eyes of the beholder, how can we draw a predictable line between what is permissible and what is illegal? Should a different line be drawn in other forms of harassment? What about the First Amendment issues making their way through the lower courts? Those questions indicate just how much heavy lifting we are asking of our employment discrimination laws. Small wonder the court demurred.

The opinion in *Harris* was handed down with astonishing speed and brevity—four weeks from the date of oral argument and mercifully devoid of footnotes, arcane legal arguments, or political and sociological posturing. One wonders if the enthusiasm with which the decision was greeted from all sides of the political spectrum was prompted by relief that so little was decided.[33]

Clearly, *Harris* has not settled every question that might be raised about what constitutes "hostile work environment." But the two-fold test provided by the Supreme Court does make it easier for persons in the kind of situation depicted by Weeks to charge their employers with sexual harassment.

V. DIFFERENCES IN PERCEPTION

Some behaviors are widely viewed by both men and women as sexual harass-ment. Rena Weeks claims that Greenstein pinned her arms behind her back in order to see which of her breasts was bigger. It is hard to imagine anyone fail-ing to see that such behavior is harassment and so does not belong in the work-place (or any place, for that matter). The issue with this alleged behavior is not about how to characterize it; the issue is whether the alleged behavior took place at all. Weeks said Greenstein really did it; Greenstein denies doing it.

While some forms of harassment are not disputed, there is a vast range of behavior that is more open to interpretation. As prevailing values and norms concerning appropriate workplace conduct evolve, the task of correctly inter-preting behavior becomes more and more difficult. "But what does sexual ha-rassment really mean? Managers of both sexes are sifting through the past and fretting about next week. Was it all right to say I liked her dress? Is it okay to ask him out to lunch to talk about that project? Should I just stop touching anybody, even if it's only a congratulatory pat on the back? For that big client meeting Houston, wouldn't it be less risky to fly out with Frank than with Francine? Or, for female managers, vice versa?"[34]

The workplace now feels like a minefield to many people; nobody knows for certain whether the next step will set off an explosion. In this kind of am-biguous situation, it is hard to map the terrain because different people can in-terpret the same behavior quite differently. It is easy to point out where there is a "gender gap" causing different perceptions among men and women. But it is also true that women disagree with other women (just as men disagree with men) about what counts as sexual harassment.

The traditional legal standard for sorting through problems of interpreta-tion is known as the "reasonable person" standard: Would a reasonable person find the behavior sufficiently intimidating, hostile, or offensive to warrant call-ing it sexual harassment?[35] The problem with the "reasonable person" standard is that, in the hands of mostly male judges, it inevitably contains a gender-based bias. For example, in a particular case one court held that a secretary was *not* harassed by her boss, even though he escorted her to and from the bath-room, standing guard while she used the toilet; even though he had the habit of dropping by her home unexpectedly, going to her bedroom, massaging her hands while waiting for her husband to return home.[36]

To counter the problems inherent in the supposedly neutral "reasonable person" standard, in 1991 several courts started to try a new standard known as the "reasonable woman" standard. According to the reasoning of the Ninth Circuit Court of Appeals:

> Because women are disproportionately victims of rape and sexual assault, women have a stronger incentive to be concerned with sexual behavior. Women who are victims of mild forms of sexual harassment may under-standably worry whether a harasser's conduct is merely a prelude to vio-

lent sexual assault. Men, who are rarely victims of sexual assault, may view sexual conduct in a vacuum without a full appreciation of the social setting or the underlying threat of violence that a woman may perceive. . . . We adopt the perspective of a reasonable woman because we believe that a sex-blind reasonable person standard tends to be male-biased and tends to systematically ignore the experiences of women. A gender-conscious examination of sexual harassment enables women to participate in the workplace on an equal footing with men.[37]

The question of interpretation was raised explicitly at the Weeks trial by Greenstein's lead lawyer Thomas Gosselin, who characterized sexual harassment as a "moving target." By this he meant that sexual harassment is not a well-defined idea. Moreover, he argued that many of the claims against Greenstein actually reflected the fact that men and women view the same action from different perspectives.

VI. THE JURY DECIDES

On August 27, 1994, after a month-long trial, the jury of the San Francisco Superior Court decided that Baker & McKenzie had turned a "blind eye" to Rena Weeks's complaints about Martin Greenstein. The jury, consisting of six men and six women, had deliberated for two and a half days before reaching its verdict. They ruled that Baker & McKenzie had failed to take appropriate steps to stop Greenstein from harassing Weeks. They awarded Weeks $50,000 from Baker & McKenzie, to compensate her for emotional distress.[38]

One week later, the jury returned and assessed $6.9 million in punitive damages against Baker & Mckenzie and $225,000 against Greenstein. Punitive damages are intended to punish and to deter especially outrageous behavior. This amount was the largest ever awarded in a sexual harassment case. However, in November 1994 a state judge in California effectively reduced by more than half the amount of the penalty, reducing the punitive damages against Baker & McKenzie to $3.5 million. The award against Greenstein was not reduced.[39] According to Judge John Munter of San Francisco County Superior Court, there was ample evidence that Greenstein had harassed numerous women, including Weeks, at Baker & McKenzie over a fourteen-year period and that the law firm "continued to employ him with a conscious disregard of the rights" of these women. But in explaining the reduced punitive damages against Baker & McKenzie, Judge Munter explained that the $3.5 million was 5 percent of the firm's net worth, the sum requested from the jury by Weeks's lawyer, who told the jurors that the law would not allow $6.9 million. Moreover, according to Judge Munter, while Baker & McKenzie had failed to take reasonable steps to protect Weeks and other women at the firm, its conduct "was not the product of a deliberate and purposeful policy aimed at violating the rights of anyone."[40]

Despite the firm's insistence that it did all it could, many experts in sexual harassment and employment law say Baker & McKenzie had ample opportunity to see a pattern of abuse and failed to do so, perhaps because Greenstein was a so-called rainmaker, one of its top income-producing partners. "If I had that many complaints, even if somebody denied it every time, I'd be very suspicious," said Alan Berkowitz, a labor and employment lawyer at Schachter, Kristoff, Orenstein & Berkowitz in San Francisco. "It's too much of a coincidence. But there's a tension about dealing with a partner who controls a large amount of business. There's a tendency to shuffle it under the rug." Paul Salvatore, a labor and employment partner at Proskauer, Rose, Goetz & Mendelsohn in New York, agreed. "Personalities are allowed to dominate and idiosyncrasies are tolerated if you're a major rainmaker," he said. "And if your idiosyncrasy is liking women, everybody says, 'That's the way he is.'"[41]

QUESTIONS FOR REFLECTION

1. Is sexual harassment a problem that can be dealt with adequately with legislation and/or corporate policy statements?

2. Will men and women ever agree on what counts as "safe" social conduct at work?

3. Concerning matters of sexual harassment, do men and women naturally have differences in perception? Or are these differences learned through their socialization? How can men and women best reach a shared perception of what counts as sexual harassment?

SUGGESTIONS FOR FURTHER READING

MacKinnon, Catharine A. *Sexual Harassment of Working Women*. New Haven: Yale University Press, 1979.

Stringer, Donna M., Helen Remick, Jan Salisbury, and Angela B. Ginorio. "The Power and Reasons Behind Sexual Harassment: An Employer's Guide to Solutions," *Public Personnel Management* 19(1) Spring 1990.

Wells, Deborah L. and Beverly J. Kracher. "Justice, Sexual Harassment, and the Reasonable Victim Standard," *Journal of Business Ethics* 12 (1993): 423–431.

ENDNOTES

1. http://www.courttv.com/national/ 1999/0812/harassment_ap.html

2. http://www.citypages.com/databank/ 22/1090/article9889.asp?page=2

3. Available at http://www.eeoc.gov/ press/8-11-99.html

4. http://www.eeoc.gov/35th/ 1990s/index.html

5. http://www.gsu.edu/~lawppw/ lawand.papers/harass.html

6. http://www.eeoc.gov/35th/2000s/ index.html

7. http://www.paweekly.com/PAW/ morgue/news/1998_May_13. RULING.html

8. http://www.iwon.com/home/ careers/company_profile/0,15623,1059,00 .html

9. Anne B. Fisher, "Sexual Harassment: What to Do," *Fortune* (August 23, 1993): p. 85.

10. The following account is drawn from the following sources: Harriet Chiang, "Sexual Harassment Charges Led to Peninsula Lawyer's Downfall," *San Francisco Chronicle* (August 3, 1994): p. A15; Dennis J. Opatrny, "Sexual Harassment Trial Against Law Firm Begins," *San Francisco Examiner* (July 26, 1994): p. A4; and Associated Press, "Baker & McKenzie Fighting a Sexual Harassment Suit," *Chicago Tribune* (August 7, 1994): Business Section p. 2.

11. Jane Gross, "Big Law Firm is Held Liable in Harassment," *The New York Times* (August 28, 1994): p. A29.

12. Jane Gross, "Law Firms Grapple with Harassment," *Daily News of Los Angeles* (July 31, 1994): p. N15, quoting Joe Schwacter, a partner at Littler, Mendelson, Fastiff, Tichy & Mathiason, a labor law firm.

13. Unless otherwise noted, the following account of Rena Weeks's charges is based on Chiang, "Sexual Harassment Charges," op. cit., and Gross, "Law Firms Grapple," op. cit.

14. Ken Hoover and Harriet Chiang, "Secretary Testifies in Harassment Suit," *San Francisco Chronicle* (August 11, 1994): p. A18.

15. Opatrny, "Sexual Harassment Trial Begins," op. cit.

16. Ibid.

17. Gross, "Law Firms Grapple," op. cit.

18. Opatrny, "Sexual Harassment Trial Begins," op. cit.

19. Gross, "Law Firms Grapple," op. cit.

20. Dennis J. Opatrny, "Lawyer Defends Himself in Sex Harassment Trial," *San Francisco Examiner* (August 2, 1994): p. A5.

21. Gross, "Law Firms Grapple," op. cit.

22. Chiang, "Sexual Harassment Charges," op. cit.

23. Dennis J. Opatrny, "Lawyer in Sex Harassment Case Says Accuser Was Incompetent," *San Francisco Examiner* (August 3, 1994): p. A4.

24. Dennis J. Opatrny, "Court TV Eyes Case Against Law Firm: S.F. Trial to Weigh Sex Harassment Charges Brought by Former Secretary," *San Francisco Examiner* (July 21, 1994): p. A2.

25. Terry Morehead Dworkin, "Harassment in the 1990s," *Business Horizons* (March–April 1993): p. 52.

26. Marilyn Machlowitz and David Machlowitz, "Hug by the Boss Could Lead to a Slap from the Judge," *The Wall Street Journal* (September 25, 1986): p. A20.

27. Fisher, op. cit., p. 88.

28. Dworkin, op. cit., p. 53.

29. Ibid., p. 53.

30. William E. Lissey, "Easier to Prove Sexual Harassment," *Supervision* 55(7) (July 1994): 20–21.

31. Larry Reynolds, "Court Rulings and Proposed Regs will Guide Harassment Policies, *HR Focus* 71(4) (April 1994): 1.

32. "A Victory on Workplace Harassment," *The New York Times* (November 11, 1993): p. A26.

33. R. Gaull Silberman, "After *Harris*, More Questions on Harassment," *The Wall Street Journal* (November 17, 1993): p. A22.

34. Fisher, op. cit., p. 84.

35. Dworkin op. cit., p. 54.

36. *Kouri v. Liberian Services*, 55 Fair Empl. Prac. Cas. (BNA) 124 (E.D. Va. 1991).

37. *Ellison v. Brady*, 924 F.2d 872, 879-80 (9th Cir. 1991).

38. Jane Gross, "Big Law Firm is Held Liable in Harassment," *The New York Times* (August 28, 1994): p. A29.

39. Margaret Jacobs, "Harassment Award Is Cut," *The Wall Street Journal* (November 29, 1994): p. B10.

40. Associated Press, "Sex-Harassment Award Reduced," *The New York Times* (November 29, 1994): p. A22.

41. Jane Gross, "When the Biggest Firm Faces Sexual Harassment Suit," *The New York Times* (July 29, 1994): p. B7.

4

Whose Job Is It to Protect Consumer Health?

Tobacco's Last Stand

Questions to Keep in Mind

1. What sort of pleasure does the smoking or other consumption of tobacco provide? Why do people use tobacco?

2. How harmful is tobacco, really? Why?

3. What is the Tobacco Institute? What does it do?

4. What is the present status of actions to limit the use of tobacco?

(You may bring matters from the chapter up to date; given the moving target of smoking regulations, you'll probably have to.)

5. On what legal theory or theories are the lawsuits based?

6. What have the lawsuits accomplished? How will that money be spent?

In early April 2002 the 3rd District Court of Appeal (a federal court that handles appeals from Circuit Court decisions) decided that John Lukacs, seventy-seven years old and dying, could indeed have his day in court against Big Tobacco.[1] Somewhere between 50,000 and 70,000 Floridians were part of a statewide class-action lawsuit against the tobacco companies, which argued that tobacco causes cancer (primarily, but also heart and other vascular disease), that the tobacco companies were well aware of tobacco's identity as a carcinogen, that tobacco is addictive, that the tobacco companies were *really* well aware of *that* and had counted on it for their sales, and that therefore tobacco companies were liable for the crushing burden of sickness that they had caused in Florida. The suit was successful, and resulted in a record award of $145 *billion* in July of 2000, for the medical care of the smokers of Florida. The verdict is on appeal, of course. If it is upheld, then all those individuals will receive some part of the award. After that verdict, it will be up to each individual to come forward and show that he or she qualifies under the terms of the verdict. But Lukacs is dying and does not want to wait.

How did we get to this point? No one ever forced Lukacs to smoke; no one claims that Lukacs' illness can come only from smoking; no one even claims that Lukacs was deceived. It is 2002, after all, and as we will discuss below, the warnings have been in place since 1964 at least. On what theory does one citizen hold another responsible for such a death? What follows is an account of a fascinating evolution of the notion of corporate responsibility in the latter half of the twentieth century.

I. THE TOCSIN SOUNDS: LUTHER TERRY'S REPORT

1. The Road to the Report

No one ever really approved of tobacco. As early as the fifteenth century, when one of Christopher Columbus's sailors lit up a pipe of tobacco brought home from Cuba, he was promptly arrested and legal proceedings undertaken against him (seeing the smoke from his nose and mouth, the townsfolk assumed he had taken up with the Devil). Two Popes made tobacco use an excommunicable offense, and an imperial edict issued in China in 1638 made the use or distribution of the weed punishable by decapitation. In the eighteenth century, tobacco was widely regarded as poisonous; in the nineteenth, organized anti-tobacco movements began in the United States. It was not just that hostesses despised the odor and mess caused by its burning. It was that a series of reformers were convinced, on the basis of observation, that it caused diseases.[2] Besides being connected with constipation, acne, insanity, tooth decay, and, even then, cancer and heart disease,

It was unnatural, unclean, unwholesome, unrefined, unattractive, ungentle-manly and messy. It caused baldness. It exhausted the soil. It was a waste of money.[3]

And so forth. By 1890, 26 states had outlawed the sale of cigarettes to minors, and further restrictions were urged on the state legislatures. The movement died out during and after World War I, when cigarettes, popular among sol-diers and increasingly popular with women, gained a measure of respectability. Cigarette consumption doubled during the 1920s. But respectability did not last long.[4]

For much of the science-oriented twentieth century, scientific evidence accumulated that smoking cigarettes was very bad for your health. Through the 1930s, concerned physicians reported observations of links between smok-ing and heart disease, high blood pressure, and forms of cancer; all evidence was anecdotal. Three crucially important publications came out in 1938—a *Journal of the American Medical Association (JAMA)* article, a report in *Science News Letter* ("Smoking Causes Cancer"), and a set of tables on family history and longevity gathered by the Biology Department of Johns Hopkins Univer-sity, assembled by statistician Raymond Pearl and published in *Science*, which showed that "Smoking is associated with a definite impairment of longevity."[5]

So the data were there, early. In the 1940s America succumbed to a passion for smoking, immortalized by Humphrey Bogart and World War II. But studies continued to pile up—varied in form (a survey of dental patients with oral cancer; reports on the carcinogenic effect of cigarette tar painted on the backs of mice) and still largely anecdotal, but all to the same effect—smoking causes cancer. Especially, noted a surgeon:

> After having had an opportunity to observe, over a period of ten years, an unusually large series of patients with cancer of the lung, in two of the large municipal hospitals in New York City, two very distinct elements were noted in these patients; first, the patients were almost always men; second, they were heavy cigarette smokers and almost always inhalers.[6]

An anecdote is no more than that—there were no controls on these patient counts; and how much, really, is "unusually," and how distinct is "very"? But the point is, that all the anecdotes pointed the same direction, and laid the groundwork for the first study that met contemporary standards, funded by the American Cancer Society and run by Evarts Graham and Ernst Wynder of the Washington University School of Medicine in St. Louis.

This is work for the statistician. We did not know in 1950, nor do we know for sure in 2003, the exact mechanism by which cells become cancerous and start to spread in the body. We do not know what cigarette smoke really does in the lung, beyond laying down a layer of tar. Meanwhile, there is no one-to-one cause-to-effect—not everyone who smokes gets lung cancer, not every-one who gets lung cancer smokes—and even when a smoker does get lung cancer, there is no telling whether he will get it ten, twenty, or thirty years after he starts smoking. At present, the only way we can show that smoking is a cause of cancer is by matching populations who smoke with otherwise very similar populations who don't and comparing them, over the long term, with regard to incidence of cancer; by matching populations who get lung cancer with populations who don't, and seeing how many in each group smoke; finding out if *heavier* smokers get *more* lung cancer, by similarly matching groups; finding out if populations who have quit smoking are closer to smokers or non-smokers with regard to lung cancer; and more of the same.[7] Graham and Wynder published the results of their work as "Tobacco Smoking as a Possible Etiological Factor in Bronchiogenic Carcinoma" in 1950 in the prestigious *Journal of the American Medical Association*. For the first time, solid scientific evidence backed up the anecdotes, and the results were out where the medical profession could see them.[8]

Studies mounted through the 1950s, prospective as well as retrospective, indicting tobacco as cause of several cancers, heart disease, emphysema and other lung disease, premature birth of infants and miscarriages of pregnancy. *Reader's Digest*, which had opposed tobacco since its inception, carried a very powerful article by Roy Norr, "Cancer by the Carton," in December 1952, which threw a scare into *Digest* readers—and there were many, many of them. Similar articles appeared late in the 1950s in *Nation, New Republic* and *Ladies' Home Journal*: now *there's* a spectrum. And deaths from lung cancer, a disease "almost unheard of" at the beginning of the century, continued to mount.[9]

By 1961 pressure on the federal government to "do something" about the cancer deaths had become intolerable. In the course of a presidential press conference in May of that year, a reporter unexpectedly asked President John F. Kennedy what he intended to do about the increased concern about cigarettes. Kennedy referred the matter to his surgeon general, Dr. Luther Terry, who promptly commissioned an advisory committee to study the matter, evaluate it, and produce a report.

That report came out on January 11, 1964. Luther Terry, Surgeon General of the United States, put the authority of his office and the United States government behind its findings: smoking is the major cause of lung cancer in men (data on women were insufficient because they had not been smoking cigarettes long enough in enough numbers), and was indicted as a cause also of heart disease, bronchitis, emphysema, and cancer of the larynx. And those pretty filter tips, increasingly popular as the threats to health became more obvious, did little good. The only way to lessen the hazard to the health was to give up smoking, now.

Terry recommended four immediate steps to combat this threat to the public's health: an educational campaign, ingredient labels on cigarette packs, health hazard warnings stamped on the cigarette packs, and restrictions on advertising copy. Meanwhile, he halted the free distribution of cigarettes at all the hospitals under the authority of the federal government and ordered all hospitals to begin educational campaigns to get people to stop smoking. All except one of the members of the committee Terry had appointed gave up smoking. Terry himself tried to give up smoking, failed, and later contracted cancer of the lung.[10] The course was set from that mark: This nation is suffering from an epidemic of lethal illnesses brought on by tobacco in general and cigarette smoking in particular, and tobacco use will have to stop.

2. The Tobacco Industry's Response: Back to Bed

That report was tobacco's wake-up call—not the moment when thinking people really began to believe that there might be something wrong with tobacco (that had happened a decade earlier) but the moment when it became clear that no thinking person could deny it. The alarm was clearly sounding, a bell that was not to be ignored. But who ever said that when the bell sounds you have to get up? It is always possible, when the wake-up call comes, to inch out of bed with the bedclothes still wrapped about, stumble to the telephone or clock, whatever the instrument emitting the offensive noise, seize the thing, and throw it out the window. That's about what the tobacco industry did with the Surgeon General's report. Then, of course, it is also possible to procure your shotgun from the closet, crawl back into bed, and defy anyone to try to wake you again. That's about what the Tobacco Institute did in 1964 and in general, with major retreats, continues to try to do.

The Tobacco Institute was founded in 1954 by the six major tobacco companies to unite the industry's response to mounting criticism. The major players in the tobacco industry, to bring the size of the problem into focus, are very major indeed, with a great deal of money to spend on defense. Philip Morris is the biggest, with estimated cigarette sales of $73 billion in 2001, for 50.5 percent of the market; R. J. Reynolds (RJR Nabisco) is second with sales of $8.6 billion and a market share of 23.4 percent in the same year. Brown & Williamson/American (with 10 percent of the market), Lorillard (8.7 percent), and others share the rest of the market.[11] (Those sales figures are sharply down from counts earlier in the 1990s.) That is a powerful war chest, and the industry used it well. Together they formed the Tobacco Institute, which contacts legislators at all levels and by all means, funds pro-tobacco initiatives from non-industry sources, rallies potential constituencies, and coordinates all activity that may help the industry.[12]

In what follows we will use "tobacco industry" loosely to refer to any of the actions of the Tobacco Institute, or any of the actions of individual companies undertaken for the Institute or for the benefit of all members. The story of this collective action is a chronicle of one way, indeed the limiting case of that way, of reacting to very bad news.

We should give very serious consideration to this reaction: When your industry *as a whole* is under attack, and there is danger that every company's profits will fall catastrophically, what is the best course to follow? Should you treat the attacks as matters of *substance*, reality, that must be dealt with by substantial change? Should you then acknowledge the truth of all that is true, undertake industry-wide changes to ameliorate the conditions that prompted the attacks, and work with your attackers to restore the industry's reputation for sound and safe products? That was the Chemical Manufacturers Association response to the attacks that followed upon Love Canal and the explosion at Bhopal, India (see chapter 9 in this text on Union Carbide and the Disaster at Bhopal). Or on the other hand, should you treat the attacks as matters of *image*, public relations, and respond with a public relations campaign? Should you deny every accusation, buy advertising space to print responses to the attacks, and generally attempt to overwhelm customer doubts with omnipresent assurances that all is safe? *If the accusations are, to your certain knowledge, totally false, that is what you must do.* Whatever the leading company executives of the tobacco industry believed about the truth of the report (and it was as solidly grounded as any such report could be), that was the response they adopted, and considering the continuing profitability of tobacco sales, almost forty years after Terry's report, the response may have a good deal to recommend it from a business point of view. Or it may not; that question will follow us through this retelling of the story.

The tobacco industry's strategy was clear and consistent from the 1964 beginning: We will not believe a word of the unfortunate report; we will denounce its conclusions as half-truths and unproven; we will attack every attempt to further tax or limit the practice of smoking as counterproductive, unconstitutional, and morally wrong; we will destroy the capacity for collective action by campaigns at every available level of public democratic institutions.

So in late 1963, as soon as President Kennedy was dead, and Lyndon Johnson was in office anticipating the arrival of the January 11 report, Philip Morris retained a Washington law firm to represent them to the government— the firm that had Abe Fortas, one of Johnson's oldest friends, as a partner. The six major tobacco firms retained a lobbyist (Earl Clements) with family ties to both President and Mrs. Johnson.[13] It helped, probably, that Johnson was a long-time cigarette smoker. Meanwhile, on Capitol Hill, all the major congressional committees were headed by legislators from tobacco-growing regions (by the traditions of Congress, committee chairs were chosen on the basis of seniority, and the southern states, with their stable one-party systems, always returned the same men to Congress), ensuring that no bills hostile to the industry would reach the floor of Congress.

The first result of the Tobacco Institute's massive congressional lobbying campaign was that Congress effectively took control of tobacco regulation away from the Federal Trade Commission. That meant that the restrictions on the distribution of this substance, now officially declared to be harmful, would be determined not by the expertise of the professionals hired by the Commission, but by political figures acting on political considerations. In such a change, democracy is served, but the public health may not be. When all the Congressional debates were done, after all that public alarm and attention, the only restriction placed on the industry in the 1965 session was a mild warning label on the packages of cigarettes. Not only was the end result disappointing to those who had hoped for the beginning of an end to tobacco consumption in the United States, but there was a devastating legal side effect: With federal "regulation" now in place, no state could demand any more restrictions of sales, advertising, or labeling within its borders—the federal rule preempted any state requirements. (That preemption was upheld by the courts until 1992.)

The gathered forces of public health had fired their salvo, and the tobacco industry had made it clear that it intended to fight to the death, literally, for access to the lungs of the world. The country settled in for a grim siege which is not yet over.

II. TOBACCO AND HEALTH

1. Mortality and Morbidity: A Medical Overview

The Tobacco Institute's theory was that all the fuss could be reduced to a public relations problem. Could it? What is the scientific basis of the belief that smoking is bad for your health? To get a handle on the state of the empirical question, let us run through some of the health findings.

Over the years, health publications have kept track of the health effects of tobacco; see, for a particularly readable example, Richard G. Schlaadt's 1992 work, *Tobacco and Health*.[14] Even then, the Center for Disease Control had begun counting the deaths of people who were not themselves smokers, but who had been exposed to other peoples' smoking.[15] Then, in April 1994, the *New England Journal of Medicine* published a two-part article on "The Human Costs of Tobacco Use," summarizing specialized data from a multitude of medical studies. Part I of the report concentrated on the medical data. The presentation is straightforward and, for the layman, all too clear and comprehensible:

> It has been 30 years since the surgeon general of the United States released the first report of the Advisory Committee on Smoking and Health. In each of the subsequent reports, cigarette smoking has been identified as the most important source of preventable morbidity and premature mortality in the United States. A total of 418,690 deaths in the United States were attributed to smoking in 1990. . . . The prominence of tobacco as a contributor to mortality prompted former Surgeon General C. Everett Koop to state that cigarette smoking is the leading cause of preventable premature death in our society and the most important public health issue of our time.[16]

In this country, 46.3 million adults (25.7 percent of the population) are smokers, most between the ages of twenty-five and forty-four. One quarter of them smoke heavily. Nearly one fifth of all deaths in 1990 could be attributed to tobacco; the number exceeds one in four of deaths of those aged thirty-five to sixty-four,[17] the years of greatest productivity and responsibility. Meanwhile, new data reveal the complications of tobacco use for others, as found in a 1992 report by the Environmental Protection Agency (EPA); "environmental tobacco smoke," composed of "mainstream" or "secondhand" smoke exhaled by the smoker and "sidestream" smoke, trailing from the lit cigarette between puffs, subjects nearby nonsmokers to the same risks (at a much lower level) that we find in smokers.

With that summary as background, the *New England Journal of Medicine* authors detail risks for the various medical conditions associated with smoking. Since the correlation between cigarette smoking and coronary heart disease reported from the Mayo Clinic in 1940, we have ample data

> that cigarette smoking substantially increases the risk of cardiovascular disease, including stroke, sudden death, heart attack, peripheral vascular disease, and aortic aneurysm. In the United States in 1990, smoking caused 179,820 deaths from cardiovascular disease. . .,[18]

an assertion hammered home with study after study after study:

> Components of cigarette smoke have been shown to damage vascular endothelium, and endothelial injury is considered a primary antecedent to atherosclerosis. The adverse effects of smoking are also related to its effects on coronary vaso-occlusive factors, such as platelet aggregation, vasomotor reactivity, and a prothrombotic state, and factors such as carbon monoxide production, increased plasma viscosity, and fibrinogen levels. Smoking is a major risk factor for coronary vasospasm. . . .[19]

It goes on. And that's just the cardiovascular disease. The section on cancer is much more devastating: "In addition to being responsible for over 85 percent of lung cancers, smoking is also associated with cancers of the mouth, pharynx, larynx, esophagus, stomach, pancreas, uterine cervix, kidney, ureter, and bladder and accounts for about 30 percent of all deaths from cancer."[20] A grim chart on the next page of this account, or indictment, reprinted from a Department of Health and Human Services publication, tracks the increase in the smoking of cigarettes from 1900 to 1990 (peaking about 1980), and the parallel track of increases in cases of lung cancer, following a discreet 20 years behind. Smokeless tobacco too—the snuff and chewing tobacco favored by the athletes—is clearly associated with oral cancers, and about 80 percent of deaths from cancer of the esophagus can be laid at the cigarette's door.[21]

Meanwhile, smokers who do not contract cancer have a litany of deadly lung diseases in store for them—pneumonia, influenza, chronic airway obstruction, and especially chronic bronchitis and emphysema.[22]

Others than the smokers suffer. The risk to nonsmokers in smoke-filled environments is repeatedly mentioned, with special warnings reserved for the unfortunate human who must spend the first nine months of its existence in the womb of a heavy smoker. Once born, respiratory infections are multiplied in young children of smokers, especially asthmatics.[23]

Certain groups are seen by the authors of the *New England Journal* study as particularly worrisome. Women are catching up with men in cigarette-caused death: Lung cancer has outstripped breast cancer as a cause of mortality in women. Combined with the use of oral contraceptives, smoking enhance the risk of cardiovascular disease in women. Smoking also increases the danger of osteoporosis, the deadly weakening of the bones in older women.[24] Minorities—native Americans, African Americans, and Hispanics—seem to have smoked less than their white Anglo counterparts until recently; only now does their cancer line begin its fatal rise. And the elderly, as a group, are as much at risk as the fetus; smoking causes stroke, cataracts, and oral cancers. "Among men and women over 65 years of age, the rates of total mortality among current smokers were twice what they were among participants who had never smoked."[25]

2. The Scientific Controversy on Smoking and Health

That is the indictment. How pleads the defendant? From the opening bell in the 1950s, the Tobacco Institute has followed a multipronged and highly effective defense—scientific, economic, sociological, constitutional, and moral. The first prong was—and is—empirical: As for the scientific evidence, as presented above, it contends that smoking has not been *proven* to be dangerous to health, that the connections between tobacco use and disease are speculative and statistical only—that we have, as it were, only circumstantial evidence, not adequate for a conviction, or at least not enough to seek the death penalty. While there was, to be sure, some data suggesting that cigarette smoking was harmful to health, the studies were not conclusive. Other studies could be found, the industry suggested, that contradicted them, and anyway, a statistical correlation need not apply to any individual—to me, for instance, should I want to continue to smoke.

Early reactions concentrated on the dissidents in the medical profession. No more than any other group, or in any other issue, do physicians respond in unison to this type of news. The industry initially made good use of scoffers such as Leroy Hyde, M.D., who scornfully compared the assertion that cigarette smoking causes cancer to the assertions that pellagra was an infectious disease and that horseback riding was good for tuberculosis.[26] Joseph Berkson, M.D., an expert in medical statistics, also doubted the causal relationship, and his doubts were well publicized. As the 1960s drew to an end, other publications urged the safety of smoking, and conflicting studies appeared to confute Terry's facts; the apparent involvement of the tobacco industry in some of these publications might raise doubts as to their validity.[27]

The empirical strategy, insistence upon a "controversy" over the facts, continued as a rear-guard action. No evidence was acknowledged until the evidence was irrefutable. Certain studies showed that cigarette tar created tumors on a mouse's back; the relevance of these studies was denied, since we (concededly) do not use tobacco that way. Then, when a series of ingenious (and inhumane) experiments that forced cigarette smoke into the lungs of beagles led to a frightening number of beagle lung cancers, the industry challenged the relevance of these studies too; there could be no "meaningful parallels between human smoking and dogs subjected to these most stressful conditions."[28] At the same time, accounts on both sides of the question showed up in a wide variety of popular media. For instance, "To Smoke or Not to Smoke—That is

Still the Question," by one Stanley Frank, in *True* magazine (1968) challenged the scientific status of the statistical studies that appeared in Terry's report. Two million copies of the article were promptly distributed to anyone—physician, journalist, Congressman—who might influence public policy. When the dust cleared, it turned out that various tobacco companies had funded the whole thing—the writing of the article, the placement in the magazine, as well as the reprints and their distribution.[29] But the existence of a perceived scientific "controversy" on the scientific data continued until very recently.

There is no longer any real dispute on the link between smoking tobacco and various forms of disease. Of course the industry can continue to *suggest* denials in their paid advertising. Most cigarette ads, for instance, feature young persons in the middle of some vigorous activity—volleyball, skiing, surfing, hiking—demanding on heart and lungs. They are the very image of cardiovascular and pulmonary health and strength, contrary to all we know about smoking. The ad clearly counters the fears that might be nudged by the warning on the package—and, of course, on the ad.

Such use of images to suggest dubious correlations is standard stuff in the ad industry. But it has been argued that the "scientific controversy" campaign waged by the tobacco industry, with such vigor, at such expense, for such a long time, goes a bit beyond puffery and image, to what we have learned on the spy scene to call "disinformation": an organized campaign of lies so massive, detailed, and self-assured that it overwhelms our ability to disbelieve.[30] Given that the objective of this massive campaign is only to sell a product, to increase profits, why could it not constitute fraud—actionable and prosecutable? We will return to this possibility in the next part of the chapter.

III. THE USES OF THE LAW

1. On Liberty

A second prong in the tobacco industry's defense against its accusers has been the replacement of the question of harm with a question of right, or liberty. It goes something like this: Whether or not smoking harms the smoker, it is the smoker's right to smoke, knowing the harm (which the warning label ensures), but choosing nevertheless to put the pleasure of smoking higher on the personal values hierarchy than healthy longevity. There are, after all, many high-risk activities (rock-climbing, for instance) that are perfectly legal. And we have known for centuries that certain substances (alcohol, for instance) are deadly to the user if consumed in sufficient quantities and *sometimes* lethal to those in the vicinity of that user, yet we tolerate them as socially acceptable. If we decide to restrict or prohibit consumption of all things we know to be harmful, we shall never have done (steak, eggs, butter, and candy would certainly have to be done away with), and we will have reduced the pleasures available to ordinary citizens, many or most of whom could have consumed at least some of those dangerous items without suffering any harm at all. Where we are dealing with self-inflicted harms, where the risk is voluntarily assumed by the sufferer, especially where small amounts of the dangerous stuff can apparently be tolerated without harm being done to anyone, surely the government is overreaching when it calls upon its police power to enact barriers and bans. John Stuart Mill argues persuasively in *On Liberty*[31] that where self-regarding behavior—conduct that affects only the person who engages in it—is at issue, we ought to leave people alone to make their own choices. While other nations might strike a different balance between the security of paternalistic protection by government and the liberty of the individual to choose, even unwisely, for himself, our nation has been founded on liberty. We are a people who put a very high value on individual choice, liberty, and rights, especially where the choices concern our own welfare and lifestyle. The choice to use tobacco, a self-regarding choice if ever there was one, should therefore be left to the smoker.

The argument is powerful, and has many analogies on the American scene; there are states where the authorities do not even compel motorcycle riders to wear helmets. The answer that has been proposed to the argument, where tobacco is concerned, is complex; for the sake of simplicity, we will divide it into three parts: First, the presumption of liberty is problematic in itself and can be defeated by arguments from societal responsibility; second, any product on the market is presumed to carry an implied "warrant of merchantability"—that is, if used as directed, it may be presumed that it will not ordinarily harm its user; and third, smoking is in no way "self-regarding," since it harms everyone near the smoker with the "environmental smoke" produced in its use. We will take these up in order.

First, the presumption of liberty is problematic. We are social animals. Liberty to do harm to oneself has never been taken as absolute; under the accepted police power of the state, public authority is always empowered to block people from certain harm. Suicide is still, strictly speaking, illegal; and if your behavior presents a clear and present danger to yourself, even if it presents none to others, you may be restrained or confined, quite legally. Further, in a society made up of families and other social organizations, can any behavior *really* be only self-regarding? Families and colleagues are always affected by self-destructive behavior. Whatever the medical effects, those who have to be around smokers might argue that their opinions on the matter should be heard.

More to the point, society as a whole has to absorb a significant portion of the burden when the behavior's risks materialize. When the motorcycle rider wraps himself around a tree, or the smoker arrives in the emergency room, uninsured and unable to breathe, he becomes society's charge—no matter what his age, his (former) competence, or the well-weighed reasoning that went into his choice to smoke or to ride helmetless. It may also be that "liberty" cannot describe tobacco consumption at all, for autonomous choice cannot take place under certain kinds of compulsion—like addiction. Citizens are forbidden to purchase addictive street drugs under any circumstances, not only for fear of the theft and violence that attends the drug trade, but also on the theory that addiction negates any presumption of a "free contract" to buy. On an associated theory that ignorance similarly negates that presumption, citizens are forbidden to acquire large numbers of perfectly safe and helpful drugs without a physician attesting that they need them. So if tobacco should fall under one of the categories, for instance that of "addictive" drugs, already accepted as requiring regulation—a category in which it is accepted that we as a society must protect individuals from themselves—there would be no novelty in prohibiting or strictly rationing tobacco. Is tobacco a drug? We will return to this possibility later.

2. On Lawsuits

The second answer to the liberty argument was written in the consumer movement of the 1960s and 1970s. People have a right, the movement maintained, not to have harmful products visited upon them without their full consent to the harm, which consent was not likely to be forthcoming. Lawsuits backed up that contention, extracting startlingly large damage payments for consumers of automobiles, lawnmowers, even excessively hot cups of coffee from fast-food restaurants. Certainly many of the suits seemed to be unreasonable, not just from the point of view of the manufacturers, but in the perception of all of us raised in an earlier understanding of the commercial transaction. No more were buyers at their own risk once they got the product home. If the product harmed them, even with the contributing factor of their own carelessness or failure to follow directions precisely, even if their use of the product violated common sense—they had a very good chance of holding the manufacturer responsible for the harm and of collecting a tidy sum for a remedy. *Caveat emptor*—"let the buyer beware"—had been replaced by *caveat vendor*—let the seller pray that no one gets hurt when his product is anywhere in sight.

Now, cigarettes harm people, even if, especially if, they are used precisely according to the company's instructions. Tobacco companies still issue denials, but most of us know that. It was only a matter of time before the consumer-movement lawsuits began. The first serious lawsuit was brought against the Liggett Group in 1983. Rose Cipollone sued because she was dying of lung cancer. She alleged that cigarette advertising had forced her to smoke. The wheels of justice grind slow, and she did not have long to prosecute her cause, but when she died, her husband Antonio continued the suit. In its defense, Liggett Group did not maintain that its ads were totally ineffective—that would have been an awkward case for them to argue—but rather, that Cipollone could easily have resisted the ads. They further argued that any state or common law requirements of merchantability—including serious warnings if serious harm could result from the use of a product—could not apply, since the federal government had already acted preemptively: In requiring warning labels, the federal authorities had already required all that could be required in the way of warning consumers.

Those contentions merit examination. What makes an ad "compelling"? (Probably most advertisers would like to know!) The tobacco industry could offer classes in effectiveness. It has expertly picked up every weakness, in the human psyche, especially failure of self-esteem, and put it in the ads. The earliest advertisements, for instance, beamed at young men, featured the suave black-tied sophisticate, the masculine ideal of the time; the earliest ads directed to women played on addiction to oral gratification and the constant desire of women for slim figures—"Reach for a Lucky instead of a sweet." Ads directed at young men asserted that "Luckies separate the men from the boys—but not from the girls," fulfilling every adolescent's fantasies in one sentence. The most recent ad campaigns featured the Marlboro Man (the most successful ad campaign in history)—the lonesome, masculine, master of the wildness of the West; the successful woman ("you've come a long way, baby," Virginia Slims reminds us); and an ultra-cool teenage camel, later banned as too appealing to children. Are they effective? The tobacco industry surely thinks so; they spend, or spent, a good deal of money on them.

The second issue turns on an abstruse legal technicality. If the federal government has undertaken to pass legislation on an industry, a state cannot enact its own additional requirements, inconsistent with federal legislation. So the tobacco industry argued that with the federally required warning label in place, no state could intervene with more requirements. The notion is called preemption: By regulating, the government preempts all other legal possibilities on the subject.

Well, *does* that federal warning label requirement preempt all state action? The first ruling came down in spring 1984: No, it does not. But on April 7, 1986, Judge James Hunter III of the U.S. Court of Appeals for the Third Circuit (1985–1986) overturned that finding, asserting that federal regulation did indeed preempt state powers. A minor "conflict of interest" quarrel erupted at this point: Hunter had worked for American Tobacco Company from 1964 to 1966, during the controversy over the Surgeon General's report. Is it possible that he should have disqualified himself? This doubt about the participation in the debate of present or former tobacco industry employees will generalize with frightening speed, since the tobacco industry now includes so many food companies. It may, in the future, become very difficult to establish the appropriate distance between witness and employee or participant in any case involving tobacco.

Meanwhile other cases came to trial: John Galbraith (no relation to the popular economist) was an officer of an insurance company who had smoked for many years. When he contracted lung cancer, in 1979, he began to lay the foundations for a lawsuit, including recruiting the famous plaintiffs' attorney Melvin Belli; after he died in 1982, his widow Elayne carried it forward. This was not a good case for the plaintiff: Galbraith was old and sick, and was shown to have had good many causes of death, some of them probably cigarette-related. Belli, hurried to trial, may have argued the case badly, and the jury reasonably found that they could not be absolutely sure of the actual cause of death. A much better case was *Marsee v. United States Tobacco Company*, which came to trial in late May of 1986. Sean Marsee, an outstanding athlete (best athlete of 1983 at his high school) did little that was harmful to his health. But he loved U.S. Tobacco snuff (Copenhagen brand) which is not smoked at all, but wedged in a small ball between gum and lip. Sean, a star runner, died at age 18 of oral cancer, which, considering the place of origin of the cancer, clearly derived from use (six years) of U. S. Tobacco snuff.[32] His mother filed a complaint on March 21, 1985, claiming that U. S. Tobacco "failed to warn" Sean of the dangers of their product, and that therefore they should be held strictly liable for his sickness and death. She lost; U. S. Tobacco created a grueling ordeal of denial and delay, tardy documents and evasive depositions, showing in unmistakable clarity the battlefield tactics of a beleaguered industry. Nothing illegal was done; but the foes of tobacco were put on notice that a great deal of sophistication would be required to get that one victory that would open the legal field to class-action suits on behalf of every smoker.

The issue of preemption had still to be settled. Did Congress, when it passed the Federal Cigarette Labeling and Advertising Act in 1965, intend that the placing of warnings on each package fully satisfied the tobacco companies' obligation to make the extent of danger clear to their customers? Did it, in fact, intend to prevent all courts this side of the U. S. Supreme Court from even *considering* whether or not the obligation was satisfied? Judge James Hunter, above, declared that it did. And the courts backed up Judge Hunter, several times: From 1986 onwards, five federal appeals courts concluded that the 1965 legislation should be read that way; some even went so far as to conclude that Congress intended to permit the companies to tell direct and deliberate lies about the safety of their products—just so long as they continued to put the mandated warnings on the packages.[33]

Then, finally, in July 1990 the New Jersey Supreme Court concluded that Congress had intended no such thing.[34] A Texas appellate court backed them up in 1991; Congress intended no preemption.[35] Then, finally, the U. S. Supreme Court agreed to review the issue in *Cipollone*. Oral arguments took place in October 1991, and on June 24, 1992, the Court handed down its decision. Typically, it denied nothing of what went before: The labeling legislation did indeed preempt state requirements of further warnings on the cigarette packs. But there was no preemption of state requirements of the use of other means of communication. And since there were plenty of other ways the companies could communicate, the companies were not protected from failure-to-warn lawsuits.[36] The field was now open for class-action suits, and the definitive action was to begin two and a half years later.

The litigation that followed featured accusations of fraud and conspiracy (occasionally invoking RICO, the racketeering statute applied to Mafia conspiracies) in addition to inherent harmfulness. The formation of the Tobacco Institute, to lobby for all tobacco causes, had only one founding reason: to mount a "defense" of the industry by insisting there was a "controversy" over the scientific evidence on the causation of cancer. As noted above, there is none, nor was there at the time the defense was mounted; the tobacco industry's "defense" amounts to a massive disinformation campaign, aimed especially at the young. This is fraud, and has inspired at least one criminal investigation into the possibility that the activities constitute mail or wire fraud.[37] Puffery and imagery aside, a concerted campaign to put falsehoods before the public is not morally permissible, and may well be legally actionable.

Yes, but does the tobacco industry *really know* that smoking is harmful to the health? It does; we come to that in a moment.

3. On Harm to Others

Smoking, ultimately, is not self-regarding behavior. When the Environmental Protection Agency studied the effects of smoking on nonsmokers who had the misfortune to be in the vicinity of a smoker, it came (in 1992) to the conclusion that the nonsmoker suffered the same diseases as the smoker, but in lesser amount.[38] (This 1992 report backed up the conclusions of the 1986 Surgeon General's report on the same subject.[39]) But then, the liberty argument does not apply at all. If nonsmokers are harmed by smoking, any municipal authority is fully empowered to ban smoking in any area where smokers may impose their smoke on nonconsenting others—for instance, all restaurants and bars, all offices and workplaces, and even a private home, if others (for instance, hired painters, plumbers, and carpenters) have no choice but to be there. Municipalities are proceeding to do just that; as of January 2003, it looks as if New Yorkers will not be able to smoke even in bars.

The implications of the EPA study were immediately clear to the tobacco industry, and the response was strong. When Jacob Sullum, managing editor of *Reason* magazine, wrote an article critical of the EPA report ("Passive Reporting on Passive Smoke") for Forbes' *MediaCritic* magazine, in 1994, Philip Morris promptly took out five straight days' worth of full-page ads on the back page of the first section of *The New York Times* to reprint the article, page by page.[40]

The thesis of Sullum's article is not implausible: The statistics cited by the EPA, that purportedly show that environmental tobacco smoke causes cancer, fail to prove their point because the cancers of those nonsmokers so exposed rise so slightly above the general cancer rate (which is somewhere between 30 percent and 35 percent of the population), and are so thoroughly implicated with other risk factors of cancer (especially low income, problematic diet, and urban dwelling) that statistical significance (less than one chance in twenty of the correlation happening by chance) is not achieved. The problem is a simple one: The general cancer rate is so high that to show a *slight* elevation of that rate in any group, the number of subjects in that group would have to be enormous. (If there is a very marked elevation in the rate, a smaller group will do.) But environmental smoke raises the risk of cancer only slightly, and there are not enormous numbers of people who do not smoke who regularly inhale large amounts of other people's smoke—not if they can help it, anyway.

Sullum points this out in a manner that readers of the ads must have found fascinating. He argues very solemnly that there is a fallacy in associating the Tobacco Institute's (and its members', joint and several) *present* position that there is no proven connection between sidestream smoke and lung cancer, which he supports, with the Tobacco Institute's *previous* position, that there is no proven connection between smoking and lung cancer for the smoker, which he does not at all support.

> By convention, epidemiologists call a result significant if the possibility that it occurred by chance is five percent or less. The associations between smoking and lung cancer are sizable as well as statistically significant: Recent studies indicate that the average male smoker is 20 times more likely to develop lung cancer than a male non-smoker, while the risk ratio for women is about 10 to one. The figures are even higher for heavy smokers.[41]

This quotation, recall, is from copy paid for by Philip Morris. Even if the Tobacco Institute was dead wrong on its earlier claims of "controversy," Sullum continues, that does not mean that it is *not* right on its later claims, and so his argument continues.

Well, there you have it, something very new and refreshing; the tobacco industry and Philip Morris are now on record as endorsing—at least, Philip Morris has paid to publish worldwide—Sullum's assertion that, as everyone knows, there is of course a very strong correlation between smoking and cancer, smokers are much more likely to get lung cancer than nonsmokers, and the heavier the smoking, the greater the risk. So the "controversy" is over.[42] Now it remains to be asked, how much of this proven harm should society permit? Is the tobacco industry to be blamed for what is arguably the public's own choice to smoke?

4. On Street Drugs and Addiction

Where is the cigarette industry at this point? Still in bed after the snooze alarm has gone off loud and clear—still denying the latest reports on the harmfulness of their product, still opposing, by foul means as well as fair, the latest measures to ban smoking in public places.[43] And where is the public? Trying to stop smoking. Out of the first 200 books listed under "smoking" in the topic index of *Books in Print,* you will find that (at least) 137—well over half—claim to teach you how to stop smoking.[44] The books must be selling well, for more keep coming out; apparently the public is buying them. Americans know they want to stop smoking cigarettes, for good. But then why do they keep buying cigarettes? If this is an issue of individual liberty or choice of lifestyle, as the liberty argument claims, why the books? There are no books on how to give up rockclimbing. Smoking, it seems, involves an addictive drug, and that changes the picture completely.

Nicotine now is legally classified as—what?—a pleasurable substance, possibly, something on the order of maple syrup. Suppose we decide, on the basis of its effects on the body if on no other basis, that from now on, nicotine shall be called a drug. What legal consequences follow? If nicotine is a drug, then the Federal Food and Drug Administration (FDA) regulates it. If it is a drug, then, by law, the FDA must find out if it is addictive. If it is addictive, then the FDA has to ban it unless it can be shown to be safe. There is no way that cigarette smoking can be shown to be safe. So *all* smoking would by law, have to be banned—not just smoking in public places, not just smoking by minors, but all smoking everywhere. At least, a start has to be made toward that end.

This approach to the smoking issue was attempted, in measured steps, by Dr. David A. Kessler. In June 1994 Kessler, then Commissioner of Food and Drugs (head of the FDA) testified at a hearing convened by Rep. Henry Waxman, head of the health and environment subcommittee of the House Energy and Commerce Committee, on company manipulation of the amount of nicotine in cigarettes and tobacco.

5. Whistleblowers

Kessler was able to testify because of some very damaging documents brought to public attention by tobacco industry whistleblowers, Merrell Williams and Jeffrey Wigand. Williams was employed by Brown & Williamson Tobacco (B&W) "to work in the document room at B&W, coding internal records and research findings that might be helpful to people suing the tobacco industry should the records come out in court. . . . 'The whole point of the exercise,' Williams says, 'was to cover it up.'" Instead of doing that, Williams copied about 4,000 pages of the documents and released them to the public.[45] The papers showed that from 1963, the company had known that it was selling an addictive drug that posed grave harm to its users; that the company had carefully selected high-nicotine strains of tobacco to keep smokers addicted; that the company had frantically attempted to develop a safe cigarette and had joined the ranks of risk-debunkers with renewed enthusiasm when they discovered it was not possible; that it had known for years that secondhand smoke was dangerous; that it had consciously marketed cigarettes to youngsters while denying doing so; and that it had even insisted that all research results go through its attorneys so that the results would not, as attorney-client privileged, be discoverable at law. There was a lot of paper, and a lot of damning evidence. Jeffrey Wigand, hired during the safe-cigarette attempts of the mid 1990s, gave those documents a human face.

> "Wigand did basically three things," said Stanton A. Glantz, a professor at the University of California at San Francisco. . . . "He brought what was in the documents into the present; the documents ended in the mid-1980s, and he showed that it was all still going on. The second thing is, he put a human face on it. . . . The third thing . . . put the whole thing out there as a hard news story that couldn't be suppressed by the cigarette companies."[46]

By the time the whistles died away, it was clear that Brown & Williamson's research division had developed a genetically engineered strain of tobacco that kept the tar level low but radically increased the nicotine; meanwhile, the company had been experimenting with ammonia additives to the tobacco that would increase the delivery of nicotine to the bloodstream.[47] The implications of the manipulation were clear to everyone: If companies manipulate nicotine levels to make sure that people keep buying, it must be that companies know that it is a hunger for nicotine—not some vapid inessential "pleasure"—that keeps the customers coming back. Then what does that make nicotine? Kessler had indicated as early as February 1994 that the FDA was considering regulating cigarettes as drugs "if the FDA determined that cigarette makers intended that people should buy their products to satisfy what he called a 'nicotine addiction.'"[48] Congressman Waxman summed up: "So, in other words, you're telling us that tobacco company executives and those in the tobacco industry have known for three decades that the nicotine in cigarettes is addictive and is causing a pharmacological reaction in people which causes them to smoke." "I was reading their words," Dr. Kessler deadpanned.[49]

The course was clear from that point. The Science section of *The New York Times* featured an article by Philip Hilts, "Is Nicotine Addictive?" on August 2, 1994, in which he presented a series of ratings of "problem substances," with nicotine in first place—higher than heroin, cocaine, and alcohol.[50] On August 3, the *Times* reported the first FDA moves toward limiting the drug (without which cigarettes do not seem to sell).[51] The only next step is legislation banning the manufacture, sale, and use of all tobacco products.

Creating that legislation—and enacting it and enforcing it—may be the political battle of this millennium. But by August 1995 it was clear that there was a more direct way to the end of the tobacco road. Recall that in 1992 the legal way was cleared for a class action suit alleging harm to smokers. Kessler's testimony provided the theory that the plaintiffs needed for such a suit, and Williams's and Wigand's evidence had brought the testimony before the eyes of every potential juror in America. "The smoker freely chose to smoke" can be no defense if the substance is addictive, and the companies have no defense if it can be shown that they knew the stuff was addictive and that they cynically manipulated the product to ensure that the addiction continued, both of which they did.

The lawsuits started slowly, picking up from where they had left off before Williams's and Wigand's bombshells had cleared the jungle. In March of 1994 Dianne Castano, widow of a smoker who died of cancer, with three other plaintiffs, filed suit in the United States Eastern District Court of Louisiana. The suit names seven major tobacco manufacturers, their related companies, and the Tobacco Institute itself, alleging negligence, fraud, and deceit in the promotion and sale of tobacco products—specifically, that the defendants "concealed knowledge that nicotine was addictive, and that they manipulated the levels of nicotine in cigarettes to keep customers addicted."[52] With a good theory in hand, all the plaintiffs needed was good financial backing and sophisticated legal representation, so that they could not be outspent, outlasted, and outmaneuvered, as plaintiffs had so many times before (remember *Marsee*). By February 1995 these resources were assembled, and Federal Judge Okla Jones, Jr., ruled that the suit was a class action on behalf of every American ever addicted, or possibly addicted, to cigarettes; "all nicotine-dependent persons in the U. S."; and their heirs and assigns—potentially tens of millions of persons.[53] By the end of 1996, Liggett Group, the fifth largest American tobacco company, had broken ranks and settled with the lawyers in the wake of a battle for control of the company. Meanwhile, the first verdict against the tobacco companies had been handed down in Florida. It looked like the dam had finally begun to burst in what would turn out to be the most expensive (or profitable, depending on your perspective) product liability action of all time.[54]

The big breakthrough came when a group of lawyers decided to stop standing "in the smoker's shoes," that is, suing on behalf of those who smoked and suffered and died. The clear defense against the "smoker's" suit was that the smoker chose to smoke (even if afterward he became addicted). To avoid that line of defense, the lawyers chose to sue on behalf of the state, which had to pick up the medical tab for the indigent smoker after he got sick. The suits were rapidly taken over by the states, to recover Medicaid expenses for indigent smokers (Florida, with the highest tab, led the way). Action to recover money for health expenses culminated in a June 1997 proposal to settle all cases on a national level for $368.5 billion. Congress didn't like it.[55] Eventually the settlement figure was inflated to $516 billion before the whole deal unraveled. By the next year a figure of $206 billion had been reached.[56] (Hubert H. Humphrey III, son of the late U.S. Senator, Vice President, and presidential candidate, led the Minnesota fight, and got $6 billion for Minnesota;[57] Florida got $11.3 billion.)

The lawsuits still came in cascades. Suffering plaintiffs sued each tobacco company, all tobacco companies, and even grocery stores for selling cigarettes; counties, cities, individual hospitals and doctors, and Blue Cross/Blue Shield all sued tobacco; everyone sued everyone; this is America. Many of those have been successful. Throughout 1998 and 1999, major lawsuits, to no one's surprise, were brought by attorneys against states, arguing for bigger fees.[58] (California lawyers were awarded $1.25 billion, a decision, said the dissenting judge, that "shocks the conscience." His conscience may have been shocked: He was the tobacco industry's nomination for the panel. The majority cited the major contribution that the lawsuits had made to American life.[59]) But the big victory had been won. No one can now doubt that tobacco is harmful when consumed as directed by its manufacturer, that the manufacturers knew that fact and subtly increased addictive substances in the tobacco in order to keep people smoking and that the manufacturers lied repeatedly in order to keep their profits high. Whether or not tobacco remains legal, all the lawsuits could make it impossible for tobacco to remain profitable.

IV. CONCLUSION

1. The Economic Issues

If nicotine is a harmful addictive drug, as the evidence suggests, that, ultimately, is the final word on tobacco use. Despite its current exemption, it *must* be regulated and probably banned; our law leaves no choice in the matter. Regulation will open new cans of worms, new issues of enforcement, therapy, and delicate negotiations with neighboring sovereign nations. But the new issues will not be problems in *business* ethics—they will not be ethical dilemmas for a successful and profitable industry dealing with the terrible news that its product kills. After regulation, the economic issues that now swirl around the tobacco industry—issues of crop subsidies, job protection, foreign trade, bans on advertising (especially to underage smokers), differential insurance rates, and the like—will become moot. It might be worth touching on these issues in passing, however, since the history of the battle suggests that it will be a long time before anything so conclusive as a ban on all use of tobacco goes into effect.

A point of contention in the tobacco wars of the recent past has been the federal "subsidy" of tobacco growing—not a direct payment, but a price support, that sets a minimum price for the sale of a measure of tobacco. Why, it has been asked, do we subsidize tobacco growing through price supports on domestic tobacco? Should the anti-tobacco army attempt to seize the congressional initiative and repeal all the federal subsidies? Such repeal would probably be counterproductive. There is a history of conflict between the tobacco industry and tobacco growers. Attempts by the industry to keep the price of tobacco low through monopoly tactics were met by a full-scale growers' strike in 1907–1908. The strike did no good (typically, it did much more harm to the growers and their organization than to the triumphant American Tobacco Company[60]) but it did persuade Congress to extend price supports to keep the price of American tobacco fairly high. Of course, if we oppose all use of tobacco, we want prices to be high. The legislation also restricted how much and what quality of tobacco can be grown. Since the tobacco companies are already increasingly buying their tobacco abroad at very low prices, without the price supports and restrictions the price of American-grown tobacco would simply drop to near overseas prices to compete, further impoverishing American farmers and lowering the price of cigarettes on the street. (Incidentally, the foreign plantations are no credit to labor practices of U.S. companies; they are tended by workers kept in filthy camps, especially in Zimbabwe and Brazil. But this is another issue, and cannot be dealt with here.)[61] All the repeal of price supports would do is lower the cost of manufacturing to the companies.

But should we not at least forbid all advertising? If cigarettes are harmful, why do we permit advertising them? Should the ban of cigarette advertising on television be extended to all forms of media use—including the commercial editorials of the sort that Philip Morris composed to counter the EPA report? Larry White (*Merchants of Death*) makes a surprising case that advertising prohibitions will solve nothing. First, newspapers and magazines depend significantly on cigarette advertising; such a ban could hurt them and therefore restrict the exercise of free speech. Of course, the industry has in the past used this fact as leverage to obstruct free speech, by preventing coverage of the dangers of tobacco.[62] But ending the tobacco advertising will not remove the leverage, since the companies have diversified. Finding themselves cash-rich in the final quarter of the twentieth century (cigarette technology matured decades ago, and all the revenue since is pure profit), they began acquiring non-tobacco related companies: RJ Reynolds acquired Nabisco, Philip Morris is the giant with General Foods as its subsidiary, others have merged also. So even if the cigarettes themselves cannot be advertised, the massive advertising of their subsidiary companies could, hypothetically, be used as the same kind of bludgeon.

The two most obvious targets for the anti-tobacco crew, then, turn out to be surprisingly counterproductive or inappropriate. Ultimately we, the American people, and our counterparts across the world, are the right target. When we stop buying, the companies will stop selling. Until then, we have a very difficult case to make in the halls of Big Tobacco.

2. The End

Sometimes the study of business ethics yields real conclusions. It doesn't happen often, but there are the occasions, and industries, where right and wrong look us in the face, and the history of the tobacco industry is one of those occasions. As we write, tobacco is smoking itself to death in a corner that gets smaller and smaller. It is beleaguered from all sides, as much in Europe as here; as much, if official government statements are to be trusted, in the developing countries as in the developed. Its course of defense, since the first warnings came out in the 1950s, has been a case study of irresponsibility. No one will go bankrupt as a result of the demise of the tobacco industry; everyone is diversified, there will be plenty of time to arrange for golden handshakes and foreign assignments as the Kessler-begun initiatives grind toward their inevitable conclusion. But a stain lies across the history of American business, left by a group of very well paid men and women who did not see that the time had come to do the right thing.

QUESTIONS FOR REFLECTION

1. By far the most common argument used against restrictions on tobacco advertising, sale, and use is the liberty argument. Review the argument, and see if it could equally be applied to other addictive drugs—heroin, for instance, or cocaine. Construct an argument for the legalization of all such substances.

2. To what extent should the manufacturer of a product take responsibility for the foreseeable medical risks associated with the product's use? Consider, for instance, the morbidity and mortality associated with skis, skateboards, automobiles, and footballs. Then consider the morbidity and mortality associated with chocolate, butter, french fries, and porterhouse steak.

3. How should the economic consequences of the ban of a product from the market be calculated—especially such massive economic consequences as would flow from the ban of tobacco products? Is there any obligation to compensate those who would suffer loss?

SUGGESTIONS FOR FURTHER READING

Schlaadt, Richard G. *Tobacco and Health.* Guilford, CT: Dushkin Publishing Group, 1992.

Whelan, Elizabeth. *A Smoking Gun: How the Tobacco Industry Gets Away with Murder.* Philadelphia, PA: George F. Stickley Co., 1984.

White, Larry C. *Merchants of Death: The American Tobacco Industry* (foreword by C. Everett Koop, M.D., former Surgeon General of the United States). New York: William Morrow, 1988.

ENDNOTES

1. Terri Somers, "Man Allowed to Sue Tobacco," *The Sun-Sentinel* (Miami) (April 9, 2002).

2. Richard G. Schlaadt, *Tobacco and Health* (Guilford, CT: Dushkin Publishing Group, 1992): p. 29, citing a July 1989 article by Cassandra Tate in *Smithsonian* (pp. 107–117). Hostesses did, of course, prefer that guests not smoke, and rapidly withdrew with the women to safer quarters when men lit up their horrid cigars.

3. Schlaadt, loc. cit.

4. Schlaadt, loc. cit.

5. *Science* (March 4, 1938). Cited in Elizabeth Whelan, *A Smoking Gun: How the Tobacco Industry Gets Away with Murder* (Philadelphia, PA: George F. Stickley Co., 1984).

6. Edwin Grace, "The Gravity of the Smoking Habit," *American Journal of Surgery* (June 1943). Cited in Whelan, op. cit., p. 77.

7. See list of epidemiological criteria, Whelan, op. cit., p. 83.

8. *JAMA* (May 1950). Cited in Whelan, op cit., p. 84.

9. Whelan, op. cit., Chapter 9.

10. Whelan, *Smoking Gun*, op. cit., p. 101.

11. 2001 industry figures from "Fortune 1000 Ranked within Industries," *FORTUNE* (April 15, 2002): p. F-64, and "Industry Profile: Alcohol and Tobacco Companies See Growth," *Alcoholic Beverages and Tobacco Industry Survey* (March 7, 2002). The latter's optimistic title notwithstanding, the word is that "Total cigarette shipments in the United States declined an estimated 3.2% in 2001. . . . ," (p. 7).

12. For instance, during the 1994 New York City Council deliberations on whether or not to ban smoking in most public places: "'Our approach is simple,' said Thomas Lauria, a spokesman for the Tobacco Institute, the industry's trade association. 'We contact City Council members, articulate what the problems are. We help coordinate the efforts made by restaurant owners and people in the hospitality industry. Non-smokers have an axe to grind, and we do, too.'" See Jonathan Hicks, "Tobacco Industry Battles Council on Smoking Curbs," *The New York Times* (September 26, 1994): p. B2.

13. Similarly, the lobbyists that the industry hired to represent it in the more recent battle over smoking in public places in New York City had, as far as possible, close ties to City Council Speaker Peter F. Vallone, who proposed the smoking ban in the Council. Hicks, loc. cit.

14. Op cit.

15. Cited in Schlaadt, op. cit., p. 14.

16. *New England Journal of Medicine* 330 (13): 907, citing "Cigarette Smoking-Attributable Mortality and Years of Potential Life Lost—United States, 1990," *Morbidity and Mortality Weekly Report* (MMWR) 42 (1993): 645–49; J. M. McGinnis and W. H. Foege, "Actual Causes of Death in the United States" *JAMA* 270 (1993): 2207–12; "Reducing the Health Consequences of Smoking: 25 Years of Progress." A report of the Surgeon General: Executive Summary (Rockville, MD: Dept of Health and Human Services 1989) DHHS publication no. [CDC] 89-8411; "Cigarette Smoking Among Adults—United States, 1991," *MMWR* 42 (1993): 230–33.

17. Ibid., citing "Smoking-Related Deaths and Financial Costs: Estimates for 1990,"

Rev. ed. (Washington, DC: Office of Technology Assessment, 1993).

18. Ibid., citing "Cigarette Smoking-Attributable Mortality," op. cit., and "Reducing the Health Consequences of Smoking," op. cit.

19. Ibid., citing W. C. Krupski, "The Peripheral Vascular Consequences of Smoking," *Ann. Vasc Surg* 5 (1991): 291–304; P. E. McBride, "The Health Consequences of Smoking: Cardiovascular Diseases." *Med. Clin. North Am* 76 (1992): 333–53; P. K. Shah and R. H. Helfant, "Smoking and Coronary Artery Disease," *Chest* 94 (1988): 449–52; M. Sugiishi and F. Takatsu, "Cigarette Smoking Is a Major Risk Factor for Coronary Spasm," *Circulation* 87 (1993): 76–79.

20. Ibid., citing "Cancer Facts and Figures—1993" (New York: American Cancer Society, 1993); "The Health Consequences of Smoking—Cancer: A Report of the Surgeon General" (Rockville, MD: Department of Health and Human Services, 1982) (DHHS publication no. (PHS) 82-50179).

21. Ibid., citing (among other sources cited in previous notes) "The Health Benefits of Smoking Cessation: A Report of the Surgeon General" (Rockville, MD: Department of Health and Human Services, 1990) (DHHS publication no. (CDC) 90-8416); "Cancer Facts and Figures—1993," op. cit., R. E. Mecklenburg, D. Greenspan, D. V. Kleinman, et al., "Tobacco Effects in the Mouth: A National Cancer Institute and National Institute of Dental Research Guide for Health Professionals" (Washington, DC: National Cancer Institute, 1992) (NIH publication no. 92-3330); P. A. Newcomb and P. P. Carbone, "The Health Consequences of Smoking: Cancer," *Med Clin North Am* 76 (1992): 305–31.

22. Ibid., citing C. B. Sherman, "The Health Consequences of Cigarette Smoking: Pulmonary Diseases," *Med Clin North Am* 76 (1992): 355–75; K. McCusker, "Mechanisms of Respiratory Tissue Injury from Cigarette Smoking," *Am J Med* (1992–93) Suppl 1A: 18S–21S; P. Menon, R. J. Rando, R. P. Stankus, et al., "Passive Cigarette Smoke—Challenge Studies:

Increase in Bronchial Hyperreactivity," *J Allergy Clin Immunol* 89 (1992): 560–66.

23. Ibid., p. 910, citing Royal College of Physicians, "Smoking and the Young," *Tob Control* 1 (1992): 231–35.

24. Ibid., p. 911, citing W. C. Willett, A. Green, M. J. Stampfer, et al., "Relative and Absolute Excess Risks of Coronary Heart Disease Among Women Who Smoke Cigarettes," *N Engl J Med* 317 (1987): 1303–39; M. C. Fiore, "Trends in Cigarette Smoking in the United States: The Epidemiology of Tobacco Use," *Med Clin North Am* 76 (1992): 289–303; J. E. Fielding, "Smoking and Women: Tragedy of the Majority," *N Engl J Med* 317 (1987): 1343–45; P. M. Layde and V. Beral, "Further Analyses of Mortality in Oral Contraceptive Users," Royal College of General Practitioners' Oral Contraception Study. *Lancet* 1 (1981): 541–46; H. H. Hussey, "Osteoporosis Among Women who Smoke Cigarettes," *JAMA* 235 (1976): 1367–68.

25. Ibid., p. 911.

26. Leroy Hyde, *California Medicine* (1963); cited in Whelan, op. cit., p. 109.

27. Lloyd Mallan, *It Is Safe to Smoke*, (Hawthorn Press, 1967). This and others cited in Whelan, op. cit., p. 110.

28. Cited in Whelan, op. cit., p. 111.

29. Ibid.

30. This is the general drift of both Whelan's *Smoking Gun* and Larry White's *Merchants of Death*, as the titles indicate.

31. See Introduction.

32. Larry White, *Merchants of Death* (New York, NY: William Morrow and Company, 1988): Chapter 5.

33. *Cipollone v. Liggett Group Inc.*, 789 F. 2d 181 (3d Cir.), cert. denied, 107 S. Ct. 907 (1986); *Cipollone v. Liggett Group Inc.* 683 F. Supp.1487 (D. N.J. 1988); *Cipollone v. Liggett Group Inc.*, 893 F. 2d 541 (3d Cir. 1990).

34. *Dewey v. R. J. Reynolds Tobacco Co.*, 577 A. 2d 1239 (NJ 1990).

35. *Carlisle v. Philip Morris Inc.*, 6.1 TPLR 2.1 Texas Ct. of Appeals, 3d Dist., (1991). Cited Roemer, op. cit.

36. *Cipollone v. Liggett Group Inc.,* 112 S. Ct. 2608, 120 L. Ed. 2d 407, 60 U.S.L.W. 703 (24 June 1992).

37. Roemer, op. cit., p. 139.

38. Environmental Protection Agency, "Respiratory Health Effects of Passive Smoking: Lung Cancer and Other Disorders" (Washington, DC: Office of Health and Environmental Assessment, 1992).

39. "The Health Consequences of Involuntary Smoking: A Report of the Surgeon General" (Rockville, MD: Department of Health and Human Services, 1986). DHHS publication no. (CDC) 87-8398.

40. Philip Morris, Inc., "Secondhand Smoke: Facts Finally Emerge," *The New York Times* (June 27–July 1, 1994).

41. Jacob Sullum, "Passive Reporting on Passive Smoke," *Forbes Mediacritic,* cited in "How Science Lost Out to Politics on Secondhand Smoke," ad placed by Philip Morris, Inc., *The New York Times* (June 28, 1994) p. A18.

42. Of course it was over long ago within the walls of the cigarette manufacturers. Prior to the appearance of the Philip Morris ads, Philip Hilts had reported for *The New York Times* ("Embattled Tobacco" (June 16, 1994): p. A1) that internal documents recovered from Brown & Williamson showed that the data had been accepted long ago, and that debate had waged fast and furious on the best counterattack to mount against the growing negative reports.

43. Jonathan P. Hicks, "Tobacco Industry Battles Council on Smoking Curbs," *The New York Times* (September 26, 1994): p. A1.

44. Survey taken October 3, 2002.

45. This section is summarized from an account by Hunt Helm of the *Courier-Journal* (May 25, 1997), from http://www.tobacco.org/News/970525 helms.html?printable=1.

46. Ibid.

47. Warren Leary, "Cigarette Company Developed a Potent Gene-Altered Tobacco," *The New York Times* (June 22, 1994): p. A1.

48. Ibid., p. A14.

49. Ibid., p. A14.

50. Philip J. Hilts, "Is Nicotine Addictive? It Depends on Whose Criteria You Use," *The New York Times* (August 2, 1994): p. C3.

51. Philip J. Hilts, "FDA Panel Takes Step Toward Setting Control on Nicotine: Addiction Chief Cause of Smoking, Panel Says," *The New York Times* (August 3, 1994): A27.

52. Glenn Collins, "Judge Opens Way For a Class Action Against Cigarettes," *The New York Times* (February 18, 1995): pp. 1, 47.

53. Suein L. Hwang and Milo Geyelin, "Tobacco Industry, Plaintiffs Square Off as Cigarette Suit Is Ruled Class Action," *The Wall Street Journal* (February 21, 1995): pp. A3, A6.

54. Benjamin Weiser, "Tobacco's Trials: Cigarette Makers Once Were so Hard to Beat in Court that Many Top Lawyers Refused to Take Them On," *The Washington Post Magazine* (December 8, 1996).

55. Bob Hohler, "Senators Assail Tobacco Pact, Cite Compromises," *The Boston Globe* (July 17, 1997): p. A7.

56. Aaron Zitner and Frank Phillips, "Clinton Endorses $206b Tobacco Pact," *The Boston Globe* (November 17, 1998): p. A9.

57. Scott Shane, "Humphrey, Tobacco Face Off Today," *The Baltimore Sun* (January 26, 1998): p. 1A; "Tobacco Lawsuit Settled; $6 Billion Agreement Avoids Defeat by Jury," Knight Ridder Newspapers (May 9, 1998).

58. Barry Meier and Jill Abramson, "Tobacco War's New Front: Lawyers Fight for Big Fees," *The New York Times* (June 9, 1998): p. A1.

59. Henry Weinstein, "Tobacco Lawsuit Fee: $1.25 Billion," *Los Angeles Times* (July 15, 2002): Metro p. 1.

60. For a very thorough account of the rebellion, see Tracy Campbell, *The Politics of Despair: Power and Resistance in the Tobacco Wars* (Lexington, KY: The University Press of Kentucky,1993).

61. White, op. cit., Chapter 3.

62. White, op. cit, p. 133; Whelan, op. cit.

5

How Shall We Know If Our Products Are Safe?

Diverse Perspectives on Tires and Automobiles

Questions to Keep in Mind

1. Concerning the Pinto crash described in this case: Which facts are known to be true? Which facts are still contested? What don't we know about the crash? What is at stake, ethically, in what we know or don't know about this crash?

2. What are the four perspectives used here to review the Pinto case? How do these perspectives overlap, and how do they differ?

3. What kind of conflict can occur between those who engineer a product and those who market it? How did that conflict play out with the Ford Pinto?

4. As a formal decision-making procedure, what are the steps of cost benefit reasoning? What are the advantages and disadvantages of this kind of reasoning?

5. Based on this chapter, how would you describe the relationship between the auto industry and the government concerning product safety?

6. What is the ethical significance of the jury decision in the Ulrich case?

We buy things to make our lives easier. All kinds of things: household appliances, sophisticated computers and digital communications tools, and machines large and small. Normally we don't give much thought to the safety of the various consumer goods we use each day. We don't worry about safety as long as everything works the way it should. But when the things we buy hurt us, we start to pay attention. In the worst cases, when many people are seriously maimed or killed by product failures, the general public can get upset and demand some kind of justice. It isn't always easy, however, to know what justice requires when products fail. If the reasons for the product failure are unclear and complex, people may have difficulty locating a simple target for their righteous anger. Businesses involved in product safety issues fear they will become ensnared in arguments about their liability. The government has the duty to protect the public welfare, but it may not be at all obvious how the government should get between consumers and business. For all concerned, it can be difficult to pin down exactly who is responsible, and for what.

Automobile tires are a classic case in point. We all rely upon them whenever we ride in a car, but we almost never give them a second thought—that is, until the tires start to kill us. It is not always easy, though, to say who is to blame and who has the responsibility for making things right.

Bridgestone/Firestone, Inc., makes tires. It has been making tires since 1900, when Harvey Firestone founded the Firestone Tire & Rubber Company in Akron Ohio. In 1990 Bridgestone USA, a subsidiary of Tokyo-based Bridgestone Corporation, acquired Firestone. Today, Bridgestone/Firestone makes and sells thousands of different kinds of tires. For many years it enjoyed a positive reputation, a solid public image supported by its long-standing relationship with the Ford Motor Company, a major and faithful customer of the Bridgestone/Firestone tires.[1]

Apparently, however, in the 1990s a big problem was brewing with Bridgestone/Firestone's ATX, ATX II, and Wilderness tires. Vehicle accidents linked to these tires have resulted in 174 deaths, more 700 injuries, and over 6,000 complaints.[2] The treads on many of these tires seemed to separate suddenly, causing blowouts and other failures, and often causing vehicle rollovers. These tires were used on various trucks and SUVs, but mostly on the Ford Explorer. The problem seemed most severe in hotter climates, with most of the North American complaints coming from Texas, Florida, and other southern states.

The media picked up the issue in spring of 2000, focusing public and governmental attention on the emerging problem. That May, a Houston television station reported that there was a connection between the Firestone tires and auto accidents in that area. Very quickly, the National Highway Traffic Safety Administration (NHTSA) was deluged with complaints about the tires and it opened an investigation that month. On August 9, 2000, Bridgestone/Firestone initiated a voluntary recall of some 14.4 million tires under investigation that were made in the preceding decade (about 6.5 million of these tires were still on the road). Since these tires were original equipment on the Ford Explorer, Ford issued its own tire recall for buyers of its SUV, an action that involved about 13 million tires. Only after the recalls did both Ford and Bridgestone/ Firestone publicly apologize.[3] Eventually Congress got involved, quickly passing the Transportation Recall Enhancement, Accountability, and Documentation Act (TREAD Act), which President Clinton signed on November 1, 2000.[4]

Recalls of this nature and magnitude are highly unusual and very costly, to both Bridgestone/Firestone and Ford. The negative business consequences extend far beyond the simple cost of the recall. There is a loss of public confidence that can linger for years, depressing future sales. In this case, the disputes surrounding the recall damaged a vital business relationship. After a nasty period of mutual criticism over questions of responsibility and liability for the problem, Ford and Bridgestone/Firestone ended their ninety-five-year contractual relationship. This messy situation was complicated by growing suspicions and accusations that either or both companies knew about the problem for some time without correcting it. During Senate hearings about the accidents, evidence surfaced that Bridgestone/Firestone had known about potential tread separation problems as far back as 1994. Internal memos from Bridgestone/Firestone and Ford showed that both companies acknowledged in 1997 that there were concerns about the tires.[5] Apparently, however, Bridgestone/Firestone and Ford continue to disagree about who was really responsible.

Nobody disputes that there is a problem when large numbers of people are injured or killed by their tires and automobiles. There is a natural and human desire to fix the problem and to seek justice for those who were wronged. We may wish for a simple "bad guy" to serve as the target of our moral outrage. But more often than not, there is no single, simple basis for problems like the Bridgestone/Firestone tires and the Ford Explorers. Though we may want to "cut to the chase" and settle these kinds of problems without delay, we should recognize and think carefully about the various ingredients in this kind of problem. In particular, it can be helpful to think about the Bridgestone/Firestone–Ford dispute from several different points of view, including those of engineering, political, and financial stakeholders.

The perspective of engineers is absolutely critical for issues of product safety, because the engineers design and help oversee the production of the products we use. Engineers share a fundamental commitment to safety and the integrity of the product. In theory, their duty to protect the public welfare comes before everything else. In practice, however, engineers fulfill their duties while working in particular contexts, which can complicate how they understand their duty. For example, all the major parties involved in the conflict over Bridgestone/Firestone tires included engineers, each of whom had a duty to protect the public. But these various engineers approached their duties with different concerns or emphases. Bridgestone/Firestone's engineers were concerned about the design of the tire itself and the conditions that would contribute to tire failure. Ford's engineers were concerned about the design of the Ford Explorer and how to reduce the chances of it rolling over during normal driving maneuvers. The NHTSA engineers were charged with helping over-see highway safety. They monitor complaints, they test tires, and, when neces-sary, they advise whether to recall products.

In principle there is a general consensus that engineers should follow their duty to promote public safety. In practice, we need to recognize that engineers come to different conclusions. Bridgestone/Firestone engineers felt their tires were safe, and blamed the failure of certain tires on Ford's recommendation to consumers to maintain lower tire pressures than Bridgestone/Firestone rec-ommended. The Bridgestone/Firestone engineers also felt that Ford was not willing to share information about its vehicles that would help everyone solve the engineering problems. Ford, in reply, claimed that its Ford Explorer was not more prone to roll overs than other SUVs, and that the Ford Explorer was not uniquely responsible for causing the tread separation on the Bridgestone/Firestone tires.[6] The NHTSA engineers claimed that the tires had passed their required tests, and that they had no way to know of the po-tential danger to the general public until they began to receive complaints from consumers.

While the engineering perspective is critically important for discussions about product safety, engineers are not the only voice in the conversation. The political perspective is important, as is the financial point of view. Politically, there is a mandate to serve and protect the public good. And yet, there may be different views of what constitutes the public good and how we should best promote it. The financial perspective would have us situate product safety within a framework of costs and benefits. From this standpoint, we might need to acknowledge the futility of manufacturing a perfectly safe automobile tire if it costs so much that hardly anyone can afford to buy it.

The wake-up call that focused all these concerns around questions of prod-uct safety was the case of the Ford subcompact automobile, the Pinto. A care-ful review of this classic case can help us respect the complexity of product safety issues, while also reminding us of the terrible price to be paid when we do not give sufficient attention to the values of human safety and human life.

I. THREE DEATHS IN INDIANA

In 1979 the Ford Motor Company was charged with criminal homicide.[7] For twenty weeks before a jury in an Indiana courtroom, Elkhart County prose-cutor Michael A. Cosentino and Ford chief attorney James F. Neal debated whether Ford should be convicted of reckless homicide. According to the presiding Circuit Court Judge Harold R. Staffeldt, Cosentino needed to show that Ford Motor Company had engaged in "plain, conscious and unjustifiable disregard of harm that might result (from its actions)." In other words, a suc-cessful criminal charge would need to establish a criminal intent on the part of Ford and its agents. Also, according to Judge Staffeldt, to support the charge of criminal homicide it would be necessary to prove that Ford's disregard of harm involved a "substantial deviation from acceptable standards of conduct."

What had Ford done to deserve such a serious, unprecedented charge of criminal homicide? Though some of the key details of the case were disputed, both sides generally agreed to the following facts:

On August 10, 1978, three young women were killed in an automobile accident involving a Pinto, a subcompact car made by Ford. They were Judy (eighteen years old) and Lynn Ulrich (sixteen years old), and their cousin Donna Ulrich (eighteen years old). They were driving a 1973 Ford Pinto on U.S. Highway 33 near Goshen, Indiana, sometime between 5:30 P.M. and 6:30 P.M. Their two-door Pinto had had several previous owners. For some reason, the three apparently had stopped their car on the highway. At the trial there was speculation that the gas cap had come off the car (they had recently fueled up at a self-service gas station), and perhaps they had stopped to retrieve it. While stopped, they were hit from behind by a van weighing almost twice as much as their Pinto. (There was a dispute over whether the Pinto was moving when it was hit. Prosecution witnesses, including the van's driver, estimated the Pinto was moving at about 50 mph. However, a hospital attendant testified for the defense that one of the three women said, as she was dying, that their car was not moving.) There were no skid marks on the road to indicate the van had tried to stop. The collision knocked the Pinto about 170 feet down the highway. Its gas tank ruptured and the car burst into flames. According to one witness to the accident, it looked "like a large napalm bomb going off."[8] All three young women burned to death: Donna and Lynn at the scene of the accident; Judy lived a few hours but then died from her burns. (To eliminate any question about the cause of death, in November 1978 the bodies of the two sisters were exhumed for autopsies.[9])

The state charges against Ford in the Ulrich case constituted the first criminal prosecution of an American corporation in a case involving alleged product defects that were responsible for the loss of human life. The prosecution claimed that Ford executives *knew* that the Pinto's gas tanks tended to explode when struck from behind, and that they did nothing to correct the problem, selling hundreds of thousands of Pintos anyway.[10] Though only monetary penalties were involved in this case—Ford faced a potential penalty of only $30,000—it had broader financial significance for the automobile company: A guilty verdict in the Ulrich case would strengthen multimillion-dollar damage suits filed by Pinto owners involved in other accidents.[11] Also, the Ulrich case was closely followed nationally because of its serious implications for public policy debates about enforcing product safety laws.[12]

To better understand this case, we need to review it from several perspectives. First, it is important to adopt a historical perspective because the Ulrich case was not an isolated incident. Second, we will look at the Pinto from an engineering perspective. Here we will seek to understand the various pressures and deadlines that bear on product development in highly competitive situations. Third, we will look at the Pinto case from an economic perspective that weighs the comparative costs and benefits of product safety decisions. Fourth, we will conclude by looking at the broader political context of the Pinto debate. Here we will focus on the development of governmental safety standards for the automobile industry. Having reviewed the issue of Pinto's safety from historical, engineering, economic, and political perspectives, we should be in a position to judge for ourselves the true lesson of the Ulrich case for ongoing issues of product safety and corporate responsibility.

II. A HISTORICAL PERSPECTIVE:
THE CONTROVERSIAL ACHIEVEMENT
OF THE PINTO

The Pinto played a vital, if controversial, role in Ford's competitive strategy in the early 1970s. At that time the American automobile industry was plagued by rapidly changing global competition, unforeseen political events, and shifting consumer tastes. The Pinto was central to Ford's strategy to survive these complicated events.

Following World War II, the American automobile industry enjoyed an undisputed global leadership. Even in the narrow, twisting streets of foreign cities, large American cars were coveted as the status symbol of choice. By many accounts, this uncontested superiority lulled the American auto industry into a false sense of complacency. American auto manufacturers were not prepared for the fundamental changes in the 1970s that challenged their ways of doing business.

Americans had a love affair with the big automobile. Gas efficiency was not even a consideration, thanks to the unquestioned availability of cheap fuel. But in the 1970s, the Arab oil embargoes and corresponding rising fuel prices sparked a new consumer interest in smaller, gas-saving cars. The four U.S. auto makers—General Motors, Ford, Chrysler, and American Motors—were all hurt by growing American imports of foreign subcompact cars. The U.S. manufacturers' large automobiles enjoyed higher profit margins compared to their smaller cars, and so the U.S. auto executives were reluctant to give up on the big car. But comparatively higher profit margins on large automobiles are meaningless when people stop buying them. The American auto industry needed new strategies for survival.

Among the four U.S. auto makers, Ford was well equipped to respond to the changes in consumer demand. Founded in 1903, the Ford Motor Company had been family-owned and managed until its first public stock offering in 1956. Against its principal competitor, General Motors, Ford was more successful in identifying and pursuing unique market niches. Traditionally, Ford had been strong in the small car market, having introduced a compact car, the Maverick, in 1969. But in the face of more aggressive foreign imports, Ford needed to go even farther and to develop quickly a sub-compact automobile.

Ford's president at that time, Lee Iacocca, put his weight behind the rapid development of the Pinto, urging that it be ready for 1971. With unusual ur-gency, Ford succeeded in producing the Pinto as a 1971 model. The Pinto be-came one of Ford's best selling cars, and helped Ford compete successfully against foreign auto imports. It was also clear that Ford's competitive strategy would need to depend on the Pinto for some time to come: Its next-generation small car, the future successor to the Pinto, would not be ready for possibly another ten years, because of the time it would take to develop the innovations necessary for a genuinely new automobile design.

The Pinto seemed to be a triumph for Ford, but it was also controversial. The Ulrich case was not the first instance in which people were injured or killed by exploding Pintos. In 1977 Mark Dowie, an investigative journalist who studied the Pinto phenomenon, wrote a classic article called "Pinto Madness" that appeared in the somewhat radical magazine *Mother Jones*. Dowie claimed:

> By conservative estimates Pinto crashes have caused 500 burn deaths to people who would not have been seriously injured if the car had not burst into flames. The figure could be as high as 900. Burning Pintos have be-come such an embarrassment to Ford that its advertising agency, J. Walter Thompson, dropped a line from the end of a radio spot that read "Pinto leaves you with that warm feeling."[13]

Ford executives were outraged by Dowie's assertions, which they dismissed as inaccurate and misleading. Some aspects of Dowie's account, especially his presentation of Ford's cost/benefit reasoning, have been strongly criticized. Shortcomings to his article notwithstanding, Dowie had started a debate that would persist until and after the Ulrich case, and thus his article will be cited and examined later in this chapter.

At the Ulrich trial, Ford defense attorney James Neal argued that it was not fair to question the Pinto's safety record against abstract or arbitrary stan-dards. To the contrary, he claimed, a particular product's safety record can be assessed only *contextually*, in relation to similar products made at that time. When the safety record of other U.S. subcompacts is taken into account, he said, it is fair to conclude that Ford followed "acceptable standards of conduct" in developing and selling the Pinto.

Neal emphasized important similarities between the Ford Pinto and other manufacturers' subcompact automobiles: Their gas tanks are made of similar materials; the gas tanks of subcompacts all tend to be placed near sharp metal parts (like the differential housing) that might puncture the tank; and subcom-pact automobile bodies are welded similarly in that they are usually made with-out what is called a "frame body." Neal even pointed out that the Pinto is superior to some other subcompacts in safety features: The Pinto has a safety guard rail built into the left side of the car, whereas the Chevy Vega has none.

According to U.S. government information, said Neal, the Pinto performed as well or better than most other subcompacts with respect to collisions and fires.

If the Pinto is viewed against more general automobile standards and performance features, it does not compare as well. The Pinto does not have the safety features of many larger automobiles. But Neal argued against comparing the Pinto to larger cars, saying such a judgment would be like comparing apples to oranges. He said:

> There is no way you can compare a Pinto with a Lincoln, a Pinto with a standard car, a Pinto with a Cadillac, or a Pinto with a Mercedes. Nor is there any way you can compare any of these other subcompacts with those kinds of cars. And, members of the jury, our world is ending for those kinds of cars.[14]

Among other contextual considerations that Ford thought relevant to the Pinto's safety in the Ulrich case was the condition of Highway 33, where the Pinto collision and explosion took place. According to defense attorney Neal, Highway 33 had an eight-inch curb, which was so high that it prevented the Ulrich car from getting completely off the road when it stopped. According to Neal, even a large automobile stuck on a highway under similar circumstances would explode if hit from behind by a large, speeding van. His point: Under normal circumstances, the Ford Pinto is reasonably safe according to "acceptable standards of conduct." It is comparatively safe when viewed against the safety features and performance of other subcompacts. True, the Pinto may not be *completely* safe, when judged against standards more fitting for larger cars. But such a comparative judgment would be unfair. The Pinto is safe for what it is—a subcompact automobile—and that is the only relevant standard for safety.

III. AN ENGINEERING PERSPECTIVE:
BUSINESS PRESSURES ON DESIGN
AND PRODUCTION

Dowie's article, "Pinto Madness," claimed that Ford was so eager to get the Pinto to market that it sped too quickly through critical design and preproduction tests. Among Dowie's charges:

- Ford engineers discovered in preproduction crash tests that rear-end collisions would rupture the Pinto's fuel system extremely easily.

- Because assembly-line machinery was already tooled when engineers found this defect, top Ford officials decided to manufacture the car anyway—exploding gas tank and all—*even though Ford owned the patent on a much safer gas tank.*[15]

What were the grounds to support Dowie's claim?

In 1967 Lee Iaccoca established the goal to have the Pinto in Ford's show-rooms by 1971. Moreover, Iaccoca imposed the "limits of 2,000" on the engineers: The Pinto must weigh less than 2,000 pounds and cost no more than $2,000.[16] Formal planning began at once in June 1967 and production was started in August 1970. According to Dowie, this twenty-five-month period was shorter than usual, as the typical time span from conception to production of a new car is forty-three months. Some of the accelerated schedule can be explained by the Pinto's simplified car design and Ford's innovations in stream-lined management.

But Dowie charged that this accelerated schedule didn't give the Ford engineers sufficient time to do their job right. Consequently, a number of critical design and engineering issues did not receive sufficient attention or were not implemented adequately. For example, one particularly controversial point concerned the safest place to put the gas tank. Like most cars made in the early 1970s, the Pinto's gas tank was behind the rear axle. But late in the Pinto's design process, a study showed it would be safer to place the tank directly above the rear axle, which would better isolate it from the point of impact by a rear-end collision. But engineers weighed this benefit against other problems: Putting the tank above the rear axle increased the threat of spilled fuel igniting in the passenger compartment. The new location also raised the car's center of gravity, making it more difficult to handle. Besides these safety issues, the new tank location would reduce the Pinto's storage space, would make it difficult to design a Pinto station wagon or hatchback, and would make the car more difficult to service. These factors needed to be weighed carefully, something Dowie claims the engineers did not have time to do because of the 1971 deadline.

Another design issue that was debated in the Ulrich trial was whether the Pinto's gas tank should have been fitted with a rubber bladder. Some studies showed that such a device lessened the chance that the tank would rupture in a car collision. But according to Ford defense attorney Neal at the Ulrich trial, no other American cars had a rubber bladder in their gas tanks, except the Corvette Stingray. The reason was, according to Ford, that such devices don't work well in actual situations, depending on the climate where the car is used and depending on the kind of collision the car experiences. Also, there was a concern at Ford about the cost of introducing effective gas tank bladders. Would this design issue have received more careful attention if the Pinto had been on a more typical production schedule?

At issue here are the contrasting fundamental values or outlooks associated with engineers and marketing-oriented executives. According to Dowie, an anonymous Ford engineer said, "This company is run by salesmen, not engineers; so the priority is styling, not safety."[17] It is not clear whether a more generous production timetable would have facilitated a consensus on design safety among the engineers and marketers at Ford. We do know, however, that Ford is not alone in having this kind of conflict in perspective.

Engineers would like to have all the time necessary to test their designs fully and to implement them without compromise. Marketers would like to put their products on the market as soon as possible, in order to beat the competition. Caught in the unavoidable tension between these two orientations is the nagging question of what counts as adequate product safety.

IV. AN ECONOMIC PERSPECTIVE: WEIGHING THE COSTS AND BENEFITS

One of the more disturbing aspects of the Ford Pinto case was Ford's use of cost/benefit reasoning to make decisions that directly affected consumer safety. The cost benefit issue was brought to public attention by Dowie's article, which published a Ford internal memorandum that weighed the positive value of human life against the cost of improving Ford gas tanks. It is important to emphasize that this Ford memo is concerned only with fuel tank fires caused by a rollover, not by rear-end impact. Also, this memo measures the costs of reengineering <u>all</u> Ford cars, not just the Pinto. Thus, contrary to how many have interpreted Dowie's report, this Ford memo was not doing a cost/benefit analysis to determine specifically how to deal with Ford Pintos that were exploding from rear-impact collisions. Nevertheless, this infamous Ford cost/benefit analysis is linked permanently in public consciousness with the Pinto issue. Also, Neal's arguments in the Ulrich case uses cost/benefit judgments to defend the Pinto's design. We need to be careful not to confuse this Ford memorandum with the arguments made in the Ulrich case. But it is appropriate here to review the way in which this Ford memorandum introduces cost/benefit reasoning to discussions of automobile safety, even if this memo was not used by Ford to make any safety decisions directly affecting the Pinto. This review is warranted by the pervasive impact of cost/benefit reasoning on business decisions in general and on product safety issues in particular. Our purpose here is to use this memorandum to display the kind of logic that is operative when an economic perspective prevails in discussions of product safety.

First, what is cost/benefit analysis? It is a formal decision-making procedure that, in the best of possible worlds, follows the following steps:[18]

1. The project or policy to be analyzed is identified.
2. All the impacts, both favorable and unfavorable, present and future, on all of society, are determined.
3. Values, usually in dollars, are assigned to these impacts. Favorable impacts will be registered as benefits, unfavorable ones as costs.
4. The net benefit (total benefit minus total cost) is calculated.
5. The decision to be made is based upon the rule that in any choice situation, we should select the alternative that produces the greatest net benefit.

Of course, in actual circumstances it is impossible to identify and to assign accurate values to *all* the impacts of a proposed project or policy. Nevertheless, cost/benefit analysis is widely used in business because it upholds capitalism's basic commitment to economic efficiency.

The underlying presupposition, that we should put scarce resources to their most valuable use, has guided informal decision-making since the dawn of humankind. But the systematic and quantitative application of cost/benefit reasoning to decisions is a more recent phenomenon. It was first employed by the U.S. government to analyze water resource projects in the 1930s and blossomed in strategic analysis methods developed during World War II. Today, nearly every organization of any size, business or otherwise, employs some kind of formal, quantitative cost/benefit reasoning procedure for project and policy decisions.

As reported in the Dowie article, Ford made a cost/benefit calculation to decide *not* to make a safety modification to the gas tanks of their automobiles (keeping in mind that the memorandum reviewed here was not written with the Pinto specifically in mind). According to a Ford internal memorandum entitled, "Fatalities Associated with Crash-Induced Fuel Leakage and Fires," which Dowie made public in his article,[19] Ford reasoned as follows:

> The issue: Should we make a technical improvement costing $11 per car that will prevent gas tanks from rupturing so easily?
>
> The memorandum indicates that <u>benefits</u> are calculated as follows:
>
> Savings: 180 burn deaths, 180 serious injuries, 2,100 burned vehicles
>
> Unit Cost: $200,000 per death, $67,000 per injury, $700 per vehicle
>
> Total Benefit: 180 × ($200,000) + 180 × ($67,000) + 2,100 × ($700) = $49.5 million

The <u>costs</u> are calculated as follows:

> Sales: 11 million cars, 1.5 million light trucks
>
> Unit Cost: $11 per car, $11 per truck
>
> Total Cost: 11,000,000 × ($11) + 1,500,000 × ($11) = $137 million.

Applying the basic rule of cost/benefit reasoning (select the alternative that produces the greatest net benefit) we see that the total cost ($137 million) clearly outweighs the total benefit ($49.5 million). Therefore, it is rational to conclude that Ford should not make the $11 per unit technical improvement to its gas tanks.

Cost/benefit reasoning is open to some powerful objections, which Dowie and others use to critique the reasoning in this internal Ford memorandum. The following extract summarizes some of the problems associated with this form of reasoning:

> Benefit-cost analysis is especially vulnerable to misapplication through carelessness, naivete, or outright deception. The techniques are potentially dangerous to the extent that they convey an aura of precision and objectivity. Logically they can be no more precise than the assumptions

and valuations that they employ; frequently through the compounding of errors, they may be less so. Deception is quite a different matter, involving submerged assumptions, unfairly chosen valuations, and purposeful misestimates.[20]

Picking up on this issue of where we get our valuations and estimates, the Ford cost/benefit analysis can be challenged on its valuation of human life, which it estimates to be $200,000. Where did Ford get this figure? From the U.S. government! In 1972 the National Highway Traffic Safety Administration issued a report that calculated a human life to be worth $200,726. It estimated as follows:[21]

Component 1971 Costs

FUTURE PRODUCTIVITY LOSSES
    Direct $132,000
    Indirect 41,300
MEDICAL COSTS
    Hospital 700
    Other 425
PROPERTY DAMAGE 1,500
INSURANCE ADMINISTRATION 4,700
LEGAL AND COURT 3,000
EMPLOYER LOSSES 1,000
VICTIM'S PAIN AND SUFFERING 10,000
FUNERAL 900
ASSETS (Lost Consumption) 5,000
MISCELLANEOUS ACCIDENT COST 200
TOTAL PER FATALITY $200,725

(Note: These figures are from a 1972 NHTSA study. In 1977 the amount was adjusted to $278,000 to account for inflation. Presumably human life would be worth more today, even with the lowered inflation rate of recent years!)

The above calculation estimates the cost to society every time someone is killed in a car accident. Is this a justified valuation of human life? In particular, where does the $10,000 for "victim's pain and suffering" come from? Dowie reports that he was unable to find anyone, in the government or at Ford, who could explain the rationale for this figure. Presumably there are people who will object to a $10,000 valuation of human pain and suffering (even if we take into account that these are 1971 dollars): First, because it is too low an amount. Second, and more devastating for cost/benefit reasoning about product safety, because it is inappropriate to put <u>any</u> price tag on human life.

One reason that we tend to accept cost/benefit calculations that affect human life is that the human lives in question are "anonymous" or "statistical." Humans have a tendency to toss out cost/benefit reasoning when the lives of known persons are at stake. Thus a community will spend a large sum of money to rescue five identified miners trapped in a mine when the same amount of money could have been used instead to install better safety features in the *next* mine that would save many more lives overall than the currently trapped five. Rationally, according to cost/benefit reasoning, we should save more "statistical" or future lives than fewer "known" lives now. But many people are uncomfortable with this kind of rationality.[22] When Ford, and other companies, make cost/benefit trade-offs between product cost and human life, they do not have particular persons in mind. Ford's executives were not thinking about, nor did they even know, the three Ulrich young women when they contemplated the $11 improvement to their gas tanks. And this oversight, says Dowie, is precisely what is wrong with cost/benefit reasoning applied to these kinds of issues. He says:

> And you could talk "burn injuries" and "burn deaths" with these guys [cost/benefit policy makers], and they didn't seem to envision children crying at funerals and people hiding in their homes with melted faces. Their minds appeared to have leapt right to the bottom line—more safety meant higher prices, higher prices meant lower sales and lower sales meant lower profits.[23]

The greater impact of "known" lives on our judgments about safety explains why Ford put its own engineers on the defense stand at the Ulrich trial. For these engineers attested that not only did they drive the Pinto, but they let their wives and children drive the car too!

V. A POLITICAL PERSPECTIVE: WHO SETS THE CONSUMER SAFETY STANDARDS?

The Dowie article claimed that Ford actually lied to the government in order to delay the enactment of government automobile safety standards, standards that would have required Ford to change the Pinto gas tank's design. An important background to the Ulrich accident is the long-running battle between Ford and the government over the auto safety standards. At issue is who should determine the appropriate level of safety for the American consumer.

For most of America's history, the fundamental business rule has been "let the buyer beware." Consumers had relatively low expectations about the reliability and safety of business products. Following World War II, the United States experienced a shift in attitude toward a more aggressive consumerism that said, in effect, "let the seller beware!" Increasingly, consumers demanded the *right* to safe and reliable consumer products and the U.S. government stepped in to enforce that right. The auto industry successfully resisted governmental safety regulation until the 1960s. Inspired by consumer advocate Ralph Nader's classic critique of the Corvair automobile, *Unsafe at Any Speed*, the American public looked for help from governmental groups like the Environmental Protection Agency and private consumer advocate groups like the Center for Auto Safety. Ford's most extended safety battles, however, were with the

National Highway Traffic Safety Administration (NHTSA) a regulatory agency in the Department of Transportation. From the start, the auto industry and NHTSA were adversaries, as reflected in the following battle between Ford and NHTSA over safety standards affecting the Pinto.

Before 1969 during the design stage of the Pinto, there were no federal government car safety standards specifically on gas leaks from rear-end crashes. In January 1969 NHTSA proposed the first rear-end fuel system integrity standard, called Standard 301. It required that a stationary vehicle should leak less than one ounce of fuel per minute, if hit by a 4,000-lb barrier moving at 20 mph. Standard 301 was called a "moving barrier" test because the barrier rams into the car, not the car into the barrier. Ford responded by supporting Standard 301, adopting it as a design objective for all its cars. It tested the Pinto against this standard and made adjustments to its gas tank to bring it into compliance.

In 1970, after Ford had already started manufacturing the Pinto, NHTSA revised Standard 301 to be a 20-mph fixed barrier standard. In this test, the car is pulled backward into a fixed barrier. The entire automobile industry opposed this revision, saying that the fixed barrier test puts nearly twice as much stress on the car as the comparable moving barrier test. Moreover, the auto makers said, the revised Standard 301 is unrealistic because cars almost never back into objects at that speed. Most rear-end collisions were at speeds of less than 20 mph (as in the moving barrier standard), and only 0.45 percent of injury-producing rear-end collisions also included a fire.[24] Ford proceeded to use its own 20-mph moving barrier standard. It also started to work on ways to pass a 30-mph moving barrier test, which it thought the NHTSA would eventually propose. In 1973, NHTSA surprised Ford by proposing a 30-mph *fixed barrier* rear-end fuel system integrity standard, effective September 1976 for all 1977 models. NHTSA also proposed a fuel system integrity standard for cars that roll over in accidents. Ford opposed this requirement, using for its argument the cost/benefit analysis cited earlier.

In 1977 Motor Vehicle Safety Standard 301 was amended to implement all provisions of the proposed fuel system integrity standard, affecting all 1977 model. Shortly thereafter, Dowie's article appeared in *Mother Jones*. Ford vehemently denied that it had purposely delayed Standard 301, saying that it had only opposed "certain excessive testing requirements."[25] NHTSA initiated an investigation into the Pinto's fuel tank system. Ford complained that the basis for NHTSA's inquiry was unfounded and that NHTSA was motivated by political, not safety, concerns.

In May 1978 NHTSA said that pre-1977 model year Pintos were subject to fuel leaks and other problems.[26] In June 1978, Ford agreed to a recall, but it did not agree with NHTSA's view that the Pinto design involved an "unreasonable risk" to safety. Ford conceded that NHTSA had identified some areas for practical improvement (like replacing the fuel filler pipe and installing a polyethylene shield across the front of the fuel tank). Ford's recall cost the company $20 million after taxes.[27] In response to Ford's action, NHTSA closed its long-standing investigation without making a final determination about the Pinto's safety.

This long-running feud between Ford and NHTSA illustrates the tension between the auto industry and the government concerning product safety. The government seeks to represent the interests of the consumer, who individually are not able to press for better safety standards. The automobile industry seeks to provide products at prices that consumers are willing to pay. Concerning the Ulrich case, Ford concedes that it *could* build a safer car—like a tank! But few consumers would desire or be able to afford such a vehicle.

VI. THE OUTCOME OF THE TRIAL

On March 13, 1980, after a ten-week trial, the Elkhart County Jury reached a verdict in the Ulrich case. The verdict came after twenty-five hours of deliberations over a four-day period, including a session lasting more than fourteen hours and ended at 3 A.M. The jury was polled twenty-five times. According to jury foreman Arthur Selmer, the first vote by the jurors was four in favor of the conviction, eight against. Eventually there was but one holdout who favored a conviction, James Yurgilas, a self-employed mobile home salesman.

> "I felt that it was a reckless automobile but on the other point you couldn't actually prove that they didn't do anything in their power to recall it," said Mr. Yurgilas, whose eyes and facial expressions bespoke agony over his decision to yield.[28]

The jury found Ford not guilty of criminal homicide in the Ulrich case. The verdict came during a meeting of Ford's board of directors, who cheered loudly at the news. This case shows that it is very difficult, perhaps even pointless, to try to convict corporations of <u>criminal</u> charges in cases like this.[29] Not only was Ford acquitted in this case, avoiding the stigma of being the first company in history to be guilty of reckless homicide, but Ford now expected to counter more easily the maze of civil suits pending against it.

The Ulrich family's response was more subdued. Earl Ulrich, father of two of the victims, said of the verdict, "I'm very disappointed. But this has nothing to do with us. This was the state of Indiana against Ford Motor Co."[30]

Even though the jury did acquit, this Pinto proceeding had a pervasive impact on the auto industry and society. According to Clarence Ditlow, executive director of the Washington-based Center for Auto Safety, "The bottom line of all this, from a consumer view, is that we will wind up with safer cars. . . . Manufacturers now realize they are in danger of criminal charges. Cost versus benefits of safety will be looked at closely."[31]

From the standpoint of ethics, the jury's acquittal has not diminished debate about product safety and corporate responsibility. Because of the stirring nature of the case, and because of the unprecedented severity of the criminal charge against Ford, this Ford Pinto case is a watershed in the evolution of public perceptions and judgments about product safety standards. Corporate critics still cite the Ford Pinto as a benchmark in their arguments about product safety.[32]

QUESTIONS FOR REFLECTION

1. What should be the basis for our standards of product safety? Should our safety standards reflect the prevailing level of safety demonstrated in particular product categories? Or should our safety standards reflect an as-yet unattained ideal?

2. How much should Americans be willing to pay for automobile safety? In your opinion, is automobile safety a sufficiently high priority for automobile manufacturers and for consumers?

3. How pervasive do you think cost/benefit reasoning is in business decision-making, in the area of product safety as well as in other areas? Are you comfortable using cost/benefit reasoning for important decisions? What are the ethical risks of relying too exclusively on cost/benefit reasoning?

    What, ethically, are the advantages associated with this kind of reasoning?

4. Who bears primary responsibility for product safety? The manufacturer or the consumer? Which value should govern our thinking on product safety: "Let the buyer beware" or "Let the seller beware?"

5. While we can assign values to particular products (we price them), can we price human life? Why or why not? As a matter of actual practice, in our everyday decisions and actions, *do* we place a value on human life?

6. Do you think that a political solution (government regulation) is the best solution to the ethical problem of people being harmed by dangerous products?

SUGGESTIONS FOR FURTHER READING

Dardis, Rachel and Claudia Zent. "The Economics of the Pinto Recall." *Journal of Consumer Affairs* 16(2) (Winter 1982).

Dowie, Mark. "Pinto Madness." *Mother Jones* (September/October 1977).

Fried, Charles. *An Anatomy of Values.* Cambridge: Harvard University Press, 1970.

Hoffman, W. Michael. "The Ford Pinto." In Thomas Donaldson and Al Gini, eds., *Case Studies in Business Ethics.* Englewood Cliffs, NJ: Prentice Hall, 1993.

Stokey, Edith and Richard Zeckhauser, *A Primer for Policy Analysis.* New York: W.W. Norton & Company, Inc., 1978.

ENDNOTES

1. http://www.e-businessethics.com/firestone.htm

2. C. Carter, "Family Sues Firestone, Ford over Fatal Accident," *SF Gate News* (February 23, 2001). http://www.sfgate.com/cgi-bin/article.cgi?file=/news/archive/2001/02/23/state2121EST0239.DTL.

3. "Second National Advertising Campaign Featuring A Safety Message from Ford CEO Jac Nasser Airs on Network Television," http://media.ford.com/article_display.cfm?article_id=5764.

4. H.R. 5164, Pub. L. 106-414, 114 Stat. 1800. See also, House Report No. 106-

954, 106th Cong., 2nd Sess. (2000) (Commerce Committee).

5. "Damaging Documents: Firestone Knew of Defective Tires Months Before Recall," ABCNews, September 8, 2000, http://abcnews.go.com/sections/us/ DailyNews/tiresPM000908.html.

6. "Ford, Firestone, and the Rolling Explorer," in Marianne M. Jennings, *Business Ethics*, 4th ed. (Mason, OH: Thomson Southwestern, 2003): pp. 352–357.

7. Unless otherwise indicated, information about this case is taken from W. Michael Hoffman, "The Ford Pinto," in Thomas Donaldson and Al Gini, eds., *Case Studies in Business Ethics* (Englewood Cliffs, NJ: Prentice Hall, 1993): pp. 218-27; and *State of Indiana v. Ford Motor Company*, U.S. District Court, South Bend, Indiana (January 15, 1980).

8. Tom Nicholson and William D. Marbach, "A Dead Stop in the Ford Pinto Trial," *Newsweek* (February 24, 1980): p. 65.

9. "Autopsies Confirm Burns Caused Pinto Crash Deaths," *New York Times* (December 1, 1978): p. 20.

10. William D. Marbach, "Ford Goes to Trial," *Newsweek* (January 7, 1980): p. 70.

11. Nicholson and Marbach, op. cit., p. 66.

12. Reginald Stuart, "Ford Auto Company Cleared in 3 Deaths," *The New York Times* (March 14, 1980): p. A1.

13. Mark Dowie, "Pinto Madness," *Mother Jones* (September/October 1977): p. 18.

14. *State of Indiana v. Ford Motor Company*, op. cit., p. 84.

15. Dowie, op. cit., p. 18.

16. "Ford Ignored Pinto Fire Peril, Secret Memos Show," *Chicago Tribune* (October 13, 1979): Sec. 2, p. 12.

17. Dowie, op. cit., p. 23.

18. The description that follows draws on Edith Stokey and Richard Zeckhauser, *A Primer for Policy Analysis* (New York: W.W. Norton & Company, Inc., 1978): p. 136.

19. Dowie, op. cit., pp. 24, 28.

20. Stokey and Zeckhauser, op. cit., p. 135.

21. Cited in Dowie, op. cit., p. 28.

22. For a discussion of identifiable versus statistical lives in policy decisions, see Charles Fried, *An Anatomy of Values* (Cambridge: Harvard University Press, 1970): pp. 207–236.

23. Dowie, op. cit., p. 28.

24. "Observations on Fire in Automobile Accidents," Cornell Aeronautical Laboratory, Inc. (February 1965).

25. Ford Motor Company news release (Dearborn, Michigan: Ford Motor Company, September 26, 1977): p. 1.

26. Rachel Dardis and Claudia Zent, "The Economics of the Pinto Recall," *Journal of Consumer Affairs* (16 (2), Winter 1982): p. 262.

27. "Ford Orders Recall of 1.5 Million Pintos for Safety Changes," *New York Times* (June 10, 1978): p. 1.

28. Stuart, "Ford Auto Company Cleared," op. cit., p. D12.

29. Richard A. Epstein, "Is Pinto a Criminal?" *Regulation* (March/April 1980): pp. 16–17.

30. Stuart, "Ford Auto Company Cleared," op. cit., p. D12.

31. Reginald Stuart, "Ford Won in Pinto Case, but the Memory Will Linger On," *The New York Times* (March 16, 1980): Sec. 4, p. 20.

32. See for example, Andrew W. Singer "Pinto Redux?" from *Ethikos* 6(4) (January/February 1993): 1–3, 6. This uses the saga of the Ford Pinto as a benchmark for assessing a more current controversy about the safety of General Motors Corporation's pickup trucks.

6

Who Should
Clean Up the Mess?

Love Canal
and Corporate Responsibility
for Old Pollution

Questions to Keep in Mind

1. How do we assess blame, or accountability for action, in general? How do we assess blame for unforeseen events in particular? What factors are most important for assigning blame for Love Canal?

2. What is risk? What kinds of risk are "acceptable," and why? How did the homeowners see their risk? How far should the government protect us against risk?

3. What was the role of the mass media in all of the events of Love Canal? Can we make sense of general duties owed to the society by the press? Were they fulfilled or breached in this case?

4. On July 1, 2002, President George W. Bush announced that funding for the cleanup of toxic sites like Love Canal would be drastically cut. What had the "Superfund" accomplished in its history (which dates from the events described in this chapter)?

LOVE CANAL, THE EVENT:
A CHRONOLOGY[1]

May 1892: William T. Love plans to build a model industrial city. Since the technology of the time allows only for transmission of power by direct current, economical only over short distances, the Niagara Falls region, rich in hydroelectric power, is ideal. He starts to dig one of several planned canals, then is stymied by recession and the development of alternating current (1894). Love goes bankrupt.

April 1942: Hooker Chemical acquires the old canal, gets the necessary permits, and in 1947 starts dumping wastes (ultimately 21,800 tons) into the canal. So do several federal agencies, especially the army. Clay lining makes the canal an ideal spot for getting rid of toxic wastes—one where human beings will never be exposed.

1951: Housing development begins near canal.

April 1953: Hooker closes the dump and seals it with a clay cap. With an increase in population of young families in Niagara Falls in the 1950s, the board of education needs more land for schools. It asks Hooker Chemical to release the Love Canal area, which, under threat of seizure, it does, for a sum of $1.

November 1957: Public hearings on use of ceded land. Hooker issues warnings not to cut into the clay cap because of danger from toxic wastes.

June 1958: By this time roads and sewers are cut through and homes have been built in the Canal area. Children are burned after chemical exposure, probably from lindane. Hooker Chemical reissues warnings about waste.

1971–1977: Presence of chemicals in basements and on grounds of school noted occasionally.

April 1978: New York State orders access to the area restricted; buried chemicals to be removed.

June 1978: After two years of occasional articles on the fears and odors of Love Canal, Michael Brown of the *Niagara Gazette* begins chronicles of ill individuals who attribute their ills to Love Canal exposures; national media attention follows.

August 1978: New York State commissioner of health declares health emergency at Love Canal, orders evacuation of some twenty families. Governor Hugh Carey announces that state will fund relocation of 236 families. Love

Canal Homeowners Association formed. Soon thereafter, President Jimmy Carter declares Love Canal a disaster area.

February 1979: Dr. Beverly Paigen of Roswell Park Memorial Institute in Buffalo urges further evacuations based on in-depth study of several families living near the pollutants. In these families, a high incidence of hysterectomies, asthma, and mental instability is found.

November 1979: Federal report indicates that odds of residents contracting cancer "are as high as 1 in 10."

December 1979: Justice Department files a $124.5 million lawsuit against Hooker.

May 15, 1980: Dr. Dante Picciano, on commission from the Environmental Protection Agency, finds an elevated level of chromosome damage among families in the Love Canal area. This report is leaked to the media on May 17.

May 19, 1980: Dr. Steven Barron, on commission from the EPA, finds some degree of peripheral nerve damage to Love Canal residents. Love Canal residents mob streets, seize two EPA inspectors hostage. Love Canal Homeowners Association President Lois Gibbs telephones White House to describe the situation.

May 21, 1980: President Carter declares State of Emergency at Love Canal. At an ultimate cost of about $30 million, 2,500 more residents to be permanently relocated.

June 1982: First of 227 houses is demolished.

July 1982: Attorney General Robert Abrams says two studies show levels of dioxin in homes next to the canal were "among the highest ever found in the human environment."

March 1983: The EPA declares that homes a block and a half or more away from the canal are safe enough to live in; members of the panel originating the report differ on the conclusions.

May 1983: Findings of chromosome damage contradicted.

September 1983: EPA finds new leaks of chemicals.

October 1983: The lawsuit that had been brought by Love Canal residents against Occidental Petroleum (the chemicals company that had acquired Hooker Chemical), the city, the county, and the Board of Education is settled for $20 million.

December 1984: A new clay cap is installed over the canal.

February 1985: Former residents receive settlement shares averaging $14,000 each.

January 1986: The cleaning of the sewer system begins.

October 1987: EPA decides to burn all dioxin-contaminated soil taken from the area.

February 1988: Judge John Curtin of Federal District Court finds Occidental liable for the cost of the clean-up, estimated at $250 million.

INTRODUCTION

For most Americans the words "Love Canal" represent the emerging awareness that a price tag is attached to the conveniences provided by the chemical technology of the twentieth century. Love Canal was the warning trickle that became a flood of chemical stews in open pits, rusting steel drums leaking toxins, dirt roads sprayed with PCB-laden oil, radioactive and chemical contamination at nuclear weapons facilities, PCB-contaminated fish in the Hudson River, Vietnam veterans contaminated by Agent Orange, and, finally, an explosion of popular protest, manifest in legislation (CERCLA, or SUPERFUND) and the self-protective fear of local pollution that we came to call NIMBY—"Not In My Back Yard."

After the first evacuation in 1978, Love Canal disappeared (temporarily) from the news—but not before entering our vocabularies as a universal designator of a new kind of evil. An article in *Time* more than a decade later, for instance, quotes the director of a Mexican research facility, speaking about mostly U.S.–owned industries on the Mexican border, "These are all Love Canals in the making."[2] In a 1990 *Newsweek* article, Anne Underwood captured the significance of the events at the Canal:

> Love Canal became a national story, a byword, because it radicalized apparently ordinary people. Love Canal severed the bond between citizens and their city, their state, and their country. The battle . . . was fought in public, through protest marches and press releases, because the public, not the state, was at risk.[3]

From another perspective, emerging in sharper focus in retrospect, Love Canal has another significance. As Elizabeth Whelan put it,

> Love Canal . . . serves well as the focal point for an exposé of the questionable, indeed, immoral and dishonest tactics of those individuals who term themselves "environmentalists" but who are in fact mostly a group of anticorporation, antitechnology advocates. Love Canal is a classic story of

half truths, distorted historical facts, unprecedented media exaggeration, and misguided government intervention, all of which caused substantially more human upset and misery than did even the most toxic of Hooker's chemicals.[4]

From either perspective, Love Canal is a symbol, a watershed, an icon—of something. What do Americans do with icons? They memorialize them. By the beginning of 2001, Love Canal Museum was in the works, prepared to entertain up to 200,000 tourists a year with an account and guided tour through the once-toxic area.[5] (When last heard from, the museum had not been faring well—typical of Niagara Falls ventures.)[6]

The two perspectives are clearly in conflict, but are not necessarily contradictory. Both may be true and valuable. Public ethics is often best understood as the skill of making judgments without assigning blame. Both perspectives should be more comprehensible at the end of our inquiry than they are at this point.

I. A BRAVE HISTORY, A SHATTERING REVELATION

1. Background

Petroleum was discovered in 1859. Soon after it was discovered, it was found that petroleum could be separated by a distillation process (cracking) into various components, such as gasoline, kerosene, and other hydrocarbons. Kerosene soon replaced whale oil as fuel for lanterns. The other hydrocarbons included the olefins[7] such as ethylene (CH_2CH_2), which became the feedstock for petrochemicals—from plastics to pesticides, synthetic drugs to synthetic fibers. In 1927 it was discovered that a combination of ethylene and benzene produced another basic petrochemical, styrene. By 1937, the chemistry of connecting these individual basic molecules to each other, in very long chains, was worked out, and polymerization was born, bringing with it polyethylene, polystyrene, polyvinylchloride, and thousands of new solvents, films, fibers, plastic, adhesives, and synthetic rubber products.

Petrochemicals began to dominate the chemical industry by in 1920, but it was World War II that brought them into prominence. With natural rubber and silk no longer available, the Allies turned to the chemical industry for synthetic rubber and nylon to provide tires and parachutes. To kill the anopheles mosquitoes that carried the malaria parasite, they rediscovered the chlorinated hydrocarbon, dichloro-diphenyl-trichloroethane (DDT), which had been gathering dust on an English chemist's shelf. In the thirty years following World War II, the petrochemical industry expanded by a factor of 60; 95 percent of organic chemicals are petrochemicals.

The problem is that many of the petrochemicals are suspected to be toxic. By the usual methods we employ to determine toxicity of various kinds, many are carcinogens; that is, substances associated with the onset of cancer. Others seem to do damage to the nervous system, the liver, or other human systems. Pesticides are clearly toxic and are designed to be so. No surprise, chemicals that are designed to kill may well kill species other than the targeted species. The story of DDT's harmful effects on wild birds, especially raptors, is well known[8] and parallels the stories of many other pesticides. (It is estimated that hundreds of thousands of pesticide poisonings occur each year, most of them to agricultural workers in the Third World.[9]) But pesticides are only a small portion of the synthetic chemicals produced by the industry—there are some 70,000 chemicals used every day, with up to 1,000 new ones added to the environment each year.

Once these chemicals, or those used in their production, are discarded, a "toxic waste" site is born. ("Toxic" because data, not usually data on human beings, suggests that some components present harm those exposed to them.) Unfortunately, hard scientific data on the vast majority of petrochemicals is lacking. According to Sandra Postel, the National Research Council "estimates that no information on toxic effects is available for 79 percent of the more than 48,500 chemicals listed in EPA's inventory of toxic substances."[10] In 546 toxic waste dumps there are an estimated 229 chemicals, but only 25 chemicals comprise two-thirds of the identified toxic waste "occurrences" (incidents in which toxic chemicals are brought to public notice by reason of some cause for alarm).[11] Of these, eleven are chlorinated hydrocarbons, accepted as toxic; four are hydrocarbons, many of which are toxic; and seven are heavy metals (lead, cadmium, mercury), which are naturally occurring (as opposed to synthetic petrochemicals), but nevertheless generally toxic. We do not know what toxicity is created when these chemicals are mixed together, as in a dump.

In the midst of this toxic stew, it should be noted that ". . . epidemiological studies have shown very little evidence of a hazard to human health resulting from exposures to chemical disposal sites." The fear that drives people from their homes is primarily fear of the unknown: We simply have no data on delayed effects of exposure to these chemicals.[12] As for that, the verdict on many aspects of the toxic waste dilemma is still wanting, as we shall see.

2. The Event

There is no typical hazardous waste site. At one point, 20,000 sites were addressed by the EPA as part of the "Superfund" legislation,[13] but they varied tremendously in geological, hydrological, ecological, physical, and chemical characteristics. There is not even an accepted definition of a hazardous waste site. The problem is too new, or rather, too recently recognized, to have generated the research that will allow us to categorize the problem; the "failure of U.S. society to assess and manage the issue of hazardous waste"[14] is shown first and foremost in the failure to engage in basic research on site characteristics.

The sixteen-acre Love Canal site is located in Niagara Falls, New York. In 1892 William T. Love began the development of an industrial site along the canal that connected the Niagara River to Lake Ontario. Two years later, the project was dropped for lack of interest. The Hooker Chemical Company took over the isolated, abandoned canal in 1947, having received permission in 1942 to use it. The company had complied with what few requirements were necessary for waste disposal at that time. The canal bottom consisted of a soil containing clay. Among natural soils, solid clay is the preferred liner for waste sites, because it is virtually impermeable to water. (Because some chemicals will diffuse through it—a three-foot clay barrier will leak mobile chemicals in five years—most modern sites use a mixture of clay and synthetic materials.) Was this natural liner cracked and permeable? Hooker Chemical certainly did not think so at the time the dumping began; but it became an issue in the legal arguments when the wrangling began. We'll get to that later. By 1952 the company had dumped 21,800 tons of chemical wastes into the site. Hooker was not the only source of chemicals in that dumpsite, by the way; several federal agencies, especially the army, arranged with Hooker to dump residues of wartime production in the same spot. Meanwhile, residential building had begun nearby, as the city of Niagara Falls expanded outward. In 1953, the canal could accept no more waste, so the company covered it, again, as they thought, with a cap of solid clay.

Soon afterwards, an expanding population required more schools in the area, so the company sold the site (reluctantly, and under threat of condemnation) to the Niagara Falls Board of Education for $1. Apparently at that time the school board wanted the site only for a playground, and that was fine with Hooker. They made sure to insert into the deed (dated April 28, 1953), a strong disclaimer regarding any injury to come from those wastes:

> Prior to the delivery of this instrument of conveyance, the grantee herein has been advised by the grantor that the premises above described have been filled, in whole or in part, to the present grade level thereof with waste products resulting from the manufacturing of chemicals by the grantor at its plant in the City of Niagara Falls, New York, and the grantee assumes all risk and liability incident to the use thereof. It is therefore understood and agreed that, *as a part of the consideration for this conveyance and as a condition thereof,* no claim, suit, action or demand of any nature whatsoever shall ever be made by the grantee, its successors or assigns, against the grantor, its successors or assigns, for injury to a person or persons, including death resulting therefrom, or loss of or damage to property caused by, in connection with or by reason of the presence of said industrial wastes. It is further agreed as a condition hereof that each subsequent conveyance of the aforesaid lands shall be made subject to the foregoing provisions and conditions.[15]

There matters stood for four years; then the school board decided to build on part of the site and sell the rest. Hooker showed up at the hearings; company officials were insistent that hazardous wastes were under that ground, and issued dire warnings about what might happen if that clay cap were pierced. The minutes of the school board's meeting on November 7, 1957, indicate that A. W. Chambers of Hooker was present at the meeting, specifically warning about the dangers of those buried chemicals should the site be disturbed. He conceded that the company had no further control over the use of the property, but urged strongly that none of that land be sold or used for building houses or other structures.

When the school board eventually decided to build an elementary school on the site, then, Hooker had informed the board that chemicals were buried there; it had not, however, told them what the chemicals were, or to what extent they were toxic; nor did it tell them what quantity of chemicals were buried there.[16] It is not clear whether Hooker officials knew any of those items of information. A later review of the situation revealed quite an assemblage:

> What lay beneath the surface was 43.6 million pounds of 82 different chemical substances: oil, solvents and other manufacturing residues. The mixture included benzene, a chemical known to cause leukemia and anemia; chloroform, a carcinogen that affects the nervous, respiratory and gastrointestinal systems; lindane, which causes convulsions and extra production of white blood cells; trichloroethylene, a carcinogen that also attacks the nervous system, the genes and the liver. . . . The list of chemicals buried in the Love Canal seems endless, and the accompanying list of their acute and chronic effects on human beings reads like an encyclopedia of medical illness and abnormality.[17]

Trouble could be expected. An elementary school was built and house lots were sold. As early as 1958 children were burned from playing in the dump, probably from the pesticide lindane, some 5,000 tons of which Hooker had buried at the site and which surfaced in a cake-like form.[18]

3. Trouble Materializes

In 1977, chemicals started to appear in the basements of nearby houses after heavy rains, leaching out of their graves like ghosts on Halloween. Michael Brown, a reporter for the *Niagara Gazette* wrote of resident complaints of dizziness, respiratory problems, a chemical stench, breast cancer, and pets losing their fur.[19] In 1978, national publicity prompted both state and federal action.

Two hundred chemicals were identified on the grounds around the school built over Hooker's protests. Among them, benzene, a known carcinogen, was prominent, and is credited for initiating government action. New York State began studies of the site, supplementing the anecdotal newspaper reports of the time. A panic atmosphere, however, is not ideal for scientific studies. Before any real study began, Robert Whalan, New York State Commissioner of Health, declared an emergency and moved to evacuate about twenty families. On August 9, 1978, New York Governor Hugh Carey visited the site and declared that all 236 families living along the streets affected would be permanently relocated, at state expense. (At that time a new clay cap was placed over the old Canal area.) As residents of the houses just beyond those purchased and evacuated by the state began to find more and more ailments among them,

Dr. Beverly Paigen, a biologist with Roswell Park Memorial Institute in Buffalo, came out with her own study of a few families and their ailments. Her evidence was largely anecdotal, but triggered enough interest to bring the Environmental Protection Agency into the case.

Early in 1980 the EPA commissioned a study by Dr. Dante Picciano on chromosome damage in the area. The study claimed to find elevated damage. Hard on the heels of this study came another, by Dr. Steven Barron, on nerve damage among inhabitants of the Love Canal area; he also claimed to find elevated levels. Coming at a time of tension as they did, these two reports incited a full-scale riot, including the taking of two EPA officials hostage by the local Homeowners Association. Within days, President Jimmy Carter declared a State of Emergency at Love Canal, announcing the relocation of another 2,500 residents—first temporarily, at a cost of $3 million to $5 million, then permanently, at a cost of $30 million.

Interpretations of these events vary. On the one hand, we can see an appropriate response, possibly a warm-up for more serious things, in the way public, press, and government worked together to address a situation that was certainly perceived to be dangerous. Between 1978 and 1980 federal, state, and local authorities, goaded by the press and encouraged, to say the least, by local voluntary organizations, worked with rare cooperation to get the people out of danger. They had moved quickly and thoroughly: New York State closed the school and started to evacuate the 236 families who lived next to the canal; President Jimmy Carter declared Love Canal a disaster area, which provided funds for additional evacuations in 1980. New York State had capped the canal with clay and installed a drainage system that pumped any leaking material to a new treatment plant, started demolishing the most contaminated houses, and started buying up the others that had been abandoned. In 1982 and 1983 the houses, the school, the parking lot, and the original playground were all demolished. By 1990, everything west of the street that backed up to the canal, for one-quarter mile, had been buried and fenced off, and the State owned 789 single-family homes. The total clean-up costs at that point were estimated at $250 million.

On the other hand, there may have been no danger. None of these studies— not Beverly Paigen's anecdotal study of epilepsy, mental illness, and reproductive difficulties (including miscarriages) in a few families; not Dante Picciano's studies, which lacked controls; nor Steven Barron's study, which was merely a pilot study but was leaked when the others became public—has withstood scientific scrutiny. A word about scientific testing is in order.

4. The Chemicals, the Illnesses, the Tests

Determining toxicity is difficult and expensive, and unless we start experimenting on humans, the results will always be controversial. The most common technique is animal testing, although some techniques use bacteria and other organisms or tissues. The smaller the population tested, and the less time taken to reach significant results, the less expensive the test, so these tests typically are conducted on animals—frequently white mice bred for genetic sameness—that are exposed to a much larger quantity of the chemical, over a much shorter period of time, than any human population ever would be.

On the basis of such testing, we are prepared to say that many of the substances found at the Love Canal site—including benzene, dioxin, toluene, lindane, PCBs, chloroform, trichlorethylene, trichlorobenzene, and heavy metals—are certainly capable of causing harm. Thirteen are known carcinogens. With the exception of heavy metals, most of the chemicals found there would be liquid at room temperature and soluble in water, increasing the chances of migration away from the site. Additionally, chlorinated hydrocarbons are denser than water and therefore would sink, migrating toward ground water.

It is very hard to prove cause and effect in these cases—to prove that exposure to a given chemical at a given time causes a specific symptom. In order to determine that, it would be necessary to know the quantity of the chemical to which the sufferer was exposed and the period of time of exposure, for each individual within the exposed population. Additionally, findings should be repeated in a number of exposed individuals, other causative factors must be ruled out, and the cause and effect should make physiological sense. There were 200 chemicals at Love Canal and an exposed population that occupied some 800 homes. Separating each chemical and symptom from others appears to be a monumental task; given the number of chemicals, synergistic and antagonistic reactions cannot be ruled out. There has never been a comprehensive study done on the health effects purported to have resulted from chemical exposure at Love Canal. And of the less-than-comprehensive studies that have been done, the ones that tried to connect the chemicals to the symptoms (those mentioned above) have, as above, not been accepted by the scientific community.

Many of the early accounts, the accounts that drew the attention of the media to Love Canal, were informal surveys done by the residents themselves. The state and federal government studies mentioned above were among the few governmental studies done. As noted above, Paigen's results were anecdotal and impossible to interpret statistically; Picciano's, on chromosomal damage, were uncontrolled. A group of seventeen scientists from the Centers for Disease Control, Brookhaven National Laboratory, and Oak Ridge National Laboratory attempted a follow-up study on chromosome damage in 1983 and found that, if anything, the chromosomes of Love Canal residents were healthier than the norm.[20] As for the miscarriages, those results were taken up specifically by Dr. Nicholas Vianna of the New York State Department of Health:

> Efforts to establish a correlation between adverse pregnancy outcomes and evidence of chemical exposure have proven negative. Comprehensive studies of three households with unusually adverse reproductive histories did not produce evidence of unusual risk of chemical exposure....We have not yet been able to correlate the geographic distribution of adverse

pregnancy outcomes with chemical evidence of exposure. At present, there is no direct evidence of a cause–effect relationship with chemicals from the canal.[21]

Meanwhile anecdotal evidence continued to accumulate, including stories of seizures, learning problems, eye and skin irritations, incontinence, abdominal pains, lung cancer, non-Hodgkins lymphoma, and leukemia. In children, birth defects, low birth weight, and hyperactivity were noted. One child born of parents in the area was deaf, had a cleft palate, deformed ears, a hole in the heart, and impaired learning abilities.

Anecdotal evidence, as above, carries little weight in scientific circles. Even if it could be shown that the incidence of such ailments is statistically higher in the Love Canal area than elsewhere, and it has not been, no connection to exposure to chemicals could be shown. But the residents, as may be imagined, dismiss all denials of that type as politically motivated (like the Tobacco Institute's disclaimers on the link between smoking and cancer), and continue to insist that the New York State Department of Health (DOH) underestimated the health effects of the event. The DOH scientists, for their part, believe that the health effects were *over*estimated by unqualified independent investigators, and that the second evacuation in 1980 was unnecessary. There seems to be general agreement that the psychological toll on the residents has been immense; for them, any slight physical symptom becomes a cause for serious concern and that is not a pleasant way to live.

5. Legislation

No one disputes that the publicity given to the symptoms reported by the Love Canal residents and to the eventual abandonment of the area was the driving force behind Congress' enactment of the Comprehensive Environmental Response, Compensation and Liability Act (CERCLA, or "Superfund"), designed to assess liability for hazardous waste sites and to clean them up. By this act the EPA is empowered to sue the owner, or the dumper, for the clean-up costs; if the site is significant, the responsibility for payment is usually settled in court. (The other piece of legislation that controls hazardous waste is the Resource Conservation and Recovery Act [RCRA, 1976, 1984] which requires dumpers to obtain permits and describe how the material is to be treated. It also requires "cradle to grave" reporting of waste, from origin to final disposal. This requirement is generally acknowledged to be unenforceable, given the estimated 750,000 hazardous waste producers and 15,000 hazardous waste carriers.) Is stimulating the EPA's mandate *why* the publicity happened?

The actions taken by the EPA in this case are subject to two readings: On the one hand, the EPA is charged with protecting the public from environmental dangers; when evidence came to their attention that an environmental hazard existed at Love Canal in Niagara Falls, New York, it acted appropriately in commissioning studies and in cooperating with state and local agencies in acting on the results of those studies. To be sure, not all the data was in when they acted, and scientific nitpickers may continue to find flaws in the research designs. However, given that lives were apparently in danger, the results, if only suggestive, were adequate basis for taking appropriate action.

On the other hand, any responsible public agency should have thought long and hard about the "panic factor" in such situations. Any such action is certain to cause fear and injury (if only to property values); why would the EPA gamble on uncertain results? The answer, suggests Hank Cox in *Regulatory Action Network*

> may lie in EPA's awareness of the growing tide of public opinion opposed to excessive regulation and the agency's desire to deflect political pressure for reform. At the same time it was creating the Love Canal panic, the EPA came out with another report showing that there were an estimated 50,666 hazardous waste sites similar to that in Love Canal around the country, thereby laying the groundwork for [the creation of] a "superfund" to clean up this alleged danger to the American people.[22]

"Were EPA's actions at Love Canal self-serving, simply to stimulate more federal laws, activities, and, most important, budgetary revenues for itself?" wonders Elizabeth Whelan.[23] Superfund was a major triumph for an agency worried about its legitimacy. We tend to think of individuals as self-interested and corporations as profit-oriented, but there is a strong sense in which government agencies can be self-interested in much the same way that private parties can be. In government as in business, success is measured not simply by salary or prominence in the press, but also by extent of office space, numbers of secretaries, computers, rugs on the floors, number of staff—in short, by total budget. An agency will stay in business only as long as it finds work to do, dragons to slay, and maidens to save. A finding that the evil that they are set up to fight is really minimal right now will lead straight to budget cuts and layoffs. The detection of violation is in the hands of those who will prosper if there are violations and who will be cut from the budget if there are none. There is a worrisome bias built into the system: The regulators are acting as judges in their own cause.

6. Liability

Of course there were and are lawsuits against the company involved in Love Canal. Let's review what a lawsuit would have to establish. Whether brought by public or private party, the kind of negligence that will be alleged requires the establishment of four points: (1) that there was injury (someone got hurt—the plaintiff, generally); (2) that the defendant was under a duty to the plaintiff, which preexisted the injury—either under existing law governing conduct or under the common law duty to exercise "due care" in all actions; (3) that the defendant breached that duty by some act or omission, which act or omission figured in the injury; and (4) that indeed, that act or omission was the proximate (nearest, most immediate) cause of the injury. Accordingly, any defense against charges of negligence will argue that there was no injury; or that no duty existed between defendant and plaintiff; or that if there was a duty, then there was no breach (i.e., that defendant obeyed the law, was within his rights, and exercised due care in what he did); or finally, that so many other causative factors are present that we could not possibly sort out the defendant's contribution from all the others.

Occidental Chemical, which had bought out Hooker in 1968, argued all of those things, and very cogently. It continued to claim that there were no documented health effects attributable to the leakage of chemicals from Love Canal, beyond the dogs with chemical burns discovered in 1977. Psychological distress counts as an injury, of course—but again, only if the company was the proximate cause of the psychological distress, and the company could argue convincingly that the publicity, not the chemicals, caused that distress. In any case, the situation worsened. Hooker was under no duty of any kind to anyone regarding that site, after the sale (under compulsion of condemnation) of the site to the City of Niagara Falls, especially given the disclaimers in the deed. It is not clear what obligation companies have to people in general regarding the safe disposal of toxic wastes. That obligation is generally determined by the law at the time the wastes are dumped (the 1940s, in this case), added to the general duty of due care, which Occidental claimed was satisfied by the choice of an impermeable clay receptacle and the placement of an impermeable clay cap when the dump was full. The landfill was perfectly secure when they sold it, and they were demonstrating good corporate citizenship by turning it over to the city without a fight and by warning the city's officials about the toxic chemicals buried there. And finally, the act that disseminated the chemicals was the piercing of that clay cap when the school and the neighboring houses were built. When that was done, there was no way to keep water from seeping into the dump. Given that the floor of the canal was impermeable clay, there was no way for it to get out except by overflowing the top—carrying all manner of dissolved chemicals with it, just as Hooker had warned at the time of the sale. Surely, the company argued, whatever happened (and it is not clear that very much did, beyond a feeding frenzy for the press), the company is not to blame for it.

The courts have not seen things Occidental's way. Companies may settle civil lawsuits for many reasons, of course, but when Occidental settled a $20 million suit brought by the residents in 1983 (disbursing payments from $2,000 to $400,000), they must have seen a court decision going against them.[24] And in February 1988, Federal District Court Judge John T. Curtin found Occidental liable under CERCLA for all clean-up and resettlement costs, about $250 million.[25] Encouraged by that result, the State of New York sued Occidental in the fall of 1990, asking another $250 million in punitive damages for "recklessly disregarding public health." The suit, later settled out of court, was brought despite the clause in the deed from Hooker to the Board of Education that protected Hooker from liability; such clauses are not binding on third parties, like New York State.

The State brought new claims to this trial. In particular, it claimed that the landfill was never secure: That the bottom is actually cracked and permeable, that sandy loam replaces clay half way up the sides, and that the covering was nothing like impermeable clay. Hooker personnel have testified that they knew the cover was not secure, and that they found the situation "scary," given the chemicals stored there.[26] It was now claimed the chemicals would have leaked even if the new construction had not opened the top, and, more to the point, Hooker knew all about it: They saw trouble coming, and were very glad to get rid of the property and all liability for it as soon as the opportunity arose.[27] The State claimed to be in possession of internal memos of Hooker Chemical that establish this knowledge.

The State is not trying to establish that specific disease was caused in specific individuals by the Love Canal event, because of the difficulty of proof, especially since so many symptoms turn up years after exposure to the chemical. (In other words, there was no attempt to prove "proximate cause" for any given injury.) But the state had extensive evidence from other research of injury caused to organic systems, especially the nervous system, by the chemicals found in Love Canal, and argues that the mere creation of a risk is a punishable action. The purpose of the suit was apparently twofold: to deter future reckless corporate behavior and to use the fine for the creation of an Environmental Remediation Fund.

7. Resettlement

After the Canal was resealed in 1978, New York State conducted a five-year study to determine the potential for resettlement of adjacent areas. Soil, air, and water samples—2,300—were analyzed for contamination and compared to control samples from comparable areas in Niagara Falls. This testing, incidentally, cost New York State $100 million, bringing to $375 million the amount spent on the event by the state.

As a result of that testing, Dr. David Axelrod, the New York State Health Commissioner, announced in September 1988 that 220 houses were safe enough to be reoccupied, whereas 250 were not habitable. The Love Canal Area Revitalization Agency (LCARA), a state agency which by that time owned some 400 houses, began to develop a land use plan and to renovate the houses, which were to be sold for between $35,000 and $100,000. The cleanup and containment would continue while the sale was going on. The announcement drew sharp reactions immediately, from "No way!" to interest from bargain hunters. But six months later soil samples from neighboring control areas were found to be contaminated with toluene and dichlorobenzene, which seemed to negate the value of the comparison. The sale had to be delayed. "The real sad message here," commented Peter Slocum of the state health department, "is that there might be no place in Niagara Falls that is not within spitting distance of chemical waste."[28]

The next year the decision was reversed again. In May of 1990, William K. Reilly, Administrator of the EPA reassessed the studies and found that the original area was safe; there had been, after all, only one contaminated sample, and that one did not originate in Love Canal. Reaction was mixed: The Mayor of

Niagara Falls and Chairman of LCARA, predictably, insisted that the houses were perfectly safe; the Natural Resources Defense Council, an advocacy group, predictably, protested that the "EPA has given a narrow, legalistic reading" of the data, and that "Love Canal is a ticking time bomb." Given that there are more than 200 toxic waste sites within 50 miles of Love Canal, 23 of which were leaking, another activist complained that comparing soil around Love Canal to soil elsewhere in the area is like "comparing rotten oranges to rotten oranges."[29]

Over the protests of six environmental groups, the LCARA went forward with its plan to sell 70 houses in the summer of 1990, the first 10 to be offered in August. More than 200 people were willing to accept the risk (and stigma) of a house at Love Canal and applied for homes selling between $30,000 and $80,000, about 20 percent below the local current market price. For many of the prospective buyers, generally working class, this sale might be their best or only chance to own their own homes. Besides, as they felt, the hazard may have been overrated in the first place, and if the government says it is safe to move in, that's probably the best guarantee they'll get. The advocacy groups' plea for an injunction was denied by the state court.

II. CONCLUDING REFLECTION

The final phase of the Love Canal clean-up was supposed to occur over a five-year period, while the rehabilitated houses continue to be reoccupied. An incinerator was built to burn the 35,000 cubic yards of dioxin-contaminated soil and sediment that resulted from earlier dredging of creeks and sewers. The residual ash was buried in a newly designed landfill. The cost was in the neighborhood of $30 million, in addition to the amount already spent and the cost of relocating 1,000 families.[30]

Niagara Falls has not fared well in the meantime. The early 1990s saw major entertainment ventures proposed and fail for lack of funding, visionary leadership, honest management, or all three. A series of master plans—the latest relying on state authorization for casino gambling that never came—broke the surface of the waters and disappeared during the last years of the twentieth century, leaving only cynicism and disappointment behind. The last project, now apparently in its death throes, was the Love Canal Museum mentioned at the beginning of the chapter. Nothing yet has worked.[31]

Yet the city has earned its place in history. The influence of the Love Canal story has been considerable. It is responsible for the emergence of popular awareness of the threat of toxic chemicals, the consequent Superfund legislation, and the strengthening of the Resource Conservation and Recovery Act. With that awareness came also increased fear, some justified and much not, that led to the syndrome known as NIMBY—"not in my back yard." It has become enormously difficult to find an acceptable place to dump toxic wastes.

As a result, we are resorting to increasingly expensive means of disposing of the stuff—a ton of hazardous waste that had cost of $10 to dispose of before Love Canal cost $500 by 1988.[32] As the expense rose, so did the incidence of illegal dumping, which has reached scandalous proportions in some parts of the country.

Ironically, while hazardous wastes are among the environmental issues that have "aroused high emotions, generated reams of reports and prodded Congress to spend billions of dollars . . . scientists rate them at near the bottom of a broad array of environmental threats."[33] The acute health threat posed by hazardous wastes is uncertain, limited, possibly inflated and generally short-lived, compared, for instance, to ozone depletion. We *still* have no more useful data than we did years ago on how, or whether, small amounts of "toxic" chemicals cause damage to human health. The National Research Council issued a report on October 21, 1991, arguing that the national effort to clean up toxic waste was "hampered by its inability to tell the difference between dumps posing a real threat to human health and those that do not,"[34] and we know precious little more today. Cleanup agencies do not know whether or not the dumps are dangerous because they do not know whether the chemicals are dangerous:

> Almost nothing is known about the effects on human health of most chemicals found in hazardous waste sites, the study said. Most people exposed to hazardous waste at those sites come in contact with minute amounts of chemicals, but very little is known about how they are affected, it continued. Another gap in the Government's data is that scientists have virtually no idea of the risks posed by two or more chemicals that react in a waste site to form another toxic compound.[35]

Yet clearly exposure to some (most?) chemicals, in high enough amount, causes health problems. The danger must be taken seriously, at some level. If there is danger at all, the greatest long-term threat posed by the wastes may be their migration to ground water, because the seepage will move as a unit, very slowly, and the chemicals are very long-lived and hard to detect, making cleanup very difficult.[36]

The hope that strict regulation would reduce the amount of hazardous waste has not been realized.[37] Figures on waste disposal are hard to come by, but with 70,000 chemicals in daily use and 500 to 1,000 new ones added each year, it is safe to assume that the 1983 figure of 266 million tons of waste per year is much higher now.[38]

What, then, is the legacy of Love Canal? It will not be completely known for years. On the positive side, the increase in difficulty and costs of disposal have brought the hazardous waste generation issue full circle to source reduction. Industries are finding that by recycling and changing some procedures, they can reduce their waste considerably and save significant dollars. One EPA study showed that of twenty-eight firms investing in waste reduction techniques, 54 percent recovered their investment in less than one year, and 21 percent more in less than two years.[39] As with many other environmental issues, the encouragement of the positive effects depends upon the negative: The fear of another Love Canal propels communities to prohibit disposal of toxic wastes except at ridiculous cost; *the cost makes it profitable for industry to experiment with new and costlier methods of manufacture that eliminate the production of that waste; and the overall result is a cleaner industry.*

On the other hand, some of the results of that fear are clearly undesirable. There are unrealistic and counterproductive requirements for the handling of any land found stained with toxins—like the requirement that all hazardous wastes found on any building site must be cleared away, transported to a disposal site, and burned, before the title can be cleared and building can begin. That particular rule results only in more hazard, as the exposed, exhumed, and transported waste is picked up by wind or rain in transit and disseminated more widely than it ever would have been if it had been left alone. And there is the NIMBY syndrome, which makes all municipal efforts to dispose safely of toxic wastes very difficult, probably for no cause at all. There is the stigma of "chemicals" and the reinforced tendency to accept any fearfulness as gospel truth, any reassurance as political coverup. All of these, especially that last, will make it difficult to adapt to the necessities of handling toxic wastes.

QUESTIONS FOR REFLECTION

1. How should we assess blame, or accountability for action, in general? How should we assess blame for unforeseen events in particular? What constellation of factors suggests that the company—or some company—ought to take the blame (and pay the price) for Love Canal? What constellation of factors suggests that the public, in the form of the city of Niagara Falls (or New York State) ought to take the blame and pay the price for the cleanup?

2. Now that you have read the chapter, what do you think risk is? What kinds of risk are acceptable, and why? What kinds are not? How much of our notion of "acceptable risk" derives from scientific probability (the probability, assessed by experts, of incurring damage of a certain magnitude), and how much derives from voluntariness (my willingness to accept that risk, whatever it may be,

   as a condition for doing or having something that I want)? Compare the case of the rock climber, who voluntarily undertakes to engage in objectively very risky activity, and the case of the homeowner near Love Canal.

3. Ordinarily we assume that the community (or state, government, or society) will protect us from certain risks, through measures such as the criminalization of provision of certain drugs or the placement of guard rails on mountain roads. How far should this protection extend? What values other than physical safety determine the limits of protection?

4. Is there a sense in which society as a whole (as opposed to any individual or individuals) can voluntarily assume a risk—for instance, for a whole new technology, like gene splicing (or, in this case, for the petrochemical industry)?

5. Now that you have read the chapter, what do you think of the role of the mass media in all of the events of Love Canal? Can we make sense of general duties owed to the society by the press? Were they fulfilled or breached in this case?

6. Is Superfund doing its job? On July 1, 2002, President George W. Bush announced that funding for the cleanup of toxic sites like Love Canal would be drastically cut. What had the "Superfund" accomplished in its history (which dates to the events described in this chapter)?

7. What was the role of government agencies (local, state, and federal) in the incidents at Love Canal? Is there any way of discerning, and preventing, the pursuit of "self-interest" by government agencies? How might agency self-interest have operated in these incidents?

8. How can corporations prepare themselves for the consequences of dealing with toxic substances?

Was there anything else that Occidental could have done to prevent the fallout from Love Canal?

9. What are the values in dispute in the case of Love Canal? What are their limitations? How can we read into the equation, and compare

The property values of the owners

The health of the residents

The public image of the town

The preservation of contractual agreements

The health of the ecosystem

The integrity of the local aquifers

Was there, in all this, a duty not to pollute, or otherwise hurt the soil, for the sake of the soil itself, in advance of legislation on the subject? If so, why? To what or whom was that duty owed?

10. Who should pay for the cleanups, now and in the future? Who was really responsible for the leaking chemicals and/or for the rest of what happened?

SUGGESTIONS FOR FURTHER READING

Beauchamp, Tom. "Love Canal" *Case Studies in Business, Society, and Ethics*. Englewood Cliffs, NJ: Prentice Hall, 1983.

Brown, Michael. *Laying Waste: The Poisoning of America By Toxic Chemicals*. New York: Parthenon, 1980.

Carson, Rachel, *Silent Spring*, Boston: Houghton-Mifflin, Anniversary Edition 1962.

Gibbs, Lois Marie, *Love Canal: My Story*. Albany: State University of New York Press, 1982.

Klinkenborg, Verlyn, "Back to Love Canal," *Harpers*, March 1991.

Levine, Adeline Gordon, *Love Canal: Science, Politics, and People*. Lexington, MA: Lexington Books, 1982.

Nader, Ralph, Ronald Brownstein, and John Richard, eds. *Who's Poisoning America? Corporate Polluters and Their Victims in the Chemical Age*. San Francisco: Sierra Club Books, 1981.

Whalan, Robert. *Love Canal: A Public Health Time Bomb*. Report of the New York Department of Health, 1978.

Whelan, Elizabeth. *Toxic Terror: The Truth About the Cancer Scare*. Ottawa, IL: Jameson Books, 1985.

Whitney, Gary. "Hooker Chemical and Plastics," in *Case Studies in Business Ethics*. Thomas Donaldson, ed., Englewood Cliffs, NJ: Prentice Hall, 1984.

ENDNOTES

1. Parts of this chronology are taken from one put together by Dennis Hevesi for *The New York Times* (September 28, 1988): p. B-1. This summary appeared in Newton and Dillingham, *Watersheds* (Belmont, CA: Wadsworth Publishing, 1994).

2. Philip Elmer-Dewitt, "Love Canals in the Making," *Time* (May 20, 1991): p. 51.

3. Anne Underwood, "The Return to Love Canal," *Newsweek* (July 30, 1990).

4. Elizabeth Whelan, *Toxic Terror: The Truth About the Cancer Scare* (Ottawa, IL: Jameson Books, 1985).

5. Bill Michelmore, "Love Canal Museum in Works," *The Buffalo News* (February 9, 2001): p. 1A.

6. Thomas J. Prohaska, "Granieri Resigns as Chairman of Love Canal 2000," *The Buffalo News* (September 10, 2001): p. B3. See also "From Love Canal through Broken Promises, Fraud; Investigations and Master Plans, a Niagara Falls Timeline," *The Buffalo News* (September 27, 2000): p. 4A.

7. Olefins are compounds consisting of carbon chains in which some of the carbon atoms are connected by double bonds, i.e., they have room for more hydrogen atoms and are therefore called *unsaturated*.

8. But if you have forgotten it, read Rachel Carson, *Silent Spring* (Boston: Houghton-Mifflin, Anniversary Edition 1962).

9. Sandra Postel, "Defusing the Toxics Threat: Controlling Pesticides and Industrial Waste," *Worldwatch Paper* (Washington, DC: Worldwatch Institute, 1987).

10. Ibid., p. 15.

11. Philip H. Abelson, "Chemicals from Waste Dump," *Science* 229(4711) (July 27, 1985).

12. Ibid.

13. In the summer of 2002, President George W. Bush cut federal funds to the cleanup effort, reducing by thirty-three the number of sites slated for cleanup.

14. "Health Aspects of Hazardous Waste Disposal" (summary of report of the same name from Universities Associated for Research and Education in Pathology), *Environment* 28(3) (April 1986): 38.

15. Deed of Love Canal Property Transfer, Niagara Falls, New York, April 28, 1953. Emphasis added.

16. Conversation with Eugene Martin-Less, Esq., Environmental Bureau of the Attorney General of New York State, Albany, New York. Senior Attorney, *New York State vs. Occidental Chemical Company* (suit pending), asking $250 million punitive damages relative to Love Canal dumpsite.

17. Ralph Nader, Ronald Brownstein, and John Richard, eds., *Who's Poisoning America: Corporate Polluters and Their Victims in the Chemical Age* (San Francisco: Sierra Club Books, 1981).

18. Gary Whitney. "Hooker Chemical and Plastics," *Case Studies in Business Ethics*, ed. Thomas Donaldson (Englewood Cliffs, NJ: Prentice Hall, 1984).

19. Michael H. Brown, "A Toxic Ghost Town Harbinger of America's Toxic Waste Crisis," *The Atlantic* 263(1) (July 1989).

20. "CDC Finds No Excess Illness at Love Canal," *Science* 220 (June 17, 1983).

21. Nicholas Vianna, Report to the New York State Department of Health. In *Science* (June 19, 1981): p. 19.

22. Hank Cox, *Regulatory Action Network: Washington Watch* (September 1980).

23. Whelan, op. cit., p. 99. For further discussion of Superfund, see Chapter 9, of this text, "What Responsibilities Do We Have for Foreign Management?"

24. Brown, op.cit.

25. Ibid.

26. Ibid.

27. "Love Canal Suit Threatens to Make Old Errors Costly," *Wall Street Journal* (October 24, 1990).

28. Quoted in *The New York Times* (April 15, 1990).

29. *The New York Times* (May 15, 1990).

30. *Science News* (November 14, 1987): p. 319.

31. "From Love Canal Through Broken Promises, Fraud, Investigations and Master Plans, a Niagara Falls Timeline," *The Buffalo News* (September 27, 2000): p. 4A.

32. Joel S. Hirschhorn, "Cutting Production of Hazardous Waste," *Technology Review* 91(3) (April 1988).

33. *The New York Times* (January 29, 1991): p. C4.

34. Keith Schneider, "U.S. Said to Lack Data on Threat Posed by Hazardous Waste Sites," *The New York Times* (October 22, 1991): p. C4.

35. Schneider, loc. cit.

36. "Health Aspects of Hazardous Waste Disposal," *Environment* (April 1986): pp. 38–45.

37. Ibid.

38. Postel, op. cit.

39. Hirschhorn, op. cit.

7

❀

How Shall We Deal with Unlimited Greed?

The Insider Trading Scandals

Questions to Keep in Mind

1. Why is there a Wall Street? How does Wall Street serve business, investors and the economy?

2. Some have argued that Wall Street today increasingly resembles a casino. Is this characterization fair?

3. What constitutes insider trading? Under what circumstances is it legally and ethically wrong?

4. What is a Chinese Wall? What kind of approach to maintaining ethical conduct does it represent?

5. Why did prosecutors arrest Wigton in the way that they did? What kind of message were they sending to Wall Street?

People seem to love hating Martha Stewart, the homemaking queen known for her ingenious decorating ideas, linens, and housewares. Perhaps they resent her seemingly inexhaustible ability to transform mundane junk into all manner of beautiful and ingenious things. Or perhaps they believe the rumors that she is a harshly demanding chief executive of Martha Stewart Living Omnimedia. Whatever the reason, an entire nation sat up and eagerly took notice when Stewart joined the ranks of CEOs charged with corporate misdeeds. More than a few observers outwardly delighted in her troubles.[1]

On December 27, 2001, Stewart sold 4,000 shares of ImClone Systems, a biotech company that was started and run by Stewart's friend, Samuel D. Waksal. According to Stewart's lawyers, she and her stockbroker, Peter E. Baconovic, had long before agreed that he should sell ImClone if the price dropped below $60 a share. Stewart denies that her decision to sell the shares was based on any inside information from Waksal or anyone else. It was simply a coincidence, she maintained, that her sale of ImClone took place just before the company released the bad news that the Food and Drug Administration (FDA) was not going to approve a new ImClone anti-cancer drug.

As of this writing, Martha Stewart has not been charged with any crime. She is currently under investigation by the Justice Department and the Securities and Exchange Commission (SEC). A Congressional committee that had been examining the ImClone sale has just turned the matter over to the Justice Department, which will determine whether Stewart may have caused "materially false representations" about her trading.[2] Regardless of the outcome of the controversy surrounding Stewart, however, her case is significant because it is a reminder that problems of insider trading are still with us.

Almost a generation has passed since the sensational insider trading scandals of the 1980s, when executives, bankers, arbitrageurs, lawyers, and even lowly financial news reporters traded illegally by using forbidden material nonpublic information. But as that "decade of greed" came to an end, the public's attention seemed to shift from Wall Street to Silicon Valley. As more and more people pursued wealth in the "New Economy" of skyrocketing dot-com companies, it no longer seemed necessary to get rich illegally with insider information. But today, just two years into the new millennium, insider trading seems to have returned—with a vengeance.

By the late 1990s, "merger mania" was once again becoming a force to reckon with. Just halfway into 1998, for example, takeovers and acquisitions engineered by Wall Street had soared past $1.2 trillion dollars, compared to just $920 billion in the entire preceding year.[3] When many companies are taken over and sold, the conditions are ripe for abusing nonpublic information that can affect the stock prices of companies. Apparently, that is precisely what has been happening in recent years.

The Securities and Exchange Commission has lately redoubled its efforts to catch insider traders. It is especially interested in the trading patterns of senior executives who have been linked to the various accounting and disclosure scandals that rocked the business world in 2001–2002. The SEC also wants to pursue anyone who profited illegally from the sudden declines in the stock market following the dot-com bust. It is hard to say whether there is more insider trading going on now than in the 1990s. Clearly, however, we now live in a troubled business climate in which the public is much less tolerant of any illegal trading that is taking place. In an effort to restore public confidence in Wall Street, the SEC is now imposing tougher penalties on those who get caught. In the fiscal year ended September 30, 1997, the Commission brought forward 57 insider trading cases.[4]

Some things about insider trading have not changed significantly since the 1980s. For example, as was the case back then, there still is no statutory definition of insider trading. The reason for this continues to be that a clear definition of insider trading would only help crafty lawyers find legal loopholes. We continue to use certain theories to interpret whether insider trading has occurred. One of these is the so-called "misappropriation theory," which says that people who acquired material nonpublic information through a special relationship with a company could not "misappropriate" this information for their own financial gain. Since the 1980s, prosecutors have had mixed success using this theory to convict inside traders. But in 1997, the Supreme Court strengthened the misappropriation theory when it upheld the insider-trading conviction of James H. O'Hagan. O'Hagan was a Minneapolis lawyer who sought to profit from information gleaned from his law firm's representation of Grand Metropolitan, a company who had tried to take over the Pillsbury Company. While O'Hagan's law firm worked for Grand Met, he bought call options and shares of Pillsbury stock. He sold these options and stock when Grand Met announced its tender offer, for a profit of more than $4.3 million. A case was made against O'Hagan. However, a federal appeals court overturned the conviction, saying that O'Hagan was neither an employee nor a fiduciary of Pillsbury. But the Supreme Court reversed the federal appeals court, saying that a person who obtains inside information, under conditions in which that person knows the information is supposed to remain nonpublic, may not use that information for trading. As a consequence, people who buy and sell securities today still need to be mindful of legal interpretive principles that were first hammered out in the 1980s.

At the same time, some things about insider trading today are very different than in the 1980s. Charges of insider trading today arise in a context of widespread public disgust with corporate scandals and ethical misconduct of senior executives. It galls many people that CEOs continue to enjoy huge salaries, bonuses, and perks while their companies' profits evaporate, employees are laid off, and long-term investors get hammered. There may be literally dozens of cases in which corporate insiders have legally sold millions of dollars of shares shortly before revised earnings projections drove down the prices of their companies' shares. It looks like insider trading. Why is it allowed to happen?

The problem was created, in part, by the growing practice of companies compensating their chief executives with generous stock options. One purpose of these options was to align the executives' self-interest with the interests of their corporations. But the executives needed a way to exercise their stock options without being accused of insider trading. By the end of 2000, then SEC Chairman Arthur D. Levitt led the Commission to adopt a rule allowing executives to set prearranged schedules for selling their stock.[5] This so-called "safe harbor" approach insulated the executives from charges of insider trading, since they were selling according to fixed, pre-arranged schedules.

Levitt's rule may have helped to curb insider trading, but it did little to soften the growing public outcry over whether executives and the markets can be trusted. Kenneth Borovina is a thirty-four-year-old carpenter whose grandmother's life savings has shrunk from $600,000 to $200,000 in 2001–2002 in the dismal stock market. Of the senior executives who recently have been investigated and arrested for shady financial dealings, Borovina says, "They're getting what they deserve. That makes me feel great."[6] He no doubt speaks for many Americans who have turned their backs on corporate America in disgust.

The stock market is fundamentally based on trust and investor confidence. If people don't have assurance in the integrity of Wall Street, it will be difficult for the U.S. capital markets to maintain their standing as the premier markets of the world. The roots of this issue run very deep. To begin to appreciate the intensity of the furor over today's insider trading scandals, it is necessary to look back to the wake-up call from Wall Street in the 1980s. Richard Wigton of Kidder, Peabody & Company was an "everyman" of the Street—far from the celebrity spotlight that illumined stars like Ivan Boesky and Michael Milken. But if we are to understand the reasons for the rancor today over a star like Martha Stewart, we need to go back to the story of what happened to "Wiggie" in the 1980s.

I. AN ARREST ON WALL STREET

On the morning of February 12, 1987, Richard Wigton reported to work at Kidder, Peabody & Co., the prominent New York investment bank. Mr. Wigton worked in the business of arbitrage, seeking to profit on the stocks of companies who were takeover targets. Arbitrage was one of the flashier aspects of the exciting world of finance in the 1980s.[7] But Wigton, "Wiggie" to his friends, was not a typical flamboyant Wall Street "player." In an industry propelled by young, aggressive competitors, Wigton belonged to the older, more conservative Wall Street of yesteryear. After all, he had started on Wall Street in 1956, before many of his coworkers had even been born!

The stock market was active and Wigton got down to business in his office next to the Kidder trading floor. He was not pleased when the bank's receptionist interrupted, calling to say that a Mr. Moreno was asking to see him. Thinking it a job seeker, Wigton told the receptionist to send Moreno away. But she responded that Moreno would not be put off.

Wigton went to the receptionist area, where he was told by two postal inspectors that he was under arrest! Wigton was frozen in shock, unable to speak or move. Before a group of stunned onlookers, one of the agents shoved Wigton against a wall, frisked him, and then cuffed his hands behind his back. The agents then led Wigton back to his office, going through the trading floor, in full view of his startled coworkers. He could not hide the tears in his eyes.

In all the confusion, Wigton didn't fully realize what was happening. Only after he was arraigned and fingerprinted did Wigton find out that he was charged with insider trading. Even worse, it was alleged that he was getting his insider information from a trusted and respected Kidder colleague, Martin Siegel.

Following the arraignment, Wigton actually returned to work, probably in a reflex action. At 5:45 P.M. he went home, same as every other night, just as if nothing had happened. In the drive back to New Jersey, the two other members of his car pool didn't say a single word about the crisis that day. But that night, Wigton couldn't sleep, tossing and turning, asking over and over, "My God, why has this happened to me?"[8]

Wigton's arrest, which sent shock waves through the financial community and beyond, was a wake-up call to Wall Street and the American public. To be sure, there would be flashier Wall Street celebrities to be accused and convicted of insider trading and financial fraud. But Wigton's dramatic arrest put everyone on notice: If it could happen to him, could it happen to me? Just how widespread is this insider trading, anyway? And what, if anything, can be done about it? To sort our way through these questions, and to understand why this happened to Wigton, this chapter will navigate some interesting terrain in the world of financial services, uncovering some practices and rules not widely understood by the business community, let alone the American public. First, we will briefly review some background about Wall Street, with particular attention to its investment banking and arbitrage functions. Next, we will describe Wigton's dealings with key associates at Kidder, principally Marty Siegel, in order to uncover his use of insider information to make profits. We will then review both legal theories and ethics arguments about insider trading, to consider whether and in what sense there is something wrong about insider trading. Armed with these perspectives, we will return to Wigton and review what happened to him since his arrest on February 12. It will be up to you to decide whether Wigton was treated justly, and to discern the implications of this wake-up call for Wall Street.

II. BACKGROUND ON WALL STREET

Wall Street may be one of the best-known but least-understood segments of the business world. For example, while nearly everyone has heard of the New York Stock Exchange—which proudly occupies the prestigious corner of Wall and Broad Street—very few can explain how the Exchange actually works. Most people's impressions of Wall Street in the 1980s were formed by popular films like *Wall Street* and *Other People's Money*, which gave one-sided accounts of what has been popularly described as "the decade of greed." One recent definition of "Wall Street" says that it has become a "term applied to most anybody in a pin-striped suit and a silk tie who looks prosperous and wears an expensive wristwatch."[9]

It is not surprising that Wall Street is something of a mystery, since many aspects of its business <u>are</u> technical, requiring sophisticated expertise. Also, many investment banks associated with Wall Street have not cared much about effective public relations. As a consequence, much of the public responds with confusion, even hostility, when abuses are uncovered on Wall Street.

To understand what happened to Wigton, it is not necessary to become an expert in all aspects of the complex financial services industry. But a few background points will help us avoid common, often misleading, stereotypes about Wigton's line of work. To help clarify this case, we can contrast Wall Street's traditional investment banking function against its more casino-like risk arbitrage activity.

First, what exactly is Wall Street? One answer is that it is a piece of real estate—a street that cuts across lower Manhattan in the city of New York. About 400 years ago it was only a dirt path that took its name from a wall running alongside it, built by the Dutch to keep the cows in their settlement and to keep Native American Indians out. Now a bustling street that spans the short distance from Roosevelt Drive near the East River to Trinity Church, Wall Street is an urban canyon flanked by the world's leading banks. True, the globalization of business has spread important financial activity all around the world: Tokyo, Hong Kong, and London all boast major markets. But Wall Street still maintains its reputation as the symbolic financial center of the world.

Thus Wall Street is more than a physical location or real estate. It is also a symbol of the <u>market</u>, the essence of capitalism. Wall Street is where the providers of money make deals with those who need money, the essential process in which business acquires the financial resources necessary to function. It makes no difference whether this process occurs on the floor of the New York Stock Exchange or "away from the floor" on computer screens of distant banks. Wherever deals are made in financial markets, there breathes the spirit of Wall Street.

The financial marketplace is based upon the "primary market," where business raises the financial capital needed for long-term growth. A key Wall Street figure in the primary market is the investment banker, who offers advice and resources to help companies meet their financial objectives. The investment banker often functions as a middleperson between the company that needs capital and the public or other institutions that provide it, by recommending an appropriate method of financing like a public offering of common stock. Often the investment banker will help underwrite and distribute a company's stock to the investing public. In addition, the investment banker can help guide a company through complex financial deals such as mergers and acquisitions. The investment banker might help a client company find a suitable target company for a corporate takeover, and then devise the strategy and secure the financing for effecting the takeover.

The relationship between the investment banker and the client company is like a marriage. The investment banker is in a position to know the company's deepest secrets and dreams. Thus not only is the investment banker expected to have specialized expertise; this person is also required to be trustworthy and to use his or her knowledge solely for the benefit of the client company's interests. Traditionally, investment bankers have displayed a high degree of professionalism in their business conduct and overall deportment. Compared to traders and salespersons in investment banks, the investment bankers seek to be the ones with the most "class" and "sophistication." This fact is critical. Strip away fancy airs and expensive suits, and what remains of investment bankers is the essential element of trust: A company must be able to trust its investment banker <u>completely</u> when it swims with the sharks on Wall Street.

The investment banking function is an important element in the Wigton case. But there is also a speculative side to Wall Street's functions. Some claim that instead of helping business raise needed capital (which in turns provides more jobs and social benefits), Wall Street makes it possible for people simply to speculate or gamble (which just makes some lucky persons richer at the expense of others). For example, in recent years there was an explosive growth in the use of complicated "derivatives."[10] Not exactly stocks or bonds, derivatives are a type of "artificial" security designed to act in a certain way in response to the price movement of some "real" security, like a company's stock. Futures or index options are examples of a derivative security. Thus derivatives allow persons to speculate about the direction of the market without actually putting their money to work productively in company operations. Many argue that derivatives help investors manage risk better, thereby making more money available overall for business' capital needs. But others argue that derivatives are but one more step toward transforming Wall Street into a legal casino for nonproductive gambling.

If Wall Street is to be viewed a casino, then we might regard the arbitrageur as one of its main members. For it is the risk arbitrageur, "arb" for short, who has adapted traditional arbitrage techniques to the more speculative, volatile character of the casino.

If you understand the logic of "buy low, sell high," then you understand the essential rationale of arbitrage, which involves buying something in one market and almost immediately selling it for more money in another market. For example, if briefly the same commodity X sells for $100.00 in New York and for $100.05 in London, a virtually risk-free arbitrage would be to buy X in New York and sell X in London. Arbitraging typically happens in the complex world of foreign currency markets or the spot markets for commodities. High-speed communications and computer-based trading programs have made it possible to find and trade on price discrepancies in a matter of seconds! Traditional arbitrage is a conservative, low-risk way to eke out profit, a trading strategy available to professionals who have quick access to key market information.

During the 1980s arbitrageurs applied their techniques to the volatile world of corporate mergers and acquisitions. These arbs would buy stock (lots of it) in a company rumored to be a takeover target. In essence, the arbs were gambling that the takeover attempt would drive up the value of their shares. The potential profits were enormous. However, some critics claimed that these arbs were merely placing big bets in the "takeover casino," calling them "river-boat gamblers."[11] For many, arbitrageurs represented the more unsavory side of Wall Street. As *Wall Street Journal* reporter James Stewart describes them:

> Arbitrageurs tended to be crass, excitable, street-smart, aggressive, and driven almost solely by the pursuit of quick profits. Their days were de-fined by the high-pressure periods between the opening and closing bells of the stock exchange, during which they screamed orders into phones, punched stock symbols into their electronic terminals, scanned elaborate screens of constantly shifting data, and placed phone calls to every poten-tial source of information they could imagine.[12]

One of the best-known arbs of the 1980s, Ivan Boesky, wrote a popular book, allegedly about his lucrative techniques, *Merger Mania* (subtitled *Arbi-trage: Wall Street's Best-Kept Money Making Secret*). Of course, the book did not disclose that Boesky's success was due to his misusing "insider information." In the world of takeovers and acquisitions, arbitrage presents an opportunity to misuse information for personal gain. Though arbitrageurs would openly at-tribute their success to superior insight or better computer programs, some ac-tually would get their news of impending takeovers from insiders involved in the deals, like bankers or lawyers. They would use this "insider information" to arbitrage the takeover targets, making huge profits at very low risk. However, as we will see, insider trading is against the law. It is also arguably unethical.

III. WIGTON'S FRIEND: MARTY SIEGEL

With this background about investment bankers, arbitrageurs, and the rise of speculation on Wall Street, we are now able to understand why Wigton was led from his office in handcuffs on February 12. Wigton, as an arbitrageur, was placing bets about possible takeover targets. He was arrested because of the al-legation that he was using insider information to determine which companies to bet on. It was alleged that Wigton received his insider information from someone with confidential information about major corporations, an invest-ment banker. That investment banker supposedly was Martin Siegel.[13]

Marty Siegel joined Kidder, Peabody & Co. in 1971, after graduating from the Harvard Business School, the youngest member of his class at age twenty-three. Though from a modest background, Siegel had all the qualities of a first-rate investment banker: a highly polished demeanor, impeccable academic credentials, and a winning way with people. His career focused on mergers and acquisitions, including hostile takeovers—something new for Kidder, Peabody, which previously had avoided such business.

As his success grew, Siegel became acquainted with some of the most pow-erful arbitrageurs on Wall Street, including Ivan Boesky. As an investment banker, Siegel had information about corporate clients that Boesky valued. It has been reported that Siegel began sharing insider information with Boesky, rationalizing it by saying he would give Boesky information only when it would also serve his clients' interests (sometimes Boesky's trades could affect stock prices in ways that would help Siegel's corporate clients). Siegel reasoned that since nobody got hurt from his giving Boesky insider information, nothing was wrong.

Sharing this insider information with Boesky was not without its risks, however. Boesky seemed to bet correctly so often on possible takeover targets, that many suspected he *must* be using insider information. In summer 1984 an article in *Fortune* magazine suggested that Boesky had a link with someone at Kidder, Peabody. The magazine article scared Siegel, who vowed to stop sharing insider information with Boesky and others before he got into *real* trouble. However, Kidder soon gave Siegel a powerful incentive to continue trading in insider information.

Though it was a prestigious investment bank, in the 1980s Kidder became less profitable. As large segments of Wall Street in that decade chased after new, highly speculative profit opportunities, Kidder stuck with its traditional lines of business, earning relatively small profits on brokerage and underwriting commissions. Kidder's conservatism reflected the desire of its chief executive officer, Ralph DeNunzio, to avoid conflicts of interest between the firm and its clients. Eventually, however, DeNunzio relented, putting Wigton and Timothy Tabor (an inexperienced Kidder employee) in charge of a newly created arbitrage desk. Their assignment was to bet on takeovers, using Kidder's own capital. The existence of Kidder's new arbitrage desk was a closely guarded secret, to prevent a bad reaction among Kidder clients who disliked this "gambling" side of investment banks.

Unfortunately, Wigton and Tabor seemed to lack the experience and knowledge necessary to run a successful high-powered arbitrage operation. DeNunzio appointed Siegel to be their secret "advisor" to ensure they would be profitable. In this way, Kidder inadvertently kept the pressure on Siegel to keep using insider information—this time, to benefit Kidder's arbitrage desk, not Ivan Boesky.

It has been reported that Siegel was also sharing insider information with Robert Freeman, head of arbitrage at Goldman, Sachs & Co., another highly prestigious New York investment bank. Freeman would give Siegel tips about takeover targets, which Siegel would then pass along to Wigton. Usually these tips led to highly profitable arbitrage bets placed by Wigton on behalf of Kidder. Wigton would place these bets through small, third-party brokers, hiding any direct link in their trading records between Freeman's calls to Siegel to trading by Kidder. Wigton called this move "hiding our hand."[14]

Thus, on the surface Wigton was not doing anything wrong. There is nothing illegal about arbitrage, even if some find it a nonproductive form of gambling. What led to Wigton's humiliating arrest was not <u>that</u> he was arbitraging; the arrest was based on an allegation about the *kind of information* Wigton used to guide his trades. It is illegal to trade on the basis of insider information. But in what sense is it illegal? And should it be illegal? Was anybody really doing anything wrong here? These questions point to deeper issues about ethics on Wall Street, the significance of which goes well beyond Wigton's arrest. To explore these questions, we need to examine what is meant by "insider information" and why using it is wrong.

IV. WHY INSIDER TRADING IS WRONG: THE LAW

Of all the sins of Wall Street in the 1980s, insider trading was among the most visible and most controversial. Insider trading was the chief tool for success used by Gordon Gekko, the Boesky-like character in the movie *Wall Street*. Millions of theatergoers learned from this film that insider trading is wrong, though probably not many can explain why it is. (The same is true for many people who work on Wall Street!) One reason for the confusion about what is wrong with insider trading is that the act of insider trading has never been specifically prohibited by federal securities laws; nor is insider trading statutorily defined.[15] In 1961 the SEC stated that corporate insiders (officers and directors of a corporation) in possession of material, nonpublic information were required to disclose that information or to refrain from trading.[16] Since then, the definition of insider trading has evolved through the course of several important court cases, including the Supreme Court cases of *Chiarella v. United States* and *Dirks v. Securities and Exchange Commission*.[17] Following these court decisions, two legal theories have arisen that have been influential in prosecuting insider trading cases: Misappropriation Theory and Tipper-Tippee Liability Theory.

Misappropriation (a nice word for "stealing") Theory applies to situations where an individual is an insider to a corporation—perhaps an employee in the corporation or an outside investment banker or lawyer hired to provide special services for the corporation. That position of trust and confidence is what we will later describe as a "fiduciary relationship." Misappropriation occurs when such an individual takes material nonpublic information from the corporation. Note the phrase "material nonpublic information," which is the more complete way to specify insider information. Information about a corporation is <u>material</u> if public disclosure of that information could affect the corporation's stock price. It would be material information if IBM were planning to buy Apple Computer; it would not be material information if IBM were to install new grey carpets in its headquarters. Information about a corporation is <u>nonpublic</u> if it has not yet been disseminated in a forum accessible by the investing public. Information shared only within the confines of a private meeting of the board of directors is nonpublic. When that information is published in the newspaper, it most certainly is public.

So, according to Misappropriation Theory, you will be guilty of insider trading if you (a) trade a corporation's security (for example, a company's stock) while in possession (b) of material nonpublic information about that corporation, which was obtained (c) in the breach of a fiduciary duty (a duty you have to the company to put the company's interests ahead of your own). Can you apply this theory to possible cases? Try this one: Sam, the president of ABC Company, learns his company is going to acquire XYZ Corporation by buying the stock of XYZ Corporation. This information has not yet been publicly announced. On his own, Sam purchases stock in XYZ corporation. Is this illegal insider trading?

You should have answered <u>yes</u>! Sam did buy XYZ's stock. He possessed material nonpublic information, namely that ABC planned to buy XYZ. Also Sam breached a fiduciary duty to the shareholders of ABC by purchasing stock in XYZ. How? Sam's purchase of XYZ may drive up the price of XYZ stock. As a result, ABC may have to pay more for XYZ than they would have if Sam had done nothing. He should have put the interests of ABC stockholders ahead of his own.

Did you think this question was easy? In a survey of stockbrokers, 98 percent got it right; 81 percent of MBA students answered correctly, as did 77 percent of undergraduate students. How did you do? Of course, in real life, many situations are much more ambiguous.

Misappropriation Theory, while central to the prosecution of many insider trading cases, applies only when there is an individual who is already an insider who trades on inside information. What about people outside of corporations, who do not occupy a position of trust and confidence in the corporation whose stock they trade? Wigton, after all, was not an insider to the corporations whose stocks he arbitraged for Kidder, Peabody. If anyone is guilty of misappropriation in this case, it would more likely be Freeman, the Goldman Sachs arbitrageur. It was Freeman, after all, who allegedly passed along to Marty Siegel material nonpublic information gleaned from his job.

To show why what Wigton allegedly did was wrong, we turn to the second major theory of insider trading, Tipper–Tippee Liability Theory. This theory refers to situations when someone in a fiduciary relationship with a company (the "tipper") gives inside information to someone outside the company (the "tippee"), who subsequently trades on the information. According to this legal theory, tippees are liable for insider trading if they know or <u>should have known</u> that (a) the information given to them by the tipper was material nonpublic information and (b) the information was given to them in the breach of a fiduciary duty owed by the tipper. (The test for breaching a fiduciary duty is whether the tipper personally will benefit, directly or indirectly, from the disclosure.)

Try applying this theory to the following case: Joe Lookdown is walking along Wall Street when he finds a slip of paper on the sidewalk containing material nonpublic information concerning CC, Inc. Joe purchases stock in CC, Inc. Is he guilty of insider trading?

The correct answer is that Joe is not guilty, because no duty has been breached. It was just by chance that he found the slip of paper. Did this seem obvious to you? Interestingly, only 60 percent of stockbrokers surveyed gave the correct answer; 57 percent of MBA students and 75 percent of undergraduate students answered correctly.

A slight change in the facts alters the picture dramatically, however. Suppose that the piece of paper that Joe had retrieved from the sidewalk had been thrown to Joe from his friend Pete, an investment banker working for CC, Inc. Then Joe might be held liable for insider trading under the Tipper-Tippee Theory.

Just how far does along this line of tipping does liability extend? After all, with Wigton, allegedly the information first came from Freeman at Goldman Sachs, who passed the tip to Siegel, who then gave it to Wigton. Certainly what Siegel allegedly was doing was wrong, but was Wigton "less wrong" because he was one step removed from the initial source? And what if Wigton were to pass the insider information along to his mother-in-law? Would she also be guilty of insider trading? Where does it all stop? Not surprisingly, after Wigton's arrest these questions echoed up and down the Street, as essentially law-abiding, but aggressive, traders reviewed the sources of their hot stock "tips."

The most important and difficult insider trading case in recent years—*U.S. v. Chestman*—tested the limits of the misappropriation and tipper-tippee theories, and provided a basis for trying to answer these questions.[18] This case involved the criminal prosecution of a stockbroker (Chestman) who had been the beneficiary of inside information disseminated by the family of the principal stockholder of a publicly traded grocery chain. The somewhat complicated flow of information is summarized by Gillis and Ciotti in a recent update on insider trading:

> In *Chestman*, material nonpublic information about the proposed sale of a publicly traded family business was communicated by a family member (a nephew by marriage) to his stockbroker, Chestman. Ira Waldbaum, president and controlling shareholder of the Waldbaum grocery chain, planned to sell his and his family's interest in a proposed tender offer from the Great Atlantic and Pacific Tea Company at a price almost double the market price. This decision was conveyed to the president's sister, who conveyed it to her daughter, who conveyed it to her husband, the nephew-in-law (hereafter nephew). Each communication included a caution about the confidential nature of the information.
>
> There was some dispute about what information the nephew conveyed to Chestman, and when he conveyed it, but the nephew testified that he had told Chestman that he had "some definite, some accurate information" that Waldbaum Inc. was about to be sold at a price substantially higher than the market price. Chestman purchased a large number of Waldbaum shares, some for the nephew.[19]

A criminal action was later brought against Chestman by a Court of Appeals, though this was later <u>reversed</u> by the a three-judge panel from the Second Circuit. This panel held that Chestman's knowledge of the tipper's breach was never established to the degree necessary for a criminal action. Chestman's convictions could not be sustained unless (1) the nephew breached a duty owed to the Waldbaum family or his wife based on a fiduciary or other similar relationship of trust and (2) Chestman knew that the nephew had done so. The Second Circuit found that Chestman was merely an aider and abetter of the misappropriation and a tippee of the information. There was no fiduciary relationship, or its functional equivalent, between nephew and the Waldbaum family.

Chestman is studied closely by traders seeking to answer the question whether they might, at times, engage in insider trading. It is likely that many questions will continue to surround this decision and its application to new situations. It is also safe to say that there are a lot of nervous traders looking over their shoulder, worrying about the long reach of the SEC. As it applies to Wigton, the critical issue is whether Wigton knew that Siegel had breached a fiduciary duty when passing along insider information from Freeman at Goldman Sachs. Wigton, of course, denied knowing that Siegel's tips were insider information. The prosecutors, however, thought otherwise. They insisted that someone with Wigton's investment banking experience should have been able to figure out that Siegel's lucrative tips were too good to be true—or too true to be good!

V. USING REGULATIONS TO ACHIEVE ETHICAL MARKETS

In the preceding section on insider trading, we saw that the absence of a statutory definition of insider trading contributes to some ambiguity about what counts as insider trading and what doesn't. This ambiguity is not entirely an accident: The absence of clear definitional boundaries for insider trading is meant to discourage crafty Wall Streeters (aided by their crafty lawyers) from sneaking through loopholes. The fuzzy boundaries thus provide an incentive to "play in the center of the court" and to avoid even the appearance of trading on the basis of material nonpublic information.

This somewhat fuzzy status of insider trading does not mean, however, that Wall Street lacks clear, enforceable regulations. To the contrary: The U.S. securities markets are the most strictly regulated in the world. Due to a variety of historical and political factors, regulations are the primary tool the government and various financial institutions use to enforce ethical conduct on Wall Street. But, as the Wigton case shows, there are limits to the reach and effectiveness of regulations. In other words, regulations are necessary for ethical conduct on Wall Street, but they are not sufficient. To explore this point, this section will briefly summarize the rapid growth of financial regulations in U.S. markets over the past sixty years. We will examine a particular tool for regulating insider information, the so-called "Chinese Wall," and consider why it didn't work in the Wigton case. Finally, we will note the effect of overly aggressive regulation on the moral climate of business, by looking again at the way in which the Feds handled Wigton's arrest and prosecution.

Today, the U.S. government is closely involved in nearly every aspect of business on Wall Street. It acts as a both a lender and a borrower; it functions as an intermediary between financial institutions, and it works as a policeman, regulating virtually every aspect of Wall Street's activities. The government's pervasive presence on the Street is directly traceable to one major historical event: the Crash of 1929.

During the 1920s the American markets, like those throughout the world, were propelled upward toward unparalleled, dizzying heights. There was excess financial capacity, meaning cash was everywhere. Stocks and bonds floated up on an extraordinary wave of risk-taking, speculating and (it was later disclosed) on self-dealing and imprudence by financial executives. Large numbers of small investors leapt excitedly on this rising wave, seeking new riches. But on Black Thursday, October 24, 1929, the stock market collapsed, plunging the nation into a severe, prolonged depression. Thousands of ordinary Americans, through no fault of their own, were ruined. The free enterprise system itself was deeply questioned as it had never been before. In a study of Wall Street's history, Ron Chernow said that "The crash was a blow to Wall Street's pride and its profits. . . . The stereotype of bankers as conservative, careful, prudent individuals was shattered in 1929."[20] A 1940 Roper Report (completed by public opinion pollster Elmo Roper) showed what Americans really thought about the world of Wall Street:

> The Roper Report showed that most Americans did not trust Wall Street. The market crash of 1929, followed by the depression and close to a decade of antibusiness rhetoric in the press and from Washington, had fixed upon the public mind the image of the stock broker as a polished crook, and the N.Y.S.E as a nest of thieves.[21]

Thus Wall Street's collapse, and with it the American economy, was viewed by Americans not merely as a technical failure of the markets. To the contrary, the 1929 crash was widely perceived as a moral failure on the part of Wall Street. In the Pecora trials, during which the government attempted to sort out what had gone wrong and whom to blame, leading financial executives confessed publicly to financial practices ranging from mere incompetence to downright dishonest. According to *The New York Times*, these revelations shocked the "moral sense of the nation."[22] By the early 1930s, Wall Street was thoroughly discredited and would have to work very hard to regain the public's trust and confidence.

But the U.S. government was unwilling to entrust Wall Street with the sole responsibility for repairing the damage. To promote the public interest, federal legislators sought to clean up the industry with sweeping reforms and controls. Their objective was to promote stability and full disclosure in the financial markets, although Wall Street tended to view these reforms as excessive government control that diminished free enterprise. Many of these pieces of legislation are unfamiliar to most Americans today—for example, the Federal

Home Loan Bank Act of 1932, the Banking Act of 1933, the Securities Act of 1933, the Securities Exchange Act of 1934, the Federal Credit Union Act of 1934, the Banking Act of 1935, the Maloney Act of 1938, the Investment Company Act of 1940, and the McCarran-Ferguson Act of 1945. Taken as a whole, however, these laws reorganized the U.S. financial system into the structure that we have today.

The SEC was established by the Securities Exchange Act of 1934. The SEC's mission is to police U.S. securities laws, thereby protecting the investing public. It seeks to enforce the laws that prohibit insider trading, manipulation of stock prices, and other kinds of fraud. What has been a major impact of the SEC on daily Wall Street life? Only half joking, financial columnist Susan Lee says that "The most visible mechanism of this enforcement is reams and reams of paperwork."[23] Consequently, every investment bank is now armed with its own compliance office, staffed with lawyers and technicians, who ensure that their companies comply with this regulatory universe. Since the mid-1930s, Wall Street has been strongly conditioned or trained by the government to use a rules or regulatory approach to deal with unethical behavior.

The "Chinese Wall" is an example of a regulatory approach to ethics, one that is especially relevant to the Wigton case. The Chinese Wall is any kind of information barrier erected within a financial firm to prevent insider trading violations by its employees and to protect the firm against potential liability.[24] Within a full-service investment bank, Chinese Walls are meant to prevent investment bankers from sharing insider information with traders in their own banks. Often, these departments are placed in different parts of the building, with separate elevators and guards stationed at key passageways to prevent "idle" wandering and/or snooping. Additional procedures, used typically in conjunction with an information barrier, include (1) restrictions or prohibitions on personal employee trading, (2) careful monitoring of firm and personal employee trading, (3) placing securities on a restricted list when the firm has or may have material nonpublic information, and (4) use of a stock watch list in the foregoing circumstances to monitor transactions in specified securities. The watch list is usually known only to a limited number of people.[25]

Just how effective are these Chinese Walls and related compliance or regulatory approaches to enforcing ethical conduct? This is difficult to measure. Nobody would seriously entertain scrapping Chinese Walls; but very few people think that external rules and regulations are sufficient to police conduct on Wall Street. It is generally acknowledged that Wall Streeters need to <u>want</u> to be ethical, at least up to a point, or they will find cracks in even the thickest Chinese Walls. According to a *Barron's* article on the effects of the Wigton case:

> But the newest cases suggest quite clearly that those self-constructed "Chinese walls" that are supposed to exist between trading and investment-banking activities on Wall Street leave a great deal to be desired. In each of the recent cases, information obtained from investment-banking clients allegedly found its way across those barriers and into the hands of traders—with no indication so far that the breach was detected by the firms' compliance operations.[26]

Important though regulations may be for establishing a relatively level playing field on Wall Street, a regulatory approach to ethics, by itself, has significant shortcomings. It is difficult to frame regulations that are sufficiently detailed <u>and</u> flexible to handle the rapid flux of Wall Street. Financial historian Robert Sobel argues that the 1934 Securities Act was designed as a "corrective mechanism for an <u>unchanging</u> securities district."[27] Thus we might wonder whether Wigton's fast-paced financial world could be controlled adequately by a purely regulatory approach to ethics.

Perhaps a more important limitation of a regulatory approach to ethics is its tendency to minimalism and conservatism. An ethics of rules tends to dwell at the level of just staying out of trouble. As long as nobody is getting caught doing something wrong, there is a tendency to assume that, ethically, everything must be OK. But the Wigton case shows what can happen when the in-house compliance officers tend to assume that everything is working as it should. The public backlash against Kidder, Peabody following the Wigton indictment shows how quickly a firm can lose its reputation for trustworthiness and honesty, a reputation that can take years to build. Thus, following the Wigton arrest, Kidder was faced with the challenge of rebuilding the public trust. To do this, it found that it needed to go beyond the letter of the law and to conduct its business in an exemplary fashion, above even the hint of suspicion. (We will see in this chapter's conclusion just how well Kidder responded to this wake-up call.) To conclude this section, however, we can say that Wall Street needs regulations and rules, but it needs more than external rules if it is to claim seriously that it has an ethic adequate to its dynamic and increasingly "gray" areas of business.

VI. IS INSIDER TRADING UNETHICAL?

Is it possible that the laws about insider trading might be wrong or out-of-date? In his study of the ethics of insider trading, philosopher William B. Irvine concludes, "All this suggests that the laws against insider trading . . . fail to mirror the moral terrain. There are cases in which engaging in insider trading is illegal but not morally objectionable; and there are cases in which withholding news of takeover offers from shareholders is legal but not morally permissible."[28] In other words, it may be that the law and ethics do not always see eye to eye on insider trading. Here, it may be instructive to summarize some of the chief ethical arguments for and against insider trading.[29]

The efficient capital market defense of insider trading claims that insider traders "pump information" into the market, with the result that stock prices more accurately reflect their true investment value. When this happens, everyone benefits, not just the insiders.

Not everyone agrees that insider trading enhances the efficiency of the markets. But even if it did, we might still ask whether insider trading is <u>fair</u>.[30] Letting only some people have material nonpublic information unfairly tilts the playing field of business. The game is "rigged" in favor of those who possess vital information over those who lack it. One harmful consequence of insider trading is that it shakes public confidence in the financial markets, prompting many investors to pull their money from productive investments. It is worth noting that much of the legislation enacted to regulate Wall Street has the stated aim of preserving investor confidence in the stability and fairness of the markets.

One of the most serious arguments against insider trading is that it violates the principle of fiduciary relationships. In our review of the Supreme Court cases and related legal theories on insider trading, we saw that the notion of a fiduciary was central to the prohibition of insider trading. Traditionally, a fiduciary is a person or company holding assets in trust for a beneficiary. The fiduciary is charged with the responsibility of investing the money wisely for the beneficiary's benefit. Fiduciary relationships are special relationships of trust and dependence, in which one party acts for the sole and exclusive interests of another.

The Supreme Court, in *Chiarella v. United States* and in *Dirks v. Securities and Exchange Commission*, used the notion of fiduciary duty to show insider trading is wrong only when it involves the violation of a fiduciary duty owed to other parties of a transaction. Insider trading occurs only when there is a fiduciary duty between two parties and that duty is breached by the misappropriation of information, or by the passing of a tip to a tippee.

Ethicist Jennifer Moore, in her analysis of the ethics of insider trading, argues that fiduciary relationships are absolutely necessary for the orderly, successful practice of business in today's society. The modern corporation cannot exist without fiduciary relationships. She says:

> Shareholders who wish to invest in a business, for example, but who cannot or do not wish to run it themselves, hire others to manage it for them. Managers, directors, and to some extent, other employees, become fiduciaries for the firms they manage and for the shareholders of those firms.[31]

The problem with insider trading, then, is that it violates the fiduciary relationships that are so essential for business to operate. When an executive uses insider information learned in the boardroom to make a profit for himself, and not for his shareholders, he violates his fiduciary duty to the shareholders, the owners of his company. When an investment banker shares a hot tip with an outsider about his client, a takeover target, the investment banker breaches a fiduciary duty to the client. With that breach, the receiver of the tip who trades on the information is guilty as well. The fabric of trust that is essential for business, which rests on both legal and moral foundations, is ripped to shreds by widespread insider trading.

Wigton comes across as a gentle, softspoken individual who generally avoided the extravagant lifestyle of many of his coworkers in the 1980s. Is this the sort of person who would knowingly harm others? Is he an unethical or unfair person?

One way to answer these questions is to consider the <u>consequences</u> of his alleged crimes, according to a teleological ethical perspective. If he were found guilty of insider trading, his company Kidder, Peabody would be liable financially for a score of regulatory infractions. From Kidder's point of view, insider trading by its employees would <u>financially</u> harm the company and its shareholders. The discovery of insider trading at the arbitrage desk would certainly cripple this new venture at Kidder. It is likely that this news would drive away Kidder clients, many of whom already had a dim view of risk arbitrage, let alone arbitrage based on insider trading.

Another approach to the question of the ethics of Wigton's actions is to take a deontological ethical perspective. Here we would note that Wigton (and Tabor) had a variety of fiduciary <u>duties</u>, among them the duty to put Kidder's interests first in their management of the "secret" arbitrage desk.

Clearly, Wigton would be unethical if he engaged in insider trading. But the key question remains: Did he actually do any insider trading?

VII. WHAT HAPPENED TO WIGGY

In February 1987 Wigton, Tabor, and Freeman had been arrested in a dramatic show of force. It was the first time that white-collar professionals had been handcuffed and arrested in their own offices. The prosecutors wanted to use the "Wall Street Three," as they were called, to set an example for the rest of Wall Street. However, the prosecutors may have overstepped themselves. Unlike other insider traders who had been caught red-handed, Wigton, Tabor, and Freeman had not done anything obviously wrong. On the face of it, all Wigton did was trade stocks of companies who became takeover targets. The prosecutors had to prove that Wigton's trading was really based on insider information. Significantly, the Wall Street Three were also the first major Wall Street figures accused of insider trading who refused to plead guilty.

In April 1987 Wigton was formally indicted for insider trading (as were Tabor and Freeman). Tabor had already left Kidder. Goldman Sachs continued to employ Freeman, paying his salary and legal fees. But Wigton suffered a different fate.

As a *Wall Street Journal* editorial put it, "Mr. Wigton became the trophy in an intracorporate tug of war."[32] Kidder apparently wanted to defend Wigton aggressively. But General Electric, which owned Kidder, had other ideas. In order to avoid a criminal indictment of its subsidiary, GE cut a deal with Rudolph Giuliani, then the Manhattan federal prosecutor. Following GE's orders, Kidder disbanded its arbitrage department and paid the government a $25.3 million penalty. Kidder chief executive Ralph Denunzio was forced out. GE's position on Wigton was equally severe: If Wigton is guilty, he should admit it and face the consequences; if Wigton should fight the indictment and lose, then GE would sue Wigton to recover the $3 million it had paid him for his Kidder stock.

On the day of his indictment, a Kidder superior told Wigton that GE had decided it would not be appropriate for him to continue running the Kidder trading department. Wigton moved to an empty office on the executive floor, away from the trading desk. Wigton was also informed that Kidder would not continue paying his salary, nor would it pay his legal fees. Wigton responded, saying, "I was hurt. Why was I being treated differently than Bob Freeman [at Goldman Sachs]?"[33] Later, Wigton moved again to another office building, isolated from the main activity at Kidder. There he kept a low profile, trading stocks for his own account.

In May 1987 Giuliani asked for a delay of the trial against Wigton, Tabor, and Freeman, saying that he did not yet have enough evidence to go to trial. At that point, Giuliani dropped the insider trading indictment against the Wall Street Three, but promised to bring a new, expanded indictment in "record breaking time."[34] Giuliani's difficulty centered on Marty Siegel's credibility. Siegel had struck a plea bargain with the prosecutors, pleading guilty to two felony counts in return for his cooperation. Siegel claimed that he had passed along insider information from Freeman to Wigton. The real issue for Giuliani was whether a jury would believe Siegel. Nobody disputed that Wigton had made the trades in question. The only issue was whether Wigton had known that Siegel's trading suggestions were based on insider information. The prosecutors argued that someone with Wigton's knowledge and experience <u>had</u> to know that Siegel's tips were illegal. But they lacked hard evidence to support this argument. Consequently, for two years Wigton (along with Tabor and Freeman) were suspended in a legal limbo. Even in January 1989, when Giuliani announced his resignation as U.S. Attorney in Manhattan (he went on to become Mayor of the City of New York), the long-standing case against Wigton was still unresolved.

In August 1989 Wigton went to work out at his health club in Short Hills, New Jersey. He knew that any minute he might get a call from his lawyer about whether the federal prosecutors would re-indict him. But he had developed a regular exercise routine during his exile from Wall Street, getting in much better shape and preserving some peace of mind. The news would have to wait: Exercise came first. Upon returning home, Wigton learned that the government was dropping its investigation. (With the indictment being dropped, General Electric paid Wigton's legal fees and back pay.)

Wigton's lawyer, Stanley Arkin, asked U.S. Attorney Benito Romano if the prosecutors could "say something nice about Dick" at a press conference, to make up for the torment they had put him through. Romano declined to make a public apology. "We're just doing our job, Stanley," Arkin recalls him as saying.[35] And what was Wigton's reaction? "'The main concern I have,' says the soft-spoken Mr. Wigton, in his first public comment since his ordeal began, 'is people that don't know me: What do they think and feel?'"[36] Wigton, after all, was not a major Wall Street "star," like a Boesky or a Milken, known to millions. Apart from this incident, he was a nondescript investment banker doing his job, about as close to a "normal guy" as one is likely to find in the industry. But now, when people think of him, it is in connection with the problems at

Kidder. Thus Wigton's main concern was about the impact of this ordeal on his reputation. He is not alone in this concern: Whether one is a major industry star or an ordinary worker, the loss of one's ethical reputation is a major career setback that is not easily overcome.

QUESTIONS FOR REFLECTION

1. Are we moving beyond the 1980s "decade of greed" or is Wall Street now just as ethical/ unethical as it ever was? Do we measure the ethical climate of an industry just by looking at the conduct of the "big name" players (like Ivan Boesky)? Or does the ethics of business also depend significantly on all the unobserved actions of lesser-known workers who might never find their names on the newspaper headline?

2. "Do no harm" is one of the most basic of ethical duties. What kind of harm, if any, was committed by arbitrageurs?

3. What should financial companies do, at the level of organizational policy, to promote and enforce ethical behavior among their members? How much of the responsibility for ethical conduct falls on the individual?

4. What should the role of the government be in safeguarding the integrity of the financial markets? Should the U.S. financial markets be regulated by standards more stringent than those governing markets elsewhere in the world?

5. What responsibility, if any, do Wall Street firms have for their workers whose careers are disrupted by indictments that are unproven? Does society in general have a responsibility to people who are harmed by unproven indictments? Should the people be compensated, and how?

SUGGESTIONS FOR FURTHER READING

Chernow, Ron. *The House of Morgan.* New York: Atlantic Monthly Press, 1990.

Little, Jeffrey B., and Lucien Rhodes. *Understanding Wall Street.* Cockeysville, MD: Liberty Publishing Co., 1982.

Sobel, Robert. *Inside Wall Street.* New York: W.W. Norton & Company, 1982.

Stewart, James B. *Den of Thieves.* New York: Simon & Schuster, 1991.

ENDNOTES

1. From CNN Web site, available at http://www.cnn.com/2002/ SHOWBIZ/News/06/25/ martha.stewart/.

2. Constance L. Hays, "House Panel Defers to Justice Dept. on Stewart," *The New York Times* (September 11, 2002): pp. C1, C11.

3. Oliver August, "Insider Dealing Returns Thanks to Merger Mania," *The New York Times* (August 17, 1998): p. C1.

4. "Insider Trading–A U.S. Perspective," Thomas C. Newkirk and Melissa A. Robertson, presented at the 16th International Symposium on Economic Crime, Jesus College, Cambridge, England, September 19, 1998. Available at http://rider.wharton.upenn.edu/~waldfogj/SEC_speech.html.

5. Stephen Labaton and David Leonhardt, "Whispers Inside, Thunder Outside," *The New York Times* (June 30, 2002): Money and Business Section 3, p. 1.

6. Warren St. John, "Sorrow So Sweet: A Guilty Pleasure in Another's Woe," *The New York Times* (August 24, 2002): Section B, p. 7.

7. By 1990 the volume of arbitrage business had declined dramatically, in large measure due to negative reaction by business and the broader public against the excesses of the 1980s. But by the mid 1990s it appeared that arbitrage was making something of a comeback. One indication of this renewed activity is the increasing level of takeover activity and related arbitrage speculation. According to Laurence Zuckerman in "For Arbitragers, the Game is Afoot Once Again," *The New York Times* (December 4, 1994): p. F6, "Through November, $150.4 billion worth of deals were announced, involving 1,298 publicly-traded United States companies—more than in any prior year, though the 1994 dollar volume may fall short of the $178.4 billion achieved in 1988."

8. Steve Swartz and James B. Stewart, "Justice Delayed: Kidder's Mr. Wigton, Charged as 'Insider,' Ends His Long Ordeal," *The Wall Street Journal* (August 21, 1989): p. A10.

9. Susan Lee, *Susan Lee's ABZs of Money & Finance* (New York: Poseidon Press, 1988): p. 208.

10. Barbara Donnelly and Craig Torres, "Sluggish Wall Street Is Rushing into 'Derivatives'," *Wall Street Journal* (November 30, 1990): pp. C1, C9.

11. Jeffrey B. Little and Lucien Rhodes, *Understanding Wall Street* (Cockeysville,

MD: Liberty Publishing Co., 1982): p. 102.

12. James B. Stewart, *Den of Thieves* (New York: Simon & Schuster, 1991): p. 31.

13. The following account is drawn from Stewart, *Den of Thieves*.

14. Ibid, p. 158.

15. Gary L. Tidwell and Abdul Aziz, "Insider Trading: How Well Do You Understand the Current Status of the Law?" *California Management Review* 30 (summer 1988): 115–123.

16. *In re Cady, Roberts*, 40 SEC 907 (1961).

17. Sources for these cases and the theories on insider trading are from Tidwell and Aziz, "Insider Trading," and *Standards of Practice Handbook*, 6th ed. (Charlottesville, PA, Association for Investment Management and Research, 1992).

18. 903 F. 2d 75 (2nd Cir. 1990). See prior holding in 704 F. Supp. 451 (S.D.N.Y. 1989). Chestman had been convicted by a jury in the District Court of (1) tender of fraud under Section 14(e) and Rule 14(e)-3(a) of the Exchange Act, (2) securities fraud under Section 10(b) and Rule 10b-5 of the Exchange Act, (3) mail fraud, and (4) perjury.

19. John G. Gillis and Glenn J. Ciotti, "Insider Trading Update," *Financial Analyst Journal* (November/December 1992): p. 59.

20. Ron Chernow, *The House of Morgan* (New York: Atlantic Monthly Press, 1990): p. 320.

21. Robert Sobel, *Inside Wall Street* (New York: W.W. Norton & Company, 1982): pp. 103–104.

22. Richard H. K. Vietor, "Regulation-Defined Financial Markets: Fragmentation and Integration in Financial Services," in Samuel L. Hayes, ed., *Wall Street and Regulation* (Boston: Harvard Business School Press, 1987): p. 16.

23. Lee, *ABZs of Money & Finance*, op. cit. p. 186.

24. The SEC first required such a barrier in a Statement of Policy in *Merrill Lynch, Pierce, Fenner and Smith Inc.*, SEC Rel. No. 34-8459 (1968).

25. *Standards of Practice Handbook*, op. cit., p. 44.

26. Diana Henriques, "Handcuffing the Street? Effects of the Inside-Trading Scandal Will Be Severe," *Barron's* 67(7) (February 16, 1987): 18–24: p. 20.

27. Sobel, *Inside Wall Street*, op. cit., p. 167. Emphasis added.

28. William B. Irvine, "Insider Trading: An Ethical Appraisal," from Thomas I. White, *Business Ethics: A Philosophical Reader* (New York: Macmillan Publishing Company, 1993): p. 396.

29. The arguments in this section are summarized from philosophers' writings on insider trading that originally appeared in different academic journals and were collected in Thomas I. White, *Business Ethics: A Philosophical Reader* (New York: MacMillan Publishing Company, 1993): pp. 373–423. Students are encouraged to consult these articles in more detail.

30. The following summarizes some helpful points about these questions that were put forward by philosopher Jennifer Moore in her article, "What is Really Unethical About Insider Trading?" in White, *Business Ethics*, op. cit., pp. 404–419.

31. Moore, "What Is Really Unethical About Insider Trading?" op. cit., p. 413.

32. "Free the Giuliani 3!" *Wall Street Journal* (May 12, 1988): p. A22.

33. Steve Swartz and James B. Stewart, "Justice Delayed: Kidder's Mr. Wigton, Charged as 'Insider,' Ends His Long Ordeal," *Wall Street Journal* (August 21, 1989): p. A10.

34. Chris Welles, "The Debris in Rudolph Giuliani's Wake," *BusinessWeek* (January 23, 1989): pp. 36–37.

35. Swartz and Stewart, "Justice Delayed," op. cit., p. 10.

36. Ibid., p. 1.

8

⊛

Which Hat Must the Engineer Wear?

The *Challenger* Case

Questions to Keep in Mind

1. What was the evidence for concern about launching space shuttles under cold weather conditions? What were the reasons for setting aside this concern?

2. What are the important features of NASA's and Morton Thiokol's histories? In what ways are they similar?

3. How does an engineer's perspective differ from that of a business manager? How does this difference play a role in the decisions concerning the *Challenger* launch?

4. What is a whistleblower? What are the ethical and practical considerations that should be weighed by any whistleblower?

5. What is "microscopic vision"? What role did it play in the decision to launch the space shuttle *Challenger*?

WHY DID *COLUMBIA* FAIL?

On February 1, 2003, the space shuttle *Columbia* disintegrated into flaming pieces upon re-entry into Earth's atmosphere. Expectant family members and friends, NASA and government personnel, and others at the Florida landing site watched the countdown clock reach zero at 9:16 A.M. They did not know there already were reports from across eastern Texas and western Louisiana of loud noises from above, followed by plummeting debris. Some observers captured the breakup on video and film. The Internet rapidly disseminated vast quantities of detailed information about the disaster, even as the more traditional media broadcast the awful news: Another space shuttle was lost.

The catastrophic event triggered an intense inquiry into its causes. Almost immediately, suspicion was directed at a piece of insulation that ripped off the shuttle's external fuel tank 80 seconds after liftoff, possibly damaging the protective tiles on *Columbia*'s left wing. Within a couple of days, however, expert investigators allowed that they had not ruled out a variety of other possible causes, which could have combined to trigger a "cascading series of failures."[1] Despite the desire of many to uncover a single "missing link" that would explain what happened, it gradually became clear that the final explanation would likely not be a simple one. There were many factors to consider.

An army of engineers and scientists mounted a technical analysis of what had gone wrong. A space shuttle is an extraordinarily complex technological achievement, and any number of things could have gone wrong. Experts speculated that Columbia's failure could have been caused by an explosion of the ship's fuels, a collapse in the shuttle's aged structure, a computer problem causing reentry navigation error, or being struck by a meteoroid or a piece of space debris. Terrorism was thought unlikely. Shuttles are exposed to such large stresses that even minor mishaps can quickly escalate into catastrophic failure. NASA officials have said that the chance of a shuttle failure is about 1 in 145 (compared to the 1 in 2 million chance of a commercial airline failure).[2]

As the investigation proceeded, other factors began to emerge. Questions arose about who knew what and when about the possible risks to the shuttle. Once *Columbia* had been lost, reports surfaced in the media of studies from as early as 1990 and 1997 about the vulnerability of the tiles and the risks from the insulating foam.[3] Nearly a month into the investigation, the public learned that NASA engineers had emailed their strong concerns to each other, while *Columbia* still orbited the earth, doing "what if" scenarios about what might happen if the tiles were indeed damaged. Lawmaker representative Anthony Weiner (D-NY) critically challenged NASA administrator Sean O'Keefe about why O'Keefe had not learned of these email exchanges until some weeks after the shuttle loss.[4] O'Keefe defended his not knowing about conversations among lower-level engineers, questioning whether senior managers should be routinely involved in technical discussions of engineers.[5] (O'Keefe himself has a financial background, not an engineering degree.) Thus the inquiry about *Columbia* moved beyond purely technical and scientific information to concerns about how that information was communicated and managed among decision-makers.

Management concerns extended to the ways in which NASA was outsourcing work on the shuttle. The primary subcontractor to NASA on the shuttle program was the United Space Alliance, which is owned jointly by Boeing and Lockheed Martin. This alliance also subcontracts NASA-related work to more than 120 other companies. It's big business for these companies: NASA awarded the United Space Alliance a $9 billion contract for the period from 1996 to 2002. This award was then extended for an additional $2.9 billion until September 2004.[6] Whatever the merits of this arrangement, critics have charged that such outsourcing made it harder for NASA to ensure that safety standards were being met.

Ultimately, questions about the *Columbia* failure moved to broader policy concerns about NASA's mission and its stature among various governmental programs benefiting the public interest. Ever since the phenomenal success of the first landing of humans on the moon, NASA has had an increasingly difficult time getting financial support from Congress. In fact, after problems on an earlier *Columbia* mission in 1999, there was a debate about whether sufficient funds were being devoted to the space program. "In the months that followed [the 1999 mission], a broad range of experts, including many from inside NASA, arrived at an alarming consensus: Years of deep budget cuts in the shuttle program—cuts that had shed more than 10,000 engineers, technicians and quality control employees—were potentially imperiling the lives of astronauts."[7]

NASA has lost two space shuttles: *Challenger* in 1986 and now *Columbia*. Obviously, the nature and details of these two failures differ dramatically. And yet it must be acknowledged that attitudes toward this most recent loss are shaped profoundly by memories of what some have called the "uneven" *Challenger* investigation.[8] At the time of this writing, we are still without an explanation for what caused *Columbia* to fail. Whatever the outcome of the current investigation, we can better appreciate the significance of its emerging findings by situating them against the backdrop of the wake-up call of the space shuttle *Challenger*.

I. THE TRAGIC EXPLOSION OF SPACE SHUTTLE *CHALLENGER*

Taken from a *New York Times* transcript of the last moments of the space shuttle Challenger, before and after liftoff:

PUBLIC AFFAIRS OFFICER: Coming up on the 90-second point in our countdown. Ninety seconds and counting. The 51-L Mission is ready to go. . . . T minus 10, 9, 8, 7, 6, we have main engine start, 4, 3, 2, 1. And liftoff. Liftoff of the twenty-fifth space shuttle mission and it has cleared the tower. . . .

MISSION CONTROL CENTER: Watch your roll, *Challenger.*

PUBLIC AFFAIRS OFFICER: Roll program confirmed. *Challenger* now heading down range. [Pause.] Engines beginning throttling down now at 94 percent. Normal throttle for most of flight 104 percent. Will throttle down to 65 percent. Three engines running normally. Three good cells, three good ABU's. [Pause.] Velocity 2,257 feet per second, altitude 4.3 nautical miles, down range distance 3 nautical miles. [Pause.] Engines throttling up, three engines now at 104 percent.

MISSION CONTROL: *Challenger,* go with throttle up.

FRANCIS R. SCOBEE, *CHALLENGER* COMMANDER: Roger, go with throttle up.

PUBLIC AFFAIRS OFFICER: One minute 15 seconds, velocity 2,900 feet per second, altitude 9 nautical miles, down range distance 7 nautical miles. [Long pause.] Flight controllers here looking very carefully at the situation. [Pause.] Obviously a major malfunction. We have no downlink [communications from *Challenger*]. [Long pause.] We have a report from the flight dynamics officer that the vehicle has exploded.[9]

January 28, 1986, was the day of the explosion of the space shuttle *Challenger.* Only 73 seconds into its flight, the *Challenger* disintegrated in a catastrophic explosion. All seven astronauts aboard died, including Christa McAuliffe, a teacher from Concord, New Hampshire, who was to have been the first ordinary citizen to travel in outer space. At the launch site and at home before their television sets, Americans watched in disbelief, scarcely able to comprehend what had just happened before their eyes. According to a reporter for the *The New York Times*:

> It seemed to be one of those moments, enlarged and frozen, that people would remember and recount for the rest of their lives—what they were doing and where they were when they heard that the space shuttle *Challenger* had exploded. The need to reach out, to speak of disbelief and pain, was everywhere. Family members telephoned one another, friends telephoned friends.
>   "It was like the Kennedy thing," said John Hannan, who heard the news when his sister called him at his office, a personnel recruiting concern in Philadelphia. "Everyone was numb."[10]

The loss of *Challenger* and its astronauts signaled more than just the ruin of an expensive space shuttle and the destruction of human life. It also constituted a profound blow to the fragile confidence of a nation that had begun to pick up the pieces after Vietnam and Watergate. At first, the *Challenger* disaster seemed to be a terrible tragedy, but only that—an inexplicable misfortune. It was reported the next day that "Debris from the explosion of the shuttle *Challenger* was scattered so widely over the Atlantic Ocean that investigators may never recover enough of it to pin down the cause of the disaster."[11] Early suspicion was directed at the large fuel tank that accompanied the shuttle in early flight.

Later, a closer examination of events surrounding the *Challenger* explosion showed that this was not just a cruel act of blind fate. To the contrary, the *Challenger* disaster stands as a monumental wake-up call to business, government, and the American public, challenging them to think more deeply about the workings of individual moral responsibility in the context of organizational practice and decision-making.

II. SOMETHING WAS NOT RIGHT

The following is an account of the final shuttle flight procedures from that morning:[12]

January 28, 1986. 1:30 A.M. to 3:00 A.M. at Kennedy. The ice crew reports large quantities of ice on pad B. The spacecraft can be damaged by chunks of ice that can be hurled about during the turbulent rocket ignition.

5:00 A.M. at Kennedy. Mulloy [Chief of Solid Rockets at NASA's Marshall Center] tells Lucas [Director of NASA's Marshall Center] of MTI [Morton Thiokol] concerns over temperature and resolution and shows the recommendation written by MTI.

7:00 A.M. to 9:00 A.M. at Kennedy. The clear morning sky formed what glider pilots call a "blue bowl." Winds dwindled to 9 mph. During the night temperatures fell to 27 degrees Fahrenheit. The ice crew measures temperatures at 25 degrees Fahrenheit on the right-hand solid rocket booster, 8 degrees Fahrenheit on the left. They are not concerned as there are no Launch Commit Criteria relating to temperatures on rocket surfaces.

8:00 A.M. at Kennedy. Lovingwood [NASA] tells Deputy Director of Marshall (Lee) about previous discussions with MTI.

9:00 A.M at Kennedy. Mission Management Team meets with Level 1 and 2 managers, project managers, and others. The ice conditions on launch pad are discussed, but not the O-ring issue.

10:30 A.M. at Kennedy. The ice crew reports to the Mission Management Team that ice is still left on booster.

11:18 A.M. A Rockwell engineer in California watching the ice team over closed-circuit television telephones the Cape to advise a delay because of the ice. Kennedy Center Director Smith, advised by the ice team that there is little risk, permits the countdown to continue.

11:28 A.M. Inside *Challenger's* flight deck (about the size of a 747), Commander Scobee and pilot Smith run through their elaborate checklists. The orbiter's main computer, supported by four backup computers, scans data from 2,000 sensors. If it detects a problem, it will shut down the entire system. In June 1984, the computer aborted four seconds before the rocket ignition. This time, it doesn't.

11:30 A.M. Thousands of motorists pull off highways to face toward the ocean.

11:37 A.M. The launch platform is flooded by powerful streams of water from 7-foot pipes to dampen the lift-off sound levels, which could damage the craft's underside.

11:38 A.M. Flight 51-L is launched. Two rust-colored external fuel tanks, each 154 feet high, carrying 143,351 gallons of liquid oxygen and 385,265 gallons of liquid hydrogen power the rocket. They will burn until the fuel runs out.

11:39 A.M. Everything looked like it was supposed to look. As one MTI engineer watched the rocket lift off the pad into a bright Florida sky he thought, "Gee, it's gonna be all right. It's a piece of cake . . . we made it."

Among those watching the launch were engineers responsible for the rocket boosters who opposed the launch, and their reactions to the initial moments of liftoff reflected their anxiety. According to another account of *Challenger's* liftoff:

> On January 28, 1986, a reluctant Roger Boisjoly watched the launch of the *Challenger*. As the vehicle cleared the tower, Bob Ebeling whispered, "we've just dodged a bullet." (The engineers who opposed the launch assumed that O-ring failure would result in an explosion almost immediately after engine ignition.) To continue in Boisjoly's words, "At approximately T+60 seconds Bob told me he had just completed a prayer of thanks to the Lord for a successful launch. Just thirteen seconds later we both saw the horror of the destruction as the vehicle exploded.[13]

As these accounts show, there had been a debate over the potential risks posed by the unseasonably cold weather that morning. In particular, there was concern about the effects of the cold on something called an "O-ring." These accounts also show that there were several parties to the debate within NASA and between NASA and Morton Thiokol, the manufacturer of the solid fuel rocket boosters for the space shuttle program. As this chapter will show, the debate about the safety of the O-rings under cold conditions had been brewing for some time. However, this debate failed to postpone *Challenger*'s January 28 launch date, for a variety of complex reasons. The Presidential Commission on the Space Shuttle Challenger Accident later described the cause of the explosion as follows:

> The consensus of the Commission and participating investigative agencies is that the loss of the Space Shuttle Challenger was caused by a failure in the joint between the two lower segments of the right Solid Rocket Motor. The specific failure was the destruction of the seals that are intended to prevent hot gases from leaking through the joint during the propellant burn of the rocket motor. The evidence assembled by the Commission indicates that no other element of the Space Shuttle system contributed to this failure.[14]

The purpose of this chapter is to describe some of the key issues concerning individual and organizational responsibility in a highly pressured business situation, with special emphasis on the problem of whistleblowing. First we will review the history of the debate about the O-rings and the shuttle's safety, within Morton Thiokol and between Morton Thiokol and NASA. Next, we will describe some of the key organizational features of NASA and Morton Thiokol that decisively shaped the contours of this debate. Finally, by looking at Roger Boisjoly's experience following the *Challenger* explosion, we will draw some important lessons for whistleblowing. This account concludes with some thoughts about the unsettling implications of this wake-up call for reconciling different perspectives on responsibility in business.

III. GROWING CONCERN ABOUT O-RINGS

It was fully one year before the *Challenger* explosion when Roger Boisjoly began to have serious questions about the safety of the solid rocket boosters that Morton Thiokol manufactured for NASA's space shuttles.[15] Boisjoly was Senior Scientist at Morton Thiokol with twenty-five years of experience as an aerospace industry engineer. On January 24, 1985, he observed the launch of space shuttle flight 51-C, as part of his responsibility for the safety of the solid rocket booster joints. The air temperature that day was unseasonably cool. The launch seemed to go normally. The solid rocket boosters separated from *Challenger* after they had burned their fuel, falling to the ocean. They were later recovered and inspected by Boisjoly. He detected something in the solid rocket boosters that worried him.

The boosters are so large that they are made up of separate segments. The connecting joints between the segments is sealed by a rubber-like material called the O-rings. These seals must not leak during launch or else an explosion is very likely. Boisjoly found, while inspecting the primary O-ring seals on two field joints, that the joints had been damaged by hot combustion gases. Part of the primary O-ring had eroded. As far as Boisjoly knew, this was the first time a primary seal on a booster field joint had been penetrated by hot gases. He found a large quantity of blackened grease between the primary and secondary seals, which alarmed him even more. Boisjoly learned from a post-flight analysis that the ambient temperature of the field joints (the temperature in the area surrounding the joints) at time of launch was 53 degrees. He remembered how cold it was the day of the launch. For the first time, Boisjoly suspected there might be a connection between the damage to the O-rings and the low air temperature. He reported his suspicions to engineers and managers at NASA's Marshall Space Flight Center. However, the association of low temperature with evidence of hot gas leakage through a field joint was termed an "acceptable risk" by key NASA officials.

In March Boisjoly conducted laboratory tests on the O-ring seals, working with Arnie Thompson, Supervisor of Rocket Motor Cases. The tests supported his theory that low temperatures prevented O-ring seals from forming an adequate seal on solid rocket booster joints. Boisjoly and Thompson did not know with certainty the temperature below which it would be too dangerous for a safe flight. They only knew that at very cold temperatures neither the primary or secondary O-rings would seal. The consequences of this double failure would be a catastrophic explosion. Boisjoly's concerns were reported to key engineers and managers at NASA and Morton Thiokol.

Even though a Seal Erosion Task Force was informally created in July, Boisjoly was increasingly frustrated by what he perceived to be a lack of progress in fixing the problem. At that point, Boisjoly wrote a memo, labelled "Company Private," which he sent to Robert (Bob) Lund, Vice President of Engineering at Morton Thiokol. The memo, which Boisjoly intended to express the extreme urgency of his views, contained the following passages:

> This letter is written to insure that management is fully aware of the seriousness of the current O-ring erosion problem. . . . The mistakenly accepted position on the joint problem was to fly without fear of failure . . . is now drastically changed as a result of the SRM 16A nozzle joint erosion which eroded a secondary O-ring with the primary O-ring never sealing. If the same scenario should occur in a field joint (and it could), then it is a jump ball as to the success or failure of the joint . . . The result would be a catastrophe of the highest order—loss of human life . . .
>
> It is my honest and real fear that if we do not take immediate action to dedicate a team to solve the problem, with the field joint having the number one priority, then we stand in jeopardy of losing a flight along with all the launch pad facilities.[16]

Following his receipt of the memo, in August Lund formally constituted the Seal Erosion Task Team. However, this team consisted of a mere five full-time engineers (there were 2,500 employed by Morton Thiokol working on the Space Shuttle Program). To some engineers at Morton Thiokol, it appeared that the Seal Erosion Task Team was never adequately supported in its implementation. Moreover, there were indications that senior Morton Thiokol managers did not take seriously the team's concerns. For example, the Seal Erosion Task Team met with Joe Kilminster (Vice President for Boosters) on October 3, 1985, to raise their concerns about the lack of corporate support. "Boisjoly later stated that Kilminster summarized the meeting as a 'good bullshit session.'"[17] During the next two months leading up to the launch of the space shuttle *Challenger*, it would appear that Boisjoly and the Seal Erosion Task Team made little headway against the indifference and even opposition that they perceived among certain Morton Thiokol executives.

IV. THE TELECONFERENCE BETWEEN MORTON THIOKOL AND NASA

The debate over the safety of the O-ring seals came to a head during a key telephone conference call between Morton Thiokol and NASA just before the launch of the space shuttle *Challenger* on January 28. The day before the launch, the weather forecast for conditions at the launch site predicted temperatures as low as 18 degrees. The situation was monitored closely by Morton Thiokol personnel at the Marshall Space Flight Center, as well as at the Kennedy Space Center. The debate over what to do culminated in a three-way telephone conference call between three teams of engineers and managers. The call took place at 8:15 P.M. Eastern Standard Time, the evening before the scheduled launch.

In this teleconference, Boisjoly and Thompson presented their scientific evidence about the effects of cold temperatures on the O-ring's ability to maintain a reliable seal. Based on their findings, they recommended against the launch of *Challenger*. The key facts supporting their position were:

> Although there was some leaking around the seal even at relatively high temperatures, the worst leakage was at 53 degrees. With a predicted ambient temperature of 26 degrees at launch, the O-rings were estimated to be at 29 degrees. This was much lower than the launch temperatures of any previous flight.[18]

It is important to note that the engineers could not state with precision the exact temperature when the O-rings would be too cold for a safe launch. It is also pertinent that engineers are trained to err on the side of caution when assessing risk.

Bob Lund summarized Boisjoly's and Thompson's report, saying that it was Morton Thiokol's recommendation that any launch should proceed only if the

O-ring seal temperature was at least 53 degrees. Kilminster supported the position of his engineers.

NASA's response was highly critical of this recommendation. One member of NASA's team, George Hardy, was reported to be "appalled at that recommendation." Larry Mulloy, Chief of Solid Rockets at the Marshall Space Flight Center, also strongly opposed Morton Thiokol's position. He objected to what he considered to be a substantive revision of the Launch Commit Criteria at what was almost literally the last minute before a launch. It is reported that Mulloy complained in exasperation, "My God, Thiokol, when do you want me to launch? Next April?"[19] Confronted by this withering criticism, Kilminster asked for a five-minute caucus with his engineers, putting the NASA side of the teleconference "on hold."

In his testimony before the Rogers Commission that later investigated the *Challenger* explosion, Boisjoly described the caucus as follows: Jerry Mason (Senior Vice President of Wasatch Operations at Morton Thiokol) insisted that a "management decision" was necessary. Boisjoly and Thompson attempted to argue their position again, but stopped when they perceived that no one was really listening to them anymore. Jerry Mason, who was reported to have said, "Am I the only one who wants to fly?" then instructed Bob Lund to "take off your engineering hat and put on your management hat." Following a brief discussion, the four Morton Thiokol managers at that discussion then voted unanimously to recommend *Challenger's* launch. Their recommendation, which was telefaxed to the Kennedy and Marshall Centers, reads as follows:

MTI Assessment of Temperature Concern on SRM-25 (51L) Launch

- Calculations show that SRM-25 O-rings will be 20 degrees colder than SRM-15 O-rings
- Temperature data not conclusive on predicting primary O-ring blow-by
- Engineering assessment is that:
- Colder O-rings will have increased effective durometer ("Harder")
- "Harder" O-rings will take longer to "seat"
- More gas may pass primary O-ring before the primary seal seats (relative to SRM-15)
- Demonstrated sealing threshold is 3 times greater than 0.038 degrees erosion experienced on SRM-15
- If the primary seal does not seat, the secondary seal will seat
- O-ring pressure leak check places secondary seal in outboard position which minimizes sealing time
- MTI recommends STS-51L launch proceed on 28 January 1986
- SRM-25 will not be significantly different from SRM-15
  [Signed: Joe C. Kilminster, Vice President, Space Booster Programs, Wasatch Division of Morton Thiokol, Inc.][20]

According to Boisjoly's account of this teleconference, he and the other engineers present were excluded from the decision making that led to this memo's recommendation to launch. The final decision came from the four senior Morton Thiokol executives present at the teleconference. Upon returning to his office, Boisjoly made the following entry in his journal:

> I sincerely hope this launch does not result in a catastrophe. I personally do not agree with some of the statements made in Joe Kilminster's written summary stating that SRM-25 is okay to fly.[21]

V. ORGANIZATIONAL FEATURES OF NASA AND MORTON THIOKOL

Critical management decisions, like the one to recommend continuing with the January 28 launch, do not occur in a vacuum. Even though we can identify individual persons making the decisions and even though we should not minimize the importance of individual responsibility, we also should not overlook the ways that organizations shape individuals' decisions and actions. To understand more adequately the debate about the O-ring seals, it is important to take into account the organizational context and history of the space shuttle program, as well as the business relationship between NASA and its suppliers. In this section we will review several important organizational features of NASA and Morton Thiokol that set the stage for the debate about the O-ring seals. First we will summarize some important features of NASA's historical development and its approach to decision-making.[22]

Until World War II, U.S. space exploration research was not well planned or very professional. It was a time when amateur scientists and tinkerers experimented widely, yielding no significant progress in rocketry science. The horrors of war, particularly the specter of Germany's devastating military rockets, pushed the U.S. government to mobilize the nation's resources to get America into space. But apart from the agenda of maintaining military and technical superiority, the United States lacked a thoughtful, systematic mission plan for space exploration.

Any complacency about America's superiority was seriously tested on October 4, 1957, when the Soviet Union launched Sputnik I into space, the first satellite to go into orbit. The United States had to scramble to compete in this new "space race." In an important early step, the National Aeronautics and Space Act (NASA) was signed into law on October 1, 1958. Now the United States had a civilian agency charged with the responsibility of bringing strategy and purpose to the country's space efforts.

For a while, NASA rose masterfully to meet its many challenges. When President Kennedy issued his historic announcement that the United States would put Americans on the moon within ten years, few doubted that NASA had the "right stuff" necessary to pull it off. Under NASA's direction, the nation took pride in a succession of highly publicized and largely successful initiatives into space: the Mercury, Gemini, and Apollo programs. And NASA made good on its promise. As the world watched in July 1969, *Apollo 11* touched down on lunar soil.

Ironically, NASA's monumental success created its biggest challenge: What to do next? In the years that followed the success of Apollo, it became increasingly clear that NASA lacked a viable long-term mission to carry it forward. That is why, in 1969, when the Nixon administration had to choose among various options for NASA's next steps, it simply went for one of the less expensive alternatives, the space shuttle (which was a lot cheaper than an orbiting space station). Unfortunately for NASA, the space shuttle program was less glamorous than the quest for the moon. As public support dwindled for government spending, NASA found that it no longer easily commanded broad support for its work. Compromises had to be made, which threatened the integrity of the space shuttle program. According to a *New York Times* article in the mid 1980s:

> To satisfy Congress, the [space shuttle] system had to pay for itself, which meant that NASA, chartered as a research and development agency, was put in the unaccustomed position of hustling business and running an orbital freight operation. The conflicting goals and pressures, as well as the complexity of the machines themselves, virtually assured that America's Space Transportation—as the shuttle is officially known—would not operate with the efficiency its original designers had planned.[23]

As this historical sketch shows, the scientists and engineers of NASA did not operate in an idealized ivory tower. Public relations had always been an important factor in NASA's actions and decisions—the original seven *Mercury* astronauts were cheered as All-Americans with the "right stuff." Especially after the success of the Apollo program, NASA had to justify its existence to increasingly indifferent, sometimes critical, political administrations. In the Reagan years, NASA had to counter the political agenda of downsizing government by showing how it could efficiently meet private-sector needs. Thus, science alone did not drive NASA's decision-making. Politics, business, and public relations all played their role in its thinking.

Some critics of NASA charge that its lack of mission and its vulnerability to bottom-line pressure contributed to shortcuts on safety. To these critics, it should be pointed out that space exploration is inherently risky. Even in its early glory days, NASA was plagued with failures. In 1959, seven of its seventeen rockets launched misfired. In 1967, in what was supposed to be a routine test, a flash fire erupted in an Apollo command module, burning to death the three astronauts strapped in their seats. Even then, some critics claim, NASA was motivated by more pragmatic interests:

Despite "official" stringent safety standards, the agency was more concerned with meeting deadlines than with safety issues. NASA used this tragedy to its best advantage. Invoking the memory of the dead, they stressed the importance of getting on with the program because that's what the astronauts would have wanted. In spite of this setback, Kennedy's challenge to land a man on the moon was met.[24]

Increasingly, decisions at NASA were made from a management and a political perspective, not just from a scientific or engineering perspective. Interestingly, a similar conflict in organizational perspective was to be found at Morton Thiokol.

Morton Thiokol, a company formed when Morton Salt Company acquired Thiokol, displayed features of two different, somewhat contrasting corporate cultures.[25] Morton, the parent company, endeavored to have an organizational structure that promoted candid, direct communication through the corporate hierarchy. It sought to implement an "open door" policy through actions like giving its workers the home telephone numbers of all its management.

Thiokol was also a hierarchical company, but it contrasted with Morton in the ways in which it funneled communication through its layers. The Wasatch division, responsible for manufacturing the solid rocket boosters for the space shuttle, has been described as an autocratic organization. In this division, employee complaints were not particularly encouraged or welcomed. In such a setting, it would be hazardous for any employee to do an "end run" around his or her boss in order to communicate a complaint higher in the organization. According to business ethicist Patricia Werhane, who is speaking about the Wasatch division:

> This rigid hierarchy led to difficulties. There was a lack of communication and with that an absence of trust between managers and engineers so a subsequent isolation of managers from proper reading of the data, and, as a result, isolation of NASA not from information, but from varying analyses of the information. The lingering effects of the old Thiokol culture demanded unquestioned loyalty from engineers such as McDonald or Boisjoly.[26]

To summarize, it was individuals who made critically important decisions that led to the January 28 launch of *Challenger*. The responsibility for that decision belongs to them. But their decision-making was shaped by long-standing traditions in organizations' policies and cultures. If the organizational patterns of decision-making had been different, it is possible that the individuals in question would have reached a different decision about whether to launch. The wake-up call of the *Challenger* explosion serves to remind us not to overlook the importance of organizations for the actions of the individuals who inhabit them.

VI. THE PROBLEM OF WHISTLEBLOWING

Roger Boisjoly was a whistleblower, in the sense that he tried to "blow the whistle" on the problem of the O-ring seals. Whistleblowing is defined as "the disclosure by organizational members of illegal, immoral, or illegitimate organizational acts or omissions to parties who can take action to correct the wrongdoing."[27] Boisjoly blew the whistle when he wrote his memo to Bob Lund labeled, Company Private, calling attention to the potential problem of the O-rings and to the perceived lack of concern by certain Morton Thiokol executives. Since Lund was an executive of Morton Thiokol, this kind of whistleblowing qualifies as internal rather than external whistleblowing. It would have been a different matter altogether had Boisjoly had sent his memo to someone *outside* the corporation, like a reporter for *The New York Times*.

After the *Challenger* explosion, Boisjoly again acted in ways that constitute whistleblowing. For example, he provided key testimony to the Rogers Commission about the debates leading up to the launch decision. This was more like external whistleblowing, since Boisjoly's views were being made public to a governmental investigating commission. This action also counts as whistleblowing in the sense that Boisjoly was trying to bring to light information that otherwise might have remained hidden from public scrutiny. Boisjoly said that Morton Thiokol's lawyers advised him to answer questions from the government only with a "yes" or "no" and not to volunteer any additional information on his own. But he felt that this kind of response would not bring the truth to light.

It is a complicated moral issue about whether to blow the whistle on an organization that one belongs to. Also important is the question of *how* one should do so. The standard view of loyalty holds that an employee has a basic duty to be <u>loyal</u> to his or her employer. Whistleblowing is an act of disloyalty and thus should be undertaken only if, morally, there are other more pressing duties. Many ethicists say something like, "Sometimes you should blow the whistle on your company, but only when you have passed certain tests or criteria for when ethically it is permissible to do so." One philosopher, Sisella Bok, has summarized a number of important considerations to take into account when deciding whether to blow the whistle.[28] According to Bok, before you blow the whistle, you should be sure that:

- A specific wrongdoing or abuse poses a present or imminent threat.

- You make every effort to consider the effects of speaking out and to ensure the accuracy of your accusation.

- You first explore existing avenues for reporting the problem within the organization (many corporations have special hotline telephone numbers or designated officers—like ombudsmen—to facilitate internal whistleblowing).

- You are fair to the persons accused of wrongdoing, making sure that your complaint is one the public is entitled to hear about.

- You are not blowing the whistle simply for self-aggrandizement, publicity, or revenge. Rather, you are acting for the public good or for the higher good of the organization.

These points underscore the important ethical dimension of whistleblowing. Beyond the purely ethical question, however, there are crucial *practical* issues raised by whistleblowing, as Boisjoly's experience bears out. One might think that Boisjoly should have been treated as a hero for trying to prevent the *Challenger* launch and for making sure the public found out the truth afterward. To the contrary: Boisjoly's actions cost him his job and nearly cost him his sanity.[29]

After the *Challenger* explosion, Boisjoly told the Rogers Commission about the prelaunch teleconference between Morton Thiokol and NASA. It was his testimony that revealed publicly that Morton Thiokol's recommendation to launch had not been unanimous. This testimony ". . . drove a wedge further between him and Morton Thiokol management." Following his testimony to the Rogers Commission, Morton Thiokol whisked Boisjoly away by jet before he had a chance to hear NASA's testimony about the prelaunch teleconference. The next day, Boisjoly was removed from the failure investigation team, on which he had played a crucially important role. Morton Thiokol returned him to Utah.

Boisjoly started having doubts about his role in the company thereafter. Morton Thiokol gave him the title of Seal Coordinator for the seal redesign effort. But Boisjoly found that he was isolated from NASA, where the real action was taking place with seal redesign. Senior Morton Thiokol executives chastised him for "airing the company's dirty laundry" before the Rogers Commission.

Sensing a major problem developing with his position at Morton Thiokol, Boisjoly and fellow worker Al McDonald met with the company's three top executives on May 16, 1986. Boisjoly felt that they were unresponsive to his concerns about his role in the seal redesign effort. In effect, he had been demoted. According to Boisjoly, the CEO told him and McDonald that Morton Thiokol "was doing just fine until Al and I testified about our job reassignments."[30] On July 21, 1986, Roger Boisjoly requested an extended sick leave, and later left Morton Thiokol. He sued the company for $1 million for personal injuries, saying that Morton Thiokol harassed him and that he experienced severe mental depression. He lost his case.[31]

The consequences for Boisjoly, though unfortunate, are not unusual. While most companies urge their employees to use appropriate internal communications channels to blow the whistle on corporate wrongdoers, many employees are reluctant to do so. They correctly perceive that, in many instances, the whistleblower is hurt by his or her actions, whether in terms of job loss, job reassignment, or something less tangible like acquiring a negative stigma that one can't be shaken. The problem of promoting constructive dissent within corporations reflects an ambivalence about whistleblowing in our broader culture. The public message in our culture tends to say something like "the constructive whistleblower is a hero." There have been many movies made that have celebrated this public message. At the same time, the implicit message of our culture is, "Don't be a tattletale," and, "Nobody likes to work with a snitch." In light of this ambivalence about whistleblowing, the would-be whistleblower faces important <u>practical</u> questions in addition to the previously mentioned ethical considerations. Put very simply, the question before us is, "How do I blow the whistle without compromising my job?" Many companies have implemented communications mechanisms to protect the constructive whistleblower, and yet it is fair to conclude that whistleblowing is a risky activity and is not undertaken lightly by many workers.

VII. PERSPECTIVE, RISK, AND RESPONSIBILITY

It would be misleading to describe whistleblowing situations as a simple conflict between "bad guys" and "good guys." There is often confusion about where to place final responsibility for what happens. With the space shuttle *Challenger*, for example, we need to recognize that different actors in this case brought different perspectives to their reading of the facts. These different perspectives do not excuse key decision-makers from taking responsibility for their judgments. But by recognizing how differences in perspective contribute to different assessments of risk, we can make a more informed judgment about where to place responsibility for the *Challenger* explosion. In addition, by learning to appreciate the moral impact of differing interpretations of the facts, we are better equipped to recognize potential conflicts of perspective, which may help us prevent catastrophes like the *Challenger* explosion from happening again.

Some experts on the *Challenger* case have concluded that the explosion was partly the result of different perceptions and priorities among the engineers and managers at Morton Thiokol and at NASA.[32] Any number of factors can affect how we view a particular ethical issue or case. Our perspective can be distorted by our own self-interest, which leads us to emphasize the features of the case that are most likely to forward our objectives. Sometimes our perspective is skewed by sheer laziness (we don't bother to collect sufficient evidence) or willful ignorance.

In the case of the space shuttle *Challenger*, no doubt many factors shaped the differing perspectives of the participating engineers and managers. For the present analysis, however, we will focus on just one very important obstacle to impartial perspective—what some philosophers call "microscopic vision."[33] With microscopic vision, sometimes people commit bad acts not because they are bad people, but because they are focusing only on a very particular aspect of their situation. Seen strictly within the parameters of their narrow perspective, their acts or judgments may appear perfectly defensible. But from a larger perspective, their acts or judgments may be more problematic. Microscopic vision may justify actions that are not justifiable from a broader perspective.

To give one example of microscopic vision at work in the *Challenger* case, let us return to the teleconference meeting between Morton Thiokol and NASA the night before the launch. Led by Boisjoly, Morton Thiokol's engineers were recommending <u>against</u> a launch under such cold conditions. Initially, Vice President for Engineering Bob Lund supported his engineers' judgment. But after NASA's strong objection to this recommendation (and while NASA was put on hold in the teleconference), Senior Vice President Jerry Mason allegedly told Lund to "take off your engineering hat, and put on your management hat." At that point, Lund reversed his position and endorsed the recommendation to proceed with the launch the next morning.

Why did Lund change his mind on launching *Challenger* during this "management caucus?" In his testimony to the Rogers Commission on February 25, Lund explained his thinking as follows:

> CHAIRMAN ROGERS: How do you explain the fact that you seemed to change your mind when you changed your hat?
>
> MR. LUND: I guess we have got to go back a little further in the conversation than that. We have dealt with [NASA Marshall Center] for a long time and have always been in the position of defending our position to make sure that we were ready to fly, and I guess I didn't realize until after that meeting and after several days that we had absolutely changed our position from what it had been before. But that evening I guess I had never had those kinds of thing come from the people at Marshall. We had to prove to them that we weren't ready, and so we got ourselves in the thought process that we were trying to find some way to prove to them it wouldn't work, and we were unable to do that. We couldn't prove absolutely that that motor wouldn't work.
>
> CHAIRMAN ROGERS: In other words, you honestly believed that you had a duty to prove that it would not work?
>
> MR. LUND: Well, that is kind of the mode we got ourselves into that evening. It seems like we have always been in the opposite mode. I should have detected that, but I did not, but the roles kind of switched. . . .[34]

How is this an example of microscopic vision? We start with the presupposition that Lund need not necessarily have been doing anything intentionally wrong when he changed his mind. There is no obvious basis for charging that he was blinded by self-interest, laziness, or ignorance. Rather, a plausible account of what happened is that when Lund removed his engineering hat and put on his management hat, he changed the microscope lens through which he viewed the launch decision. Viewing the matter strictly through the highly focused lens of the engineering perspective, Lund saw the launch decision one way. Then, viewing the matter from the narrow perspective of the manager, he saw it another way. It is important to recognize that engineers and managers are trained to view things differently. Engineers tend to focus on risk while managers tend to focus on profit. In their assessment of risk, engineers traditionally take a conservative stance, "better safe than sorry." In their calculation of profit, managers traditionally seek to maximize benefits over costs. As one philosopher describes the microscopic vision of engineers:

> Often they work from tables approved by the appropriate professional association or other standard-setting agency. When they do not have such tables, they try not to go substantially beyond what experience has shown to be safe. Engineers do not, in general, balance risk against benefit. They reduce risk to permissible levels and only then proceed. Managers, on the other hand, generally do balance risk against benefit.[35]

Lund was trained both as an engineer and as a manager. He had the capacity to view decisions through both lenses. But in the heat of the pressured decision situation of the *Challenger* launch, he apparently did not take a broader view and try to view the launch decision simultaneously from both perspectives. One way that humans deal with complexity is to limit their focus to a narrow range of pertinent facts. It would seem that Lund handled the challenge of this situation by isolating the two perspectives in his thinking, resulting in two quite different judgments.

> Of course, a complicating factor in this case is that Lund was both an engineer and a manager. The normal expectation is that he should wear both hats, thus having the apparent advantage of being able to see into two microscopes, lift his head, and place matters in a larger perspective than either alone permits. Yet, on this occasion, he was encouraged to look into only one microscope. Accepting the invitation, apparently Lund no longer saw what he normally, as an engineer, would see—and, thus, he lost sight of his basic engineering responsibility to microscopically focus on safety.[36]

Of course, there were compelling reasons to adopt a managerial perspective in this situation. NASA was saying that it wanted very much to launch. NASA was a major customer and source of significant profits for Morton Thiokol; to oppose NASA would be tantamount to denying what the customer wants. From a purely management perspective, which weighs costs and benefits and tends to side with the wishes of the customer, the justifiable response to the situation here is to recommend that the launch proceed.

There are advantages to microscopic vision. Its close attention to a narrow range of detail permits us to see things that otherwise would escape our attention. Microscopic vision naturally accompanies advanced division of labor—something generally regarded as a positive feature of an advanced economy. But microscopic vision has its disadvantages too. While we gain accurate, detailed knowledge at the microscopic level, we may fail to keep before our view the bigger picture. The *Challenger* catastrophe provides a grim lesson in what can happen when we do not recognize and test the adequacy of the particular microscopic perspectives that inform our decisions. One important lesson from this wake-up call is that people making business judgments must pause occasionally to lift their eyes from their microscopes, to remind themselves of what the big picture looks like.

QUESTIONS FOR REFLECTION

1. What are the strengths and weaknesses of various perspectives that can inform ethical business judgment?

2. How can we encourage "macroscopic" vision in an age that promotes increasing specialization and microscopic vision?

3. Why do we have mixed feelings about whistleblowers? What can be done to encourage constructive whistleblowing in our businesses? What ethical values are consistent with constructive whistleblowing?

4. How can we acknowledge the undeniable impact of organizational culture on individual ethical decisions, without losing a commitment to individual ethical responsibility?

SUGGESTIONS FOR FURTHER READING

Boisjoly, Russell, Ellen Foster Curtis, and Eugene Mellican. "Roger Boisjoly and the Challenger Disaster: The Ethical Dimensions." *Journal of Business Ethics* 8 (1989).

Davis, Michael. "Explaining Wrongdoing." *Journal of Social Philosophy* 20(1, 2) (Spring/Fall 1989).

Harris, Jr., Charles E., Michael S. Pritchard, and Michael J. Rabins. *Engineering Ethics*. Belmont, CA: Wadsworth Publishing Company, 1995.

Marx, Robert, Charles Stubbart, Virginia Traub, and Michael Cavanaugh. "The NASA Space Shuttle Disaster: A Case Study." *Journal of Management Case Studies* 3(4) (Winter 1987): pp. 316–18.

Report of the Presidential Commission on the Space Shuttle Challenger *Accident*, Washington, DC, June 6, 1986.

ENDNOTES

1. John M. Broder, "Debris Is Now Leading Suspect in Shuttle Catastrophe," *The New York Times* (February 4, 2003): p. A1.

2. Jame Glanz, "Space Flight's Dangers Are Raised by Speed," *The New York Times* (February 2, 2003): p. 28.

3. James Glanz and Edward Wong, "'97 Report Warned of Foam Damaging Tiles," *The New York Times* (February 4, 2003): p. A1; William J. Broad and David E. Sanger, "NASA Was Told in 1990 About Vulnerable Tiles," *The New York Times* (February 5, 2003): p. A1.

4. Kenneth Chang and Richard A. Oppel, Jr., "NASA Pressed on When Officials Learned of E-Mail About Shuttle," *The New York Times* (February 28, 2003): p. A1.

5. Warren E. Leary, "NASA Chief Disputes Idea That Shuttle Was Hopeless," *The New York Times* (March 1, 2003): p. A15.

6. Edward Wong with Leslie Wayne, "Boeing and Lockheed, Prime Builders, Face Questions in Shuttle Inquiry," *The New York Times* (February 3, 2003): p. A22.

7. David Barstow and Michael Moss, "Amid Quest for a Safer Shuttle, Budget Flights and Policy Shifts," *The New York Times* (February 9, 2003) p. 1.

8. David E. Sanger, "Lessons from Uneven Challenger Investigation Help Create Attitude Change," *The New York Times* (February 3, 2003) p. A23.

9. *The New York Times* (January 29, 1986): p. A1.

10. Sara Rimer, "After the Shock, a Need to Share Grief and Loss," *The New York Times* (January 29, 1986): p. A1.

11. Malcom W. Browne, "How Could It Happen? Fuel Tank Leak Feared," *The New York Times* (January 29, 1986): p. A1.

12. Drawn from Robert Marx, Charles Stubbart, Virginia Traub, and Michael Cavanaugh, "The NASA Space Shuttle Disaster: A Case Study," *Journal of Management Case Studies* 3(4) (Winter 1987): pp. 316–18.

13. Russell Boisjoly, Ellen Foster Curtis, and Eugene Mellican, "Roger Boisjoly and the *Challenger* Disaster: The Ethical Dimensions," *Journal of Business Ethics* 8 (1989): p. 223.

14. *Report of the Presidential Commission on the Space Shuttle* Challenger *Accident* (Washington, D.C., June 6, 1986).

15. Unless otherwise indicated, the following account of Roger Boisjoly's experience concerning the O-ring and Morton Thiokol is taken from Boisjoly, Curtis, and Mellican, op. cit.

16. Roger M. Boisjoly, Applied Mechanics Memorandum to Robert K. Lund, Vice President, Engineering, Wasatch Division, Morton Thiokol, July 31, quoted in Boisjoly, Curtis, and Mellican, op. cit., p. 220.

17. Ibid., p. 220.

18. Charles E. Harris, Jr., Michael S. Pritchard, and Michael J. Rabins, *Engineering Ethics* (Belmont, CA: Wadsworth Publishing Company, 1995): p. 1.

19. Malcolm McConnell, Challenger, *a Major Malfunction: A True Story of Politics, Greed, and the Wrong Stuff* (Garden City, NJ: Doubleday and Company, Inc., 1987).

20. *Report of the Presidential Commission on the Space Shuttle* Challenger *Accident,* (Washington, D.C., June 1986): p. 97.

21. Boisjoly, Curtis, and Mellican, op. cit., p. 223.

22. Background on NASA taken from Marx, Stubbart, Traub, and Cavanaugh, op. cit.

23. J. N. Wilford, "After the *Challenger:* America's Future in Space," *The New York Times* (March 16, 1986): p. A1.

24. Marx, Stubbart, Traub, and Cavanaugh, op. cit., p. 308.

25. As Pat Werhane observes in her article on *Challenger,* it is appropriate now to speak of Morton Thiokol in the past tense because in 1989 Morton divested itself of the rocket booster divisions of Thiokol. Patricia H. Werhane, "Engineers and Management: The Challenge of the *Challenger* Incident," *Journal of Business Ethics* 10 (1991): pp. 605–616.

26. Ibid., p. 611.

27. Marcia P. Miceli, Janet P. Near, and Charles R. Schwenk, "Who Blows the Whistle and Why?" *Industrial and Labor Relations Review* 45(1) (October 1991): p. 113.

28. Sissela Bok, "Whistleblowing and Professional Responsibility," in Thomas Donaldson and Patricia H. Werhane *Ethical Issues in Business*, 4th ed. (Upper Saddle River, NJ: Prentice Hall, 1993): pp. 320–328.

29. The following account of the aftermath for Boisjoly is from Boisjoly, Curtis, and Mellican, op. cit., p. 223.

30. Ibid., p. 223.

31. Werhane, "Engineers and Management," op. cit., p. 607.

32. See, for example, Werhane, "Engineers and Management," pp. 23, 605.

33. Michael Davis, "Explaining Wrongdoing," *Journal of Social Philosophy* 20(1, 2) (Spring/Fall 1989): pp. 74–90.

34. *Report of the Presidential Commission on the Space Shuttle* Challenger *Accident*, p. 94.

35. Davis, op. cit., p. 82.

36. Harris, Pritchard, and Rabins, op. cit., p. 73.

9

What Responsibilities
Do We Have for
Foreign Management?

Union Carbide
and the Disaster at Bhopal

Questions to Keep in Mind

1. Had the Union Carbide plant been in the United States, would safety standards and work practices have been different? Why or why not?

2. Would the reaction of the government have been different in the United States? Would the Indian government reaction have been different if the company had been culturally—as it was legally—an Indian company rather than an American company?

3. How did the fact that the company was American in origin and culture influence the press and the lawyers for the plaintiffs? How would the press and lawyers have treated a similar incident in a native company?

4. What are the ethical imperatives binding on an American company abroad? How do we strike a balance, neither exploiting nor being exploited?

5. How do we assess blame in such catastrophes? Who should be held accountable for the damage? How should money damages be assessed?

I. THE STORY OF A DISASTER

On December 2, 1984, at about 11:00 P.M., a discontented employee (who is known, but has not been named) removed the pressure gauge from MIC Storage Tank 610 on the grounds of a pesticide plant run by Union Carbide India Limited (UCIL). He knew, or had very good reason to know, that the tank contained MIC (methyl isocyanate), about 41 metric tons of it, and that it was very important not to let water get into it. He almost certainly did not know *why* contact with water should be prevented; his home and family (most probably) were nearby, and injury to the people of the area was surely furthest from his mind. But he knew that water would ruin the batch of pesticide being prepared from that MIC, and that is apparently what he intended when he attached a hose, already connected to a faucet in the corner of the yard, to the hole left where the pressure gauge had been, and turned on the water.[1] Within hours, the ensuing chemical reaction had blown the safety valve in the tank and allowed poisonous gas to spread over (ultimately) about twenty-five square miles of the area downwind of the plant,[2] killing about 4,000 people[3] and causing an undetermined number of injuries.[4]

The aftermath of this simple-minded act of destruction left the name of Bhopal engraved on the international scene as a synonym for the senseless, unexpected, disastrous injury that can follow upon industrial accidents in advanced industrial settings—and for the economics, law, and politics of compensation for that injury. The drama attracted a disproportionate amount of public interest and acrimony. Within a few years of the incident, even as lawsuits continued, at least three books had been written about it, none of them friendly to Union Carbide and corporate enterprise generally. Two of them, Dan Kurzman's *A Killing Wind* and David Weir's *The Bhopal Syndrome*, have been consulted extensively, along with materials from Union Carbide, as primary sources in the account that follows.

In considering the ethical dimensions of the Bhopal incident, we will divide the discussion in three. We begin with an examination of the conditions and events at the time of the incident, a disaster, as one author put it, waiting to happen.[5] We will trace the fateful events themselves. We will go on to consider the sequel to the accident, a sad chronicle of finance and politics that loses the victims in the shuffle, to see what might be learned from the experience for future cases of this type.

1. Union Carbide in India:
Chemistry for Disaster

Why was Union Carbide in India to begin with? What is methyl isocyanate. What makes it worth manufacturing despite its known tendency to explode and kill people under certain circumstances? And given the use of such a lethal chemical, was it right to maintain the relatively low level of security that permitted the sabotage to take place? Could the incident have been prevented?

Despite its American name, the company whose gas exploded into that lethal cloud was largely Indian-owned and completely Indian-operated. It was founded (as a branch of an American corporation) almost fifty years ago to provide pesticides for India's agricultural "green revolution"; the plant at Bhopal dated from 1969.[6] There was nothing exotic or extraordinarily dangerous in the operation of its plants. The most common kind of pesticide produced in them is carbaryl, an ester of carbamic acid, a reliable and relatively safe product, marketed in the United States under the brand name SEVIN.[7]

There is no doubt that the chemicals employed in the process of making the pesticide are dangerous. Phosgene, the deadly gas briefly used in World War I on the battlefield (and also in the gas chambers of the Third Reich) is a precursor of SEVIN. The UCIL process for the manufacture of SEVIN uses phosgene ($COCl_2$) and a methyl (CH_3) amine (NH_2) to produce the intermediate compound methylcarbamoyl chloride ($CH_3NHCOCl$). The latter compound breaks down with heat into MIC and hydrochloric acid (HCl).

Methyl isocyanate (CH_3NCO) is a variation of the cyanide group (NCN^{-2}) of which the highly poisonous hydrogen cyanide (HCN) is probably the most famous. MIC is extremely unstable and dangerous, and as such is not ordinarily studied in a laboratory situation. Its boiling point is 39° C (102.4° F). Lighter than water in liquid form, but heavier than air in gaseous form, it hugs the ground when released. Its breakdown products include carbon dioxide and stable amines (organic compounds of carbon, hydrogen, and nitrogen), but the process is explosively exothermic—it releases a vast quantity of heat in a very short time. It reacts violently with water (producing breakdown products and high temperatures). Therefore it is an extremely dangerous human poison— and there is no known antidote.[8] U.S. Occupational Safety and Health Administration (OSHA) regulations allow human exposure at 0.02 parts per million (ppm) over an eight-hour period. Irritation is felt at 2 ppm and becomes unbearable at 21 ppm.[9] Five ppm will kill 50 percent of an experimental rat population (LD_{50}).[10] Of course no one measured the concentration of the escaped gas at Bhopal, but as 50,000 pounds of it escaped,[11] the heart of the cloud must have greatly exceeded those limits.

The MIC is then used as an intermediate in the production of SEVIN, which is considerably less poisonous than its chemical precursors.[12] Incidentally, MIC is not the only route to SEVIN. SEVIN can be produced with the addition of methylamine to a reaction of phosgene and napthol. Or it can be produced without using phosgene. In Germany, Bayer makes MIC by combining dimethyl urea and diphenyl carbonate. What considerations led to UCIL's choice of this particular method of making SEVIN? Is another method preferable?[13]

Why make the pesticide in India, in the middle of a dense colony of people, instead of in some remote area in the United States, from which the relatively safe finished product could be exported? Because it made sense to manufacture SEVIN in India instead of in the United States and exporting it: Transportation costs (and dangers) were eliminated and labor costs were a good deal lower in India, making the whole operation safer and more profitable as far as Union Carbide was concerned. The Indian economy was chronically depressed, so the Indian governments sought, welcomed, and catered to American companies willing to locate plants in their country, providing tax revenue and very good jobs. The land on which the plant in question was built was given to Union Carbide by the Indian government for an annual rent of $40 per acre, as part of the plan to bring industry into the area. (Bhopal is the capital city of Madhya Pradesh, the largest and one of the poorest states in the nation.)

2. The Factory in a Foreign Land

At the time of the accident, there were fourteen Union Carbide plants in India. Here as elsewhere, the host nation insisted on assuming a large share of the ownership of "foreign" plants; in the case of Union Carbide, India did not insist on a majority holding, since the plant was a "high technology" enterprise.[14] The Indian government held about 25 percent of the stock. The rest was held by Indian citizens.[15] The management of the plant was wholly Indian; the last American employee had left the Bhopal plant in 1982. Even so, the operation was widely seen (at least for political purposes in that election year in India) as an American intrusion into the Indian economy, an outpost of foreign colonialist capitalist greed in a sovereign state.

Well, which was the company, Indian or American? The division of responsibility for the safety of the plant—the Americans responsible for the design, the Indians responsible for implementation—fostered an attitude of complacency and unconcern for the details of the safety arrangement and of mutual suspicion for decision-making authority. Those attitudes predict the tragic chain of events that followed the explosion: recriminations, litigation, continuing political hyperbole, threats of further litigation—and no relief at all to the actual sufferers.

Union Carbide (UCC) is not the only American multinational corporation to experience a reversal of the welcome mat. What, really, is the obligation of an American corporation in such situations? When nationalism insists that the plant must be run by national managers, and Americans can no longer exert the kind of control that may be necessary to ensure safety, are they obligated to withdraw the whole operation? Was there a "double standard" at Bhopal?

II. WHAT WENT WRONG?

Union Carbide was very well aware of the instability of MIC and of the potential for any of a wide variety of contaminants, including water, to set off an explosive and lethal chain reaction. To prevent that reaction, UCC had a meticulous series of systems and rules all "aimed at preventing MIC from escaping, getting overheated, or being contaminated."[16] In general, the procedures work.

Similar plants in the United States have excellent safety records, and there had been only one fatal accident at the Bhopal plant (a worker died of phosgene inhalation after cleaning out a pipe without a mask). But investigations after the incident revealed a litany of collapsed systems. Weir gives us a partial list:

> Gauges measuring temperature and pressure in the various parts of the unit, including the crucial MIC storage tanks, were so notoriously unreliable that workers ignored early signs of trouble.
>
> The refrigeration unit for keeping MIC at low temperatures (and therefore less likely to undergo overheating and expansion should a contaminant enter the tank) had been shut off for some time.
>
> The gas scrubber, designed to neutralize any escaping MIC, had been shut off for maintenance. Even had it been operative, post-disaster inquiries revealed, the maximum pressure it could handle was only one-quarter that which was actually reached in the accident.
>
> The flare tower, designed to burn off MIC escaping from the scrubber, was also turned off, waiting for replacement of a corroded piece of pipe. The tower, however, was inadequately designed for its task, as it was capable of handling only a quarter of the volume of gas released.
>
> The water curtain [high-pressure spray], designed to neutralize any remaining gas, was too short to reach the top of the flare tower, from where the MIC was billowing.[17]

What had gone wrong? One of the major problems throughout the decision-making prior to the incident was the slim budget available for maintenance. The Bhopal plant had never made very much money; its projected market never materialized. Designed to produce 5,000 tons of pesticide a year, it had produced 2,308 tons in 1982, 1,647 in 1983, and in 1984, it dropped below 1,000 tons.[18] Cost-saving measures were mandated; shutting down the refrigeration unit was one of them. As in all cases of cash flow problems, routine maintenance was deferred. And suggested remodelings (to increase the height at which the "water curtain" could work, for instance) or moves (to the "obnoxious industry" zone outside of town) were impossible.

But pesticide manufacture is a hazardous industry, and the warnings were readily available. A Union Carbide investigative team had visited the site two years prior to the incident, had discovered many flaws in the safety arrangements, and had recommended changes, which had not been implemented. An enterprising journalist, Raj Kumar Keswani (who uncovered the UCC report), had written a series of exposés in the local newspaper on the safety problems at the plant. "Why didn't the insurance companies covering Union Carbide in the event of a chemical disaster require that the Bhopal plant fortify its safety systems? Why didn't the Indian authorities heed the repeated warnings sounded by [Keswani] of the impending danger posed by the Bhopal plant?"[19] Where, in short, was everybody else who was supposed to be watching the store?

The problem underlined by Bhopal, from the company's point of view, is one of proximity and control. For instance, there was no reason, in advance of the accident, to believe that the Indian managers were unable to maintain the same safety standards that would be maintained in a similar plant in the United States (the plants were built to the same specifications). Nevertheless, when the accident happened, the managers on that shift were taking a tea-break together, contrary to company rules and explicit instructions.[20] Was that foreseeable? In retrospect, should Union Carbide have terminated the operation as soon as it lost effective control—whatever the loss of jobs for the area and whatever the damage to the immediate financial interests of its shareholders?

1. The Victims, Workers, and Squatters

Why were all those people in the way of the gas? The plant had been built in a small city, with perhaps a million souls in it before the establishment of the pesticide operation. The plant soon found itself surrounded by people. Employees found housing near the plant and brought their extended families with them. Meanwhile, a veritable army of India's homeless constructed shantytowns near the plant, occasionally against the plant walls themselves, conveniently solid and vertical. These clusters of shacks, amounting to villages with identities and names of their own (J. P. Nagar, Kazi Camp, Chola Kenchi, Railroad Colony) had grown into crowded slums since the plant arrived, and largely because of it.[21] These were the people so horribly gassed when the tank exploded. What were those people doing there, where they did not "belong"? Presumably it makes no moral difference that the people were poor and uneducated. But does it make any difference that the people had no particular "right" to be there?[22] Is it appropriate to introduce the notion that people squatting on land that is not theirs (government land, in this case) are there somehow "at their own risk"?

The suffering of the victims was beyond question. The MIC "reacted furiously with moisture in exposed tissues."[23] The moisture in the lungs was first and most affected, although burns also occurred in the eyes. Cardiovascular, gastrointestinal, neuromuscular, reproductive, and immune tissues were all also affected.[24] Respiratory symptoms were the most common (choking and shortness of breath) in the survivors, and may extend to the long term in some of the victims. Also common was eye watering, lid edema, and corneal ulcerations, but no irreversible eye damage. Here as elsewhere in Bhopal, good data may be hard to come by; clinical studies that have been done on the medical sequelae of the incident apparently lacked controls, impugning their validity, and show evidence of inherent biases in design and conclusion.[25]

Once the reaction began, there was no stopping it. The introduction of water to the MIC tank started the "runaway" reaction. That produced the heat of an intensely exothermic reaction. Apparently chloroform ($CHCl_3$), used as a solvent throughout the process, had already contaminated the MIC; it had not been removed by distillation earlier, due to a higher than normal temperature in the still.[26] That compound evidently provided the chlorine ions (Cl^-) that attacked the steel lining of the tank, which in turn released the iron ions (Fe^{++}) that acted as a catalyst promoting the trimerization (three molecules of MIC reacting with each other in a polymerization reaction), which is also exothermic. MIC, usually held at 20° C (ideally at 4.5° C) finally reached 120° C.[27] By now, of course, the MIC had boiled (vaporized), and the pressure blew the tank, releasing a cloud that covered forty square kilometers. None of the safety devices had worked, and the emptying of the huge tank—and the resulting devastation—was inevitable.[28]

The workers in the plant were as much at a loss as the squatters outside it. Kurzman documents[29] the frantic efforts of plant managers home at the time of the leak to get to the plant through the mobbed streets, and the efforts of the employees on the spot to find out what was going wrong with the MIC tank, to drain that tank when they realized that a reaction was out of control, to get the caustic scrubber, flare tower, and water curtain working—and incidentally, to inform their superiors, organize remedial efforts, and prevent panic. Not much of this effort was to any avail; the plant and workers were simply not up to stopping the killer cloud from completing its journey.

III. THE IMMEDIATE REACTION: THE CORPORATION'S RESPONSE

Union Carbide Corporation's response was instantaneous: Warren B. Anderson, chairman of the board and chief executive officer of the company, announced that the company took full moral responsibility for the disaster, and that the victims would be compensated. He departed immediately for Bhopal, authorized by his board of directors to offer anywhere from $1 million to $5 million in aid on the spot, and pledged to find out how the company could best help the victims. Did this reaction signify a real horror at the human suffering, a genuine compassion and a sincere desire to help, or was it simply public relations, dramatic gestures to protect the shareholders—to evoke sympathy for the company and perhaps a little leniency in the lawsuits sure to follow? Who knows? Who cares? Let us take those questions one at a time.

Who knows? Probably no one, including Warren Anderson. Most human motivation is a mixed bag. There is no reason to doubt that simple compassion and a desire to help was a significant part of his reason for the trip. There is also no reason to doubt that he knew that *his* going would make a clearer statement of the company's compassion than sending any middle manager, no matter how expert in the chemistry and medicine of gases, and also that he wanted to use this gesture to place the company in control of handling the aftermath of the disaster. More than likely it also went through his head that it was important to protect the shareholders' equity, and that the company would be in better shape in the long run if he was seen to concentrate on getting aid to the victims rather than circling the legal wagons. After all, CEOs are paid to have such thoughts go through their heads at frequent intervals.

Who cares? We do. We want very much to be able to attach a moral label to the public acts of those who influence our lives, like the CEOs of major companies. The moral character of a single act is determined less by the effects it has than by the motive on which the agent acted. So we want to find out not only what the consequences of an act are likely to be, but also from what law it flowed—not why anyone should or should not do it, but why the agent in fact *did* do it. We are, in the language of ethics, at least as much deontologists as we are teleologists—Kantians as much as Utilitarians. So depending on what we believe about Warren Anderson's motivation in making the trip to Bhopal, we will regard that trip as a courageous and compassionate pilgrimage, appropriately designed to put the source of money on the spot where it needed to be spent and praiseworthy beyond the call of duty for an elderly corporate statesman—or as cheap public relations grandstanding, crocodile tears for the masses concealing a blatant attempt to get India to accept a small payment immediately in lieu of the larger payment that UCC would have to make when all the facts had been ascertained.

1. Response and Frustration: Dealing with India

Our conclusions on those two questions will dictate our reaction to Anderson's arrest by the Indian authorities when he stepped off the plane at Bhopal, to be detained in a company guest house for a few days. He never got to interview the victims or his managers from the plant nor to offer help. Promised interviews with the governor and the prime minister never materialized; not even the environmental minister would talk to him. Either that arrest was a vicious bit of Indian political grandstanding, playing to the nationalistic crowd in an election season, tragically counterproductive for the actual victims, or it was just what Anderson deserved, and good medicine for a conceited corporate mogul who was trying to manipulate public opinion to save his profits and his job. Further, he was forbidden to talk to the press, which was one of his major objectives in the trip. That prohibition itself was either a cynical move to ensure that the victims would never know that Union Carbide was entirely ready from the outset to compensate them for injuries sustained (because the politicians wanted to make any eventual settlement look like a triumph for them), or simply a refusal to let Anderson turn the press, as he wanted, into an arm of the UCC public relations department—again, depending on your reading of the trip to begin with. (One trouble with the gag rule was that, as both the Indians and UCC had anticipated, contemporary sources read Anderson's failure to contact the press as deliberate evasion.)[30]

Thereafter, UCC had to conduct its response to the incident from afar, hindered by lack of access to the plant (the Indian equivalent of the FBI had closed it for its criminal investigation) and, for many months, by a prohibition against interviewing the employees on duty that night. They devoted an immense amount of time and energy to the task. The company's management split in two: While Anderson and many others assembled a team of scientists and administered the investigation into the causes and cures of the uncontrolled emission of gas, a caretaker administration ran the rest of the company. The major part of their effort, for some time, was to get relief for the victims.

The tale of UCC's efforts to give money to those who really needed it at Bhopal is a chronology of frustration. As above, Warren Anderson's initial offer, days after the explosion, of several millions of dollars was rebuffed. By February 1985 the UCC Employees' Bhopal Relief Fund had collected more than $100,000 for the victims, but had no one to give it to. That April India again rejected "out of hand" any comprehensive settlement. Litigation began, initiated by teams of lawyers who wanted to represent the victims in damage suits against UCC, before U. S. District Court Judge John Keenan, with the object of having the cause tried in the United States. Judge Keenan accepted on behalf of the victims $5 million from UCC, the first money actually to be routed toward the sufferers. More significantly, he ordered the cases back to India, on grounds that that was where the accident was, as were the victims, witnesses, documents, applicable laws, and most of the lawsuits. The government of India promptly invalidated all the lawyers' claims, taking on itself the right and duty to speak for the victims. After more litigation, dragging on for three more years, Chief Justice R. S. Pathak of India's Supreme Court directed a final settlement of all Bhopal litigation in the amount of $470 million, to be paid by March 31, 1989; full payment was made by the end of February.[31]

In the course of the litigation, UCC had made repeated attempts to get funds to the victims through channels other than the law, including at least the Red Cross and Mother Teresa; all potential channels turned down the money, on grounds that the political flak that would accompany any appearance of cooperating with UCC would hurt their own work.

Why did it take so long to get money to the victims? The answer seems to be a combination of politics and calculation. On the political side, much advantage seemed to be flowing from portraying Union Carbide as "murderers," who had knowingly foisted a terribly dangerous operation on an unsuspecting community. The political players were soon competing with each other in hyperbole of condemnation and blame of the company, in scornful rejection of any proposed settlement as a tiny fraction of what was really owed, and in posturing as saviors from the unimaginable dangers of anything the company might ever again do with regard to Bhopal. In what may have been the supreme act of cynicism in the entire Bhopal affair, Arjun Singh, governor of Madhya Pradesh, created a full-blown panic in Bhopal when UCC vice president Van Mynen led a technical team in on December 18, 1984, to convert the remaining MIC to SEVIN (the safest way to dispose of it). Singh urged residents to evacuate the town if they could, but pledged that he personally would guarantee that these "murderers" would do no harm during this routine operation, by personally ordering the appropriate safeguards—which included shutting all the schools and colleges, which were in the middle of examinations. He then announced that wet cloths would be draped over all the fences, a tent of wet cloths would be erected over the MIC tank, and continually sprayed with water, and, just to make sure, "Indian Air Force helicopters would hover overhead and periodically spray the plant with water."[32] The conversion operation was perfectly safe, but in the panic, more lives and much more property were lost. In such an atmosphere, who would dare sit down at a negotiating table with Union Carbide, and presume to talk about a "fair" settlement?

Nor was that the only time that political frustration resulted in real damage to the residents. Union Carbide funded a Vocational Training School to relieve the poverty of the area, and the government had it closed. Thwarted in their attempts to go through the government to reach the victims, UCC provided more than $2 million to Arizona State University to build and operate a rehabilitation center for the injured. "The center was built, and operating well, but when the state government learned that Carbide money had funded it, bulldozers were sent in to knock the building down."[33] UCC and UCIL together offered to fund a hospital to treat the victims over the long term and provide more jobs and better medical care for the area; that hospital was built and opened to receive victims—in the year 2000, long after the need for it had passed. It now stands, "a gleaming white elephant on 87 acres on the city's outskirts, filled with the latest medical equipment but rarely more than half full."[34] On the one hand, in the light of the political situation, the obstructive actions are not surprising, and they were expected to produce a larger compensation in the long run (that was where the calculation came in). On the other hand, the victim of the killer cloud, the impoverished Indian sickened by the gas, might have been helped by the vocational school and prompt medical aid, but could not possibly benefit from acts whose import was only symbolic.

2. The Investigation, Within and Without

On his return from India, Van Mynen led the technical side of UCC's response to Bhopal—the effort to determine just what had happened. By mid-March the scientific team had determined that the reaction had been triggered by a large volume of water, confirmed in July when they were able to obtain core samples from the plant. By August they had determined that the only way that water could have got into the tank was by a deliberate act.[35] (That had also been the first impression of the managers of UCIL, the night of the explosion.[36]) UCC had no access to human sources of information until the government of India sued Union Carbide for damages later that year. The court action allowed UCC to request the records from the factory, which the U. S. District Court (S.D. N.Y.) ordered India to make available them in November. In December 1985, they obtained access to the logs of the plant, and immediately noticed a pattern of change and falsification. That pattern was confirmed when they were finally, almost a year and a half after the incident, permitted access to plant employee witnesses.

Three obstacles hindered the fact-finding through interviews. First, after a year and a half, given that the plant was now closed and all employees laid off, simply finding the employees on duty that night, and persuading them to talk to the UCC investigators, was a major task. Second, for those only peripherally involved in the incident, memories fade, a sense of what was really relevant dissipates, and accounts must be reconstructed slowly and patiently through the sifting of countless details. Third, those very partial accounts from peripheral observers, once reassembled, turned out to be the most reliable sources of information, for the most centrally involved parties had a tendency to lie. Ashok Kalelkar, one of the investigating team, describes the team's experience during the interviews:

> . . . as the interviews with the operators and supervisors directly involved progressed, it became apparent that there were massive contradictions in their stories. For example, operators and employees from other units and another plant downwind of the MIC unit, together with some MIC operators, reported sensing small MIC leaks well before the major release occurred, and they notified their shift supervisors. However, those Bhopal plant supervisors denied hearing any reports about earlier leaks. In addition, the supervisors were unable to plausibly account for their activities during the 45-minute period prior to the release. They placed themselves with people and in locations for reasons that were entirely different from those that had been given by those individuals they were supposedly with.[37]

Why the discrepancies? Apparently, to cover up the fact that several of them, contrary to instructions, had taken their tea break together. The other discordances in the logs and in the interviews, too, can be explained all too readily as consistent attempts to place the person giving the account as far away from the scene as possible, or as completely ignorant as possible, as long as possible, of any trouble brewing.[38]

3. Accident or Sabotage?

Meanwhile, a long time had passed, and the readers of the world had accepted a totally misguided theory of the causation of the accident. Unlike UCC officials, journalists had full access to anyone they could find to talk to, and they brought their own agendas. Journalists love a story. They want it to be exciting and they want it to be true, and if the two conflict, the exciting at least gets a shot at acceptance. Above all, they want it fast, and they settle on their conclusions quickly, for deadlines await at home. These imperatives of journalism worked against UCC and the truth in the complex aftermath of Bhopal. Isolating all UCC spokesmen from the Indian press ensured that unlimited speculation would rule the "background" stories. "It is remotely possible," Alfred de Grazia pointed out (writing less than a year after the incident), "that the research facility [on the factory grounds] was being used or intended for use to test the chemical warfare potential of MIC or to develop other chemicals that would be hazardous in themselves or when compounded. Indian journalists have raised such issues, and have found a large audience receptive to the theories."[39]

More bothersome than these fantasies was the early acceptance, prior to exhaustive investigation, of the theory that worker negligence was the cause of the water entering the tank. For months, the account of the incident faulted a missing "slip blind" for the explosion. (The slip blind, a circular disc inserted in a pipe while it was being washed, was supposed to isolate the piping being washed to keep the water from leaking backward past the valves into the tanks of chemicals.) The first report issued by UCC (March 1985), for that matter, was noncommittal about the source of the water that would have been needed for that reaction to take place, and noted that the slip blind appeared to be missing.

In this period, theories jostled for newsmagazine space. The amount of water necessary to trigger the reaction became a serious question, as was the timing of the entry of the water. The Indian investigation team hypothesized that only a small amount of water would be necessary to cause the reaction via a different chemical route (and therefore it could have easily been an accident), while the Union Carbide team hypothesized that 120 to 240 gallons of water must have entered the tank and that therefore it had to be a deliberate act.[40] Additional questions arose as to the amount of time necessary for the reaction to produce the temperature necessary to corrode the steel tank and release the catalytic iron ions. If, as one Union Carbide manual had described, it would take more than twenty-three hours, the saboteur would have to have allowed the water to enter the tank the day before (and presumably be found out). Union Carbide stated that as large an amount of water as they hypothesize entered the tank would cause the reaction in two hours.[41]

At this point, journalists had every reason to accept the "accident" theory and to suspect the "sabotage" theory. An analyst who followed Union Carbide for ten years for the First Boston Corporation, Anantha K.S. Raman, commenting in April 1985 on Union Carbide's conclusion that the cause of the disaster was sabotage, said it was "a carefully orchestrated attempt to influence the upcoming legal hearings."[42] By August, however, when UCC had been able to obtain core samples, UCC realized (and proved) that the sheer amount of water needed to cause that kind of reaction could not have come from leaks from pipe-washing. (There were many other reasons to reject the slip blind or "water-washing" theory.[43]) But two years later, when access to plant workers for interviews had spotlighted the missing pressure gauge and made the cause of the accident quite clear, some journalists still defended the slip blind, apparently under the impression that UCC's responsibility for the accident would be lessened if it were established that the water had been introduced to the tank deliberately.[44]

Would sabotage lessen UCC's responsibility? Some say that it would: that in the case of the leak from the water-washing (involving faulty valves and the like) "the plant" was to blame primarily and the careless worker only secondarily; that in the case of sabotage the perpetrator was to blame and it was simply a regrettable shame that no one caught him at it. That view rests easily with the criminal law and the *mens rea* ("guilty mind," or intent to do wrong) that, except in rare instances, is necessary for the existence of a "crime." Responsibility in the criminal law thus rests on the saboteur himself, and on no one else. In cases of ordinary negligence, no one is held to be "guilty" (although the negligent tortfeasor may have to pay the bill for the damages) and it is psychologically easier to blame the surrounding circumstances, in this case the factory, for whatever happened.

But from the perspective of the civil law and Union Carbide, there is no distinction between responsibility in the one case and in the other. In both cases we have sloppy procedures (careless washing and omission of the slip blind versus no security around a tank full of dangerous chemicals) and bad personnel practices (inadequate training and supervision of the washer versus inept handling of an employee demotion), both of which are culpable deficiencies in the plant management. Besides, UCC had been prompt to admit full responsibility for the disaster; it remained only to establish what the actual, real, damages were, and they would be paid in full.

IV. SORTING OUT THE DEMANDS
FOR COMPENSATION

Of course, as in every case in torts, not everyone was interested in having UCC pay only the actual, real, damages. Efforts to attribute fair liability and determine compensation, in the aftermath of the leak, rapidly drowned in exaggerated estimates of the amount of money available from the company. Partly because India is a poor country, the amounts demanded in "compensation" were not at all in line with the experience of the Indian justice system. Since justice is the issue here, the controversy deserves a closer look.

First, the estimates of damages payable were high by any standards. Within a year after the incident, de Grazia, writing on behalf of the India–America Committee for Bhopal Victims, devoted a chops-licking chapter to "Damages and Compensation," and concluded that UCC owed the victims and their survivors $1,318,650,000 (American).[45] And de Grazia did not know that more were to die. Families and individuals discovered or invented reasons for thinking that they were owed particularly large amounts. Depending on political advantage, Indian officials alternately dangled and withdrew promises of much more money for the victims.[46] Since records of deaths and injuries were woefully inadequate, it was impossible to verify who had actually suffered from the gas, and who had suffered only (only!) from the preexisting poverty, malnutrition, and disease.[47] Since emergency measures that were supposed to save lives, at the hospitals and in the town, were impossible to coordinate in the heat of the incident itself, it was impossible to attribute blame for injury and death with any reasonable certainty. After the incident, attempts to register who deserved compensation were shot through with bureaucratic inefficiency and blatant corruption; with UCC money looming in the background to repay all debts, there seemed no reason why every official and secretary—and even the occasional doctor or policeman—should not seek maximum financial reimbursement for performance of his duty.[48]

1. The Entrance of the Lawyers

The lawyers—international ambulance-chasers of the stripe of Melvin Belli, John Coale, and eventually Stanley Chesley—claimed that they only wanted to represent the helpless widow and orphan, to make sure that the poverty-stricken victims got what was due them. But their plans to take 30 percent of each award, or at least as much of that as they could persuade a judge to allot them, were openly mentioned and discussed from the time they laid foot in India. First on their own behalf, going from door to door persuading the poor of Bhopal to sign retainers appointing them as attorneys, and then (after the Indian government took over that role) in the efforts to persuade the Indian government to hire them as representatives in the American courts, the lawyers had mentioned sums beyond anyone's imagination: millions for the victims, billions for the government. They were taken all too literally.

It may be too easy to be cynical about the lawyers. In private conversation with one of the authors of this text, on a memorable bus ride through San Francisco, Stanley Chesley described himself, with all apparent sincerity, as a man who just cannot resist a chance to help the underdog. The author believed him. Surely it is part of the American tradition that one can do good and do well at the same time. The lawyers were just doing their job.

More important, it is certain that if American lawyers did not bring the victims' cause to the fore, no one else would. No Indian lawyer, or indeed the Indian government, showed real interest in compensation for the victims until the American lawyers arrived.[49] In a telling comment to the press soon after his arrival in India, Melvin Belli explained why he wanted the cases tried in the United States: ". . . in court, you don't appreciate the dignity of a man as much as we do."[50] By "dignity," he meant worth: worth as an autonomous individual, worth as a human life, worth in court in terms of monetary compensation. For this is India, "steeped in poverty, apathy, corruption, and greed, an India that, while laudably dedicated to democratic freedoms, still judged the value of a life by the kind of work a person did."[51] And where tort law is concerned, that judgment is crucial. Tort law is undeveloped in India, for "compensation for injuries" is not a matter of fundamental right where injuries occur so often to so many. "Since there are no civil juries in India, judges determine liability and damages, and they are not overly impressed by calamities that kill thousands and simply punctuate the rough rhythm of survival in India."[52] According to all sources, India is not the place for a tort action on behalf of the poor: The poor are expected to accept their lot, victim and judge agree that most injuries are a matter of fate and could not have been avoided, and in any case, the value of what was lost—scraps of property, time, health, limb, life—is so small in the social reckoning that the suit is hardly worth the lawyer's effort. Until the Americans arrived, and talked of infinite money, no one else was talking about the infinite value of a human life. No doubt the lawyers were very interested in high fees. But they also represented, and championed, the Western law's historic recognition of the rights and value of the individual; and if Warren Anderson can have mixed motives, so can the lawyers.

2. The Incident Continues

The situation did not notably improve after the first shock of the accident. Indian fatalism may be the most appropriate philosophical orientation for the poisonous human waves of disruption and destruction that followed the chemical killer cloud—the maneuvering of the politicians, the assaults of the lawyers, the arrival of the political activists who took over part of the UCIL grounds (temporarily) to set up a People's Hospital, the bestselling journalistic accounts of the incident, some of which have been used extensively in this account, all of them hostile to business in general and UCC in particular, and the hostile takeover attempt by GAF Corporation that drained UCC's energies and coffers just when they were most needed by the victims. A decade after the event, there was little that had been done for those victims, UCC was having problems with the recession, Bhopal activists were threatening more litigation to have the settlement overturned, more Indian citizens had put in claims for compensation for injuries than were present in Bhopal at the time of the accident, and the government of India was still seeking to bring criminal charges against Warren Anderson. There was no peace.

Five years later, that last effort bore strange fruit. An account appeared in *The New York Times* of March 5, 2000: "Warren M. Anderson, chairman of the Union Carbide Corporation during the 1984 chemical disaster at Bhopal, India, has apparently gone into hiding to avoid a summons to appear in a Manhattan federal court as part of civil proceedings against him and the company, say lawyers who have hired a private investigator to locate Mr. Anderson."[53] As of March 4, 2000, he was apparently not at his last known address in Florida, and Union Carbide, with corporate headquarters in Danbury, Connecticut, had refused to accept a summons on his behalf. (*Sierra* helpfully published a "Wanted" poster of him in its July/August 2000 issue.) How could these new proceedings have happened? For the terms of the settlement included the vacating of all "criminal charges" against Anderson and any other individuals, and released Union Carbide from any further liability with regard to the accident. But apparently no one had thought, given the clear facts of the case, that Anderson personally might be the object of a civil suit, so that possibility had not been ruled out by the settlement, and the lawyers were still hungry.[54] By the time of the final settlement, Anderson had already resigned from the board of directors and retired, dividing his time between Bridgehampton, New York, and Florida.

By September of 2002, the pursuit of Anderson was again in the news. Among a people who had little motive and less ability to ferret out the real truth underlying the political posturing, political truth replaced actual truth soon after the accident. A generation of Bhopalese have now grown up thinking that Anderson was the callous murderer who killed their families. "Hang Anderson" slogans abound on signs, on walls, in the minds of the people, and the criminal charges are back. Settlement or no, local authorities are attempting to extradite him to stand trial for "culpable homicide," and attempts by the Indian government to downgrade the charges to a nonextraditable offense (so

as not to discourage foreign investment) have failed.[55] Nongovernmental
Organizations (NGOs) of various stripes have joined the hunt; some private
investigators tracked the eighty-one-year-old Anderson down at his
Bridgehampton house early in September, and took a revealing video of him
watering his flowers. It is not clear what is to be gained by this effort.

3. Some Provisional Conclusions

Just from this vantage point, Bhopal has a lesson to teach us. First, the
U.S.–based multinational corporation will have to rethink its relation with the
Third World or withdraw its operations. Warren Anderson, surveying the problems of the Bhopal plant, concluded that multinationals "must not simply make
improvements; they must demand more control of the plants, especially in the
Third World, even if the host government balked," and if that were not possible, then they should withdraw from the project completely.[56] Anderson was
distressed that any UCC plant should operate, as the one at Bhopal had, "with
such total disregard for procedures."[57] With nationalism on the rise all over the
world, the prospect for control of, and for untroubled operation in the developing nations, seems remote indeed. Yet the major "globalization" issues of the
day—sweatshops, land sales, pollution, poverty—turn on the ability to solve
the problems created by increasing technological complexity in a business environment of decreasing political control.

V. THE CHEMICALS INDUSTRY'S
REACTION: RESPONSIBLE CARE

1. The History of the CMA

Trade or industry associations are generally formed for limited purposes—as
mutual support groups among the companies of their trade or industry, to
serve their members by providing technical support and advice, and most important, to protect their members from unwelcome government attention.
The public perception of the trade association is surely that they have no purpose at all beyond the enhancement of the profits of their member companies;
the chronicle of the Tobacco Institute, while extreme, typifies the species. A
major activity for such an association is lobbying the federal government on
behalf of its members, to keep taxes down, image up, and regulation at bay. By
nature they are self-praising boosters, cheerleaders for their members. When a
company is paying good money in dues to an association, the payback had
better be visible on the bottom line, and the last thing it expects is image-
damaging criticism.

The industry association for the chemicals industry was no exception to
that rule for most of its career. Founded as the Manufacturing Chemists
Association in 1872 as an industry club and forum for information and opinion, it transformed itself into the Chemical Manufacturers Association (CMA;

now the American Chemistry Council, ACC) in 1978, for the express purposes of lobbying and technical support for its member companies. But by the early 1980s the industry faced problems that went deeper than the next round of lunches with legislators.

By that time Love Canal (see Chapter 6) was a household word. In August 1978 the New York State Commissioner of Health declared a health emergency at Love Canal and ordered the first of several relocations of families from the area; through 1979 the tales of chemicals-caused illness continued. In 1980, the U. S. Congress passed a bill called the Comprehensive Environmental Response Compensation and Liability Act (CERCLA, or more popularly, "Superfund") to empower the EPA to make sure that hazardous substances were not released into air, water, or earth, and above all to clean up the old toxic waste disposal dumps. The chemical industry had opposed it, but given the headlines from Love Canal, opposition was unlikely to succeed. By the terms of that legislation, all toxic dump sites had to be cleaned up—and the chemical companies had to pay for the cleanup.

Love Canal continued to create problems for the chemicals industry in the year that followed. Then CERCLA came up for reauthorization. The CMA had opposed it the first time around, but realistically decided this time to offer to edit its provisions to make it more realistic and enforceable. Through 1984, the services of CMA experts on technical matters were available to Congress. Just as that debate was winding down, Bhopal blew up, and the chemical industry faced a very dark hour indeed.

In part because of the means chosen by the Indian government to handle the disaster, the drama of Bhopal attracted a disproportionate amount of public interest and acrimony. Edward Holmer, president of the CMA, took the position that the crisis was not Carbide's alone, but affected every one of the CMA's members. So in 1985 he assembled a committee, a special-purpose study group, and embarked on the task of a response to Bhopal. From this work eventually emerged the initiative now known as Responsible Care.[58]

2. Bhopal Imperatives

Sifting through the wreckage, one point became very clear. There had been no communication with the community. All the safety provisions, operable or not, stopped at the factory gate. No one had ever tried to make the people in the crowded town around the factory aware of what to do should an accident occur at the plant. As it was, many of the citizens of Bhopal apparently ran *toward* the plant when they heard all the noise—to see what was happening. And when the injured began to turn up at hospitals, no one knew what to do for them. The disaster was compounded, as far as the extent of mortality and morbidity is concerned, by the inability of the medical community to offer any real help. MIC poisoning was all but nonexistent; indeed, the gas was widely believed to be harmless, as Union Carbide's medical director continued to claim for some time after the gas had escaped.[59] Drops for the eyes, oxygen for the ravaged lungs, was about all anyone could come up with. Some physicians administered sodium thiosulfate, a known antidote for hydrogen cyanimide, or cyanide poisoning. Later it was alleged that there was official reluctance to implicate this most famous poison (for fear of causing panic?), but that some attending physicians thought that it had been involved and the antidote should be given.[60] Again, no clinical evidence is available on one side or the other.

Could injuries have been prevented by more attention to public warnings? Had the people in the path of the gas known even to put a wet cloth over their noses and mouths, hundreds of lives might have been saved, but no one had thought that that might be a useful thing for them to know. There had been no drills or information. Should there have been? The probability was that there would never be any need at all to know what to do in the case of a massive gas leak, and attempts to "educate" the people might just cause panic. How do you balance the known and certain disadvantages of fearful warnings, with the unknown and unproved disadvantages of chancing a disaster without the warnings? With Bhopal in their faces, the issue changed perspective. As far as the CMA was concerned, Bhopal landed with the weight of 4000 corpses on the side of public awareness and education.

VI. RESPONSIBLE CARE

1. CAER: The First Step

Bhopal set the agenda: The immediate problem was the safety of the community. How could the industry assure the safety of the towns in which chemical plants were located, in the face of proof that they were terribly dangerous? In 1985 the CMA was given a draft of a set of requirements for voluntary adoption by the membership. Called the Community Awareness and Emergency Response program (CAER), it reflected a solid commitment on the part of the study participants to cooperation with localities for the protection of the public. The CAER code required members to communicate with the public outside the plant—not just to answer questions truthfully, but to reach out to the community to begin the dialogue. They had to tell the public what sort of safety provisions the plant had made against various possible accidents, and above all they had to discuss with the local police and fire departments just what sorts of disasters might occur, how to cope with them, and how the chemical company might be of assistance. In a radical development, they were required to work out with local governments some means of conducting a disaster drill once a year. The essence of the program was communication: within each plant (to make sure all emergency procedures were known to all employees), with all local authorities—especially police and fire—and with the public at large, to make sure that the community was aware of the overall plan.[61] The program was well received, and member companies began incorporating its recommendations.

Then, in mid–1985, as if in response to those who attributed the Bhopal accident to a carelessness unique to a backward place like India (it could never happen here), Union Carbide's plant in Institute, West Virginia, also had a malfunction that released MIC into the air. No one was hurt, but the noise of that bell was unmistakable. This was not some foreigners' problem. Union Carbide was a leader of the chemical manufacturing industry, the plant was owned, run, and monitored by Americans in America, and if it happened in Institute it could happen anywhere. Evidence piled up that the public mistrusted the chemical industry, feared the chemicals, and doubted the word of the industry's representatives and its ability and willingness to keep the citizens safe. "The public was frightened and angry, because decisions about risk regarding exposure to chemicals were being made for them without their knowledge," observed one of the participants. "They saw decisions being made behind plant fences, in company labs, in skyscrapers. Corporations were saying, 'These are acceptable levels of risk and the public at large wouldn't understand the technical issues anyway.' The industry had found itself awash in a sea of mistrust and misunderstanding."[62]

In this climate CERCLA was reinstituted under the title of Superfund Amendment and Reauthorization Act (SARA), appropriating $8.5 billion to renew for five years the hazardous waste cleanup program. The funds were to come from a tax on all manufacturing companies (not just from the chemicals industry); initial estimates set the cost of a total cleanup of just the existing hazardous waste sites at $100 billion.

Included in Title III of SARA were unprecedented legal provisions for public accountability. The public mistrusted all corporate claims of "absolutely safe," and the horrors in the train of the nuclear explosion at Chernobyl in the Soviet Union (April 25, 1986) had given unparalleled force to the demand for full information about operations within the gates. Accordingly, by Title III, all U.S. plants that made or used more than a certain amount (which changed from version to version) of a set list of chemicals (also changeable) had to report all emissions from the plant—kind and amount—in detail. Further, they had to report typical inventories of dangerous chemicals to the local communities and work with police and fire departments to prepare plans for any spill, explosion, sabotage, or other emergency that could endanger the community's welfare. Most significantly Title III, dubbed "The Community Right-To-Know Act," empowered localities to adopt whatever environmental regulations seemed sensible to them to protect their citizens' health and safety, without waiting for the EPA.

CAER was already published and in the early stages of implementation when SARA was on the drawing board. To the CMA's delight, the legislators adopted whole sections of CAER for Title III, almost word for word. A few years later Jon Holtzman of the CMA commented on this development:

> It taught us that if we were willing to attack a problem that the public is interested in—where government wants success—government will cherry-pick our program and write it into law. Government will buy into our experience because they don't want to fail either.[63]

2. The Canadian Modifications

Meanwhile, the Canadian Chemical Producers Association (CCPA) had come to the conclusion that radical changes were needed in all aspects of its operations if it was to regain the trust of the public. The CCPA considered CAER as a model because it was specific as well as general, mandating certain practices and certain reporting procedures on those practices and because even though it was voluntary, the U.S. industry had accepted it and was actively in the process of implementing it. The Canadians adopted CAER and then went beyond it in three significant ways:

1. They generalized CAER to encompass all activities of the chemical industry, projecting management codes for research, transportation, distribution, health and safety, manufacturing processes, and disposing of hazardous wastes, as well as emergency response to accidents. They called this very comprehensive program "Responsible Care."

2. From these practices they derived a set of "guiding principles," a short list of imperatives that would govern the whole enterprise of manufacturing principles.

3. They made adherence to this plan mandatory for all members of the association. There is no misreading the last sentence of the "Statement of Commitment": "The most senior executive responsible for chemical operations in each member company of CCPA has formally accepted these principles and endorsement is a condition of membership."[64]

3. The Adoption of Responsible Care

When the CMA conducted surveys among its members in 1986 and 1987 to learn how it might be more useful to them, it found that the first item of concern was the public image of the chemicals industry. So among the task forces CMA launched in 1987 to address the concerns of the industry was a Public Perception Committee (PPC). Possibly the membership hoped that a really effective public relations campaign would emerge from the PPC. But the PPC took a totally different route: It determined that the "public perception" problem was not one of public impressions but of industry performance, and to change those perceptions the industry would have to change its performance—radically, permanently, and visibly.[65]

The Canadian program provided a viable model. Anything that worked in Canada was likely to work in the United States; for the most part, Canadian chemical companies are branches of U.S. companies, or of European companies that also have plants in the United States. The CMA Executive Committee looked over the Responsible Care provisions, liked what they saw, and decided to import it wholesale. In the summer of 1988, the officers of the CMA built consensus in the industry through a series of meetings with chemical company executives. All of the objections were raised during those meetings; when the CMA board (composed of forty-five executives of member corporations) took a vote in September, the decision was unanimous in favor of adopting Responsible Care as mandatory for all members.

Members were required to sign a statement of principles known as the "Guiding Principles," and they had to agree to implement any requirements or "Codes of Management Practice," that the organization might develop in the future.[66] No guarantees were available, save that CAER seemed to work and the CEOs of many companies had bought into the idea—and the knowledge that every firm would have to participate or be forced out of the association.[67] What they had, in short, was trust. On the strength of that trust, the entire membership voted to change the CMA bylaws to make Responsible Care a condition of membership. Despite lingering doubts about everything from legal liability to equity for smaller firms, the corporations that make up the chemical industry in the United States had handed their trade association a mandate to write rules to protect safety, health, the natural environment, community involvement, and fairness in allotment of burdens, especially where hazardous wastes were concerned, rules that the CEO of each company promised in advance to adopt, publicize, sell to his employees, adhere to, and be judged on—by his company, his peers in the CMA, and the public at large. On the whole, this is an extraordinary commitment for a market system.

4. Preliminary Reflections

Now, *why* did the members of the CMA vote such potentially onerous requirements on their own heads, even before they were available for detailed inspection by their legal staffs? Was it because they just recognized that this was the good, honest, responsible thing to do? Or did it have something to do with dollar signs? Was it because the negative public "image" boded ill for future regulation, lawsuits, customer loyalty, and the ability to hire good chemists, and the bottom line needed protecting? We may recall, from the Introduction, the distinction between doing something for ethical reasons or out of respect for the law (deontological motivation) and doing exactly the same thing for economic reasons or to achieve an advantageous end (teleological or utilitarian reasoning), and the tendency to suspect hypocrisy when claims to ethical reasons are made in circumstances where the same actions would be economically advantageous. We recall also the complications of ethical behavior in business. In publicly held companies, where the officers are working with other peoples' money, they have no *right* to do anything for ethical reasons—unless those actions can *also* be shown to have a positive effect on the bottom line.

In the matter of public image and reputation, ethical and economic motives theoretically fuse. Assuming that the public approves of morally good action and that its money one way or another follows its approval and further assuming that widespread durable deception is impossible, doing that which is morally right will improve market position—or at least, doing that which is morally wrong will hurt it. Since it was precisely the reputation of the chemical industry that was at stake, the question of whether the CMA established Responsible Care for the sake of justice or for the sake of profit, is probably not worth asking. A survey of industry literature, incidentally, shows industry spokespersons going back and forth between deontological and teleological reasoning in the justifications they give for the initiative.

And that is not surprising, for while we can hold deontological motivation and teleological motivation separate in abstraction, in the concrete reality of executive decision-making, they are psychologically inseparable. No person who does the right thing, in any situation that presents the wrong thing as an alternative, can be absolutely sure that all his or her motives were absolutely "pure," devoid of self- or company interest. Human motivation is mysterious at best, and the business executive must consider not just moral codes but the legitimate expectations of his or her role in the company and the fiduciary responsibility to the economic benefit of the shareholders. The moral puzzle created by the assumption that moral motive and economic motive are mutually exclusive is rarely solved at any level, and logically cannot be solved when, as in business, the individual has a contractual obligation to serve the interests of an economic entity. Then how can we urge corporate executives to be moral? Presumably, by ordering our institutions in such a way that the conflict between corporate interest and the public good never arises. This is precisely what the Responsible Care initiative attempts to do with all the companies of the industry.

QUESTIONS FOR REFLECTION

1. What does Bhopal teach us about responsibility or accountability for things that go wrong? Is it inevitable that attributions of blame will be politically influenced?

2. What is the difference between the way we ascribe blameworthiness to individuals and to corporations? How does the early controversy on whether the Bhopal incident was an accident or sabotage illustrate this difference?

3. What would have been the best way to ensure that the victims got speedy and effective treatment? What should be done in future incidents of this sort?

4. What should American companies that wish to operate abroad do to avoid future Bhopals? Must we reach the conclusion that capitalism, of the United States variety, is simply unworkable in third world nations?

SUGGESTIONS FOR FURTHER READING

de Grazia, Alfred. *A Cloud over Bhopal.* Bombay, India: Kalos Foundation, 1985.

Kurzman, Dan. *A Killing Wind: Inside Union Carbide and the Bhopal Catastro-*phe. New York: McGraw-Hill Book Company, 1987.

Weir, David. *The Bhopal Syndrome: Pesticides, Environment and Health.* San Francisco: Sierra Club Books, 1987.

ENDNOTES

1. Ashok S. Kalelkar (Arthur D. Little, Inc.) "Investigation of Large-Magnitude Incidents: Bhopal as a Case Study." Presented at The Institution of Chemical Engineers Conference On Preventing Major Chemical Accidents, London, England, May 1988.

2. Alfred de Grazia, *A Cloud over Bhopal* (Bombay, India: Kalos Foundation, 1985).

3. Denise Lavoie, writing for the Associated Press, "Bhopal Still Haunts Former Carbide Chief," *Hartford Courant* (April 5, 1992): pp. D1, D7. Union Carbide estimates 3,800 deaths in "Union Carbide Corporation Bhopal Fact Sheet," available from Union Carbide Corporation, Corporate Communications Department, Section C-2, Danbury, CT 06817-0001. Hereinafter, documents obtained from that source will be identified as "UCC." Dan Kurzman, in *A Killing Wind*, estimates 8,000 "at least" and has bodies dumped anonymously in the river to account for the lack of evidence for more. Kurzman, *A Killing Wind: Inside Union Carbide and the Bhopal Catastrophe* (New York: McGraw-Hill Book Company, 1987): p. 77. De Grazia estimates 3,000 killed (*A Cloud over Bhopal*, p. 15), but wrote before the toll of indirect death was complete.

4. Lavoie (supra) estimates 20,000; Union Carbide estimates closer to 3,000 with measurable injury after the fact (Ibid.; UCC). Kurzman (supra) estimates 300,000; de Grazia has 30,000 disabled and 180,000 "affected to minor degrees," supra loc. cit. Such discrepancies are the rule in this issue and will be taken up in the text below.

5. Weir, op. cit., p. 36

6. Warren M. Anderson (former chairman, Union Carbide Corporation), "Bhopal: What We Learned," distributed by Union Carbide Corporation (Danbury, CT, 06817-0001; UCC Document # 158). Kurzman, op. cit., p. 21.

7. Ashok S. Kalelkar, "Investigation of Large-Magnitude Incidents: Bhopal as a Case Study," presented at The Institution of Chemical Engineers Conference on

Preventing Major Chemical Accidents, London, England, May 1988, p. 11.

8. "India's Tragedy: A Warning Heard Round the World," *U.S. News and World Report* (December 17, 1984): p. 25; Pushpa S. Mehta et al., "Bhopal Tragedy's Health Effects: A Review of Methyl Isocyanate Toxicity," *Journal of the American Medical Association* 264(21) (December 5, 1990): p. 2781.

9. Mehta et al., op. cit.

10. Kurzman, op. cit., p. 41.

11. Union Carbide Corporation, *Bhopal Methyl Isocyanate Incident Investigation Team Report*, Danbury, CT, March 1985.

12. Ibid.; Ehrlichs et al., *Ecoscience* (San Francisco: W. H. Freeman & Co., 1977); Kurzman, op. cit., p. 22; Weir, op. cit., p. 31.

13. Kurzman, op. cit., p. 22.

14. Weir, op. cit., pp. 30–31.

15. Anderson, op. cit.; UCC, "Union Carbide Corporation: Bhopal Fact Sheet," p. 1.

16. Weir, op. cit., p. 33.

17. Weir, op. cit., pp. 41–42.

18. Weir, op. cit., p. 35.

19. Weir, op. cit., p. 49. See also de Grazia, op. cit., p. 44.

20. Kalelkar, op. cit, p. 21.

21. De Grazia, op. cit., p. 12. Weir relates a personal interview with M. N. Buch, former planning director for the state of Madhya Pradesh, in which Buch claimed that old maps of the city showed the existence of these slums prior to the arrival of the plant; Union Carbide claims that the squatters arrived after it did. The two accounts are not incompatible. Weir, op. cit., pp. 36–37.

22. "Others accuse the victims of being illegally in the path of the poisonous gases, of being 'illegal squatters,' as if they had no business existing or should have been on holiday at the seashore when the cloud came over Bhopal." De Grazia, op. cit., p. 46.

23. John Rennie, "Trojan Horse: Did a Protective Peptide Exacerbate Bhopal Injuries?" *Scientific American* (March 1992): p. 27.

24. Ibid.

25. Mehta et al., op. cit.

26. Ibid., p. 184.

27. Kurzman, op. cit., p. 47.

28. UCIL's tanks were unusually large for such an operation, which (in retrospect) has occasioned criticism. The UCIL tank's capacity was 57,120 liters and was almost full. In Germany, the United States, and Korea, MIC tanks have a capacity of 17,500 liters and are filled only to 50 percent of capacity as a safety precaution. Mehta et al., op. cit., p. 2781.

29. Kurzman, op. cit., especially pp. 37–57.

30. See, for example, de Grazia, op. cit., p. 19.

31. UCC, "Union Carbide Corporation, Bhopal Chronology."

32. Kurzman, op. cit., p. 142.

33. Warren M. Anderson, "Bhopal: What We Learned." Distributed by UCC, Danbury, CT.

34. Amy Waldman, "Bhopal Seethes, Pained and Poor 18 Years Later," *The New York Times* (September 21, 2002): p. A3.

35. UCC, "Union Carbide Corporation: Bhopal Chronology."

36. Kurzman, op. cit., p. 106.

37. Kalelkar, op. cit., p. 21.

38. Loc. cit.

39. De Grazia, op. cit., p. 34.

40. J. Peterson, "After Bhopal, Tracing Causes and Effects," *Science News* 127 (March 30, 1985): p. 196.

41. Ibid., p. 188.

42. Neal Carlan and Peter McKillop, *Newsweek* (April 1, 1985): p. 35.

43. Kalelkar, op. cit., pp. 14 ff.

44. Weir, op. cit., pp. 48–49.

45. De Grazia, op. cit., p. 116.

46. Kurzman, op. cit., p. 157.

47. Ibid., p. 159.

48. Ibid., 161 ff., and Chapter 4 generally.

49. De Grazia, op. cit., p. 50.

50. In Kurzman, op. cit., p. 175.

51. Kurzman, p. 155.

52. Kurzman, op. cit., p. 195.

53. Chris Hedges, "A Key Figure Proves Elusive in a U.S. Suit Over Bhopal," *The New York Times* (March 5, 2000): p. 4.

54. For the lawyers, the case never ended. In June 1989, F. Lee Bailey, Stanley M. Chesley, and others filed in the same court for an order directing reimbursement of "their legitimate costs and expenses" related to Bhopal litigation, to be paid from the $470 million that India had just been awarded. They were turned down (S.D.N.Y. 1989, U.S. Dist. LEXIS 6613, Decided June 14, 1989). They tried again to collect their fees in December 1993, in the same court, asking this time for "an attorney's lien against respondent, the Union Carbide Corporation." They were turned down again (S.D.N.Y. 1993 U.S. Dist. LEXIS 18227, Decided December 27, 1993).

55. Waldman, op. cit., p. A3.

56. Kurzman, op. cit., p. 173.

57. Kurzman, op. cit., p. 185.

58. CMA, *Bhopal: The Industry Stands Together, Communicates, Prepares Action Plan* special report, 1985.

59. Kurzman, op. cit., pp. 81–82.

60. Rennie, op. cit., p. 27.

61. Christopher Cathcart, "CAER Means Educating Communities," *CMA NEWS* (April 1985).

62. Interview with Bob Kennedy, Chairman and CEO, Union Carbide Corporation, Danbury, Connecticut, May 3, 1990. Cited in Rayport and Lodge, "Responsible Care," Harvard Business School Case Study, President and Fellows of Harvard College, 1991. Case N9-391-135: 1/15/91.

63. Interview with Jon Holtzman, Vice President-Communications, Chemical Manufacturers Association, Washington, DC, May 23, 1990.

64. Canadian Chemical Producers Association (Ottawa), "Responsible Care."

65. Interview with Jonathan Holtzman, cited in "Process Safety: Underscore Safety from Start to Finish: The Chemical Industry Responds with "CAER" and the "Responsible Care" Initiative," *1992 Safety Manager's Guide*, Bureau of Business Practice, pp. 320–332; Interview with Clyde H. Greenert, director, Public Issues and Contributions, Union Carbide Corporation, Danbury, CT, May 3, 1990, cited in Rayport and Lodge, "Responsible Care," op. cit., p. 9.

66. Interview with Holtzman, ibid., p. 324.

67. Rayport and Lodge, op. cit., p. 10.

10

Who Will Watch
the Watchers?

The Savings and Loan
Disaster

Questions to Keep in Mind

1. What role has the savings and loan (S&L) industry traditionally performed in the U.S. economy? What economic and political factors have changed this traditional role, and how?

2. How would you describe the accounting firm Ernst & Young? What are the ethical challenges it faces in its dealings with client S&Ls?

3. What has been the role of the media in reporting this issue? Has the media distorted the public's understanding of the accounting industry's ethics?

4. What were some of the reported abuses of Charles Keating and Lincoln Savings of California? In what ways were these *ethical* abuses?

5. What are the standards that ensure the professional objectivity and ethics of auditors? Are these sufficient for today's competitive business environment?

By 2002, many Americans were asking whether there was any integrity left in the executive offices of major U.S. corporations. Their concerns began in 2001 when Enron, the Houston-based oil company, slid into one of the largest corporate bankruptcies in U.S. history. Enron was undone by a complicated maze of thousands of partnerships that it used to conceal some $1 billion of debt and to inflate profits. As a result, thousands of employees lost their retirement savings. Small investors and pension funds alike took a major financial hit. People everywhere were suitably and justifiably appalled.

If the problem had ended with Enron, most Americans might simply have picked up the pieces and moved on, possibly wiser for the experience. But the problem was not limited to just one company. Since the Enron fiasco, the public has been assaulted by a seemingly unending series of corporate scandals: WorldCom, Global Crossing, Adelphia, and Tyco quickly followed. Every few weeks it seemed there was another white-collar defendant in the news, hand-cuffed and escorted to the courthouse—a kind of corporate "perp walk."[1] Even executives not directly charged with illegal actions felt the heat. Corporate superstar Jack Welch, who was guilty only of enjoying tremendous financial rewards and perks for his leadership at GE, was stung for the perceived extravagance of his company-financed lifestyle. Taken as a whole, the litany of corporate wrongdoings and excesses has made a substantial and lasting impact. Public confidence in corporate America has been severely shaken, perhaps more profoundly than ever before in the history of U.S. business.

By summer 2002, Congress decided that serious steps were warranted to stem the damage and to begin restoring public trust in business and the U.S. financial system. Under the sponsorship of Senator Paul S. Sarbanes, Democrat of Maryland, Congress created a new regulatory agency, the Public Company Accounting Oversight Board. Its purpose was to clean up the accounting industry. After all, the accountants were supposed to alert investors and the public of corporate financial problems. (To be fair, it wasn't just the accountants who were seemingly asleep at the watch. There also were countless others— Wall Street analysts, credit-rating agencies like Standard & Poors and Moody's Investor Service, even the Securities and Exchange Commission (SEC)— who should have been more watchful.) Arthur Andersen, Enron's auditor of sixteen years, not only failed to expose Enron's problematic practices, it was charged with obstruction of justice for destroying thousands of Enron audit documents.

The board was given a powerful mandate to set new standards for ethics and conflicts of interest. It would discipline wayward accountants, when necessary. It would conduct annual reviews of the biggest accounting firms. This was tough love, indeed. To give the board the financial independence necessary to overcome resistance from the accounting industry, Congress determined that it would be financed from assessments charged against the accounting firms' corporate audit clients.

But who could provide the leadership necessary to run this board? It would have to be someone of unquestioned ethical stature, someone who knew the business, someone with the conviction to fight for what's right. A natural candidate was Paul A. Volcker, the former chairman of the Federal Reserve, who earned the reputation in the 1980s for being one of the most honest men to emerge from that so-called "decade of greed." The SEC offered Volcker the job of leading the board, but he declined.[2]

The position was next offered to John H. Biggs, the chairman and chief executive of the TIAA-CREF pension investment plan. TIAA-CREF is the largest pension system in the United States for education institutions and has a reputation for conservativism in business dealings. Biggs is well known for his outspoken criticisms of the accounting industry and its role in the recent spate of corporate scandals. For example, he has called for a more strict accounting of the lucrative stock options that many companies lavish on their senior executives.

Significantly, Biggs has criticized accounting firms for providing both auditing and consulting services to the same corporate client. Traditionally, accounting firms provided only auditing services to client corporations. Over recent decades, however, they have increasingly added consulting services to their offerings to companies. The simple reason is that more money is to be made from consulting services. In 2001, 1,240 American corporations surveyed reported that they had each paid, on average, $3.2 million in consulting fees to their accountants. This compared favorably to the $1.3 million they paid on average for auditing fees.[3]

Biggs was concerned that this practice created conditions for conflicts of interest. It would be very difficult, after all, for auditors to challenge the accounting practices of a big client, if that client happens also to be the source of substantial consulting income. For this reason, under Biggs's leadership, TIAA-CREF did not use the same accounting firm for both auditing and consulting services.

For a while, it looked like Biggs had the job sewn up. He received strong endorsements from many business and congressional leaders, including Paul Volcker and Arthur Levitt, a former chairman of the SEC. All the signs were go.

In October 2002, however, Harvey L. Pitt, the chairman of the SEC, withdrew his support of Biggs. Just the previous month he had assured Biggs that he was behind his candidacy to lead the board. What had happened to change Pitt's mind?

According to one report, leaders of the accounting industry and at least one senior Republican lawmaker complained that Biggs was simply too tough on accountants. According to Lynn E. Turner, a former chief SEC accountant during the 1990s, "It appears that the accounting firms, the Republicans and now Chairman Pitt are trying to circumvent the Sarbanes legislation by making certain that the board does not include any reform-minded persons. If we lose Biggs, we lose a reform-minded board."[4]

The selection of the leader of the Public Company Accounting Oversight Board carries great symbolic weight. Americans need more than the arrests of a few executives to feel justified in trusting business again. They need to be assured that the rules of the game are fair, and that there is a capable umpire monitoring the game. Clearly, the selection of a leader for this board is deeply caught up in politics, regardless of who is finally selected. What emerges from the story, as it has unfolded thus far, is a picture of an accounting industry unsure about its functions and responsibilities. Accountants need to function as professionals to ensure that the public is well served by their judgments. The objectivity of the accounting profession is a necessary condition for re-establishing trust and confidence in business. At the same time, accountants need to stay in business. When professional duties clash with the economic realities of an increasingly competitive marketplace, we see the kinds of disputes that have erupted over the leadership of the Public Company Accounting Oversight Board.

To understand what is happening today, it is vital to recall the crisis of the savings and loan industry in the 1980s. That wake-up call alerted us to important underlying changes in the general culture of business and specifically in the culture of accounting. These underlying changes helped to set the stage for the ongoing wave of corporate scandals that we're witnessing today.

I. A $400 MILLION SETTLEMENT

Not too long ago, the S&L industry had been viewed as a necessary, if unglamorous, part of the U.S. financial system that helped millions achieve the American dream of home ownership. The savings and loan in Frank Capra's classic movie, *It's a Wonderful Life*, symbolized all that was good about neighborhood lending institutions. But during the 1980s something had gone seriously wrong with the S&L industry. Seemingly overnight, newspapers across the country disclosed shocking failures of one S&L after another. The sums of money lost or stolen were astronomical. Furious citizens and legislators demanded to know why regulators didn't see the crisis coming.

The Office of Thrift Supervision (OTS) was established in 1989 as the successor to the Federal Home Bank Board. It joined a small group of regulatory bodies responsible for handling the S&L crisis.[5] In light of the growing public resentment about the S&L failures, this might not seem like a good time to be a federal regulator. But on November 24, 1992, the tide seemed to turn for the OTS.[6] On that day, the major accounting firm of Ernst & Young agreed to pay the U.S. government $400 million to settle claims that it had improperly audited federally insured banks and S&Ls that later had failed. According to the government, Ernst & Young had worked as an auditor and accountant for at least 300 banks and S&Ls that eventually went bankrupt. The government claimed that the prestigious accounting firm should have detected and reported the S&Ls' financial problems before they had gotten so out of hand. All of the more than 700 S&L failures presented the American public with an outrageous price tag that one estimate put at $220 billion.[7]

What was the impact of the settlement on the American public? It is estimated that the government spent tens of billions of dollars to protect just the depositors at the collapsed S&Ls that had been audited by Ernst & Young.

According to Arthur D. Bowman, editor of a monthly trade publication called *Bowman's Accounting Report*, "As a taxpayer, I am upset, because if the potential settlement were in the billions of dollars, then that shortfall has to be made up some other way."[8] But the government's perspective on the settlement was that the American taxpayer also had been spared the cost of fighting Ernst & Young in court, and there was no guarantee that the government would have prevailed in court. (In August of 1992, a federal appeals court upheld a decision to dismiss a large case against Ernst & Young that involved the audit of a Texas savings institution.) At least the settlement ensured that the American public would recover *some* money from the accounting firm.

In fact, the $400 million settlement was the largest amount the government had won in its effort to punish accountants and other professionals who, according to the government, had not done their jobs as auditors. This settlement was second in size only to the $500 million penalty paid earlier that year by the investment bank Drexel Burnham Lambert and its junk bond wizard, Michael Milken. "This is going to be pointed to as a watershed event in the altered view of professional responsibility," said Stephen Gillers, a professor of legal ethics at New York University. "This represents a new magnitude of exposure for professional firms. Now maybe we'll get auditors who audit and lawyers who put their foot down when they see wrongdoing."[9]

In this chapter we will review several dimensions of the immensely complex S&L crisis, paying special attention to the professional duties and ethics of the accountants who were the auditors of these banks. First we will describe the functions of the S&L industry and the dynamics that led to its financial crisis. To help focus the analysis, we will look at the audit of a particularly notorious bank, Lincoln Savings. Ernst & Young, the accounting firm responsible for this particular audit will be described. With that narrative in hand, we will review issues related to changing accounting standards and the new accounting "culture" that are important to consider when trying to assign responsibility for the S&L scandals. The objective here is to cover enough material to help us appreciate the seriousness and complexity of the judgment against Ernst & Young, which is described in the chapter's conclusion.

II. THE SAVINGS AND LOAN INDUSTRY

During the 1980s very few observers grasped the full implications of the rapid changes in the S&L industry. As the astounding magnitude of the crisis emerged, so did finger-pointing to put the blame *somewhere else*. As the following account seeks to show, the S&L crisis was practically a foregone conclusion, given the rules of the game and certain economic and political developments that had reshaped American business.[10]

The S&L industry traditionally served the important role of supporting the housing industry, one of the biggest spheres of economic activity in American society. When people want to buy a house, they usually need to borrow most of the money for the purchase. When homeowners get a mortgage from an S&L, they are borrowing money, usually to be repaid at a fixed rate of interest over a long period of time. This mortgage interest is <u>income</u> to the S&L.

Where does the S&L get the money to lend to homebuyers? From depositors. When a person opens a savings account at an S&L, that person is lending money to the S&L. The interest rate paid on the savings account is actually the interest that the depositor charges the S&L for the loan. (Traditionally, this rate was fixed by law, not negotiated by the depositor!) Thus the savings account interest rate is a <u>cost</u> to the S&L.

Mortgages are long-term loans by S&Ls to homeowners, usually to be paid back over thirty years. Savings account deposits are short-term loans by citizens to the S&Ls. Thus, traditionally, S&Ls borrowed short from depositors and lent long to mortgage holders. As any basic finance text or experienced gambler will attest, this combination of transactions is among the riskiest of financial ventures. The S&Ls were gambling that short-term interest rates (their costs) would stay lower than long-term mortgage rates (the source of their profits). For a long time, their gamble paid off because interest rates tended to be stable and predictable.

But in the 1970s, the U.S. economy experienced considerable inflation. Several consequences followed. Interest rates in general rose with inflation. The fixed interest rates S&Ls could offer for savings deposits started to look less attractive and people began to pull their money from S&Ls. To help out the S&Ls, the government let them raise the interest rate they could offer for savings deposits. This helped stem the flow of money out of S&Ls. However, the S&Ls' interest expenses began to exceed their interest income. Since mortgage interests rates were fixed for the long term, the S&Ls were stuck with rising costs and fixed income. They were paying out more than they were taking in, with no solution in sight.

Thanks in large measure to pressure from S&L lobbyists and Democratic congressional supporters of federal housing assistance, the Reagan administration advanced a number of new policies and practices meant to help the S&Ls:

- First, the government allowed the S&Ls to diversify their investments. No longer would S&Ls be restricted to thirty-year fixed mortgages for family homes. From then on, S&Ls could lend funds for the purchase of commercial real estate, which traditionally had been the turf of commercial banks.

- Second, the government let regulators use a new set of regulatory accounting principles (RAP). These principles were generally viewed as more lax than the traditional generally accepted accounting principles (GAAP) that regulators and accountants had previously used to audit S&Ls. Under the new RAP, S&Ls could do things like defer for years losses on loans sold. Simply by switching from the old accounting principles to the new ones, it was possible to make an insolvent S&L appear solvent again.

- Third, the government also encouraged regulators to lighten up. It is generally acknowledged that during the Reagan years, supervision of the S&Ls was not as strict as it had been previously.

- Fourth, Congress increased the deposit insurance limit from $40,000 to $100,000 for each account, through the Depository Institutions Deregulation and Monetary Control Act of 1980. According to Seidman, former chairman of the FDIC, "This in effect made the government a full partner in a nationwide casino, first speculating mainly in real estate, later in extremely volatile mortgage securities, junk bonds, futures and options, and similar Wall Street exotica."[11]

Understandably, people want to get the highest return on their investments. But rational investors exercise some care in where they put their money, depending on the comparative risks and rewards of investment opportunities. Everyone has his or her own risk/reward preference. But imagine what would happen if there were <u>no</u> difference in risk among various investment opportunities. Then people would put their money where they could get the highest return.

When the government raised the deposit insurance limit to $100,000, it in effect encouraged people to invest their money in the S&Ls that offered the highest rate of return, because it was promising they couldn't lose their money (up to $100,000). But the S&Ls offering the highest rates of return were often those taking the greatest risks. The S&Ls were encouraged to compete aggressively for deposits because they weren't disciplined by market risk. Concludes Seidman, "The government, for its part, was deregulating as a matter of economic faith in the free market, forgetting that its own full faith and credit had castrated the market's regulatory strength."[12]

By the end of the 1980s, it became clear that S&Ls had sought "brokered deposits" by trying to offer the highest interest rates. To make the money necessary to pay these interests rates (and to have some left over for profit), the S&Ls began investing in risky real-estate ventures and investments like junk bonds. When these ventures and investments failed, the S&Ls lacked the means to pay back their depositors/investors. The government had to pick up the tab for the bank failures. The result was the S&L crisis. Were the S&Ls' executives simply out of their league, acting stupidly or ignorantly? Were they shrewd crooks looking for a quick scam? Were they innocent victims of a complex financial game that was rigged against them? Each interpretation has its supporters and each probably is true for certain cases.

III. THE AUDIT OF LINCOLN SAVINGS

The Ernst & Young watershed settlement pivoted on Ernst & Young's work with a few notorious S&Ls that had allegedly crossed the line into criminal activity. We will look at one infamous S&L, Lincoln Savings of California, which figured prominently in Ernst & Young's troubles.

Charles Keating acquired Lincoln Savings in early 1984.[13] Until that time, Lincoln Savings had invested primarily in local home mortgages, and Keating's business plan for the S&L indicated his intention to continue the same kind of business. In the first half of the 1980s, however, the Home Loan Bank Board was counseling S&Ls to diversify their investments, a piece of advice that Keating apparently was more than happy to act on. "In five years the only home mortgages Lincoln made were to its favored employees. But during that period, Lincoln grew tenfold from approximately $600 million in loans to near $6 billion."[14] Lincoln attracted the money for these loans through brokered deposits. It used this money to underwrite a diversified program of speculation that included takeover stocks, junk bonds, hotels, financial futures, and high-risk loans. By mid-1986, these speculative investments accounted for 62 percent of Lincoln's assets. The S&L reported profits in every quarter from 1984 to 1986.

The Phoenician, an unbelievably extravagant hotel built at Keating's direction, is a fitting symbol of what went wrong at Lincoln Savings:

> At a cost to build of half a million dollars a room, it was a palace of unparalleled conspicuous consumption. It was an extraordinary display of what fun you can have spending other people's money. . . . A monument to Keating's ego, its opulence guaranteed that it was never going to be profitable unless the hotel could charge the unattainable sum of $500 a night for every room in the house.[15]

Beneficiaries of Lincoln money included certain S&L employees who received special perks and salary bonuses from Keating. The highest paid employee at Lincoln Savings was Keating's son, a twenty-nine-year-old former bartender who was paid just under $1 million per year to run the real estate operation.

As it turned out, most of Keating's investments through Lincoln Savings were no good. In 1989, when the Federal Savings and Loan Corporation examined the assets of the failing bank, it found the following investments on Lincoln's books: ". . . vacant land in Arizona that wasn't worth half what Lincoln had paid for it, a weak junk bond portfolio, half-built hotels in overbuilt markets, and inventories of unsold homes."[16] OTS seized control of Lincoln Savings in August 1989.

The most important charges against Ernst & Young involved its work with Lincoln Savings and three other infamous failed savings institutions: the Vernon Savings Association of Dallas; the Silverado Banking, Savings and Loan Association of Denver; and the Western Savings Association of Phoenix. Just these four bank failures cost the government at least $4.5 billion.[17] Ernst & Young's audit of Lincoln Savings was actually done by the accounting firm of Arthur Young and Company, which later became Ernst & Young. Jack D. Atchison, an Ernst & Young partner, had primary responsibility for the Lincoln Savings audit work. In 1987 Atchison issued an unqualified opinion of Lincoln, a clean audit that did not point to significant trouble spots at the thrift. Also during that year, while Keating was battling with federal regulators, Atchison appealed to five U.S. senators for help; they later intervened on Keating's behalf. An interesting point about Atchison's professional objectivity: Very shortly after he signed the Lincoln audit, Atchison resigned from Arthur Young and went to work for Lincoln Savings' parent company, American Continental Corporation. His salary more than tripled.[18]

Atchison's audit helped Lincoln Savings market risky investments, like junk bonds, to a trusting public. By one estimate, investors lost $250 million on those high-yield securities.[19] The audit also made it more difficult for the board of directors to gain a complete picture of how badly Lincoln's financial health had deteriorated. If Lincoln's dire financial situation had been known at an earlier time, before 1987, it would have been possible to stop the S&L's losses from escalating out of control. Lincoln could have been liquidated at a comparatively modest cost. But because very few people seemed to know the true scope of Lincoln's financial troubles, the S&L kept doing business, spending $1.6 billion on Arizona land in 1987 and 1988, most of it worth very little today.

IV. BACKGROUND ON ERNST & YOUNG

Ernst & Young is one of the largest and best-known accounting firms in the world. It was created in 1989 by a merger of Ernst & Whinney and Arthur Young, themselves two large firms that were among the "big eight." Ernst & Young was born in a period of consolidation and change that rapidly was changing the face of the accounting industry. In 1992, at the time of the $400 million financial settlement, Ernst & Young generated about $2 billion in annual revenues.[20] At about that time, the firm had more than $500 million in partners' equity, 120 offices, and about 23,000 employees.

Some of the most serious S&L charges brought against Ernst & Young concerned auditing work done by Arthur Young prior to the merger. According to the SEC, Ernst & Young is, as the successor partnership, liable for all acts of Arthur Young.[21]

The $400 million settlement, while unprecedented for Ernst & Young, was not an isolated event. Like a number of other accounting firms, Ernst & Young had had ongoing problems with lawsuits concerning its role and responsibilities in the S&L crisis. The following account summarizes some of the firm's troubles in this area.

In late 1990, the accounting industry was swept by rumors that Ernst & Young might file for bankruptcy court protection because of its exposure to potentially huge lawsuit liabilities concerning its S&L audit work.[22] In December of that year, Ernst & Young ran, at a cost of $250,000, full-page ads in major newspapers, which read that the firm was "in very strong financial condition." The ads also thanked clients and employees for helping to make Ernst & Young a "leader" in the professional services industry, boldly predicting that the firm would continue to be a leader.

Ernst & Young denied that the firm was in trouble or that the unusual ads had anything to do with its bankruptcy rumors. Said Michael Grobstein, vice chairman, "The whole thing is just off the wall. We're not contemplating nor discussing any plans whatsoever related to bankruptcy. It's absolutely not true. We have no significant liabilities from litigation claims. We do, however, have pending cases like any big firm."[23] Also, shortly after *The Wall Street Journal* reported on the rumors, the financial newspaper printed a strongly worded letter from Ernst & Young's co-chief executives. They accused the newspaper of helping to spread what they called groundless rumors about their firm's financial health. They complained: "Although you weren't able to substantiate the rumor and must have known after all your reporting that the rumor was untrue, you nonetheless chose to run the article. Another of your reporters even told us that a competitor of the *Journal* had created a 'feeding frenzy of negative news' on accounting firms. . . . Our experience with the story raised the question: 'When is a rumor a matter of public concern?' There will always be rumors—about us, about our competitors and about other businesses. But if you are unable to verify the rumor, publishing it is a disservice."[24]

This squabble about the Ernst & Young bankruptcy rumors is important because it shows just how precarious and volatile conditions had become in the accounting industry. The rumors automatically gained some degree of plausibility simply because so many firms were in financial distress. Just two weeks before Ernst & Young ran their ads, the seventh largest accounting firm, Laventhol & Horwath, had filed for Chapter 11 protection from creditors. In its filing, the firm said that it had more than 100 claims amounting to $2 billion. Also at the same time the New York-based firm of Spicer & Oppenheim also disbanded. These events were indicative of the industry's turmoil in 1990, the same year that the FDIC had first filed its lawsuit seeking $560 million in damages from Arthur Young for its 1984–85 audit work with Western Savings Association in Dallas, a thrift that was ruined by its speculative real estate loans.

In early 1991, *The Wall Street Journal* reported that the California Board of Accountancy said it was seeking to revoke Ernst & Young's license for "gross negligence" in its audits of the Lincoln S&L. There were also reports that February that Ernst & Young and the Resolution Trust Corporation (RTC) had reached a tentative agreement about a $41 million settlement for what the government called its poor audit of the Lincoln S&L.[25]

In April 1991, The California State Board of Accountancy announced that Ernst & Young had agreed to settle charges it was negligent in its audit (through its predecessor Arthur Young) of Lincoln S&L. At that time, the settlement was the largest ever achieved by a state regulatory agency. Ernst & Young denied any wrongdoing; it claimed that the settlement merely reflected its desire to avoid costly litigation.[26]

In June 1991 the SEC filed a lawsuit in federal court in Washington, charging that there had been improprieties between the Dallas office of the accounting firm of Arthur Young & Co. and a Texas bank, Republic Bank (which later went bankrupt). The SEC charged that some of Arthur Young's partners had received more than $20 million in loans from the bank. The SEC also claimed that the accounting firm filed misleading audits of Republic Bank Corp during a time when some of its partners had $21.8 million in loans from the bank (for personal use or used to invest in apartments and shopping centers). Ernst & Young, the accounting firm's successor, did not disclose that its independent auditor status had been compromised by these loans.

It was the SEC's argument that this "failure to disclose" compromised the independent judgment that is central to auditing. According to SEC top litigator Thomas Newkirk: "Here you have intimate business dealings between partners in an accounting firm and a client they are auditing, where partners are in debt, the amounts are significant and yet they still claim to be independent. Investors rely on the independence of accounts to invest in a company."[27]

Ernst & Young contested the legality of the SEC suit, filing court papers arguing that external regulations should not bar its members from accepting such loans, since the firm now has internal policies prohibiting such loans. Ernst & Young further argued the SEC was abusing its powers by seeking to broaden the rules on auditor independence.[28] (At the time of this suit, the American Institute of Certified Accountants proposed a rule barring members from taking new loans from audit clients.)

V. STANDARDS IN THE ACCOUNTING INDUSTRY

On the face of it, Atchison's close relationship with Lincoln Savings would seem to compromise his capacity to display the disinterested objectivity expected of accounting professionals. Moreover, the seemingly widespread failure of the accounting industry to help detect and prevent the S&L crisis has contributed to growing public sentiment that accountants aren't doing their job. But what exactly are the duties and responsibilities of accountants? *Should* they be held responsible for the S&L crisis? And what are the pressures on accountants today that may make it difficult for them to meet their responsibilities? In this section we will discuss some essential characteristics of accounting as a profession, with special attention to its central standards and procedures. Though it would seem that these standards and procedures tend to evolve in response to changes in the business and political environment, there are those who would argue that the profession's standards are still adequate for today's competitive business environment. This section concludes with a defense of the accounting profession against blame for the S&L scandal and other business failures.

The standard textbook definition of accounting as a business practice lists the following essential characteristics: the identification, measurement, and communication of financial information about economic entities to interested persons.[29] External regulations compel financial entities like S&Ls to report publicly important financial information. It is the accountant's job to help supply the managers of the S&Ls with this information. In so doing, accountants provide financial statements that report on vitally important information like the balance sheet, income statement, and statement of cash flows.

Accountants are necessary because our economy has become so large and complex. Before 1900, when the U.S. economy consisted mainly of single ownerships, accounting reports were much more simple than they are today. It wasn't until the 1920s, with the growth of large corporations, that stockholders and the public required more detailed financial information about business. The stock market crash of 1929 and the ensuing great depression put pressure on the accounting industry to develop more stringent accounting standards. Over time there evolved a number of organizations that helped develop modern accounting standards, contributing to a higher degree of professionalism in the industry. These organizations included the American Institute of Certified Public Accountants (AICPA); Financial Accounting Standards Board (FASB); Governmental Accounting Standards Board (GASB); Securities and Exchange Commission (SEC); American Accounting Association (AAA); Financial Executives Institute (FEI); and, Institute of Management Accountants (IMA).

One might suppose that with this kind of oversight, the accountant's responsibilities would be clearly stated and understood. Instead, the accountant's job is complicated by external political pressures as well as changing patterns of competition among the accounting firms.

The accounting industry has developed a common set of standards and procedures called generally accepted accounting principles (GAAP). These have substantial support across the profession. For example, the AICPA Code of Professional Conduct requires that members prepare financial statements that accord with generally accepted accounting principles like GAAP. Accountants subscribe to these principles in order to minimize the potential dangers of bias, misinterpretation, and conflict of interest.[30]

But accounting is not a static discipline. Its standards and procedures have evolved over time, partly in response to changes in the business and political environment. And, in turn, the information that accountants provide to the public alters the business and political environment. This mutual interplay is the source of continuing changes in the discipline of accounting. The following is a textbook illustration of how changing economic conditions in the S&L industry fuel an ongoing debate over the appropriate standards:

> To acquire more liquidity, many S&Ls would like to sell of part of their investment portfolio. If they did so, however, large losses would be reported because the market value of these investments is considerably below their book value. As a consequence, these losses would reduce stockholders' equity to such an extent that many S&Ls would be in violation of regulatory requirements. The S&Ls argue that they should be permitted to defer these losses and amortize them over an appropriate future period. The accounting profession, on the other hand, argues that under generally accepted accounting principles, a loss should be reported currently because the transaction is completed.[31]

Debates of this nature about appropriate standards and procedures tend to complicate the task of determining precisely the accountant's responsibilities in relation to S&Ls. To some observers of the industry, however, accountants have been unfairly blamed for the business problems of the savings industry.

Two professors of accounting, Lowell S. Broom and Steven C. R. Brown, have argued that the investing public's criticism of the accounting industry is mistaken, as it fails to distinguish between business failure and audit failure.[32] Consequently, there is a tendency to think that if a business fails, then the independent auditor must have failed also. But a close examination of key accounting standards shows that accountants are not obligated to detect every possible piece of evidence of poor (or even illegal) business practice, particularly when the business carefully conceals this evidence.

For example, auditing standard SAS 54 (Illegal Acts by Clients) states that auditors are not responsible for assuring that all possible illegal acts will be detected. SAS 39 (Audit Sampling) does not require that *every* transaction in an account balance, or that all transactions, be audited. To the contrary, auditors are expected to select and evaluate a *sample* from an account balance or a class of transactions that is judged to be sufficient for reaching a conclusion about the transactions overall.

Should the accounting industry have done a better job of detecting the problems in the S&L industry before they got so out of hand? First, there is the question whether certain accountants did substandard work, missing evidence of fraud or poor business judgment that should have been identified early on. If the S&L mess happened because certain people weren't doing their jobs, then the issue is mainly one of identifying and punishing the appropriate individuals. But another question should be distinguished from the issue of individual culpability: whether the accounting standards themselves are part of the problem. Could the S&L scandal have gone undetected for so long if the accountants were performing competent audits <u>as defined by the standards</u>? If the answer to this question is "yes," the issue may be deeper—whether the standards themselves are inadequate.

VI. A CHANGING CULTURE

Besides these somewhat abstract issues about professional standards, in recent years there have been some unusual changes in the culture of accounting that further strain the industry's capacity for professionalism and objectivity.

Before the 1980s, the accounting industry was something like a comfortable gentleman's club (the same could be said of other areas in financial services, like investment banking). But since the 1990s, some argue, the industry has been transformed from a dignified profession to something more like a "Darwinian jungle."[33] The major accounting firms have been rocked by big changes, including a dramatic increase in competition, shrinking audit business because of corporate client mergers, litigation from unhappy clients, and un-precedented layoff and partner defections.

In times past, accountants nearly kept bankers' hours, working forty-five hours per week. In 1991 the average workweek was fifty-five hours. Partnership income, however, has stayed flat at $100,000. According to Jay Nisberg, a behavioral consultant who has more than 100 accounting firms as clients, a survey of 50 accounting firms shows that the incidence of coronaries, ulcers, and back problems among partners has risen 30 percent from 1989 to 1991. In 1990 Charles Kaiser Jr., who had led Pannell Kerr Forster (the eleventh largest accounting firm), suddenly resigned chairmanship of the American Institute of Certified Public Accountants, three months before his year-long term expired. In 100 years, no previous chairman had quit early. The reason? Kaiser said that infighting at his firm prevented him from fulfilling his duties as AICPA chairman. There is also the example of accountant Lawrence Nelson, who worked for ten years at Ernst & Whinney, becoming a partner in the West Palm Beach office. But in 1988, in his mid-40s, Nelson quit to join a smaller local firm. According to Nelson, "[I] . . . could hardly get into my car to go to work every day. My weight ballooned to 215 pounds from 165 and I did a lot of reading at 3 in the morning. I got burned out, very depressed and overate to relieve pressure."[34]

These examples indicate generally how the industry's culture puts its members under great stress. The impact of this stress on accountants' professional-ism and clear sense of duty is not yet fully understood. But it would seem likely that a more aggressive, demanding work ethos might lead accountants to play close to the edges of acceptable practices in order to stay competitive.

VII. CONSEQUENCES FOR ERNST & YOUNG

At the time of the headlines about Ernst & Young's record-setting $400 mil-lion settlement, few people knew that several months earlier it was the ac-counting firm itself that had proposed the settlement. It had negotiated the terms of the settlement with the FDIC, which took the $400 million, and the OTS, which would continue to monitor Ernst & Young's efforts to clean up its practices.[35] (In addition to the financial settlement, Ernst & Young promised to increase training for its auditors of depository institutions, to submit certain work of audit partners to external third-party review, and to watch more closely its practices in high-risk, sensitive areas of business. Also, partner George Derr and two previous partners, Jack Atchison and Edward F. Flaherty, were prohibited from ever again providing services for federally insured finan-cial institutions.)

According to Ernst & Young's chairman Ray J. Groves, the settlement was not an admission that the accounting firm had done anything wrong. (He also claimed that the accounting industry overall was being used unfairly by Washington as a "scapegoat" for the collapse of the S&L industry.[36]) Ernst & Young had compelling business reasons to take the settlement. If the accounting firm had fought the charges in court, the years of costly litigation could have generated legal fees of at least $150 million. Also, it was hoped that the settlement would spare the firm from facing claims in other major cases brought against Ernst & Young, which could run as high as $1 billion. According to Chairman Groves:

> Although this is a costly settlement, it's the only realistic solution to an endless stream of lawsuits that would have been even more expensive to defend. Resolving all outstanding and potential government claims relating to failed financial institutions allows Ernst & Young to continue to devote its resources and energy to the business of serving our clients.[37]

Despite the large sum of the settlement, some industry observers feel that Ernst & Young came out of the experience with a "bargain," not a punishment.[38] Thanks to the settlement, the government would receive only a fraction of what it might have won in this case and many others. Ernst & Young was spared from facing numerous other legal cases that could have threatened the very existence of the firm. Also, while $400 million is a lot of money, about $300 million was paid by Ernst & Young's insurers. The firm's 2,000 partners were allowed to pay their $100 million share of the penalty over a four-year period, with borrowed money, and they would be allowed to deduct that from their taxes as a business expense. It was estimated that the penalty would cost each partner per year an average of $8,000. (Their average annual salary was $200,000.) And finally, as part of the settlement, no senior Ernst & Young executive was directly punished for the firm's alleged failure to supervise its auditors in the field. Instead, two former partners and a relatively junior partner were barred from working with depository clients. According to Abraham J. Briloff, a professor emeritus of accounting at the City University of New York:

> The assumption is, when the firms get clients they get them because of the totality of the firm. But then, when things go wrong, they say: Don't blame us. It's the guys in the Arizona office of the Firm."[39]

The issue here works at several levels: systemic, institutional, and personal. Seidman brings it all together with this observation:

> The S&L crisis was born in the economic climate of the times. It was nurtured, however, in the fertile ground of politics as usual and the political mentality of "not on my watch." The system may have given rise to the crisis, but human beings, with all their faults, ultimately determined the scope of the debacle.[40]

QUESTIONS FOR REFLECTION

1. What does it mean to be a professional? Is professionalism a function of formal standards, or
personal character, or both?

2. What room is there for professionalism and ethics in an increasingly competitive, even
cut-throat, business environment?

3. When people risk their money in
investments and lose, is it appropriate or fair for them to try to
recoup their losses by suing those
with "deep pockets"—like accounting firms? Who should bear
responsibility for business risk?

SUGGESTIONS FOR FURTHER READING

Eichler, Ned. *The Thrift Debacle*. Berkeley:
University of California Press, 1989.

Long, Robert Emmet. *Banking Scandals:
The S&Ls and BCCI*. New York: The
H.W. Wilson Company, 1993.

Mayer, Martin. *The Greatest-Ever Bank
Robbery*. New York: Charles Scrib-
ner's Sons, 1990.

Seidman, L. William *Full Faith and Credit*.
New York: Random House, Inc.,
1993.

White, Lawrence J. *The S&L Debacle:
Public Policy Lessons for Bank and Thrift
Regulation*. New York: Oxford Uni-
versity Press, 1991.

ENDNOTES

1. Kurt Eichenwald, "Even if Heads Roll,
Mistrust Will Live On," *The New York
Times* (October 6, 2002): Sec. 3, p. 1.

2. Stephen Labaton, "Chief of Big Pension Plan Is Choice for Accounting
Board," *The New York Times* (October 1,
2002) p. C4.

3. Gretchen Morgenson, "On Reform,
It's Time to Walk the Walk," *The New
York Times* (October 6, 2002): sec. 3, p. 1.

4. Stephen Labaton, "S.E.C. Chief
Hedges on Accounting Regulator," *The
New York Times* (October 4, 2002):
p. C20.

5. The Federal Home Loan Bank Board
had regulated the S&Ls until public outcry
about the scandals and political pressures
warranted the creation of the new regulatory unity, the OTS. The Federal Deposit
Insurance Corporation regulated savings
banks, located mostly in New England. It
had kept these savings banks on a tighter
regulatory leash, so that fewer major
scandals afflicted these savings institutions.
The Resolution Trust Corporation was
created to help sell the assets of the failed

S&Ls, in an attempt to recover some of
the losses.

6. Sources for the account of this settle-
ment include Kenneth H. Bacon and Lee
Berton, "Ernst to Pay $400 Million Over
Audit of 4 Big Thrifts," *The Wall Street
Journal* (November 24, 1992): pp. A3,
A16; John Cushman, Jr., "$400 Million
Paid by S.&L. Auditors, Settling U.S.
Case," *The New York Times* (November
24, 1992): pp. A1, D2; and Susan
Schmidt, "Ernst & Young Pays $400
Million to Settle Thrift Regulators'
Claims," *The Washington Post* (November
24, 1992): pp. A1, A5.

7. Bacon and Berton, "Ernst to Pay $400
Million," op. cit., p. A1.

8. Stephen Labaton, "$400 Million Bar-
gain for Ernst," *The New York Times*
(November 25, 1992): p. D1.

9. Cushman, "$400 Million Paid by S.&L.
Auditors," op. cit., pp. A1, D2.

10. This account is based on the summary
by L. William Seidman, former chairman
of the FDIC, in *Full Faith and Credit* (New
York: Random House, Inc., 1993).

11. Seidman, op. cit., p. 178.

12. Seidman, op. cit., p. 181.

13. Unless otherwise indicated, information for this account of Lincoln Savings and Charles Keating is from Martin Lowy, *High Rollers: Inside the Savings and Loan Debacle* (New York: Praeger Publishers, 1991).

14. Seidman, op. cit., p. 229.

15. Seidman, op. cit., p. 230.

16. Lowy, op. cit., p. 148.

17. Cushman, op cit., p. A1.

18. Staff reporter, "Judge Dismisses Lawsuit Over Lincoln S&L Audits," *The Wall Street Journal* (August 12, 1991): p. A6.

19. Associated Press, "Ernst Wins Ruling in Suit," *The New York Times* (July 12, 1991): p. D6.

20. Schmidt, op. cit., p. A5.

21. John M Doyle, "Auditing Firm Accused of Improprieties," *The Washington Post* (June 14, 1991): pp. D1, D2.

22. Peter Pae, "Ernst & Young, in Full-Page Ads, Seeks to End Rumors It May Seek Chapter 11," *The Wall Street Journal* (December 3, 1990): p. A5.

23. Pae, op. cit., p. A5.

24. William L. Gladstone and Ray J. Groves, a letter to the editors of *The Wall Street Journal*, *The Wall Street Journal* (December 11, 1990): p. A19.

25. Staff reporter, "Ernst & Young Said to Set Pact with U.S. on S&L Job," *The Wall Street Journal* (February 6, 1991): p. B4.

26. Staff reporter, "Ernst & Young Will Pay $1.5 Million to Settle Case," *The Wall Street Journal* (April 26, 1991): p. A3.

27. John M. Doyle, "Auditing Firm Accused of Improprieties," *The Washington Post* (June 14, 1991): pp. D1, D2.

28. Kevin G. Salwen, "Ernst & Young Faces Lawsuit from the SEC," *The Wall Street Journal* (June 14, 1991): p. A3.

29. Donald E. Kieso and Jerry J. Weygandt, *Intermediate Accounting*, 7th ed. (New York: John Wiley & Sons, 1992): p. 3.

30. Kieso and Weygandt, p. 7.

31. Kieso and Weygandt, p. 19.

32. Lowell S. Broom and Steven C. R. Brown, "Public Accountancy: A Profession at Risk?" *The National Public Accountant* (October 1991): pp. 30–34.

33. Lee Berton, "The CPA Jungle," *The Wall Street Journal* (July 24, 1991): pp. A1, A5. The following account of the accounting industry is taken from this article.

34. Lee Berton, "The CPA Jungle," op. cit., p. A1.

35. Cushman, op. cit., p. D2.

36. Schmidt, op. cit., p. A5.

37. Bacon and Berton, op. cit., p. A3.

38. Labaton, "$400 Million Bargain," op. cit., pp. D1, D10.

39. Labaton, $400 Million Bargain," op. cit., p. D10.

40. Seidman, op. cit. p. 196.

Epilogue

The ten foregoing chapters are stories of ten times that the post-Watergate alarm went off—that the tocsin rang in the night for some bastion of American industry. When the morning came, business had to be done differently. As we pointed out in the Introduction, these are only a very few of the many cases that come to mind when we try to chronicle the rapid changes in business practice from the mid-seventies to the present. Perhaps these will be enough to get us started.

For now, the major message seems to be "we will do business differently." Some principles have emerged from the cases:

1. **We will include ethical principles explicitly in our business justifications, as part of our bottom-line mentality.** We speak often of the necessity for <u>proaction</u> rather than a reliance on <u>reaction</u>: Time and again, in these cases, we have found businesses <u>reacting</u> to attack after attack from unexpected outsiders, unable to articulate a position, carry it to the world, and defend it coherently. Corporations with excellent reputations are seen to stagger from confrontation to confrontation, looking like nothing so much as a pedestrian blindsided by a city bus, unable to keep his feet or hold a position. The only way to move from reactive to proactive postures is to be clear ahead of time on what attacks might be forthcoming, and how the choices of the corporation may be shown to be the right ones in the face of those attacks. Above all, as the only way to begin anticipating such attacks, the corporate officers must be aware of what harms might be

done by their services or products, in their use or abuse. That point brings us to the second component of the ringing:

2. **We must assume cradle-to-grave responsibility for the safety of our products.** Plans for products can no longer begin when the component materials are in house, and end when a merchantable product reaches the shelves of the retail outlet (or whatever other destination). Before the start of the manufacturing process, corporate officers will be asked to warrant that the materials and parts they buy were manufactured responsibly and transported safely and are in no way the product of outrageous injustice—of child, political prison, or slave labor, for instance. Long after the products have left the retailer's shelves, these officers may find themselves held responsible for injuries to users or bystanders, for the toxic fumes given off in their burning (should they be caught in a fire), or for the damage to the environment when they are ultimately sent to the landfill. There is no way to prepare a defense against such new attacks, except to study the product itself, its origins and its probable end, and to ask in what forms of evil might it unintentionally participate.

Compounding the problem of anticipating new responsibilities is the problem of anticipating new methods of communication. Publicity does not always depend on the flaw in the product; sometimes the publicity itself is the problem. That brings us to the third component of that noise in our ears:

3. **We will discuss and resolve our problems in public, with all the world watching.** We will have to get used to dealing with issues on the streets, in the newspapers, and on the talk shows, as well as in the board room and marketplace. The elders of the community may recall the publication of Ralph Nader's *Unsafe at Any Speed* (1965), the first of the systematic consumerist tracts critical of an American product and of the company that made it. By now the books seem tame. The consumerist or policy-oriented picket line, borrowed from the labor unions, looked familiar enough around the factory, but startlingly out of place around the suburban corporate headquarters—or the CEO's home. When the critiques spread to the talk shows as a barrage of unscreened anonymous commentary on any company, practice, or product in the land, all ability to anticipate criticism and plan a line of defense against it disappeared.

A paradigm case of the "new critique" of business appeared in the front pages of the daily newspapers three years ago, after a caller on a talk show explained that his wife had died of brain cancer caused by the electric field from her cellular telephone. The company that made the telephone conceded that it had not, indeed, conducted any research on the carcinogenic properties of cellular telephone use, nor had it any reason ready at hand as to <u>why</u> no such research had been conducted, save that no one had ever suggested it, since there did not seem to be any possibility that telephone use was linked to cancer. That reason was generally regarded as inadequate; sales and the company stock plummeted. It turned out, as we now all know, that the caller was in the process of suing the company for his wife's death, that there was no evidence at all of any connection between the telephones and cancer, and that no responsible medical or public health spokesman would even credit the possibility of such a connection; the caller had simply spread the rumor to bolster his case. But before all the facts came out, how much damage had been done? Did as many people hear the retractions as heard the accusations? Will the damage continue indefinitely? And how on earth could any responsible company head it off?

That last case underscores the moral ambiguity of the world in which the contemporary corporation is expected to operate. Among the discouragements of the times we may include first and foremost the empowerment of the irresponsible consumer/citizen—through instant access to the media, as above, and also through access to the streets in political-style protest and ready and subsidized access to the civil courts.

The streets became more available after the armed conflict in Vietnam wound down in the mid-1970s. A generation of activists turned in their picket signs and returned from Washington to their communities—politically sophisticated, wise in the ways and uses of the mass media, and accustomed to confronting problems directly and publicly. In many ways, the "political dialogue" valued by Aristotle and Thomas Jefferson had been replaced by "political theatre"—the shameless manipulation of the media to publicize a cause that otherwise might not have commanded the attention of the press and the citizenry. It was never clear that bringing public pressure to bear on corporate officers to change a product or policy had quite the efficacy, or legitimacy, as the same type of public pressure on an elected official. But the temptation to use the techniques of the anti-war movement against the corporation proved irresistible. Political psychologists might have pointed out that a youth invested in a certain constellation of ideology, the rhetoric to express it, and the activist practices to advance it, may yield predictable dividends when the cause that inspired that constellation has gone by. Causes, after all, are psychologically interchangeable, at least when the "bigness" of government or the corporation is part of the issue.

The speed with which the new consumer resorts to the courts should not have come as a surprise. When the American bar relaxed its prohibitions against the contingency fee, the only restraints that remained to keep lawyers from taking every conceivable case of harm to court were the lawyers' rules of good taste and accepted practice, which shunned litigation if at all possible, poured contempt on "ambulance chasers," and absolutely forbade advertising. These rules in turn depended on the ability of the vast majority of lawyers to make a decent living in "respectable" practice. When the law schools failed to copy the medical schools in enforcing "professional birth control," and allowed any students who were qualified to enter and complete law school and obtain a license to practice, they ensured that those rules would not long endure. Now the explosion of litigation has changed the course of all professions (law included!) and business, and not necessarily for the better.

The empowerment of the irresponsible members of the society by the social acceptability of political theatre, litigiousness, and discourse, as on the talk shows, that defies society to hold anyone accountable, has undoubtedly changed the moral context of the society. That context had problems apart from any that involve business: There is an alarming rhetoric of victimization in the popular politics, encouraging citizens to blame anyone but themselves for whatever discomfort is found in their lives. The atmosphere engendered by that rhetoric enables irresponsible consumers and citizens to take advantage of their new access to streets, courts, and airwaves without social disapprobation—and makes them much more likely to do so. A world that never claimed to embody perfect justice must seem to the harried CEO to have become much less fair, much more quickly than anyone could have foreseen.

Yet there is much to hope for in this new configuration of social forces. It is, after all, the product of a genuine idealism. Consumerism, and the confrontation tactics that generally accompany it, are simply part of the larger change in levels of expectation in this land. We are seeing more hope, less resignation, less acceptance of what is shoddy or careless. This must be for the good. An informed populace demands a higher level of performance; we are as much a part of that populace as Ralph Nader, and we will be dealing with and through it for all our working lives. The litigiousness is frustrating but it is, after all, primarily an inevitable byproduct of the change in locus of authority, in all professions as well as in business: Ask not what a reasonable company (or physician or lawyer) would do; ask what a reasonable consumer (or patient or client) would want. We have gone from communities of professionals (and conspiracies of silence in the courtroom) to the autonomous empowered individual—from *caveat emptor* to *caveat vendor* and on to *caveat factor* ("maker beware"), pushing back the line of responsibility and spreading the burden of care. Surely there is a moral advance in this change. The street theatre, in its turn, need not be seen as the death of the political dialogue, but as its most recent incarnation. We are not, as a people, hostile to showmanship, and the picket line is as American as the picket fence.

The bottom line for the businessperson in this millennium is the imperative to deal with the rising expectations, the legal shifts in burden of proof, and the unpredictable media, while keeping his or her balance and, we hope, a sense of humor. We have provided aids for that task in the models shown in this book; a brief review of two of them will conclude our exploration.

A good model will satisfy the requirements set out above, that it be proactive and intentional, that it deal directly with a public accustomed to direct action, and that it be aware of media influences and constraints on its policies and practices. Chapters 4 and 9, on the tobacco and chemical industries, describe such models.

The two models are very like each other in their structure and form: Both industries were plagued with terrible publicity and public image, both had strong industry associations, supported by the member companies, both immediately chose to work through the industry association, uniting the efforts of the member companies to counter the problem as perceived more efficiently. Both understood that in order to improve the public image they had to deal intelligently and effectively with media, with customers, and with the government. After that point, their paths could not be more diverse.

As you will recall, the Tobacco Institute decided that there was no problem, at least none worth addressing with their product, and no harm that tobacco was responsible for happening to their customers. After that, conflict with the critics of tobacco was waged as so much warfare, frontal assaults (the criticism, for example, of the findings that environmental—sidestream and secondhand—smoke was hazardous to the health of nonsmokers) alternating with guerrilla warfare in the halls of Congress and psychological warfare in the advertising pages. Rearguard actions parried the increasing litigation, advance probes experimented with high-nicotine tobacco in third world markets, and the acquisition of cracker companies helped them to blend in with the occupied population. At no point (and this is *our* point) did the industry raise questions about its own fundamental performance, about the nature and effect of its own product. (Although the recent development of a "smokeless" cigarette, which delivers a nicotine hit to the user without emitting smoke into the environment, certainly addresses some of the substantive problems of nonsmokers.) Not until the courts finally handed down the verdicts that forced a huge settlement did the industry back down from its righteous stance.

Is this the way to go? Before we condemn this course of industry action, we should note that these tactics have succeeded in keeping this product profitable for more than forty years since the nation's highest-ranking physician announced that smoking was dangerous to the health and should be stopped.

The other model, the development of Responsible Care by the Chemical Manufacturers Association, took precisely the opposite tack. The initiative began with the announcement from the president of the CMA that the chemical companies' practices were indeed to blame for the bad public image, and with a suggestion for immediate remedial action, not on the image, but on the problem itself—go find a toxic dump and clean it up. After that, we can see the development of the program as a persistent effort to enlist the cooperation of media, government, and the public at large—as well as its own membership, and their suppliers and customers—in addressing the real problems of chemical pollution and hazard. Responsible Care invented "cradle-to-grave" responsibility for products. It not only adopts the highest possible standard for protection of customers, community, and employees, it also insists that there must be continuous improvement after all standards are met. CMA's response to the public demonstration is the Community Advisory Group, a mechanism for inviting the public to come in from the picket line and become a part of management decisions in the earliest stages of formulation.

It is too early to speak of concrete results from Responsible Care, in terms of the perceptions that triggered its beginnings. In terms of its own purposes, there is certain success: these proactive programs have indeed made chemical companies safer manufacturers, employers and neighbors. But it will not be clear for years whether these excellent measures have succeeded in improving the image of the industry. Given the complexities and the inherent risks in all its processes and products, that improvement may be a long time coming.

No one is ready to write the last page of the success story of either model. International competition, as we pointed out in the Introduction, may beat down all initiatives that do not yield instant profitability. Even if all attempts to do business differently, more ethically, founder on the rocks of international competition, there can be no doubt that we are under way; after these bells, we will never sleep so soundly again.